Grammar for English Language Teachers

Martin Parrott

CAMBRIDGE
UNIVERSITY PRESS

D1211028

CAMBRIDGE UNIVERSITY PRESS
Cambridge, New York, Melbourne, Madrid, Cape Town, Singapore, São Paulo

Cambridge University Press
The Edinburgh Building, Cambridge CB2 2RU, UK

www.cambridge.org
Information on this title: www.cambridge.org/9780521477970

First published 2000
10th printing 2005

Printed in the United Kingdom at the University Press, Cambridge

A catalogue record for this publication is available from the British Library

ISBN-13 978-0-521-47797-0 paperback
ISBN-10 0-521-47797-2 paperback

Cover design by Mark Diaper

Contents

Short cut to what you're looking for

Phonemic symbols

Vowels

symbol	example
/iː/	eat /iːt/
/i/	happy /ˈhæpi/
/ɪ/	it /ɪt/
/e/	when /wen/
/æ/	cat /kæt/
/ɑː/	hard /hɑːd/
/ɒ/	not /nɒt/
/ɔː/	sort /sɔːt/; all /ɔːl/
/ʊ/	look /lʊk/
/uː/	too /tuː/
/ʌ/	cup /kʌp/
/ɜː/	first /fɜːst/; turn /tɜːn/
/ə/	about /əˈbaʊt/; mother /mʌðə(r)/
/eɪ/	day /deɪ/
/aɪ/	my /maɪ/
/ɔɪ/	boy /bɔɪ/
/aʊ/	now /naʊ/
/əʊ/	go /gəʊ/
/ɪə/	here /hɪə(r)/
/eə/	chair /tʃeə(r)/
/ʊə/	tourist /ˈtʊərɪst/

Consonants

symbol	example
/p/	pen /pen/
/b/	big /bɪg/
/t/	two /tuː/
/d/	do /duː/
/k/	look /lʊk/; cup /kʌp/
/g/	get /get/
/tʃ/	China /ˈtʃaɪnə/
/dʒ/	Japan /dʒəˈpæn/
/f/	fall /fɔːl/
/v/	very /ˈveri/
/θ/	think /θɪŋk/
/ð/	then /ðen/
/s/	see /siː/
/z/	zoo /zuː/; is /ɪz/
/ʃ/	shoe /ʃuː/
/ʒ/	measure /ˈmeʒə(r)/; decision /dɪˈsɪʒn/
/h/	who /huː/; how /haʊ/
/m/	meet /miːt/
/n/	no /nəʊ/
/ŋ/	sing /sɪŋ/
/l/	long /lɒŋ/
/r/	right /raɪt/
/j/	yes /jes/
/w/	will /wɪl/

This book is dedicated to the memory of Ian McFetridge and Georges Bouscasse, lovers and teachers of language.
It is also dedicated to the memory of John Malham, whose friendship and support were greatly missed in the latter stages of writing this book.

Thanks

The following people have all provided me with either support during the writing of this book or with data that I have used in the examples of spoken English. My thanks to all of you and to anyone I have forgotten to mention here.
Susan Barduhn; Frances Eales; Diana England; Alice Lester; Jenny McAslan; John Malham; Geraldine Mark; Lindsay Nash; Albert and Beth Neher; Valdemar Paradise; Barbara, Brian, Chris, Nick and Pamela Parrott; Colleen, Jack, Lauren and Pete Sheldon; Sybil Spence; Jon Tennant; Olivia Thorne.
My thanks also to Jeanne McCarten, and Alison Sharpe at Cambridge University Press for editorial support and help.

Acknowledgements

The author and publisher are grateful to the authors, publishers and others who have given permission for the use of copyright material identified in the text. It has not been possible to identify sources of all the materials used and in such cases the publisher would welcome information from copyright owners.

Radio Times 6–12 May 1995. Film review; *Evening Standard 16th June 1994*. Page 43. © Solo Syndication; *Radio 3. 5th November 1994*. © BBC; Skynner, R. and J. Cleese. 1993. *Families and How to Survive Them*. Page 232. With permission of Random House Group Ltd and © Oxford University Press: New York; Blyton, E. *The Rockingdown Mystery text* © 1949 Enid Blyton Limited. All Rights Reserved; Park, G. 1989. *The Art of Changing*. Ashgrove Publishing. Page 7; Holliday, A. 1994. *Appropriate Methodology and Social Context*. Cambridge University Press. Pages 67, 110 and 161; Handy, C. 1994. *Understanding Organisations*. Penguin Books. © C. Handy, 1993. Page 154; *The Guardian 18th May 1996*. Page 10. 2 extracts; *Indulgence Ice Cream Advert*. © Sainsbury's; Spectrum Brochure 1996–7. Page 19; *Radio Times 31 August – 6 September 1996*. Recipe from Ready Steady Cook; Radio Times 25 February – 3 March 1995. Dean Cain interview; *Radio Times 16–22 April 1994*. Quote from Des

© Harper Collins. Page 191; Allwright, R. and C. Bailey. 1991. *Focus on the Language Classroom*. Cambridge University Press. Page 17; Tyler, A. 1996. Ladder of Years Vintage. With permission of Random House Group Ltd. Pages 247 and 318; McCarthy, J. and J. Morrell. 1994. *Some Other Rainbow*. Corgi. © Transworld; *English Language Teaching Journal 48 (4) October 1994*. Oxford University Press; *The Guardian. 31st July 1994*. Page 1; *Radio Times 18–24 September 1993*. Bennet and Collingwood's Kind of Day author Anne-Marie Sapsted; BBC Proms 1993. Pages 4 and 6. © BBC; *Evening Standard 22nd October 1993*. Page 9. © Solo Syndication; *Liverpool Echo 30th December 1993*. Page 6 and 12; *Wigmore Hall Programme 24th January 1995*. McAslan, J. and J. Tennant. *BBC English Pilot Programme*. © BBC; *Evening Standard 22nd October 1993*. Page 16 © Solo Syndication; Davies, R. (ed.). 1994. *The Kenneth Williams Diaries*. © Harper Collins; *Radio Times 7–13 September 1996*. Justin Webb's TV Dinner © Mark Lewisohn; Ian Burnside. Radio 3. © BBC; *The Observer 10th November 1996*. Page 21; BBC 2 14th May 1996 *The Works*. © BBC; 21st September 1996; *Radio Times Christmas 1994*. Interview with Cilla Black © Mark Lewisohn; Louis de Berniérès. 1995. *Captain Corelli's Mandolin*. Minerva. With permission of Random House Group Ltd.; Volkswagen advertisement; *The Independent 27th November 1993*. Article by Rick Parfitt; Fowles, J. *The Collector*; *Desert Island Discs: Trevor McDonald*. BBC Radio 4. 24th April 1994. © BBC; *Gardener's World BBC 2*. 29th April 1994. Bob Flowerdew. © BBC; Independent on Sunday. 21st July 1996. Review. Page 74; Willey, D. 1993. *God's Politician*. © Faber and Faber Ltd/; *The Observer 31st July 1994* Page 6 and 17; *Evening Standard 16th June 1994*. Page 47 © Solo Syndication; *The Sunday Express 23rd May 1993*. Page 82 © Express Newspapers; Maupin, A. 1991. *Sure of You*. Black Swan. © Transworld and © Writers House New York; *The Observer 5th May 1996*. Page 12; *The Guardian. 3rd July 1996*. Page 19 (tabloid section). *Weatherwatch* by Bob Pritchard; Christiansen, R. 1984. Prima Donna. © Penguin Books; Kerouac, J. 1994. *On the Road*; Vine, B. *A Dark Eye* (adapted). © Penguin Books; Forbes, C. 1992. By Stealth. Pan. © Macmillan; Willis and Willis. 1996. *Challenge and Change in English Teaching*. Heinemann. Page 114; *English Language Teaching Journal 49 (3) July 1995*. Oxford University Press Page 27; UCLES regulations 1993. Page 7 by permission of University of Cambridge Local Examination Syndicate; Swan and Smith. 1991. *Learner English*. Cambridge University Press; *Management in English Language Teaching*. 1991. Cambridge University Press; Minette Walter's *The Scold's Bridle*. Pan © Macmillan; *Girl about Town* 16th December 1996; *The Evening Standard 1st September 1996*. page 21 © Solo Syndication; *The Guardian. 18th February 1995*. Page 34. Article on Pilsner; *The Guardian. 5th November 1994*. Page 50. Article by Richard Ehrlich; *The New Cambridge English Course*. Page 75. Cambridge University Press; Faulkes, S. 1994. *Birdsong*.

Introduction

Aims

Grammar for English Language Teachers has two primary aims:

- to help you develop your overall knowledge and understanding of English grammar.
- to provide a quick source of reference in planning lessons or clarifying learners' problems.

The book provides a broader perspective of grammar than that presented to students in course materials. It encourages you to appreciate the complexity (and, where relevant, the *ambiguity*) of grammatical description, and to recognise the limitations of the 'rules of thumb' presented to learners in course materials.

It also seeks to nourish a love for and fascination with English grammar.

Who this book is for

This book is intended for:

- prospective and practising teachers studying language as part of a degree in English or on courses such as those leading to teaching certificates and diplomas.
- teachers who want to continue learning and exploring the grammar of English on their own.
- teachers who do and teachers who do not speak English as a first language.

Content and organisation

People sometimes associate the term 'grammar' with the different parts of speech or 'word classes' that words can belong to (*adjective, noun, preposition* etc.). Materials produced for studying English over the last three decades have, however, reflected and promoted an obsession with another aspect of grammar – the verb phrase (tenses, conditionals etc.).

The chapters in Part A look at grammar from the starting point of word class, and those in Part B deal with the verb phrase. Parts C and D, however, look at more neglected aspects of grammar, and you may want to take more time to work through these parts of the book progressively and systematically. Each of these four parts begins with a general introduction to the topic.

Each chapter in Parts A–D begins with a review of 'Key considerations' relating to its topic. It explores the topic in depth in the subsequent sections, including the 'Typical difficulties for learners' that this area of grammar causes. Information in these chapters is expanded in the relevant sections of Parts F and G.

Each chapter ends with exercises to help you consolidate what you have learned. These *Consolidation exercises* use real texts, transcriptions of conversation and examples of learners' writing; possible answers to each of the exercises are suggested in Part H. Part E (*Extension exercises*) encourages you to research how language is used in different contexts, and to evaluate classroom and reference materials. (More detailed chapter-by-chapter *Extension exercises* (and *possible answers* to these) can be found on the Cambridge University Press Website http://uk.cambridge.org/elt/gelt/extension/).

Data

Authentic data has been used extensively in:

- formulating and checking generalisations about language use.
- obtaining and adapting examples.

Finding the information

The section headed *Short cut to what you're looking for* at the beginning of the book is organised alphabetically and enables you very quickly to locate information about a specific feature of grammar.

In the longer term, there is no 'quick substitute' for systematically reading, studying, accumulating knowledge and developing awareness of grammar. The content of the book is organised thematically, and if you want to use it for systematic study, the *Contents* page will help you to find the chapters you need.

PART A

Words

Introduction to Part A

Words and grammar are often thought of as being separate entities. In fact, in learning any word we are also learning something about its grammar.

Words belong to different grammatical classes (e.g. *noun, verb, preposition*), and the class of a word determines:

- what other kinds of words we can combine with it.
  Example: We can say *a beautiful day* but not * *a beautifully day*.
  Explanation: We use adjectives not adverbs to qualify nouns.

- the order in which we combine words.
  Example: We can say *a beautiful day* but not * *a day beautiful*.
  Explanation: We put adjectives *before* the nouns they qualify.

Grammar also determines, for example:

- which form of a word we choose.
  Example: We say *two days* and not * *two day*.
  Explanation: After numbers greater than *one* we use a plural form of the noun.
  Example: We say *more beautiful* and not * *beautifuller*.
  Explanation: We use *more* to make the comparative form of long adjectives and add *–er* to make the comparative form of short adjectives.

As teachers we need to know and to be able to explain and illustrate:

- the grammatical class of words: *beautiful* or *beautifully*?
- the grammar of words: *day* or *days*?
- the implications of 'word grammar': We can't say: * *a beautifully day*; * *a day beautiful*; * *two day*; * *beautifuller*.

In Chapters 1–8 (Part A) we look at words that belong to the following grammatical classes:

	Examples	**Chapter**
Nouns:	*book(s), child(ren), information, life.*	1
Adjectives:	*easy, old, open-ended, possible.*	2
Adverbs:	*easily, sometimes, very.*	3
Articles:	*a, an, the.*	4
Quantifiers:	*any, every, a few, some.*	5
Comparative forms:	*more beautiful, easier, fewer.*	6
Superlative forms:	*most beautiful, easiest, fewest.*	6
Prepositions:	*at, in, on top of, since.*	7
Verbs:	*speak, go, can, will, drinking, been.*	8

Because the difficulties that learners have in using pronouns is closely related to judgements about how much information needs to be stated explicitly, and how much can be left out, and because choosing pronouns also involves decisions not only about number and gender but also about grammatical function (e.g. *subject* or *object*), we look at pronouns in Part C (p. 264).

Recognising word classes

In some languages the word itself tells us a lot about what class it belongs to (for example, the spelling and pronunciation of the end of a word may show that it is a noun). In English there are very few clues in the word itself, and we usually have to look at the context. The following gives examples of different parts of speech:

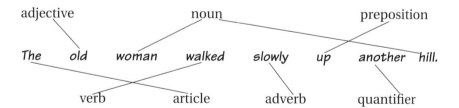

Words that belong to more than one word class

A lot of words can function as a member of one word class in some contexts and as a member of another word class in other contexts.

Examples	Word classes
abstract, adult, antique, green	nouns, adjectives
wonder, rupture, sequence, drive, play, function	nouns, verbs
fast, hard	adjectives, adverbs
around, down, up	adverbs, prepositions
come, given, considering	prepositions, verbs
boring, open, locked	adjectives, verbs

All quantifiers apart from *no* can also function as pronouns.

Quantifier	Pronoun
I saw *several* kangaroos.	He asked for a volunteer and got *several*.
I don't know *many* girls.	Teachers are poorly paid . . . *many* leave the profession.

Single words and multiword items

The simplest way to define a word is by looking at the written language. If there is a space before and after a group of letters, this group of letters constitutes a word.

If we look at meaning rather than at form, we see that some combinations of two or more words are equivalent to single words. These are multiword items.

> *fed up* (adjective = 'unhappy')   *give up* (verb = 'stop')
>
> *with regard to* (preposition = 'about')

Grammar in course materials and in academic grammars

The grammatical terms and concepts used in course materials differ in some respects from those used in academic grammars, and in this book we follow the pragmatic distinctions and classes found in course materials. Thus, for example, we look at adverbs (single words) in Chapter 3, and consider phrases with a similar function as adverbials in Chapter 19; we look at articles in Chapter 4 and quantifiers in Chapter 5. Most academic grammars consider adverbs within the wider class of adverbials, and articles together with quantifiers within the wider class of determiners.

1 Nouns

cat   cats   elite
capacity   dustbin   steak
people   Wednesday

1.1 Key considerations

Most learners are more concerned with the meaning of nouns than with
their grammar. However, in learning to use a noun, they need to pay
attention to a variety of grammatical factors. In particular they need to
know whether a noun is countable or uncountable, and if countable, what
its plural form is. More generally, learners also need to be able to:

- use nouns to modify other nouns.
- choose and construct appropriate possessive forms.

1.2 What are nouns?

What do they do?

The popular definition of a noun is that it 'describes a person, place or
thing'. In fact we use nouns to express a range of additional meanings
such as concepts, qualities, organisations, communities, sensations and
events. Nouns convey a substantial proportion of the information in most
texts.

In the previous paragraph, the following words are nouns: *definition,
noun, person, place, thing, fact, nouns, range, meanings, concepts,
qualities, organisations, communities, sensations, events, Nouns,
proportion, information, texts.*

What do they look like?

Endings

A small proportion of nouns have identifiable 'noun endings'. These
include:

> *tradition, ability, instrument, excellence, significance.*

Many plural nouns end in *s*, e.g. cat*s*.

7

Proper nouns and capital letters

Words which begin with capital letters and are not at the beginning of sentences are often the names of people, places or institutions. These are also called 'proper' nouns.

> both **Lauren** and **Jack** came   in **Africa**   a course at **International House**.

1.3 Where do nouns come in sentences?

Nouns can:

- act as the subject of a verb: **Cats** *kill mice.*
- act as the object of a verb: *Cats kill* **mice**.
- act as the complement of a verb: *They are* **men**.

They often end a phrase which begins with an article such as *a(n)*, or a quantifier such as *either, any,* or *many.* They also often follow adjectives.

> *a* **drunk**   *either* **way**   *a much older* **elite**   *large* **mice**

1.4 Countable and uncountable nouns

What are countable and uncountable nouns?

Countable nouns ([C]) have a singular and a plural form, e.g. *book – books.* Uncountable nouns ([U]) have only one form, e.g. *furniture* NOT * *furnitures.*

[C]		[U]
Singular	**Plural**	
Another **biscuit**.	*Three* **apples**.	*Not much* **success**.

The distinction between countable and uncountable is based on whether or not we can count (1,2,3,4 . . .) what the nouns describe. Nouns which describe separate and separable objects (e.g. *book(s), centre(s), computer(s)*) are usually countable while those which describe liquids, materials, substances and abstract qualities (e.g. *milk, marble, putty, success*) are characteristically uncountable.

Although the distinction between countable and uncountable is based on the reality of what the nouns describe, the distinction is a grammatical one rather than a real one. Some learners of English are surprised to discover that, for example, the following are uncountable:

accommodation hair information money news spaghetti travel weather

Words which come before and after countable and uncountable nouns

The words we use before and after nouns are determined by whether the noun is singular (countable), plural (countable) or uncountable:

before the noun	[C] singular	[C] plural	[U]
indefinite article (*a, an*)	*a* book	–	–
numbers	*one* book	*two* people	–
certain quantifiers, e.g. *both, each, either, many, a few, every*	–	*many* people	
certain quantifiers, e.g. *much, a little*	–	–	*much* interest

after the noun	[C] singular	[C] plural	[U]
singular verb forms	a child *has*	–	*information is*
plural verb forms	–	insects *are*	–

Closely related countable and uncountable nouns

Some uncountable nouns have a countable equivalent which is a different word.

work [U] : *job* [C]   *travel* [U] : *journey* [C].

The things some uncountable nouns describe can be 'broken up' into countable components.

[U]	[C]
money	*pounds, dollars, yen*
time	*hours, minutes, seconds*
furniture	*table, chair, desk*

With some uncountable nouns we can use particular words to itemise or count what they describe.

three **blades** of grass   an **item** of news

Nouns which can be countable as well as uncountable

Some nouns are countable with one meaning, and uncountable with a different meaning.

*We got lost in a **wood**. [C]   **Wood** burns more easily than coal. [U]*

Sometimes countable and uncountable forms represent two closely connected uses of one word.

*I told her a few **truths** about herself. [C]   We'll never learn the **truth**. [U]*

Some nouns that were originally plural are coming to be uncountable.

*the **data** are ⇒ the **data** is   the **media** are ⇒ the **media** is*

We can use a lot of generally uncountable nouns as countable nouns. For example, to describe:

- a kind/type of something.
  a new French cheese   a fresh orange juice
- a quantity/unit of something.
  a beer   two sugars

Countable nouns are also called mass nouns, and uncountable nouns are also called unit nouns.

1.5 Regular and irregular plural forms

Regular forms

Most countable nouns have a plural form that ends in *s*.

See page 408 for spelling rules and page 402 for pronunciation rules.

Irregular forms

Many irregular plural forms involve a change in vowel.

man ⇒ men   tooth ⇒ teeth   foot ⇒ feet

Learners sometimes find it difficult to remember which form is singular and which is plural.

Some nouns have the same singular and plural forms (nouns that end in *s* often fall into this category).

a sheep ⇒ *two sheep*   *a series* ⇒ *two series*
a crossroads ⇒ *two crossroads*

A few irregular plural forms are very different from the singular form. The most common and problematic example is *person* ⇒ *people*.

Nouns which have been absorbed into English from other languages sometimes keep their original plural form.

plateau ⇒ *plateaux*   *cherub* ⇒ *cherubim*   *mafioso* ⇒ *mafiosi*

Language change

The standard plural form of some words is changing from a 'foreign' form to an anglicised one.

foci ⇒ *focuses*   *syllabi* ⇒ *syllabuses*.

The original plural form of some words is coming to be used as singular.

a criteria   *a phenomena*

Using dictionaries

Because there is no way of telling whether a singular noun has a regular or an irregular plural form, we need to encourage learners to use a dictionary to check and learn the plural spelling and pronunciation of words that they come across as a matter of course.

1.6 Quantifying phrases

A range / variety / majority / proportion / number of . . .

We use these expressions before nouns to express something about quantity, e.g. *a variety of issues*. They are all followed by plural nouns. If the expression is followed by a verb, this is also usually in a plural form.

*A wide range of people **were** invited.*

However, some people prefer to use a singular form of the verb, particularly in formal written English.

*A variety of issues **was** raised.*

A pair of . . .

Some nouns which exist only in a plural form can be qualified by *a pair of*, e.g. *a pair of trousers / scissors / glasses.*

1.7 Collective nouns

Collective nouns are words which represent groups of people, e.g. *the* **team**, *the Conservative* **Party**. These nouns are singular in that we can talk about *an awful government* or *a big staff.*

Some people believe that these nouns should be followed by singular verb forms (*The staff* **was** *happy*) and that singular pronouns should be used (*The team won* **its** *first match*). However, most people use plural verb forms and pronouns.

> *The management team* ***want*** *to make* ***themselves*** *more accessible.*

People sometimes choose either singular or plural verb forms according to whether they are thinking in terms of a unified 'body' or of the various people who make it up.

> *The army provide**s** an excellent career.*
> *The army* ***are*** *investigating the incident.*

The names or initials of many organisations (*The Halifax Building Society, NATO*) also function like collective nouns.

> *Coca Cola are rapidly expanding.*
> *The UN are sending in peace-keeping troops.*

1.8 Combining nouns

Using nouns to modify nouns

We frequently use two nouns together

> *an insect repellent*   *a computer virus*   *a daffodil bulb*

The first 'modifying' noun usually tells us what kind of a thing the second noun describes (an *insect repellent* is a kind of repellent; a *computer virus* is a kind of virus).

When two nouns are frequently used together, they may be separated by a hyphen (-), e.g. *a battle-ground,* or written as a one-word compound noun e.g. *weekend, dustbin.* Learners may want to use a dictionary to check this.

Possessive forms

Possessive 's

We add *'s* to nouns or noun phrases (groups of words containing a noun that can replace a single noun) to show that what follows belongs to them, e.g. *the teacher's car.*

The last word in a noun phrase is not always a noun. However, we can still attach *'s* to the last word in the phrase.

> *It's that girl I told you about's book.*

Although we call this form the 'possessive *'s*', we add *'s* to the end of nouns and noun phrases to express a number of relationships as well as possession.

possession	*Jackie's disk.*
family relationships	*The other girl's twin.*
parts of the body	*The patient's leg.*
creation	*Van Gogh's 'Sunflowers'; Einstein's theory.*
places	*Asia's largest capital cities.*
time	*Two days' holiday.*

See page 413 for rules about the position of the apostrophe.

'Something' of 'something'

We can use the 'something of something' structure as an alternative to *'s*, to express family relationships, creation and place

family relationships	*The twin of the other girl.*
creation	*The fifth symphony of Beethoven.*
place	*The largest capital cities of Asia.*

We generally choose this alternative when we want to draw attention to what we put at the end of the phrase (*Beethoven, Asia* etc.). It is also more common in formal and written English

When we are concerned with abstract and inanimate things, we can't use **'s** (We say *the depths of despair* and *a pile of rubbish* or *a rubbish pile*, NOT * *the despairs' depths* or * *a rubbish's pile.*

We generally don't use this structure to express possession, e.g. *Jackie's disk* NOT * *the disk of Jackie.*

1.9 Typical difficulties for learners

Comprehension

For many learners, not knowing the meaning of specific nouns they come across is a major problem. Problems with the grammar of nouns, however, rarely impedes understanding.

Speaking and writing

Word endings

Many adjectives have related noun forms (e.g. *beautiful: beauty, cautious: caution*). Learners sometimes make plausible and intelligent guesses about the form of these nouns, but their guess may be mistaken (e.g. * *jealousness*; * *angriness*; * *youngtime*).

Countable and uncountable nouns

Learners sometimes use uncountable nouns as though they were countable (e.g. * *Two inputs*,* *How many money?* * *an information,* * a good weather*).

Learners may be misled by their own language (e.g. the equivalent of an uncountable word in English such as *money* may be countable), or something may simply seem logical to them (e.g. *information* 'ought' to be countable).

They sometimes use plural nouns as though they were singular (e.g. * *The people is here*).

With *people* there are the additional problems that:

- the word doesn't look like its singular equivalent (*person*).
- some languages have a very similar word which is singular (e.g. French *peuple*).
- with a different but related meaning, *people* can be singular in English.

   The French are a *people* who enjoy good food.

They sometimes use plural nouns as though they were uncountable (e.g. * *Her clothes was torn*).

Choosing the wrong plural form

Learners may make regular plural forms of nouns that are irregular (e.g. * *a lot of womans,* * three childrens*).

Using nouns to modify nouns

Many learners avoid placing two nouns together in any circumstances, preferring to create (inappropriate) alternatives.

They sometimes over-use **'s** (e.g. * *a computer's keyboard*, * *a wine's glass*). They sometimes use 'something of something' (e.g. * *A flight of British Airways*).

Learners who do use nouns to modify other nouns may make the modifying noun plural (e.g. * *some pencils sharpeners*) when in fact (like adjectives) they always remain singular.

Choosing the wrong possessive form

Learners often avoid the **'s** form.

   * *It's the book of my friend.*

The form this learner has chosen is used to express other kinds of relationship in English (e.g. *glass of water*) and may be a translation of how possession is expressed in her own language.

Unusual cases

Learners are sometimes puzzled by the following, and are either reluctant to use them or make mistakes (e.g. * *the news are . . .*):

Uncountable nouns which end in **s**:	The **news** is bad.
Some singular nouns which end in **s**:	a **means** of getting there.
Nouns which exist only in a plural form:	serious **arrears / arms / clothes**
Nouns which end in **s** that can be either plural or uncountable:	. . . his **politics** reveal(s) . . .

1.10 Consolidation exercises (see p. 428 for possible answers)

Pronunciation (see p. 402)

a Divide the following nouns into two categories: (i) Those whose plural form is pronounced /s/ or /z/. (ii) Those whose plural form is pronounced /ɪz/.

   wedge   wish   orange   move   knife   lunch

b What rule underlies your choices?

c Divide the following nouns into three categories: (i) Those whose plural form is pronounced /z/. (ii) Those whose plural form is pronounced /s/. (iii) Those whose plural form can be pronounced either /s/ or /z/.

lock   bath   hearth   pillow   pin   scruff

pit   cloth   cough   growth   mouth

d What rule underlies your choices?

Language in context (see p. 428)

Many nouns that are generally uncountable can often also be used as countable nouns (e.g. *Would you like a coffee?*).

a Look at the nouns in the two boxes below.

fish exposure meat steak breast lamb	unhappiness dissatisfaction society life understanding misunderstanding soil

1 For each noun decide whether it is: generally countable [C], generally uncountable [U], or both [C, U].

2 If you answered *both* for any of these words, how is the meaning generally affected by whether the use is countable or uncountable?

b Two texts follow. The first is from a cookery book and the second text is from a book that is critical of psychotherapy. Read the texts and then answer the questions below.

Grilling is a fierce and uncompromising technique, since the food is cooked by direct exposure to intense heat. Only prime cuts of meat can stand up to this barrage of heat and still emerge tender and juicy. Thus steaks, chops and cutlets are the obvious choice, although a cheaper cut like breast of lamb can be braised first, then grilled, to give a crisp exterior.

Fish presents no such problems, however, since it is never tough. Even the cheaper, oily fish such as sardines and mackerel are good cooked in this way.

Most therapists believe that the unhappiness over which patients come to therapy is not socially caused, but is self-created, that the patients are at least partially responsible for the dissatisfaction that is felt. The therapist will often state that he or she is not in a position to alter society, to change a patient's past, or to intervene in the life of the patient. What the therapist claims to offer is understanding. But implicit in this offer is the belief that the understanding is an internal one, an understanding of what the patient has brought to the situation to create unhappiness or at least to intensify it. Here we have a rich soil for creating deep and lasting misunderstandings, and even greater misery.

1 Check your answers to **a**1 to see if you predicted the countable or uncountable uses of the same words here.
2 Explain any uses you didn't predict.
3 Underline all the nouns in the texts.
4 Identify nouns which are used here as countable nouns.
5 Identify nouns which are used here as uncountable nouns.

Changing attitudes (see p. 429)

Look at the following and answer the questions about the underlined words.

(i)   The <u>media is</u> becoming very interested.
(ii) <u>Alitalia have</u> adopted a policy of apologising for any delay.
(iii) My <u>criteria</u> for making this decision <u>is</u> personal.
(iv) They have produced several <u>syllabuses</u>.

a Do you use this form yourself?
b Would you consider the form a mistake if produced by an educated native speaker?
c Would you correct the form if produced by a learner of English?

2 Adjectives

old unhappy
asleep boring
determined quick-witted
fed-up

2.1 Key considerations

Learners are generally more concerned with the meaning of specific adjectives than with their grammar. When the grammar does cause problems, this is often related to:

- ordering two or more adjectives that occur together.
- constructing comparative and superlative forms.
- deciding what words or combinations of words we can use directly before and after adjectives (e.g. where we can and can't use *very*; where we can and can't follow an adjective with an infinitive such as *to eat*).

2.2 What are adjectives?

What do they do?

Adjectives are often called 'describing words' because they provide information about the qualities of something described in a noun, a noun phrase, or clause.

> noun: *an **old** film*
>
> noun phrase: *an **interesting** experience for everyone*
>
> clause: *It's **unbelievable** that we haven't seen each other for so long.*

Adjectives provide much of the 'colour' in any description, as the following passage illustrates. This text introduces a film called *Deliverance* to television viewers. The adjectives are printed in italics:

John Boorman's *provocative, violent* and *compelling* thriller takes *American* poet James Dickey's novel to *giddy* heights of *suspenseful* stress and proves that Burt Reynolds can act. *Central* to the success of Boorman's culture clash nightmare, and what makes it resonate with such a *rare* intensity, is the *powerful* theme of *red-blooded* masculinity under *hostile* threat.

What do they look like?

Adjectives related to nouns or verbs

A lot of adjectives are closely related to nouns or verbs.

beautiful : *beauty* (noun)   *dangerous* : *danger* (noun)
drinkable : *drink* (verb)   *talkative* : *talk* (verb)

These adjectives often have one of the following endings or 'suffixes'.
Sometimes, as in the case of *impeccable,* the adjective survives long after
the noun or verb it has been related to is forgotten.

–able	impeccable	*–ent*	intelligent	*–ory*	obligatory
–al	paternal	*–ful*	truthful	*–ous*	courageous
–ate	immaculate	*–ist*	Communist	*–some*	winsome
–an	Anglican	*–ive*	impressive	*–wise*	streetwise
–ant	fragrant	*–less*	useless	*–y*	misty

Words which are not adjectives can also have these endings.

We can attach *non-, pro-* and *anti-* to the beginning of some nouns, and
-like and *-friendly* to the end to create adjective forms, e.g. *a pro-/anti-
democracy movement, a business-like manner, a user-friendly computer
manual.*

Participle forms

In the following examples *boring* and *bored* are parts of the verb *(to) bore.*

Am I boring you? I haven't bored you, have I?

Boring is the present participle and *bored* is the past participle. Many
adjectives have the same form as participles (e.g. *boring, bored, broken,
closed, exciting, excited*).

Multiword adjectives

Many adjectives are made up of two parts (usually connected by a
hyphen). These two-part adjectives are multiword adjectives.

The second part of multiword adjectives is often a past participle form.

adverb and past participle: *well-liked, well-intentioned, beautifully-
written*
noun and past participle: *feather-brained, self-centred, people-oriented*

We also derive adjectives from multiword verbs (e.g. *wear* someone *out*, *tie* someone *up*). In this case the first part is usually a past participle form (e.g. *worn-out, tied-up*).

Other multiword adjectives don't involve participle forms at all, e.g. *two-piece, birds-eye* and *slip-on* in the following description.

> His *two-piece birds-eye* suit is impressive, his blue shirt with its rounded collar immaculate, his thin, faintly European *slip-on* shoes impeccable.

Adjectives don't change before plural nouns, e.g. *two green books* NOT * *two greens books*.

Comparative and superlative forms

We add *–er* (/ə /) to the end of most short adjectives to make the comparative form, and to make the superlative form we add *–est* (/əst / or /ɪst /).

comparative: *I'm **older** than you imagine.*
superlative: *Which city is the **coldest** in the United States?*

With longer adjectives we usually add *more* or *most* (*more intelligent, most beautiful*).

Some adjectives have irregular comparative and superlative forms.

good   better   best   bad   worse   worst

Chapter 6 looks at comparative and superlative forms in greater detail.

2.3 Where do adjectives come in sentences?

Single adjectives

There are two usual sentence positions for single adjectives:

* before a noun (within a noun phrase).
* after a noun or pronoun and a verb.

Before a noun

When we use adjectives before nouns they are usually the last but one item in the noun phrase.

noun phrase			
determiner	**intensifier**	**adjective**	**noun**
some		***enchanted***	*evening*
a	*very*	***old***	*story*

We can usually leave adjectives out of a noun phrase without making nonsense of the sentence.

A few adjectives can only be used before a noun (e.g. *entire*):

> *I watched the entire performance.* NOT * *The performance was entire.*

Apart from *central*, all the adjectives in the film review on page 18 come before the noun as part of the noun phrase.

After a noun or pronoun and verb

We also use adjectives after nouns ('predicatively'). In this case the adjective is linked to the noun (or pronoun) it qualifies by a complement verb (see p. 24).

	complement verb	**adjective**
He	*is*	*cold.*
It	*'s getting*	*dark.*

When we use adjectives predicatively, they usually express the main point of the clause, and we can't leave them out.

A few adjectives (e.g. *alive, asleep, awake*) are used only after nouns.

> *She's asleep.* NOT * *We found an asleep child in a basket on our doorstep.*

We look at when adjectives can immediately follow nouns on page 23.

Using more than one adjective

Order

The following is a helpful rule of thumb to use when two or more adjectives occur before a noun:

- general before specific (e.g. *a large French car* NOT * *a French large car*)

- opinion before description (e.g. *a wonderful high ceiling* NOT * *a high wonderful ceiling*)

Learners sometimes appreciate more detailed guidance such as the chart below (however, precise information like this is only a rough guide and is not foolproof):

	1	2	3	4	5	6	noun
	size	shape	colour	origin	material	use	
a	*large*		*white*				*loaf*
a		*sleeveless*	*blue*		*woollen*		*pullover*
	Small			*Spanish*		*serving*	*dishes*

See page 413 for information about punctuating lists of adjectives.

Linking adjectives with *and*

In theory any number of adjectives can be used together, although most people avoid long strings of descriptive words, particularly in writing and particularly when they come before the noun.

Before a noun, we don't need to use a conjunction to separate the adjectives we put together.

> *They came to a **terrifying, dark, gloomy** clearing in the wood.*

However, after a noun (or pronoun) we have to use *and* before the last of two or more adjectives.

> *She was cold and hungry.*   *She was cold, tired and hungry.*

We can choose to use *and* before the final item in a list of three or more adjectives used before a noun. In this case *and* emphasises the final adjective, and allows us to change the usual order of adjectives.

> *They came to a **dark, gloomy and terrifying** clearing in the wood.*

Adjectives followed by prepositions, infinitives and *that*

When we use adjectives predicatively we can sometimes follow them with a preposition, infinitive or *that* clause

> *unaware of speaking, happy to learn, eager that you should go*

Learning what follows the adjective is an essential part of learning to use the adjective – and sometimes the most difficult part. Learners need to develop the habit of using a good learners' dictionary such as *Cambridge International Dictionary of English* to check what can follow any particular adjective. Sometimes there is more than one possibility.

A few adjectives can only be used if they are followed by a preposition i.e. they can't be used on their own.

> *I'm fond of him.* NOT * *I'm fond.*

2.4 Gradeable and ungradeable adjectives

Gradeable adjectives

Gradeable adjectives describe qualities that we can measure or grade in some way. Things can be *wet, cold, interesting* or *disappointing* to different degrees; we can say something is *quite wet, very wet* or *terribly wet*. Gradeable adjectives include *calm, flexible, happy, ill* and *jealous*.

We can use intensifiers (e.g. *very*) and downtoners (e.g. *fairly, rather*) with gradeable adjectives.

> *A very irritating development.*   *She's fairly certain.*

See page 37 for more information about intensifiers and downtoners.

Ungradeable adjectives

Some adjectives express:

* extreme qualities (e.g. *terrified, furious, starving*).
* absolute qualities (e.g. *alive, correct, dead, male, human*).

With these extreme and absolute ('ungradeable') adjectives we use only intensifiers which stress the extreme or absolute nature of these adjectives, and we don't use downtoners.

> *He's utterly terrified.* NOT* *He's very terrified.*
> *She's completely dead.* NOT* *She's fairly dead.*

See page 37 for more about intensifying ungradeable adjectives.

2.5 Exceptional sentence positions – when adjectives immediately follow nouns

Learners often work hard to remember that adjectives have to come before nouns, and are then puzzled to discover that there are apparent exceptions to this rule. The exceptions are due to:

- object complement verbs (See below and also p. 97.)
- ellipsis (See below and also p. 319.)
- adjective phrases (See below and also p. 255.)

After object complement verbs

Object complement verbs are followed by an object (often a noun or pronoun) and then a complement (often an adjective).

	verb	object	complement
Don't	*make*	*me*	*angry.*
He	*left*	*the door*	*open.*

Here the adjective as complement describes something about the object.

Ellipsis

We also use adjectives immediately after nouns when we leave something out of the sentence (i.e. when ellipsis occurs).

Usually what we leave out is a relative pronoun (e.g. *who, which, that*) and a form of the verb (*to*) *be* (e.g. *am, is, are, was, were*). This kind of ellipsis is particularly common after pronouns like *something, someone, somewhere, sometime,* and *anything*.

	pronoun	adjective	
You should wear	*something*	*warm.*	(i.e. *something* [which is] *warm.*)
Take me	*somewhere*	*nice.*	(i.e. *somewhere* [which is] *nice.*)

Forms of the verb (*to*) *be* can also be left out to avoid repetition, as in the description on page 20, where *is* has been left out before *immaculate* and *are* before *impeccable*.

Adjective phrases

Learners may be particularly confused by cases such as the following description of a musician's piano technique, where adjectives seem to follow a noun:

> *It has all the grip, **technical and intellectual**, that you would expect.*

Here the adjectives form a phrase that extends the information in the noun, and can follow it (examples like this may also be classified as verbless clauses – see also p. 364). Although at any level learners may come across and may need to understand examples like this, it is probably only at very high levels that we would want to teach them.

2.6 Typical difficulties for learners

Comprehension

If adjectives usually follow nouns in the learners' first language, learners may need time and considerable exposure to English in order to become familiar with the usual sequence of information in English noun phrases (adjectives *before* nouns). Even though they may know and be able to verbalise the 'rule', they may be wrong-footed by specific instances.

This may cause them difficulty in processing information, particularly in listening to English (in reading they have the opportunity to stop in order to study phrases and work out how information is ordered), and particularly when they come across a string of two or more adjectives before a noun.

Speaking and writing

Plural forms

Learners may create a plural adjective form.

* *They are olds books.*

This is particularly common among people whose first language has a plural form of adjectives.

Comparative and superlative forms

Learners may over-generalise the rules which determine the comparative and superlative forms of adjectives.

* *She is more old than me.*
* *That was the reasonablest I've ever seen her.*

Sentence position

Some learners often place adjectives after the noun where this is inappropriate in English.

* *It is a building very old.*

This mistake is particularly common among learners whose first language places adjectives after the noun as a matter of course.

Adjective order

Learners may use adjectives in a sequence that native speakers would instinctively avoid.

> * *It is an old beautiful building.*

Combining adjectives

Learners sometimes use conjunctions (e.g. *and*) inappropriately in a sequence of adjectives.

> * *They were playing with a big and red ball.*

Learners may be confused by the fact that the rule is different according to whether or not the adjectives come before or after the noun.

> *The ball was big and red.*

Gradeable and ungradeable adjectives

Learners may not know which adjectives we can (and can't) intensify.

> * *She was very furious when she heard the news.*

2.7 Consolidation exercises (see p. 430–431 for possible answers)

Language in context (see p. 430)

The passage which follows is from a novel. It describes London in the 1930s from the point of view of someone who has just arrived in Britain, in winter, from India. Read the passage and then answer the questions:

> She hated London – hated it at the very first sight of the foggy streets filled with drab crowds hurrying home, the shop windows glowing feebly in the misty twilight, the huge buses reduced to dim red rumbling shapes that seemed to appear from nowhere out of the smoke and fog. She particularly hated this dingy, dark, ugly room, with its broken-down furniture and the hissing gas heater in the fireplace that went out if you forgot to keep enough shillings to feed into the coin slot. She thought about struggling into a heavy skirt and cardigan and pulling on a pair of thick stockings: she hated the feel of wool against her skin. Her wool gloves, which she disliked even more, were suspended from a wire in front of the pale-blue flames of the gas heater, drying from another hopeless morning of job hunting and giving off an odour which Queenie found loathsome. Everything in England seemed to smell of damp wool, as if the entire population consisted of wet sheep.

a Identify all the adjectives in this passage.

b Imagine this passage without the adjectives. How much difference would this make to the description ? What kind of difference?

c Which of these adjectives are also participles?

d Which of these adjectives are derived from nouns?

e Which of these adjectives are derived from verbs?

f Which of these adjectives are multiword forms?

g What does *loathsome* in the last sentence but one refer to? Account for its position in the sentence.

h Identify any prefixes or suffixes which are characteristic of adjectives.

Learners' English (see p. 431)

The following was written by a learner. Identify and explain any mistakes in the form and use of adjectives.

> I am a person very working-hard and seriously. I am tall one metre
> thirty nine and I have blonds, longs hairs, blues eyes and a nose
> little and crooked. I like to wear clothes with brightly colours so
> you can always see me and easy to recognise my smilingly face. I
> wear make up with lips brightly reds and I am usually a character
> with passionately.

3 Adverbs

carefully warily hopefully
often soon there
now yet very
quite

3.1 Key considerations

The term 'adverb' refers to different kinds of words with quite different functions. For teaching purposes it is generally necessary to specify particular types of adverb (e.g. adverbs of manner), rather than refer to adverbs all together as though they were a unified class of words.

Adverbs can occupy a range of positions in the sentence, and choosing where to place them is often a major problem for learners.

The meaning of certain adverbs (e.g. *yet, already, ever*) is complex, and we may want to avoid teaching these at the same time as other major grammatical features (for example, tenses).

3.2 What are adverbs?

What do they do?

The popular definition of adverbs as words that 'modify a verb, an adjective or another adverb' is neither accurate nor very helpful. Whereas it is relatively easy to define and describe what a noun or an adjective is, we can only usefully define and describe different *categories* of adverb. It is sometimes helpful to think of 'adverb' as a 'dustbin' term – all the types of word that don't fit neatly into other categories such as noun, adjective, verb, preposition are lumped together as adverbs.

The following is a useful way of dividing adverbs:

Categories	Examples
manner	*carefully; slowly*
frequency	*always; often*
time and place	*now; here*
relative time	*already; recently; soon*
degree	*extremely; rather; very*
quantity	*a lot; a little*
focusing	*even; also; only; particularly*
attitude markers	*apparently; fortunately*

Focusing adverbs and attitude markers can also be classified as discourse markers (see also Chapter 22). Many types of adverb can be seen in the following text spoken by a family therapist who is being interviewed about jealousy.

The adverbs in the text are printed in italics. Each of them is classified below so that you know how these terms are used in this chapter.

John: So was jealousy a bit of a problem amongst you and your brothers?

Robin: *Absolutely* (**1**). Jealous squabbles were *always* (**2**) bursting out between us, and our parents could *never* (**3**) find a way of handling it *successfully* (**4**). 'We can't understand why they're all *so* (**5**) jealous,' they'd say to people. 'We try to be fair.' And they were. But because jealousy frightened and worried them *so* (**6**) *much* (**7**), we never got the chance of being *properly* (**8**) jealous, finishing it, going through it, and letting the feeling find its normal, natural place in our personalities. Still, I've learned from this, and *nowadays* (**9**), when families I see complain of jealousy in their children despite the fact that they *always* (**10**) cut the cake *equally* (**11**) with a ruler and give everyone penicillin when *only* (**12**) one child has a sore throat, I know what to do. I *usually* (**13**) tell them that, though they are such a nice, successful family in many ways, they're *obviously* (**14**) not very good at being jealous and need more practice before they come to see me next time.

1	attitude marker	**8**	degree
2	frequency	**9**	time
3	frequency	**10**	frequency
4	manner	**11**	manner
5	degree	**12**	focusing adverb
6	degree	**13**	frequency
7	quantity	**14**	attitude marker

Grammars and dictionaries often disagree about what words are adverbs and what aren't. One-word textual discourse markers such as *firstly, however* and *nevertheless* (which we consider only in Chapter 22) are sometimes classified as adverbs. Some grammars don't use the term 'adverb' at all. This chapter follows the way the term is used in most popular coursebooks.

We look at what specific adverbs and types of adverbs do on pages 33–40.

What do they look like?

–ly

We form a lot of adverbs by adding –*ly* to an adjective (see p. 408 for detailed spelling rules), e.g. *ably, busily, calmly, oddly, probably, usually.*

In most cases the meaning of the adjectives and adverbs are very close.

adjective: *He's a **careful** driver.*
adverb: *He drives **carefully**.*

Although many adverbs end in –*ly*, not all words which end in –*ly* are adverbs. The following are adjectives: *friendly, manly, leisurely, likely.*

These do not have a standard adverb form. Some people say, for example,

   * *He smiled at her very friendly.*

but most people simply avoid sentences like this. It is more usual to use an expression such as the following: *in a friendly / masterly / leisurely way.*

Other adjectives (e.g. *difficult*) have no adverb equivalent (* *difficultly*). We use the expression: *with difficulty* in place of an adverb.

A few adverbs which are closely related to adjectives in form don't mean the same as the corresponding adjective (e.g. *hardly, hugely, simply*). This can be a source of confusion for learners.

Other adverbs

Some adverbs (e.g. *often, very, even*) can't be identified as adverbs by their spelling or pronunciation.

A number of adverbs have the same form as adjectives and there is no *–ly* alternative, e.g. *fast, hard, next, freelance*.

adjective: *A freelance designer*

adverb: *She's working freelance.*

Other adverbs have two forms – one is the same as the adjective and the other (which many people prefer and may consider to be the only correct form) ends in *–ly*, e.g.

commonly used	used formally and in written language
*Hold it **tight**.*	*She held the bag **tight**ly.*
*Come here **quick**.*	*She ran **quick**ly.*
*Try to sing less **loud**.*	*He always spoke **loud**ly.*
*Is the plug sold **separate**?*	*Additional RAM can be purchased **separate**ly.*

Well is the adverb that corresponds to the adjective *good*:

*He's a **good** driver.* (adjective)

*He drives **well**.* (adverb)

3.3 Where do adverbs come in sentences?

General points

The rules which govern the position of adverbs in sentences are complex. They take into account what kind of meaning the adverb expresses and what information the speaker or writer wishes to highlight. Some adverbs are an intrinsic part of phrases (e.g. adverbs of manner, of degree, of quantity and some focusing adverbs), and their position is relatively inflexible. Other adverbs (e.g. attitude markers, adverbs of time and place and adverbs of frequency) may refer to whole clauses or to larger parts of clauses and their position is more flexible.

We look in detail at the sentence position of specific adverbs and types of adverb on pages 280–281. The following provides only a general overview of sentence position. The examples are all taken from the text on page 29.

Before a whole clause:	*nowadays, when families . . . complain . . .*
Before the verb:	*We **never** got the chance*
Before the main verb and after an auxiliary verb:	*could **never** find a way*
At the end of a clause:	*a way of handling it **successfully***
Before adverbials:	*Cut the cake **equally** with a ruler*
Before an adjective:	***properly** jealous; **very** good*
Before an adverb:	*jealousy frightened and worried them **so** much*

Although there is considerable flexibility in the position of some adverbs, and although learners will come across examples that contradict this, a good rule of thumb is that we do not put adverbs between verbs and their direct objects or between verbs and non-finite or *that–* clauses:

* She made quickly the lunch.

* He volunteered obsequiously to help.

Particularly in formal written language, some people disapprove of placing an adverb between the particle and verb in a 'full' infinitive form (i.e. splitting infinitives).

(*) *I want you to carefully open the door.*

I want you to open the door carefully.

Although learners will frequently come across examples of split infinitives, they may be penalised in examinations if they do this themselves.

'Negative' adverbs and word order

Some adverbs can be preceded by *not* (*not once, not often, not ever* etc.), and others are intrinsically negative or restrictive in meaning (e.g. *never, rarely, seldom, hardly (ever), scarcely (ever)*).

When we place these at the front of a clause for emphasis, we use the word order of a question form. This is more common in writing than in speaking.

*Not once **did she call** in to see me.*

See also page 276.

3.4 Types of adverbs

Adverbs of manner

In the following text, the adverbs of manner are printed in italics. (Diana, Roger and Snubby are children, and Loony is a dog.)

> Diana and Roger had no wish to fling themselves *joyfully* on Snubby; but Loony flung himself on them so *violently* that he almost knocked Diana over. He appeared from under the table, barking *madly*, and threw himself at them.
>
> 'Hey – wait a bit!' said Roger, very pleased to see Loony. The spaniel licked him *lavishly*, whining *joyfully*. Miss Pepper looked *crossly* at them.
>
> 'Diana! Roger! You are very late.'
>
> 'Well' said Diana *indignantly* . . . 'It wasn't our fault!'

Meaning

Adverbs of manner usually express how something is done.

> *Open it **quickly**!*   *He hit me **hard**.*

They can usually provide one-word answers to questions beginning *How . . . .*

> *How did she approach them? — **Warily**.*

Sentence position

The most common place to use adverbs of manner is at the end of a clause.

After a verb:	*You spoke **convincingly**.*
After an object:	*You described everything **convincingly**.*
After an adverbial:	*You described everything to the board **convincingly**.*

However, we can vary the position of adverbs of manner according to what we want to emphasise.

Before a subject:	***Carefully**, she put it on the shelf.*
Before a verb:	*She **carefully** put it on the shelf.*
Between an object and an adverbial:	*She put it **carefully** on the shelf.*

We also use adverbs of manner immediately before past participles.

> *The new roof was **carefully** lifted into position.*

We generally avoid placing these adverbs between a verb and its object.

> * *She extracted surreptitiously the key.*

This may be a useful rule of thumb in teaching, but it is not an absolute rule.

> *. . . by learning to change our use [of the self] we affect fundamentally every aspect of our experience.*

Adverbs of frequency

Meaning

We use adverbs of frequency to indicate how often we do things or how often things happen. Adverbs of frequency include: *always, usually, often, sometimes, occasionally, hardly ever, seldom, rarely, never.*

> *We always / usually / never get up early on Sundays.*

Sentence position

Before the main verb

We usually tell learners that we place adverbs of frequency 'immediately before the main verb'. This rule of thumb describes most cases where the verb phrase is a one-word form (e.g. *goes, spoke*) or where it comprises one auxiliary verb and a main verb (e.g. *has spoken, don't believe*).

> *She **never** speaks.*   *They don't **always** believe what I say.*

Two auxiliary verbs

If there are two auxiliary verbs before a main verb (e.g. *has been speaking, would have eaten*), we generally place the adverb of frequency between the two auxiliary verbs.

> *They would **often** have eaten before we arrived.*

(To) be

When we use one-word forms (*am, is, are, was, were*), we usually place adverbs of frequency immediately before the complement.

> *I was **always** the best student.*
> *Is she **often** ill?*

Front and end positions

For emphasis we can also choose to place *usually, often, sometimes* and *occasionally* at the beginning of a whole clause.

> **Sometimes** *her attitude is rather off-putting.*

We also place *often* and *sometimes* at the end of a clause, after the verb, object or adverbial.

> *I wash up **sometimes**.   I don't go out **often**.*

Adverbs of time and place

We use adverbs, to specify both times (e.g. *yesterday, today*) and places (e.g. *outside, underneath*), and to stand in place of adverbials (phrases such as *on Wednesday* or *at the bus stop*) which make the precise time or place known.

The following four adverbs are very common: *now, then, here, there*.

> *I need to see her **now**.*
> *I'm seeing him at 6.00. I'll tell him **then**.*
> *While we're **here**, can we see the garden?*
> *You can't stay **there** too long.*

We generally place these adverbs at the end of a clause.

When we use adverbs of time and place together, we usually specify the place before the time.

> *She's coming here now.*

Adverbs of relative time: just, afterwards, soon, currently, presently *and* recently

Meaning

These adverbs provide information about the time of an action or event in relation to some other point of time (often 'now').

> *He's **currently** working in Namibia.   They're **just** coming.*
> *I'll be there **soon**.*

Sentence position

Just

We use *just* immediately before the main verb or between two auxiliary verbs.

*I **just** saw him.   They have **just** arrived.   I have **just** been looking for you.*

Afterwards and soon

We usually use *afterwards* and *soon* at the end of a clause.

> *We're leaving **afterwards**.*
> *We'll be at the station **soon**.*

Currently, presently and recently

The position of *currently*, *presently* and *recently* is more flexible. These adverbs often:

- come at the end of a clause: *She's trying to finish the book **currently**.*
- precede a main verb: *I'll **presently** be going out.*
- come between two auxiliary verbs: *She has **recently** been getting back late.*

These adverbs can also come at the beginning of a clause, particularly in written and more formal styles of English.

> ***Presently**, she got up from the bench and wandered down to the edge of the stream.*

Special adverbs: already, still and yet

Meaning

The meaning of these adverbs is difficult to tie down independently of context – it often depends on assumptions we make about the knowledge and expectations our readers or listeners share with us.

Consider the difference in meaning between the sentences in the following pair:

> *Do you know the result?*
> *Do you know the result **yet**?* (i.e. We are both waiting for it).

In teaching these adverbs it is often helpful to refer to how these meanings are expressed in the learners' first language(s).

Sentence position

We usually place *already* and *still*

- immediately before the main verb:
  *I **already** know.   I am **still** using it.*

- between the verb (*to*) *be* and the complement:
  *They're **still** teenagers.*

We can also place these adverbs at the end of a clause.

   *I know **already**.*   *I am using it **still**.*

We use *yet* at the end of a clause.

   *Has she finished **yet**?*   *They haven't eaten **yet**.*

In British English we use *already* in affirmative statements, and *yet* in negative statements and questions.

Adverbs of degree

Meaning

We divide adverbs of degree into *intensifiers*, which make adjectives and other adverbs stronger, and *downtoners*, which make them weaker.

Intensifiers e.g. *extremely, very, really* (*real* in American English), *so*	We are *very* hungry. I am *totally* confused.
Downtoners: e.g. *fairly, quite, rather*	We ran *fairly* quickly.

The intensifiers we choose depend not only on the degree of intensification (e.g. *extremely* is stronger than *very*) but also on the meaning of what we want to intensify, the grammar of what is intensified (e.g. adjective or verb) and on style.

Some adjectives are gradeable, and we choose intensifiers such as *very* or *extremely*. With ungradeable adjectives we choose intensifiers which express absoluteness such as *absolutely, completely* or *totally*. Other intensifiers such as *largely* and *wholly* comment on the completeness of something. We use some intensifiers only to describe abstract qualities (e.g. *massively successful, hugely ambitious*).

The intensifiers we use with gradeable adjectives can also be used with adverbs (e.g. *extremely badly, really soon*), and we can use a few adverbs with verbs (e.g. *I really like it, I totally agree*).

Some common intensifiers such as *awfully, really* and *terribly* are used mainly in informal spoken English.

We use downtoners only with gradeable adjectives such as *angry, cold, hot* or with related adverbs such as *angrily*.

We can use *quite* with both gradeable and non-gradeable adjectives (and related adverbs), and its meaning changes accordingly. *Quite* functions as a downtowner with gradeable adjectives and adverbs, and expresses absoluteness with non-gradeable words. We also use different stress and intonation with the different meanings of *quite*.

She was quite tired. (gradeable)

She was quite exhausted. (non-gradeable)

Sentence position

We generally place adverbs of degree immediately before the word they qualify, e.g. *very old* (adjective), *terribly quickly* (adverb), *really like* (verb).

When the verb phrase contains a modal verb (e.g. *can, may, might, should*) we can use the adverb before the modal verb or before the main verb according to which word it qualifies.

Before the modal verb: *You **really** must look at the garden.*
Before the main verb: *You must **really** look at the garden.*

We usually place adverbs of degree immediately before the main verb when auxiliaries are used to form the tense.

*I have **quite** enjoyed the holiday.*

As well as placing *very much* before the verb, we can also place it at the end of the clause.

*I appreciate your help **very much**.*

Adverbs of quantity: a lot, a little, much

A lot, a little and *much* tell us something about quantity. We consider the expressions *a lot* and *a little* in this chapter (which is mainly concerned with single-word forms) because they have no one-word equivalent.

We generally use *a little* only in affirmative statements and *much* in negative or question forms. We can use *a lot* in affirmative and negative statements and in questions.

*She cried **a little**/**a lot**.   She doesn't eat **much**/**a lot**.*
*Do they complain about the service **much**/**a lot**?*

We generally place these adverbs at the end of a clause.

Focusing adverbs

Meaning

We use focusing adverbs:

- to single out information (e.g. *especially, even, particularly, specifically*).
- to express some kind of restriction (e.g. *just, merely, only, purely*).
- to refer back to something (e.g. *also, either, too*).

These adverbs help us to structure what we say or write, and in this way they are closely related to discourse markers (see Chapter 22).

The meaning of focusing adverbs is particularly dependent on the context we use them in and the knowledge we share with our readers or participants in conversation. Each adverb has its own rules about what kinds of words it can be used with and where it comes in the sentence, and we can use a good dictionary to check these factors.

In this section we concentrate on three examples of focusing adverbs: *even, only* and *also*.

Even

We use *even* to indicate that something is unexpected or surprising, or that it reaches an unexpected or surprising degree or extreme.

> *Everyone is lying to me – **even** you.*

Only

We use *only* to express some kind of restriction.

> *I was **only** asking you a simple question* (i.e. I was asking you a simple question and doing no more than this.)

Also

We use *also* to draw attention to the fact that we are adding information about something.

> *You have to teach the positive form of verbs and **also** the question form.*

Sentence position

The position of *even, only* and *also* in sentences is particularly flexible (although different positions may change what the sentence means). We usually place them immediately before the item they qualify.

Before the sentence subject: ***Even*** *the doorman was smiling as they left.*

Before the main verb: *The doorman was **even** smiling as they left.*

Before conjunction + clause: *The doorman was smiling **even** as they left.*

Focusing adverbs can refer to single words, which may belong to any word class, or to phrases or longer stretches of language.

Pronoun: *She invited even me.*

Verb phrase: *I also want to leave.*

Clause: *She left only what she didn't need.*

Attitude markers

Among the words that can function as attitude markers are: *apparently, blindly, clearly, hopefully, fortunately, frankly, naturally, obviously, ostensibly, really, stupidly, surprisingly, unfortunately.*

Meaning

We use attitude markers to interpret the events we describe or to convey our attitude towards them. Attitude markers usually refer to a whole clause or longer stretch of speech or writing.

> *I'll invite you **naturally**.*   ***Clearly*** *we'll want you to sign a contract.*
> ***Apparently*** *they tried to call the doctor several times.*

Most words which can be attitude markers can also function as an adverb of manner.

> *The dog wagged her tail **hopefully**.* (adverb of manner)
>
> *They'll be here, **hopefully**, by 5 o'clock.* (attitude marker)

Some people disapprove of the use of *hopefully* as an attitude marker.

Sentence position

The position of attitude markers in sentences is very flexible. For example, we can place them:

- at the beginning of a clause: ***Obviously*** *no one is going to blame you.*
- at the end of a clause: *They called the doctor several times, **apparently**.*
- before a complement: *She's **obviously** a born teacher.*
- between a subject and verb: *You **naturally** want to get recognition for what you achieve.*

We consider attitude markers more fully on page 310.

3.5 Typical difficulties for learners

Comprehension

Not knowing or identifying adverbs often poses less of a problem to learners than not knowing or not identifying nouns and adjectives, although occasionally the meaning of an adverb may be crucial. For example, adverbs of manner can convey essential information as in

Open it *gently*.

Problems with the grammar of adverbs rarely impede understanding.

Speaking and writing

Using adjectives instead of adverbs

Learners sometimes use adjectives in place of adverbs of manner.

* *She paints beautiful.*   * *She improved rapid.*

Over-using –ly endings

Learners sometimes over-generalise the rule that adverbs are created by adding –*ly* to the corresponding adjective, not knowing or realising that there are a number of exceptions to this.

* *She works hardly.*   * *She speaks ghastly.*

Adjectives with no corresponding adverb form

Although in some varieties of English examples like the following are common, most teachers would consider them to be mistakes:

(*) *She greeted us really friendly.*   (*) *She teaches very lively.*

Sentence position

Learners very often place adverbs after a verb and before a direct object.

* *I like very much music.*   * *She opened carefully the door.*

Mistakes of this kind are particularly common among learners in whose first language (e.g. many European languages) this would be the correct order.

Many other mistakes may occur where there are fixed, and seemingly arbitrary, rules which govern the sentence position of particular adverbs.

* *Have you yet been there?*   * *I have too tried ice-skating without success.*

Learners may also be unaware or may forget that the subject and verb phrase are inverted after a 'negative' adverb placed at the beginning of a sentence for emphasis.

* *Rarely we ever saw him.*   * *Not often she managed to get here on time.*

'Not . . . never'

Never (= '*not ever*') is already negative and in standard English we can't make it negative again.

* *I haven't never seen him.*

Using intensifiers with ungradeable adjectives

Students sometimes use intensifiers inappropriately.

* *I'm very starving.*   * *It's very excellent news.*

Using intensifiers with verbs

In the following cases we can use *really* to intensify the verb, but not *very* or *extremely*.

* *I very like it.*   * *Do you extremely miss me?*

yet *and* already

Learners may not know or may forget that *yet* is normally used only in negative and question forms, and *already* only in affirmative statements.

* *I have yet finished.*   * *I haven't already done it.*

3.6 Consolidation exercises (see p. 432–433 for possible answers)

Language in context

1 (see p. 432)
The following text is from a 'circular letter' sent to old friends. The adverbs have been printed in italics. Read the text and answer the questions that follow.

It's nearly Christmas – a time when I *traditionally* (1)
make efforts to renew contact with friends *individually*
(2) and when I think about you all and about what is
particularly (3) special about each and every one of you.
  This year, however, I am afraid I am writing to you
collectively (4) – I'll be thinking of each of you
individually (5) as I sign and address your card, but I
hardly ever (6) seem to have the time to sit down *nowadays*
(7) and *partly* (8) I thought this would be better than
nothing and *partly* (9) I *also* (10) want to practise my
word processing.

a What category of adverb (e.g. adverb of degree etc.) does each of these
items belong to?

b What alternative words or expressions could be used?

c Which adverbs could be used in an alternative sentence position?

2 (see p. 433)

Look at the following brief texts and answer the questions:

He explains grammar effectively and simply.

I'm interested in the quality of the product and not
simply how many units we can sell.

It went completely over my head.

I still make mistakes when I'm tired.

Woody Allen boldly goes into new territory – a Fatal Attraction-
style thriller with laughs – to produce an elegantly written,
beautifully acted film.

> The slight hum of a motor vibrates softly in the air as if the hospital was a huge ship ploughing confidently through the darkness. We sit for a while in reception in the big vinyl chairs and watch the revolving doors before going outside and taking a turn around the empty visitors' car park, laid out like a huge hop-scotch.

a Which words are adverbs?

b What category of adverb (e.g. adverb of degree etc.) does each of these words belong to?

c What effect would removing these adverbs from the texts have?

Changing attitudes (see p. 433)

a Do you consider any of the following to be unacceptable?

b If so, why?

    (i)   Hopefully, it will keep dry for the match.

    (ii)   I want to further develop my skill.

    (iii) The gradient descends very steep.

    (iv) I can't walk as quick as her.

4 Articles

a an the

4.1 Key considerations

Every time we use a noun we have to decide whether or not to use an article, and if we decide that an article is necessary, we then have to decide which one. We base these choices on a complex interaction of factors including meaning, shared knowledge, context and whether the noun is singular, plural or uncountable.

In many cases, however, fixed expressions and idioms require us to use a particular article (or not to use an article at all), apparently contradicting these 'basic rules'. Knowing these expressions is a significant factor in using articles correctly.

In helping learners to understand and use articles (particularly if their first language is a non-European language and does not have a broadly equivalent article system), we need to focus their attention constantly on how articles are used in texts they read, beginning with the most accessible and generalisable principles. There is little point in correcting mistakes and giving learners practice exercises and activities until they have developed a good awareness of how we use them.

4.2 What are articles?

What do they do?

Articles belong to the wider class of 'determiner', words or phrases that come at the beginning of a noun phrase and signal whether the information is new or familiar, or which tell us something about quantity. (Chapter 5 deals with other kinds of determiner.) We deal with articles separately here because this is how they are normally taught in course materials.

What do they look like?

The articles are:

- 'indefinite' article: *a* and *an*
- 'definite' article: *the*

We can think of *a* and *an* not as two words but as two forms of one word. This is because fixed pronunciation rules determine our choice between them (see pp. 403–404).

Where do they come in sentences?

Articles are part of noun phrases and come at the beginning of them, either immediately before a noun or an adjective, or before a combination of adverb, adjective and noun.

> *I heard* **a** *noise.* (noun)
>
> *I heard* **an** *eerie noise.* (adjective + noun)
>
> *I heard* **the** *strangely muffled noise of an animal in pain.* (adverb + adjective + noun)

4.3 How do we choose articles?

Singular, plural and uncountable nouns; other determiners

The kind of noun that follows the article affects our choice.

We can leave out articles before:

- plural nouns: *[ ] Dreams often come true.*
- uncountable nouns: *Give me [ ] money.*

We can only leave an article out before a singular noun if we replace it with another determiner:

- possessive adjectives: *her brother.*
- demonstrative adjectives: *that book.*
- many quantifiers: *any occasion, each day.*

This table shows the choices we can make:

	singular nouns	plural nouns	uncountable nouns
a/an	a book		
no article		[ ] books	[ ] rice
the	*the* book	*the* books	*the* rice

Basic rules, shared knowledge and context

A/an – introducing what is new

We use *a/an* with singular nouns to indicate that something is not common ground, to announce that we are introducing something new, something unexpected or something that our listener/reader is unaware of.

For example, imagine we meet by chance in the street. I'm upset and I blurt out *I've just seen an accident.* I choose *an* (and not *the*) because this event is something you don't know about. It tells you that I don't expect you to look around you or to root around in your memory to identify which accident I'm referring to. It's unfamiliar to you.

The – indicating 'common ground'

We use *the* to signal to our reader or listener that they know or will soon know what we are referring to. It triggers the listener or reader to search for the most obvious area of common ground in order to identify this. Context is usually the most important factor in helping us to complete this 'search' successfully.

We use *the* with a noun to refer backwards or forwards in a text or conversation, and also to refer to our shared experience or general knowledge. In each of the examples which follow, *the* (*the children*) signals that we know *which* children. We use the context to help us to identify who they are:

- referring backwards
  When I was out I passed a young couple with two little girls and a boy. I thought I knew the parents but I didn't recognise the children at all. (i.e. the two little girls and a boy)
- referring forwards
  Take prizes for the children who win. (i.e. those children who will win)
- external reference
  Shouldn't we pick up the children soon? (i.e. our children (shared knowledge))
  Herod killed the children. (i.e. the Israelite children in the Bible story (general knowledge))

No article – generalisations

We leave out articles before plural and uncountable nouns when we are referring to something general.

> *I usually have [] sandwiches for lunch.*
>
> *[] English parsley has curly leaves.*

Rules of thumb

Course materials often make little reference to these key basic rules, instead providing more specific rules of thumb, particularly with regard to using *a/an* and *the*. Some learners may find these helpful, but they can also make the basis for choosing articles unnecessarily complicated.

They teach that we use *a/an*:

- with *there is*: *There's **a** beer in the fridge.*
- the first time we mention something: *I bought **a** sandwich and **a** cake. The cake was mouldy.*
- after *have* and *have got*: *Have you got **a** mountain bike?*
- in naming things: *It's **a** rhinoceros.*
- with occupations: *I'm **a** teacher.*

They teach that we use *the*:

- when we have already mentioned what we're talking about:
  *I bought a sandwich and a cake. **The** cake was mouldy.*
- when there is only one of something:
  ***The** Moon* (i.e. the moon which revolves around our planet)
  *Can you lay **the** table?* (i.e. the table in the room we're both in)
- with defining relative clauses:
  *Shoot **the** kid who derailed the train.*
- with *of* – before something which is defined or restricted by a preposition phrase beginning with *of*
  *We're enjoying **the** benefits of early retirement.*
- in superlative expressions: *It's **the** best city in the country.*
- in comparative expressions with *same*: *Give me **the** same as usual, please.*
- with particular adjectives: ***the** first; **the** next; **the** last*

Contradictory 'sub-rules'

The problem with the 'basic rules' for choosing articles is that there are plenty of exceptions, and learners need to learn additional 'sub-rules' that may contradict these. For example:

A/an

We use *a/an* with the sense of 'every' in expressions of time and quantity such as the following:

*Forty times **an** hour.   Thirty dirhams **a** kilo.*

The

Leisure activities/forms of entertainment/travel.

We use *the* in lots of fixed expressions, where there is no obvious element of 'common ground' at all. Learners may find it helpful to consider these in 'topic' groups.

Entertainment	*I went to*	***the** cinema.*
		***the** pub.*
		***the** shops.*
Transport	*I arrived at*	***the** airport.*
		***the** bus stop.*
		***the** station.*
Musical instruments (British English only)	*I play*	***the** piano.*
		***the** violin.*
		***the** acoustic guitar.*

Proper nouns

We use *the* in the names of items in the following categories:

rivers	*the Ganges*
mountain ranges	*the Andes*
oceans and seas	*the Atlantic*
deserts	*the Sahara*
groups of islands	*the Maldives*
hotels	*the Hilton*
cinemas	*the Odeon*
political bodies	*the Labour Party, the Government*
countries whose names include political terms or plural nouns	*the United Kingdom, the Czech Republic, the Philippines*
newspapers	*The Guardian*

(When no article appears in the title of a newspaper, we use one in referring to the paper: *I read it in the Daily Mirror.*)

No article

'Belonging' to institutions

We don't use an article before the name of certain kinds of *institutions* (*hospital, church, school, prison, college, university, 'sea'* meaning 'the navy' etc.) when we want to show that someone is part of that institution.

Is she still in [] hospital? (i.e. as a patient)

He went to [] sea when he was only fourteen. (i.e. as a sailor)

Meals

We don't usually use an article in expressions which involve the names of meals.

She came to [] lunch.

Time expressions

We use no article in most expressions of time.

next [] week   *last [] year*   *on [] Sunday*   *at [] six o'clock*

Work, home and *bed*

We leave out *the* after verbs of motion in expressions with *work, home* and *bed*.

She left [] work.   *I got [] home.*   *She went to [] bed.*

Proper nouns

There is generally no article in the names of:

- people: *[] Dominique*   *[] Arthur Ashe*
- places such as villages, towns, cities, parks, streets, woods, forests:
  [] Knoxville   *[] Parsonage Lane*   *[] Sherwood Forest*
  (See p. 49 for some exceptions to this.)

Idioms

In a lot of idiomatic expressions articles are used or left out for no apparent reason other than that they belong or don't belong in the expression. Learners need to learn these like items of vocabulary, and have to remember the whole phrase, ignoring general rules or sub-rules.

***a** bit of*   *in **a** hurry*   *make **a** start*   *have **a** drink*   *do **a** turn*

*on **the** coast*   *in **the** pink*   *off **the** record*   *through **the** nose*
*go to **the** wall*   *play **the** blues*

in [] debt   *on [] loan*   *out of [] action.*

4.4 Typical difficulties for learners

Comprehension

We often pronounce articles in a very weak form, and learners may fail to recognise or distinguish them, even when they know and can predict where they should occur. For this reason, learners who listen to a lot of spoken English but who rarely read may be at a disadvantage in learning how articles are used.

Serious misunderstanding is rarely caused either by failing to hear articles or by not knowing the rules that govern how we use them. However, learners have to work much harder to understand what other people say or write if they fail to notice or understand the signals that articles give and the help they provide in processing information.

We can help learners by drawing attention to articles and to their functions in materials they use, and by guiding them to distinguish them in their very weakened forms in rapidly spoken English.

Speaking and writing

How serious are problems with articles?

Individual mistakes in using articles rarely lead to serious problems of communication. However, when learners consistently make mistakes in using them, their readers or listeners have to work much harder to understand.

Reasons for making mistakes

Learners often make mistakes because they don't know or haven't internalised the rules, or they haven't learned the fixed expressions. They may also transfer rules for using articles in their own language, inappropriately, to English.

Missing articles out

Even when learners do know the rules they may miss out articles in the struggle to communicate and to remember and use the correct information-carrying words. Indefinite articles are particularly likely to get 'squeezed out' in these circumstances.

> * Have you got pen?   * I'd like to buy new car.

Learners may also miss out articles in certain expressions where they are missed out in their own languages. *A/an* before occupations is a frequent casualty.

> * She is tax inspector.

Using articles where they aren't needed

Problems arise because the learners don't know fixed expressions or relevant 'sub-rules'.

  * *I didn't have a lunch yesterday.*   * *I watched a television.*

Learners may also use *the* in generalisations (in many European languages definite articles are normally used for this purpose).

  * *She likes the sport.*   * *The life in my country is getting harder and harder.*

Other mistakes may be the result of not realising that a noun is uncountable. Learners may treat uncountable nouns as though they are singular and therefore require an article.

  * *She plays the tennis.*   * *She has a flu.*   * *It was a good fun.*

Mistakes in using an article before a possessive adjective are usually made by people whose first language (e.g. Italian) requires this.

  * *Where is the my book?*

Using *one* instead of a/an

In many languages the equivalent of 'one' can be used to express indefiniteness before singular nouns. Learners may transfer this to English.

  * *We went to one party last night.*

4.5 Consolidation exercises (see pp. 434–436 for possible answers)

Language in context (see p. 434)

The text which follows describes an unreliable workman. The numbers indicate where articles have been used or left out. For each number explain the use (or non-use) of the article.

He was a (1) glum, unsociable person with a (2) raucous voice and (3) very thick eyebrows, and as a (4) mason he suffered from the (5) defect that he could not be depended on. He would promise to start (6) work on a (7) certain day, all the (8) furniture would be moved to the (9) far end of the (10) house, and then he would not turn up.

Learners' English (see pp. 435–436)

In the first paragraph below, a learner of English has written about a trip to the cinema, and the second is about a TV programme she had seen. The numbers indicate mistakes and especially interesting instances of how she uses articles. In each case identify correct alternatives and speculate about her use of articles.

The (1) last week I decided to go to a (2) cinema. It was difficult to choose an interesting film which I could understand without a (3) problem. I looked in a (4) newspaper and found a film. It was "Cinema Paradiso". The actors played in (5) Italian Language. I don't understand the Italian language but fortunately the subtitles were written in English. It is a wonderful film about many interesting aspects of the world of cinema and the (6) life.

I watched on a (7) TV about the (8) tuberculosis. It was (9) very interesting film. Many years ago they had to go in the (10) hospital. It was like a (11) jail. At this time many people were treated among the (12) family.

5   Quantifiers

all   another   any
both   each   either
enough   every   few
no   several   some

5.1   Key considerations

Choosing the correct quantifier is complicated, and learners often leave them out altogether or choose the wrong one.

Each time we use a noun we have to decide if a quantifier is necessary and, if it is, which one. This choice involves the meaning of what we want to express, a range of grammatical factors and also formality.

Course materials usually introduce quantifiers systematically in small groups (e.g. *some* and *any*; *much*, *many* and *a lot of*; *a few* and *a little*), and teach different uses of the same quantifier at different times.

5.2   What are quantifiers?

What do they do?

Like articles, quantifiers belong to the wider class of 'determiner', i.e. words or phrases that come at the beginning of a noun phrase and signal whether the information is new or familiar, or (in the case of quantifiers) which tell us something about quantity.

What do they look like?

See the list on page 62.

Where do they come in sentences?

We use quantifiers at the beginning of noun phrases.

Before nouns: *some thoughts.*
Before adjective+noun: *many enterprising people.*
Before adverb+adjective+noun: *any very good ideas.*

We can use noun phrases in a variety of sentence positions.

5.3 How do we choose quantifiers?

Types of noun

Whether the main noun in the noun phrase is countable (singular or plural) or uncountable limits our choice of quantifier.

- singular nouns: *another book*
- plural nouns: *a few drinks*
- uncountable nouns: *a little interest*

We use some quantifiers only when we refer to *two* things (e.g. *both occasions*, *(n)either solution*).

Is the sentence affirmative, negative or a question?

We choose some quantifiers mainly in affirmative statements, and others in negative statements or questions.

- affirmative: *I've got some time.*
- negative or question: *I can't see any problem. Do you have any ideas?*

Course materials often suggest that this is a hard and fast rule, but as we see on pages 56–58, there are many exceptions to this.

Formality

How formally we are speaking or writing can affect our choice of determiner.

Formal style	Neutral or informal style
***Much** interest was shown.*	***A lot of** interest . . .*
*They made **little** progress*	*They didn't make **much** progress*

Position of the noun phrase in the sentence

We use some quantifiers at the beginning of a sentence (in the *subject*), but generally avoid them in other positions.

> ***Much** interest was shown.*   **? They showed **much** interest.*

Meaning

Meaning determines whether we choose a quantifier instead of an article, and which of the possible quantifiers we choose.

> *Can you pass me **the** books?* (i.e. the ones we both know about)

*Can you pass me **some** books?* (i.e. an indeterminate quantity of them)

*Can you pass me **a few** books?* (i.e. a small quantity of them)

5.4 Examples of quantifiers

Some *(unstressed)*

When *some* is unstressed it is pronounced less loudly and less clearly than the words around it in the sentence, and the vowel is /ə/ (/s ə m /). Both the meaning of this unstressed form and the kinds of sentence we can use it in are different from the stressed form (see below).

General use

We use unstressed *some*:

*   to suggest an indefinite quantity but not a large amount.
    I taught them some vocabulary.
*   to introduce new information.
    He's got some money.
    Compare *He's got the money* (i.e. a precise sum we both know about).

We use *some* before plural and uncountable nouns, usually in affirmative sentences.

Learners generally learn this use of *some* at elementary level, when they learn to use *have* (e.g. *I have some cigarettes*) or *there is/there are* (e.g. *There are some eggs in the fridge*). However, we can also use *some* in the subject of a clause.

Some people came to see you.

Some in offers and requests

We can use *some* in offers even though the sentence is a question.

Would you like some custard?   (We can also say: *Would you like any custard?*)

In requests we have to use *some*.

Could I have some sugar, please? (NOT * *Could I have any sugar, please?*)

Some *(stressed)*

When we stress *some*, in southern British English the vowel is /ʌ/ (/sʌm/).

Stressed *some* can suggest a restricted or limited quantity or type of something.

> *I like SOME music.* (but by no means all!)

We use stressed *some* in questions and negative sentences as well as affirmative sentences.

> *I can't eat SOME types of fish.*

We also use stressed *some* to emphasise that precise identity is irrelevant. In this case it is often followed by a singular noun.

> *I spoke to SOME idiot in your front office.*

Any

General use

Before plural or uncountable nouns:

*   we use *any* in questions to ask about the existence of something (quantity is unimportant).

    Do you know any good jokes?

*   we use *any* after negative forms of the verb to indicate the non-existence of something (again quantity is unimportant).

    I won't bring any wine.

Learners generally learn this use of *any* at elementary level, as the question or negative alternative to *some* (e.g. *I have some cigarettes*; *I don't have any matches*).

We can use *no* instead of *not . . . any*:

> *He has **no** interest in education.* (He doesn't have any interest . . .)

We tend to prefer *no* to *not . . . any* in formal and written English, and we have to use *no* as the subject of a verb.

> ***No** students offered to help with the cleaning.* (NOT * Not any students helped . . .)

Unrestricted or unlimited quantity

Stressed *any* suggests an unrestricted quantity or unlimited choice.

> *I don't like ANY red wine.* (I think all red wine is horrible.)
> *You can take ANY book.* (The choice is entirely open.)

We use stressed *any* with singular as well as plural and uncountable nouns, and in affirmative sentences as well as negative ones and questions.

When we use *any* as part of the subject of a clause, it suggests unrestrictedness (the particular identity is unimportant) even if it isn't stressed.

> ***Any*** *music would be better than this horrible noise!*

Much, many, *and* a lot of

General use

We use *much, many,* and *a lot of* to suggest a large quantity:

> *Do you need* **much** *space?   I've lived here for* **many** *years.*   ***A lot of*** *soft drinks contain sugar substitutes.*

We use *much* with uncountable nouns and *many* with countable (plural) nouns. At elementary level we usually teach that we use *much* and *many* in questions and after negative forms of the verb (although, as we see below, we can also use *much* and *many* in affirmative sentences).

> Uncountable: *Do they have* **much** *money?   I haven't got* **much** *time.*
>
> Plural: *Do you have* **many** *things still to do?   There weren't* **many** *trees left standing.*

At elementary level we generally teach *a lot of* as a neutral, affirmative form for both plural and uncountable nouns.

> Plural: *There are* ***a lot of*** *people outside.*
> Uncountable: *They have* ***a lot of*** *charm.*

Much and *many* after *so, too*, and *how*

After *so, too* and *how* we use *much* before uncountable nouns and *many* before countable nouns.

> *I've got* ***so many*** *things to do.   You're wasting* ***too much*** *time.*
> *Tell me* ***how many*** *people have arrived.*

Much and *many* in affirmative statements; *a lot of* in questions and negative statements

We often use *many* in noun phrases that are the subject of an affirmative clause.

> ***Many*** *people arrived early.*

We can also use *many* in a noun phrase which is the object or complement of an affirmative clause, particularly in formal and written English.

*She felt **many** emotions.* (complement)

*People raised **many** doubts.* (object)

We use *much* in affirmative sentences, generally only in very formal, written registers.

*There has been **much** research into universals in the effective group behaviour of students.*

We use *a lot of* in questions and in negative statements to give extra emphasis to the amount.

*Do they have **a lot of** friends?*   *I don't have **a lot of** time.*

Several, a few, *and* a little

We use *several, a few*, and *a little* to suggest a small quantity. *Several* implies more items than *a few*.

*I've sent out **several** cards but I've only received **a few** confirmations.*

We use *several* and *a few* with *plural* nouns and *a little* with uncountable ones.

*There are **several/a few** people waiting.* (Plural)

*Just give him **a little** attention.* (Uncountable)

We tend to use these quantifiers in affirmative statements and questions, rather than in negative statements.

Few *and* little

We use *few* and *little* (without *a*) to suggest a strong sense of reservation, with a hint of 'not enough'.

***Few** people came.* (Plural)

*He had **little** success.* (Uncountable)

We tend to use these quantifiers in formal, written English. We are more likely to use *not . . . many/much* informally.

***Not many** people came.*   *He did**n't** have **much** success.*

More, fewer *and* less

These are comparative forms which correspond to *a lot of/many/much, a few* and *a little*. We use *more* with both plural and uncountable nouns, while *fewer* is used only with plural nouns and *less* is generally used with uncountable nouns.

See also Chapter 6 for discussion and illustration of these comparative forms.

All, each *and* every

We use *all, each* and *every* to emphasise the *completeness* of a group or class of things.

> *We've considered **all** opinions.*   ***All** wine contains alcohol.*   *They defused **each** bomb.*   ***Every** night was the same.*

All looks at things from a collective view and is followed by a plural or uncountable noun. *Each* and *every* have a more individual, one-by-one point of view, and are followed by a singular noun and verb.

Each and *every* are often interchangeable when they refer to three or more of something.

> *They checked **each/every** table before the guests arrived.*

We use *every* to refer to frequency and times.

> *every day*   *every minute*   *every time the phone rings*

We tend to use *every* for large numbers.

> *She had to greet **every** person in the room.*

We can use *each* (but not *every*) to refer to only two things.

> *Did you examine **each** side of the coin?* (NOT * *every* side of the coin).

Unlike most quantifiers, *all* can immediately precede *the* or a possessive adjective (e.g. *all the time; all my family*).

Both, either *and* neither

We use *both, either* and *neither* to refer to two people or things.

> *They examined **both** sides.*   *They made no attempt to rescue **either** dog.*   *They were able to make contact with **neither** parent.*

Both looks at things from a collective view (this one *and* this one).

> *She betrayed **both** parents.*

Either looks at things from the point of view of alternatives (this one *or* this one).

> *You can choose **either** option.*

Both is followed by a plural noun (*both sides*) and *either* and *neither* by singular nouns and verbs (*either dog is . . .; neither parent has . . .*).

We use *either* in questions and negative statements. *Neither* is in itself negative (*neither = not either*).

We use *neither* in formal and written English. In informal contexts, we often prefer *not . . . either* (*They didn't like either film* rather than *They liked neither film*).

Unlike most quantifiers, *both* can immediately precede *the* or a possessive adjective (*both the children; both my parents*).

Enough

We use *enough* to emphasise that a quantity is sufficient for some purpose.

> *You haven't had **enough** lessons.*

We use *enough* with plural and uncountable nouns.

> *I've been in **enough** hospitals to know.* (Plural)
> *Are you getting **enough** help?* (Uncountable)

Another

We use *another* to emphasise that something is additional to an existing number or quantity.

> *We're having **another** baby.* (This baby is not our first)

We use *another* with singular nouns and with numbers followed by plural nouns.

> *Have **another** drink.*   *I've got **another** three days.*

Overview

This table provides an overview of the grammatical considerations we take into account in choosing quantifiers:

	singular	plural	uncountable	
all		✓	✓	*All can immediately precede the or a possessive adjective.*
another	✓			
any (unstressed)		✓	✓	*We use this mainly in questions and negative sentences.*
any (stressed)	✓	✓	✓	
both		✓		*We use this to refer to two of something. It can immediately precede the or a possessive adjective.*
each	✓			*We can use this to refer to two or more of something.*
either/neither	✓			*We use this to refer to two of something.*
enough		✓	✓	
every	✓			
few/fewer/a few		✓		
little/less/a little			✓	
many		✓		*We use this mainly in questions and negative sentences.*
more		✓	✓	
much			✓	*We use this mainly in questions and negative sentences.*
no	(✓)	✓	✓	
several		✓		
some (unstressed)		✓	✓	
some (stressed)	✓	✓	✓	
a lot of		✓	✓	

5.5 Using quantifiers with other determiners

We generally don't use quantifiers immediately before or after other determiners.

However, *all* and *both* can immediately precede *the* or a possessive adjective (and in this case they are known as pre-determiners).

> ***All your*** *students came.*   *They welcomed* ***both the*** *speakers.*

We can combine the following quantifiers:

every + few	*I travel* ***every few*** *weeks.*
a few + more/less	*He needed* ***a few more*** *votes.*
a little + more/less	*I received* ***a little less*** *money.*
few/little + enough	*We get* ***few enough*** *treats.*

We can also link all the words and expressions we have looked at in this chapter apart from *every* and *no* to nouns or pronouns by using *of the* or *of*+possessive adjective. In this case the words are classed as pronouns rather than quantifiers.

of + *the* + noun	*Give it to* ***either of the*** *children.*
of + pronoun	*I didn't understand* ***much of it.***
of + possessive adjective + noun	***Many of our*** *friends came.*

5.6 Typical difficulties for learners

Comprehension

When learners don't know or don't notice quantifiers, this rarely leads to significant misunderstanding.

Speaking and writing

It is relatively easy for learners to learn the meaning of quantifiers, but more difficult for them to grasp and remember the grammatical restrictions that control their use.

Leaving out quantifiers altogether

Learners are particularly prone to leave out the more 'neutral' quantifiers (e.g. *some* and *any*).

> * *There aren't parks in the centre of my city.*   * *Could I have help?*

Inappropriate use of any

Learners sometimes use *any* in affirmative sentences instead of *not . . . any* or *no*.

> * *I can't pay. I have any money.*

Over-using quantifiers

Learners also sometimes use two quantifiers together or a quantifier next to an article.

> * *Do you have enough some money?*   * *It rained every the day.*

Pronunciation: stressed and unstressed forms of some *and* any

Learners sometimes stress *some* or *any* inappropriately, unintentionally suggesting an element of restrictedness. This can give rise to damaging misunderstandings about attitude – for example, in the first of these examples the stress on *some* can give the impression that the speaker is only grudgingly allowing time. In the second example, the stress on *any* can make the question sound demanding or whining:

> *I've got SOME time to spare.*   *Do you have ANY time to spare?*

Using much *and* many *instead of* a lot of

Learners sometimes over-use *much* and *many* because they are concentrating on whether the noun is countable or uncountable, and they forget that they also need to consider whether the sentence is affirmative.

> * *I have much money.*   (*) *You'll be sick if you eat many sweets.*

Countable and uncountable nouns

Learners mistake uncountable for countable nouns and use *many* instead of *much*.

> * *I don't have many money.*

Singular-plural confusion

Sometimes learners use plural nouns after *each* and *every*.

> * *Each regions are distinct.*   * *Every people are here now.*

Learners also sometimes want to use a singular form of the verb after *a lot of*.

> * *A lot of animals is becoming extinct.*

A lot of appears to be singular, but this use is wrong.

Quantifiers and pronouns

Learners often use *all* as a pronoun (instead of *everybody, everyone* or *everything*):

> * *He gave money to all.*

5.7 Consolidation exercises (see pp. 436–439 for possible answers)

Language in context

1 (see p. 436)

The sentences that follow are from a lecture about managing change in education.

(i)   All the references are on the handout.

(ii)   All teachers have their own implicit theories of learning.

(iii) Most teachers in Britain resisted the National Curriculum.

(iv)   Every teacher has a fund of experience and received knowledge.

(v)   Few teachers would like to be typecast as the teachers who just repeat what they do.

(vi)   Some people are so resistant to change that they just throw up their hands in horror.

(vii) He outlines a large number of steps which are concerned in change.

---

a Identify all the quantifiers.

b Identify any words or expressions that are similar to quantifiers or that can function as quantifiers in other contexts.

c Comment on any instances where another quantifier might be used in place of the one which is used here. What difference would this make if any?

2 (see p. 437)

Read the following sentences.

---

(1) sides accepted the decision.

(2) European countries apart from Britain have gymnasia systems.

(3) teachers refuse to abandon the belief that grammatical competence is the essential component of communicative competence.

The Tyneside transport system was a source of (4) pride.

She'll be with me and chase (5) spider away.

---

a Choose the most appropriate quantifier to fill each of the numbered gaps.

b Explain/justify your choices.

Differences in meaning *(see p. 438)*

Look at the following sentences. For each pair/group consider the questions below.

(i)   Have you got any paint for concrete floors?
      Have you got some paint for concrete floors?

(ii) I can't find it. I've searched through every drawer in the office.
      I can't find it. I've searched through each drawer in the office.
      I can't find it. I've searched through all the drawers in the office.

(iii) I can't find either of the books you told me to look for.
      I can find neither of the books you told me to look for.

(iv) I don't have any more strength.
      I have no more strength.

(v)   Has he scored a lot of goals this season?
      Has he scored many goals this season?

(vi) I think she's got some photos to show you. (*some* unstressed)
      I think she's got SOME photos to show you. (*some* stressed)

(vii) He's got a little sense.
      He's got little sense.

---

a Is one of these sentences incorrect or inappropriate?

b What differences (if any) in meaning and effect are there between the sentences?

Learners' English *(see p. 439)*

Look at the following sentences and in each case consider the questions:

(i) She got much money for her birthday.

(ii) She was given many presents when she left her job.

(iii) Many people congratulated her on her success.

(iv) They gave her a lot of opportunities.

(v) Much interest was shown in the project.

(vi) Neither children are going to know about it.

(vii) They invited all to visit them.

a Would this use be acceptable by a native speaker?

b Would you correct this if a learner of English wrote it in a composition? Why?

6 Comparatives and superlatives

bigger than
more interesting than
much more   many more
far better than   the worst

6.1 Key considerations

The grammar involved in expressing comparative and superlative meaning is more complex in English than in many languages.

Not all languages make a distinction between comparatives and superlatives, and some learners may find the distinction an awkward one to grasp.

Learners usually like teachers to introduce this topic bit-by-bit (e.g. initially teaching comparative forms and superlative forms separately, teaching the use of *more* separately from . . . *–er*, and *most* separately from . . . *–est*).

Coursebooks tend to teach very idealised comparative and superlative structures, to provide learners with a useful set of 'rules'. In fact, comparatives and superlatives occur only rarely in these idealised patterns. In time learners will also need to recognise the large variety of forms which occur, and to use some of the variations.

6.2 What are comparatives and superlatives?

At the simplest level:

- comparatives are adjectives and adverbs that end in *–er* (e.g. *bigger, richer, faster*).
- superlatives are adjectives and adverbs that end in *–est* (e.g. *biggest, richest, fastest*).

Because in learning to use these forms learners also need to learn when they can't be used and what to use instead, in this chapter we also consider:

- *more* or *less* followed by nouns, adjectives and adverbs (e.g. *more time, more successful, less attentively*).
- *most* or *least* followed by nouns, adjectives and adverbs (e.g. *most time, most successful, least attentively*).

6.3 How are they formed?

Long adjectives and adverbs

We use *more* and *most* before adjectives and adverbs when these words are long – almost always if they have three or more syllables.

> *expensive*: *It was the **most expensive** wine in the shop.*
>
> *energetically*: *She talks **more energetically** when she's with people she knows.*

Short adjectives and adverbs

We generally teach that we add *–er* or *–est* to the end of shorter adjectives and adverbs – almost always if they have only one syllable.

> *fast*: *He drove **faster** this morning.*

Although we may choose not to teach this – at least until a much higher level, in fact we sometimes have to use *more* and *most* with one-syllable adjectives.

> With adjectives that are also past participles, e.g. *burnt, drunk, forced, lost, spoiled, tired, torn*: *I'm getting **more** and **more tired***
>
> With adjectives that are not gradeable, e.g. *dead, male, royal*: *I feel **more dead** than I did yesterday.*

We also sometimes choose to use *more* and *most* with one-syllable adjectives.

To make a specific contrast with 'less':	A: *Did she say it was **less cold** in the north of the country?* B: *No. She said it was **more cold**.*
'One-off' individual choices:	*Don't blame me if you feel **more ill** when you've eaten all that!*

Two-syllable adjectives and adverbs

With many two-syllable words (e.g. *able, clever, common, frosty, happy*) we can choose whether to use *more/most* or to add *–er/est* to make the comparative and superlative forms.

> *Are you feeling **happier**? / **more happy**?*

With other two-syllable words, we have to use *more/most*. Sometimes there is nothing in the spelling or pronunciation of the word which helps us to know this, but there are also a number of useful rules of thumb:

Adverbs that end in –*ly*, e.g. *promptly, quickly, thinly*:
*She stood up the **most promptly**.*

Adjectives that are the same as present or past participles, e.g. *boiling, boring, damaged, freezing, needed, smiling*:
*Today's lecture was even **more boring** than usual.*

Adjectives that have 'typical' adjective endings such as –*al*, –*ant*, –*ard*, –*ate*, –*ect*, –*ed*, –*en*, –*ent*, –*ful*, –*id*, –*ite*, –*ive*, –*less*, –*ous*, –*some*, e.g. *awkward, candid, careful, careless, crucial, finite, gifted, gorgeous, loathsome, mental, spacious, recent*:
*The **most crucial** thing is to arrive in good time.*

Less *and* the least

We can use *less* and *the least* with all adjectives and adverbs, regardless of the number of syllables in the words.

> *I was **less free** in my last job.*   *Lets pick **the least complicated** solution.*

However, we often avoid using *less*, particularly in speech and more informal writing. We tend to use *not as/so . . . as* instead.

> *He is**n't as/so** keen **as** he used to be.*

Irregular comparative and superlative forms

This table shows some of the most common irregular forms:

	comparative	superlative	notes
good	better	best	
well	better	best	
bad	worse	worst	
badly	(worse)	(worst)	We can also say *more/most badly*.
far	farther farther further	farthest furthest	We use *farther* and *farthest* usually to refer only to distance. *Further* and *furthest* can also have abstract meaning (e.g. *I don't want to discuss this any further*).

old	elder	eldest	*Older* and *oldest* are the standard forms. We use *elder* and *eldest* only to talk about family relationships, and only normally before a noun (e.g. we say *my elder brother* but NOT * *My brother is elder than me*).

Expressions of Quantity

We use *more* and *most*, *fewer* and *fewest*, and *less* and *least* to make statements about quantity, in which case they clearly refer to something we can count or measure. This is usually expressed by a noun.

> There are **more people** in British prisons than there were in 1990.
>
> Many European cities have problems of traffic congestion but Athens is supposed to have **the most**. (problems)
>
> **Fewer** and **fewer school leavers** want to study classics.
>
> I have **the least** financial **expertise**.

We can think of these words as the comparative and superlative forms of quantifiers:

quantifier	comparative	superlative
a lot/much/many	more	most
a few	fewer	fewest
a little	less	least

We generally use *most*, *fewest* and *least* in expressions with *have* (e.g. *have the least financial expertise*).

Although we usually teach that *less* and *least* can't be used with countable nouns (* *less pounds*, * *the least books*), this is very common in speech and increasingly common in writing.

> Groups produce less ideas, in total, than the individuals in those groups working separately.

Some people consider this to be unacceptable in written English.

6.4 Where do comparatives and superlatives come in sentences?

At an elementary or intermediate level, coursebooks usually present comparatives as part of the following pattern:

X	verb	comparative	than	Y
Maths	was	more difficult	than	spelling.

They usually present superlatives as part of the following pattern:

Z	verb	the	superlative	type	specific class
Everest	is	the	highest	mountain	in the world.

If we look at how people really use comparative and superlative forms in speaking and writing, we find examples similar to these. The following is from a newspaper interview with a child who has just taken a national school test:

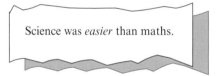

Science was *easier* than maths.

In the same newspaper article, however, there are more examples that *don't* follow this pattern, and they are more typical of how we use comparatives and superlatives generally. These comparatives are *not* followed by a phrase beginning '*than . . .*' because what the thing is being compared with is clearly implied in the context (e.g. *I thought they would be a lot harder **than they actually were***). Equally, the superlatives aren't followed by the type + class because, again, the context implies the class that the thing belongs to (e.g. *the most brilliant thing **in my life at the moment***):

Comparative structures	Superlative structures
I thought they would be a lot *harder*.	The *most brilliant* thing is that now it's all over.
They seemed hard at first but *easier* as you got used to them.	*Most important* was to divide up the work sensibly.
Usually I go to bed about 9 pm but it was *earlier* during SATS.	Science and spelling were *easiest*.
Maths started easy but got *harder*.	My mum said to me: 'You just try your *best*', and that's what I did.

In teaching, we need to draw our students' attention to comparatives and superlatives however they occur in conversations and texts, and to encourage them to identify information that is only implied. We also need to ensure that they practise these forms in simple statements and questions (e.g. *It's hotter; Who's the tallest?*) as well as in the idealised patterns.

6.5 What do they do?

We use comparatives to compare some common feature of two or more things or people in terms of degree or quantity. We use superlatives to single out one thing or person as being special in relation to others on some kind of implied scale.

Coursebook examples

Coursebooks usually focus very heavily on the *form* of how we make comparative and superlative statements, often taking the *meaning* of these forms for granted.

Coursebook examples usually suggest that we use comparatives to compare *two* things.

The Porsche is more expensive than the Toyota.

They often don't recognise that we use a comparative to compare something with more than one other thing.

The Porsche is more expensive than the Toyota and the Rover.

The Porsche is more expensive than all the other cars.

Coursebook examples often ignore that what we are comparing something with is often left unsaid.

Cars are getting more expensive (than they used to be).

Coursebook examples usually suggest that we use superlatives to compare more than two things. There may be three pictures of cars and a superlative example sentence, e.g. *The Porsche is the most expensive car.*

As we have seen, we could also say: *The Porsche is more expensive than the Toyota and the Rover.* We choose the superlative here because we aren't really interested in the other cars, only with the Porsche.

The following sentences come from an advertisement for an ice cream called 'Indulgence' produced by the British supermarket Sainsbury's. Comparatives and superlatives are used extensively in advertisements, and as we see here, they are often very different from the examples found in coursebooks:

> To complement its rich flavour, Sainsbury's Indulgence has *a far denser texture than ordinary ice creams*.

(The comparative is used to compare 'Indulgence' not with one other thing but with all 'ordinary ice creams'.)

> Just like those rich American ice creams, Sainsbury's Indulgence is made with real dairy cream and *the highest quality, freshest ingredients*.

(The superlative is used to show that the quality and freshness of the ingredients in this ice cream (and some American ones) could not be surpassed.)

Coursebook examples also sometimes suggest that we use comparatives to compare anything with anything, and exercises involve transforming sentences like *China is larger than India* to *India is smaller than China*. In fact, the second of these sentences is very unlikely as neither country is small. Coursebook examples such as *China is larger than Switzerland* are even more unnatural as we don't generally compare things at the opposite end of a scale.

Teaching

At low levels it is unwise to teach all the ways in which we use comparatives and superlatives and to explore all the factors involved in choosing them. However, ignoring meaning and focusing attention only on form is equally unhelpful, and we need to draw students' attention to the contexts in which these forms occur, and ask them context-related questions to focus on meaning (e.g. *Are any of these cars cheap? Are these countries both large?*).

6.6 Other factors

Ways of intensifying and 'downtoning' comparative forms

We use a range of words and expressions before comparative forms to make them seem stronger or weaker. Those marked with an asterisk are used mainly in spoken and informal contexts.

far *	*considerably*	*slightly*
much	*by far*	*barely (any)*
(quite) a lot *	*a little*	*hardly (any)*
a great deal	*a bit* *	*scarcely (any)*

> *The project has been **a great deal less successful** than we had hoped.*
>
> *I feel **a bit happier** now than when I last spoke to you.*

We can also use a number of expressions after comparative forms, particularly in spoken and informal contexts: *by miles, by far, by a long way, by a long chalk.*

> *Hong Kong is more humid than New York **by far**.*

Ways of emphasising superlative forms

We use a range of words and expressions before the superlative form of adjectives to make them seem stronger. We generally don't use them before the superlative form of adverbs (* *She ran altogether the fastest*).

> *simply*
> *easily*
> *altogether*
> *quite*
> *by far and away*

*She's **easily the best** candidate.*

*It was **simply the most wonderful** performance I ever heard.*

We can also use a number of expressions after superlative forms, particularly in spoken and informal contexts: *by miles, by far, by a long way, by a long chalk.*

*We've just played our worst match this season **by a long way.***

–er and –er; more and more . . .

We often repeat the same comparative form, separated by *and*. Usually this is to emphasise the speed or inevitability of a process. We often use the expression *get . . . -er and . . . -er.*

*The traffic's getting **worse and worse.***

Exact measurements

We sometimes compare things in terms of exact measurements. In this case we generally specify the quantity immediately before the comparative form.

It's thirty per cent/twenty times bigger.

When we use a fraction on its own, we generally don't use a comparative form. Instead we use *as* + adjective.

It's half as big.

6.7 Rules of thumb (and their limitations)

The *with comparatives*

'Don't use *the* before the adjective or adverb in comparisons' is a good rule of thumb for elementary learners. At a subsequent stage, however, we need to consider the following kinds of comparison, where *the* is used:

- Where *of the two of them* is stated or implied:
  He is the taller (of the two of them).
- In expressions which describe complementary processes. (*The* comparative . . ., *the* comparative . . .)
  ***The more** you eat, **the more** you want.*

The *with superlatives*

Elementary coursebooks usually teach 'Use *the* with superlatives'.

*She's easily **the most** talented of this year's graduates.*

There are also plenty of cases, however, where we don't need or can't use *the*.

- In the expressions *try your best/hardest*; *do your best* we have to use a possessive adjective (*my, his* etc.) instead of *the*:
  She tried her hardest.
- When the specific instance belongs to a small, finite class of things that is implied or understood:
  Science and spelling were easiest.
- In expressions where we infer *the . . . est thing (to do) is. . . .*
  It's safest to leave before the rush hour.
- In superlative expressions within defining relative clauses:
  Give it to the children who are oldest.
- Where the superlative form is an adverb of manner:
  Susie writes most clearly.

Beyond elementary level we need to take account of examples without *the*.

In *and* of

We generally use *in* to relate a superlative item to its 'class'.

> *The largest city **in** South America.*

We need to be aware, however, that we use *of* to relate a superlative item to *other items* in its 'class', and at some point may need to teach this.

> *The largest **of** all South American cities.*

Relative clauses

We often use superlative expressions immediately before a relative clause. The verb in the relative clause is often in the present perfect (or past simple in American English) or past perfect.

> *Tell us about the best meal **you've ever eaten**.*

It is convenient to revise superlatives when we want students to practise relative clauses.

6.8 Stylistic choices

Adjectives in place of adverbs

In both written and spoken English many people use the comparative and superlative form of adjectives in place of adverbs. This happens particularly with the *–er/–est* comparative/superlative form of one-syllable adjectives.

> *He walks a lot slower than he did.* (He walks a lot more slowly . . .)
>
> *She escaped the quickest.* (She escaped the most quickly.)

Some people dislike and avoid this use of adjective forms, particularly in written English.

Pronouns

When we use a pronoun after *than* in comparative structures, this is usually an object pronoun (*me, him, us, them*, etc.).

> *They are richer than **us**.*

Some people prefer to use the subject pronoun followed by an auxiliary verb (or a form of *be*), particularly in written English.

> *I ran faster than **he did**.*   *They are richer than **we are**.*

6.9 Typical difficulties for learners

Comprehension

In listening learners may fail to recognise comparative and superlative forms, particularly if they are unaware of or unused to the way in which we characteristically pronounce *than* and the *–er* and *–est* endings very weakly. They may, for example, hear *bigger* and *biggest* as *big*, and may hear *than* as *the*.

The final /t/ in words like *biggest* and the final /n/ in *than* often disappear before another consonant (*biggest place* — / bɪgɪs - pleɪs /; *than me* — /ðəmiː /). This may also lead to students failing to recognise the forms.

Speaking and writing

Over-using more *and* most

Learners often use *more* or *most* when it would be more normal to add *–er* or *–est* to the word.

> * *He is more tall than me.*

They also sometimes use *more* or *most* in addition to *–er* or *–est*. Whereas *more tall than* is only odd (rather than incorrect), the following is clearly wrong: * *They are more better than us.*

Over-use of –er and –est

This problem is rarer than the over-use of *more* and *most*.

Learners may not know the appropriate irregular forms.

    * *I am wearing my goodest pair of shoes.*   * *I don't want to walk farer.*

They may use *–er* or *–est* with long as well as short adjectives.

    * *Minsk is the beautifulest city in my country.*

Leaving out the

We need to use *the* in most superlative statements. Learners sometimes leave it out.

    * *She's most important person in my country.*

Using more in superlative statements

Learners sometimes use *more* instead of *most*.

    * *She's the more obstinate child in the class.*

This is particularly characteristic of learners whose first language is Latin-based (French, Italian etc.).

Using of instead of in

Learners sometimes feel uncomfortable using *in* to relate superlative items to their class or group.

    (*) *China has the largest population of the world.*

Problems with than

Learners sometimes use other words instead of *than. That* is often used, perhaps because the two words are so similar in appearance. *As* and *of* are also sometimes used.

    * *I work harder that I used to.*   * *She's older of me.*

6.10 Consolidation exercises (see pp. 440–442 for possible answers)

Learners' English (see p. 440)

What would you tell the learner who made the following mistakes, so that she understood the mistake and could avoid making it again?

(1) thinest

(2) more bigger

(3) happyer

(4) more good

(5) beautifulest

Language in context

1 (see pp. 440–441)

Comparative and superlative forms have been indicated by numbers in the two passages that follow. Study each of these and answer the questions:

" . . . the *bravest (1)* and *most correct (2)*, the *firmest (3)*, the *most loyal (4)* and the *most ardent (5)* national hero"

FAST MUSIC makes you shop *faster (6)*, classical music makes you buy *more expensive (7)* wine and country music drives you to despair, psychologists said today.

"Certain types of music can influence the degree to which people are open to persuasion," Adrian North of Leicester University told the British Association Annual Science Festival at Birmingham University today. "Music tempo can influence the speed of customers' activity."

After a study that showed that fast music led to shoppers moving around a supermarket *more quickly (8)* than did slow music, a follow-up showed that fast music caused diners to eat *more quickly (9)*.

Another study showed a similar effect with fast music in a bar – drinking was *quicker (10)* than it was to slow music. In a cafeteria, diners took *more (11)* bites per minute than they did to slow.

Playing classical music and a selection from the Top 40 in a wine cellar revealed that people buy *more expensive (12)* bottles to classical, while sad music in a stationery shop led to a *bigger (13)* purchase of greetings cards.

Sad music also led to people being *more helpful (14)* than did other types.

a Is this form a comparative or a superlative?

b Is this form an adjective, adverb or quantifier?

c Would an alternative form (e.g. *bravest* ⇒ *most brave*) be possible? Would this change the meaning in any way?

2 (see p. 441)

The following is an extract from a newspaper article, comparing Britain in the early 1950s with Britain in the early 1990s. Read the passage and then answer the questions.

Deaths from cancer and heart disease were *30 per cent lower (1)*. However, tuberculosis claimed nearly 9,000 lives compared with 400 in 1991, infant mortality was more than three times as high and people died, on average, *seven years earlier (2)*.

One myth is how cheap things were. Yes, a pint of beer cost only 6p (1s 2d) a pint and the Ford Popular* cost £350 including tax. But the average industrial worker earned £8 a week and would have had to toil for nearly a year to buy *the cheapest car (3)*. Only 14 per cent of households had cars against 70 per cent today.

Air France advertised return flights to Paris for £16. That is more than £200 in today's money.

More people died in road accidents in 1953 (4,200) than they did last year, even though there were *far fewer cars (4)*.

a Explain what is implied but not made explicit in each of the phrases printed in italics.

b In the last sentence further information could be left out without harming the meaning. Which two words could be left out?

3 (see pp. 441–442)

a Identify and classify all examples of comparative or superlative structures in the following.

b In each case comment on any features that distinguish these examples from the 'basic' patterns described on page 72.

* *Ford Populars* were small and relatively cheap cars produced for the mass market.

(i)

> The Wilsons were better educated than the Robertses and, some of the time, slightly richer. . . . The Wilsons took more holidays . . . Moreover, the psychological roles of husband and wife in the two families were to some extent the reverse of each other: Ethel, a teacher, was the strongest character in the Wilson household, whereas Margaret's mother . . . was colourless and downtrodden.

(ii)

> Men are three times more likely than women to burn out their brain tissue, according to a study by the University of Pennsylvania. Apparently women are better able to control their brain usage, while men "overdrive" their brain cells, leading to cell death. Men aged 18–45 lose cells fastest in the frontal lobe area – the part responsible for mental flexibility and reasoning.

(iii)

> Having a nasty part is a big responsibility because it is usually the person that can be nastiest who defines and determines the emotional tone, quality and direction of a relationship.

7 Prepositions

*across   at   from   in   of
until   after   beyond   despite
in terms of   in spite of
given   regarding*

7.1 Key considerations

Learners often see prepositions as a major problem. This is because:

- there are so many prepositions in English (many more than in a lot of other languages), and learners often have to make choices and distinctions that are not necessary in their own language.

- many choices have little or nothing to do with meaning, and are therefore particularly difficult to remember.

Mistakes in using prepositions rarely cause problems in communication. Some learners may choose to put up with making mistakes in prepositions in order to concentrate their energy and attention on other aspects of English.

If learners really want to use prepositions correctly, good dictionary-using habits may be as useful for them as 'preposition lessons'.

7.2 What are prepositions?

What do they look like?

Many of the most common words in English are prepositions, and many of them are very short words (e.g. *at, for, in, to*). However, longer words and short phrases (e.g. *despite, except, according to, out of, in terms of, in the event of*) can function as prepositions too. A number of participles (e.g. *assuming, concerning, given, granted, regarding*) can be used as prepositions.

> **Given** *your schedule, I think you should book decent hotel rooms.*
>
> *I wrote to you last week* **concerning** *your offer . . .*

We can't recognise prepositions just from the form of the words.

Where do they come in sentences?

General use

Prepositions:

- usually occur immediately before a noun or -*ing* form (e.g. *to work, of cooking*) or at the beginning of a phrase including a noun (e.g. *at the cinema*). These phrases can occur in various sentence positions.

- often occur immediately after a verb (e.g. *arrive at*), adjective (e.g. *fond of*) or noun (e.g. *interest in*).

When prepositions precede a verb, this is always an -*ing* form (e.g. *I'm afraid of **crying***).

In other positions

In the following cases we can use prepositions at the end of clauses:

Questions with *what, who* or *which*:	*What are you staring **at**? Who do you live **with**? Which one is it **like**?*
Passive constructions:	*Every possible surface had been drawn **on**.*
Relative clauses:	*I don't know who you were playing **with**.*
Infinitive clauses:	*It's a funny thing to ask **about**.*

We can also use prepositions before a question word in direct questions but this is very formal and old-fashioned.

With whom did she come?   *At what time did she leave?*

Some learners make questions like this whenever a preposition is involved, in which case we should encourage them to put the preposition at the end of the question (e.g. *Who did she come with?*).

We can also use prepositions before a relative pronoun in formal contexts (this may seem affected in speech or informal writing).

*A company **with whom** we have successfully been conducting business.*

*The master **under whose** guidance he had been studying.*

7.3 What do they do?

Place and time

Some prepositions have a concrete meaning that we can show or demonstrate. These often define place, position or movement, e.g. *between the columns, towards the door.*

Many of these prepositions can also refer to *time*.

> **Place**: *at the bus stop, in the room*
> **Time**: *at 10.00, in March*

Prepositions which can refer to both place and time generally have a similar meaning in both cases. However, in expressions which refer to the future, *in* can mean 'later than now', e.g. *in six months, in a few minutes.*

Learners may misunderstand this meaning of *in* when they first come across it and often avoid using it.

Other prepositions (e.g. *after, before, by, during, since, till, until*) can refer to time, but not usually to place, e.g. *after Saturday, during the week.*

Logical relationships

A number of prepositions express key logical relationships.

- cause and effect (e.g. *because of, due to, owing to, as a result of*)
  I left as a result of his speech.
- contrast (e.g. *despite, in spite of*)
  You slept despite the noise.
- exemplification (e.g. *like, such as*)
  Go somewhere like Crete or Corfu.
- exception (e.g. *apart from, except*)
  Ask anyone apart from me.

Multiple meanings

A number of prepositions have several meanings. These are not necessarily closely related.

> *They went for a walk **by** the canal.* (i.e. near/along) *It has to be ready **by** the weekend.* (i.e. on or before)
>
> *She made it **with** eggs and cheese.* (i.e. using) *She went there **with** her mother.* (i.e. accompanied by)

Dependent prepositions

After many adjectives, nouns and verbs we need to use a particular preposition. Often this preposition is just a linking word which contributes no meaning. When learners learn these adjectives, nouns and verbs, they also need to learn the correct 'dependent' preposition.

adjectives: *afraid **of**, crazy **about***
nouns: *process **of**, difficulty **in***
verbs: *combine **with**, listen **to**, accuse sb **of**, protect sb **from***

Learners often find it difficult to use *to* as a dependent preposition (see p. 89), e.g. *I've got used **to** walking again.*

These are some common words and expressions that we follow with *to*:

look forward   (be/get) used   object   (be) committed   consent.

Idiomatic preposition phrases

We frequently use prepositions in fixed, idiomatic expressions containing a noun. The noun may be singular, plural or uncountable, and may or may not be separated from the preposition by *a/an, the, some* or an adjective (often *good* or *bad*).

at times	*on good terms*
beneath contempt	*out of use*
for the time being	*to some extent*
in (good) time	*under offer*

Learners need to learn these and similar phrases as complete expressions which include prepositions.

7.4 Variation

Choice

We can sometimes choose between two prepositions without making any difference to the meaning.

*Come and see me **in**/**during** the week.   I got covered **with**/**in** paint.*

Style

Some prepositions are used primarily in a formal and generally professional or academic context, e.g. *notwithstanding.*

Till tends to be a spoken form and *until* a written one.

Geographical, social and individual variation

We use prepositions differently according to where we come from and what kinds of people we usually talk to. What is standard in Britain is not necessarily standard in other English-speaking countries – for example in the U.S.A. *through* is used in place of *till* and *until* (*through Friday*), *than* is used after *different* (*different than*), and often there is no preposition used before days of the week (*I'll see you Monday*). In Australia *on* is the normal preposition to use before *the weekend* (*Let's meet on the weekend*).

Some people have very strong views about which prepositions are and are not correct. Usually they object to social variants that are associated with working-class rather than middle-class speech. They criticise the very common *go up/down town* (instead of *go into town*) and *get/step off of the bus* (instead of *off the bus*) but may (or may not) be more tolerant of variants which are less obviously related to social class:

variant	standard
different *to*	different *from*
speak *with*	speak *to*
similar *with*	similar *to*
oblivious *of*	oblivious *to*
intimidated *with*	intimidated *by*

Some people make fine distinctions that aren't necessarily universal. For example, some people distinguish between *is made from* and *is made of* . They generally use *of* to describe simple 'source' materials (e.g. *The table is made of pine*); *from* when the materials are combined or transformed in the production process (e.g. *I make the cordial from raspberries, redcurrants, sugar and a little lemon juice*). Course materials may choose to concentrate on niceties such as this even at low levels. Teachers sometimes gloss over these sections.

7.5 Word class

Some words can function both as prepositions and as adverbs.

Prepositions	Adverbs
*They ran **along** the stream.*	*They passed it **along**.*
*He ran **past** the house.*	*He ran **past**.*

A few words can function both as prepositions and as conjunctions.

Prepositions	Conjunctions
*They phoned **after**/**before** dinner.*	*They phoned **after**/**before** they got home.*

Several prepositions have 'conjunction equivalents', e.g. *despite/although*; *because of/because*;   *during/while*.

Prepositions	Conjunctions
*They went out **despite** the rain.*	*They went out **although** it was raining.*
*They stayed in **because of** the foul weather.*	*They stayed in **because** the weather was so foul.*

7.6 Typical difficulties for learners

Comprehension

Unless they convey crucial information (this is unusual but possible, e.g. *before or after 1.00*; *above or below freezing point*) we often pronounce prepositions so quickly and softly that they are barely perceptible, particularly if they consist of only one syllable. Vowels often disappear altogether, and some consonants may also disappear, particularly if they immediately follow or are followed by another consonant, e.g. *of* /ə/ in 'Bottle of wine' and *for* /f/ in 'They went for a drink'.

Learners may not hear many prepositions at all (and so their knowledge and memory of correct preposition choices isn't necessarily helped by listening to spoken English).

Speaking and writing

General causes of difficulty

When we look at the mistakes that learners make, it's often difficult to be sure why they have made them – often there could be several reasons. These are some of the factors that may cause learners difficulty:

- Prepositions may be very similar in meaning (e.g. *in, into, inside, within*), and the learner's first language may not make equivalent distinctions.
- Verbs, adjectives and nouns with similar or related meanings may require different prepositions (e.g. *arrive at/go to*; *fond of/keen on*).
- Some verbs may require a preposition while other verbs, which are similar in meaning, may not (e.g. *talk about / discuss*; *arrive at / reach*).

- Verbs in the learner's language may require a particular preposition whereas a similar verb in English may require no preposition or one which is used in contexts the learner finds surprising (e.g. learners may expect * enter <u>in</u> the room).
- Prepositions often have little intrinsic meaning.
- Different parts of speech of the same word may require different prepositions (e.g. independent <u>of</u>/ independence <u>from</u>).

Some common errors

Learners may miss out a preposition:

  * I like listening music.   * Can I look your photographs?

They may use the wrong preposition:

  * I have a lot of problems about my English.   * They have lived there since 16 years.   * The play was written from Shakespeare.   * She left it into the room.   * I'll tell him. I'm going there after 5 minutes.
  * She got married with a much younger man.

They may use a preposition where one isn't needed:

  * They discussed about the news.   * I was tired in last night.

They may use a preposition to express purpose.

Many learners systematically use *for* + bare or full infinitive.

  * In my country we use two short sticks for eat.   * I came to Sydney for to study English.

Many languages express purpose by a preposition that is roughly equivalent to *for* followed by an infinitive. Learners may also be influenced by the fact that in English itself we can use *for* and an *-ing* form (e.g. *It's a thing for opening bottles*).

They may use an infinitive instead of *to + -ing*.

Learners often use an infinitive (with *to*) where we would normally use the preposition *to + -ing* form.

  * I look forward to hear from you soon.   * She objected to work in those conditions.

This may be because *to* often occurs with the infinitive (e.g. *I want **to go**),* and learners may find it difficult to think of it as being a preposition as well.

They may inappropriately use infinitives after nouns.

Some learners feel that it is 'wrong' to follow a noun by a preposition + *-ing* form combination, even when they have learned the appropriate rules.

> * *She had a lot of difficulty to learn her part in the play.*

This may be because an infinitive would be used in a similar context in their own languages. Learners may also be influenced by the fact that in English itself we can follow some nouns with an infinitive (e.g. *She had a lot of opportunity to learn . . .*).

7.7 Consolidation exercises (see p. 442 for possible answers)

Learners' English (see pp. 442–444)

Look at the following text written by a learner of English.

> My name is Zlena Zabovic and I am the manager from a bank's branch. My hobbies are swimming, dancing, listening music and travelling around the world. I am very interested about sport; basketball, volleyball and tennis. I have taken part at many training weekends of these sports.
>
> In my holidays I have visited many places and last year I went in America and I want to return in there in the end of this year.
>
> After the next two weeks I want to have more knowledge in grammar and in speaking English and I want to discuss political relevant's issues.

   a Identify any problems with prepositions (other mistakes have been corrected).

   b Speculate about the causes of these.

Language in context

1 (see p. 444)

   The following describes the character and (un)reliability of a workman. Six prepositions have been removed.

He was a glum, unsociable person *[1]* a raucous voice and very thick eyebrows, and as a mason he suffered *[2]* the defect that he could not be depended *[3]*. He would promise to start work *[4]* a certain day, all the furniture would be moved *[5]* the far end *[6]* the house, and then he would not turn up.

a What words are missing?

b What information enables you to identify the missing words?

c What generalisations does this exercise enable you to make about the importance of prepositions?

2 (see pp. 444–445)

The text which follows is the beginning of an article about the Internet. Read the text and then answer the questions which follow:

Given the level of hype that has surrounded the Internet in the past year, you could be forgiven for thinking that the whole thing is just one big gimmick which, like The Bay City Rollers or the hula hoop, has no real use and will soon fade into oblivion.

Media coverage of the information super highway has tended to focus either on the more outlandish, 'Tomorrow's World' realm of technology – how to do your shopping from your home computer or access a NASA database – or on the sleazeball end of the scale, with horror stories of child porn networks and obscure devil-worshipping chat forums. While the sleazy and the outlandish both have a presence on the Net, what is often ignored is that much of its content is simply good fun, with a lot of useful information thrown in. It won't change your life, but it could change the way you spend your leisure time.

Getting started on the Internet doesn't cost a fortune, but there are certain basic things you will need before voyaging into cyberspace – a computer for instance. Technically, any old computer will do, but to run some of the snazzier Internet software you'll need at least 4 Megs of RAM.

The other essential is a modem, a nifty device which connects your computer to the phone line and allows it to access other computer networks. A modem transforms your computer into a digital magic carpet capable of whisking you away to the four corners of the globe.

Bay City Rollers – a band who were very popular in the early 1970s
hula hoop – a toy that was popular during the late 1950s

a Identify all the prepositions in this text.

b Identify any words which are not prepositions in the text but which can be prepositions in other contexts. What function do they have in this text?

c Which prepositions are part of 'fixed', idiomatic expressions?

d Which prepositions are dependent on a verb, adjective or noun?

e How much meaning (if any) does each of these dependent prepositions convey?

f Which prepositions could be replaced by another preposition without changing the meaning of the phrase?

Differences in word class (see p. 445)

In the following sentences some words have been italicised, which can all function as prepositions. What is their word class here?

(i)   He walked *off*.

(ii)   She ran *down* the hill.

(iii) He stepped *off* the kerb.

(iv)   She used *to* sing.

(v)   He made *up* a story.

(vi)   She's committed *to* taking part.

(vii) He looked *up* the road.

(viii) She sat *on* the table.

(ix)   He switched *on* the radio.

(x)   She was frightened *by* the noise.

(xi)   He agreed *to* an encore.

8 Verbs (introduction)

am   be   been   believes
do   is dreaming   live   must
need   speaks   spoke   were

8.1 Key considerations

Learners need to understand various features of verbs in order to construct and choose between appropriate tenses and in order to use other basic sentence constituents (e.g. subject, direct and indirect objects) in the right order. This chapter outlines these features and the chapters in parts B and C expand this information.

Forming questions and negative statements involves making changes to the form or sentence position of verbs. Learners often have difficulty with this, and may continue making mistakes long after they have understood the 'rules'.

While all languages have verbs, many make no grammatical distinction between, for example, modal verbs and main verbs, or event verbs and state verbs. Many languages don't have tenses, or don't use auxiliary verbs in forming them.

8.2 What are verbs?

What do they do?

People often think of verbs as 'doing words' or 'action words'. While many verbs do describe actions (e.g. *hit*, *paint*), we also use verbs to express other meanings such as existence (e.g. *be, become, exist*), mental conditions and processes (e.g. *believe, deduce, enjoy*), and relationships (e.g. *depend, determine*).

In terms of meaning, their importance varies considerably. In the first text below, most of the verbs convey important information that couldn't be guessed if they were left out. Sometimes, however, nouns convey the essential meaning, and the verbs may only 'support' them, conveying little information (e.g. *I had breakfast*) or conveying information which is already clear in the context. Many of the verbs in the second text below illustrate this (e.g. *make, sauté, add, bring*).

What do they look like?

In many languages it is possible to identify at least some verbs from unique features of their spelling and pronunciation. This is not the case in English.

In the following, the verbs have been printed in italics:

> Wisdom *is* the ability to *see*, *understand* and *know* clearly and deeply, and to *speak* and *act* from that understanding. Wisdom *sees* into the heart of things. It *comes* from a deep connection with oneself, and also *connects* us with all life.

> To *make* the barbecue sauce, *sauté* the chopped garlic in the oil for one minute. *Discard* the garlic and *add* the vinegar, wine, Worcestershire sauce, tomato ketchup, a few drops of Tabasco and water to the pan. *Bring* to the boil and *simmer* for 6 minutes, *stirring* occasionally.

Where do they come in sentences?

We normally need to include at least one verb in every sentence. If we compare English with other languages, we can generalise that (as in most European languages) the verb follows the subject and precedes everything else. However, the type of verb we choose and the type of sentence we use it in also affect the order of sentence constituents. (We look at sentence position in more detail in Chapters 12–21.)

8.3 Types of verb

Main verbs

Main verbs

- don't need to be accompanied by other verbs.
- convey the key meaning in any group of verbs.

All the examples of verbs given in 8.2. above are main verbs (*is* can also act as an auxiliary verb as we see below). Main verbs have at least three different forms – for example *drives, drove, driving* and *driven* are all forms of *drive*.

Main verbs can combine with other verbs, called *auxiliary verbs* or simply *auxiliaries*, to form phrases of two or more words (e.g. *has been driving; may receive*).

Event and state

Main verbs can describe events or states. The distinction between events and states is important because we generally avoid using state verbs in continuous tenses (see below).

Break and *eat* are event verbs; they describe an action, something we consciously do.

> I **broke** the nozzle.   Why aren't you **eating**?

Belong and *know* are state verbs; they describe a passive condition.

> Does this **belong** to you?   I don't **know** the tune.

We avoid certain possible forms of the verb when we use it to describe a state. We say: *I don't know* rather than * *I'm not knowing*.

Many verbs can function as both event verbs and state verbs. For example, here, *smell* and *have* are event verbs, respectively describing a sniffing action to detect odour and a physical activity:

> I always **smell** cooked meat to make sure it hasn't gone off.
> I **have** a shower in the mornings.

We can also use *smell* and *have* as state verbs, in which case the meaning of the verb changes from describing something we do to describing an inherent characteristic or quality of something or somebody.

> The river always **smells** foul.   You **have** beautiful eyes.

When these are event verbs we can use them in a wide range of forms. For example, we can say:

> I'm just smelling the meat.   I've been having a shower.

When we use them as state verbs, we use them in a more restricted range of forms. Even if the characteristic is temporary, we have to say *The river smells foul today* (NOT * . . . is smelling . . .) and *You have a spot on your nose* (NOT * . . . are having . . .).

This table classifies a selection of verbs in these terms:

Event verbs *break, describe, eat, hit, paint, talk*
State verbs *be, exist* (existence) *belong, possess, own* (possession) *believe, know, understand* (long-term mental states)
Verbs which can describe both events and states *feel, smell, taste* (senses/testing actions) *have* (possession/doing) *appear, look* (appearance/actions)

Objects and complements

Some main verbs need to be accompanied (usually followed) by further information. In the following examples we feel that something is missing, and want to respond with w*hat*? or *how*?: *I killed, I felt.*

Kill is an object verb – it needs to be followed by an object, often a noun, pronoun or a phrase which contains a noun:

Subject	Verb	Object
I	*killed*	*a cockroach.*

Feel in the following sentence is a complement verb – it needs to be followed by a complement, often an adjective or a phrase which contains an adjective:

Subject	Verb	Complement
I	*felt*	*ill.*

Other verbs stand on their own and cannot be followed by an object or complement. These are no-object verbs such as *slip* and *talk*:

> *I slipped.*   NOT * *I slipped my foot.*
> *Who's talking?*   NOT * *Who's talking the facts?*

As well as these object verbs, complement verbs and no-object verbs, many verbs can take two objects or an object and a complement:

Subject	Verb	Object	Object
I	*sent*	*the children*	*a card.*

Subject	Verb	Object	Complement
I	*consider*	*the government*	*responsible.*

We can use many verbs in more than one of these categories. For example:

Eat	No-object verb Object verb	*Have you eaten?* *Have you eaten the chocolates?*
Get	Complement verb Object verb	*Don't get cold.* *Can you get another drink?*

We look at subjects, objects and complements in more detail on pages 255–260. Page 260 considers the difference between objects and complements, which can sometimes appear to be similar. When looking at coursebooks and other materials note the following:

Object verbs are also called *transitive* or *monotransitive* verbs.

Complement verbs are also called *linking* or *copular* verbs.

No-object verbs are also called *intransitive* verbs.

Two-object verbs are also called *ditransitive* verbs.

Object-complement verbs are also called *complex transitive* verbs.

Auxiliary verbs

'Tense' auxiliaries

We use auxiliary verbs in forming all tenses other than the affirmative form of the present simple and the past simple. The key verbs we use are forms of *be* (*am/is/was/were/been* etc.) and *have* (*have/had/having* etc.).

*She **has** arrived.*   *They **have been** walking.*

For teaching, *will, shall, be going to, used to,* and *would* are also sometimes considered as tense auxiliaries. We look at the form of tenses in detail in Chapters 12–16.

Question and negative forms

We make questions by changing the usual order of the subject and the (first) auxiliary verb.

Auxiliary	subject	auxiliary	main verb
Is	*he*		*dreaming?*
Have	*you*	*been*	*crying?*

We make sentences negative by adding *not* or *'nt* to the (first) auxiliary verb.

Subject	auxiliary + **not** or **'nt**	auxiliary	main verb
He	*isn't*		*dreaming.*
I	*have not*	*been*	*crying.*

Since the affirmative form of present simple and past simple tenses involve no auxiliaries (*see, saw*), we need to introduce one to make questions and negative statements. We use *do/does/don't/doesn't* in the present simple and *did/didn't* in the past simple, e.g.

Auxiliary	subject	main verb	
Do	*you*	*like*	*music?*
Did	*they*	*eat*	*fish?*

Subject	auxiliary	main verb
She	*doesn't*	*smoke.*
He	*didn't*	*answer.*

We look at question forms in more detail on pages 273–274.

Emphasis and contrast

We often stress auxiliary verbs for emphasis, for example, when we are contradicting.

A: *Why weren't you here?*   B: *I WAS here.*

We add *do/does* or *did* to achieve the same effect when we use the present simple or past simple tenses.

I DO love you.   *I DID phone.*

Substitution

We often use auxiliary verbs to avoid repeating a whole phrase.

> *Why weren't you helping the others?—I WAS.* (i.e. helping the others)
>
> *I hadn't planned to speak to her about it but I DID.* (i.e. I spoke to her.)

We look at substitution in more detail in Chapter 23.

Modal verbs

Modal verbs such as *can, could, may, might* and *should* are another class of auxiliary verb.

We look at these in detail in Chapter 10.

8.4 Form

Infinitive forms

We refer to verbs as infinitives when they are not part of the tense of a verb, and they have no subject.

> *I saw him **cross** the road. I don't want **to leave**.*

We look at infinitives in detail in Chapter 11.

-ing *forms*

The following are *-ing* forms of verbs: *being, cutting, doing, leaving.*

We look at *-ing* forms in detail in Chapter 11.

Past tense forms and past participles

Main verbs all have a past tense form.

Present	*bring*	*am/is/are*	*paint*	*go*
Past	*brought*	*was/were*	*painted*	*went*

Many past tense forms end in *–ed* (e.g. *loved, painted, talked*), and we call these regular verbs.

A lot of the most commonly used verbs, however, have past tense forms that don't end in *–ed*, and we call these irregular verbs. For example, in the list above, only *paint* is a regular verb. One of the problems for learners is that there is nothing in the form of the infinitive (i.e. how it is spelled or pronounced) which indicates whether or not it is regular.

Past participles are the words we use in tenses after forms of the verb *have* (e.g. *we have **eaten**)* and in passive constructions after forms of the verb *be* (e.g. *someone was **hurt***).

Regular verbs have identical past tense and past participle forms.

Past tense	*We **lived***
Past participle	*We have **lived***

Some irregular verbs also have identical past tense and past participle forms.

Past tense	*He **brought***
Past participle	*He has **brought***

Other irregular verbs have past participles which are different from the past tense forms.

Past tense	*We **drove***
Past participle	*We have **driven***

Some irregular verbs have past participles which are the same as the present tense forms.

Present tense	*We **come***	*We **run***
Past tense	*We **came***	*We **ran***
Past participle	*We have **come***	*We have **run***

Learners usually welcome lists of irregular verbs that they can take away and study, and most coursebooks contain an alphabetical table of verbs. Elementary level learners may prefer a list only of some of the most common and most useful verbs, and it is helpful to organise verbs into groups which have similar characteristics.

Present	Past tense	Past participle
drink	*drank*	*drunk*
swim	*swam*	*swum*
bring	*brought*	*brought*
catch	*caught*	*caught*
throw	*threw*	*thrown*
know	*knew*	*known*
tear	*tore*	*torn*
wear	*wore*	*worn*

A few verbs have alternative past tense and participle forms.

> *burned / burnt*   *learned / learnt*   *dreamed / dreamt*

Irregular verbs be *and* go

Be and *go* are very different from other irregular verbs in that there is little or nothing in the spelling and pronunciation of their present, past and past participle forms to show that they are related.

	Be	*Go*
Present tense	*am/are/is*	*go(es)*
Past tense	*was/were*	*went*
Past participle	*been*	*gone*

We generally teach that *go* has two past participles – *gone* and *been*.

Gone indicates a simple movement away from a particular point.

> *She's gone.* (She's not here)
>
> *She's gone to China.* (She's in China now)

Been indicates a movement both to and from a particular point.

> *She's been to China.* (She's now somewhere else)
>
> *She's been to China.* (And now she's back home again)

The difference in meaning between *gone* and *been* is simple but some learners are puzzled by this, particularly since *been* has the same form as the past participle of *be* (e.g. *I've been ill*).

See page 410 for spelling rules for -*ing* of forms, pages 410–411 for the rules for regular past forms, and page 412 for the rules for the simple present 'third person s'.

See page 405 for pronunciation rules for regular past forms and pages 406–407 for the rules for the simple present 'third person s'.

8.5 Typical difficulties for learners

Comprehension

Recognising and understanding verbs is an important part of comprehension, but problems with their grammar don't generally prevent learners from understanding what they read or hear.

Speaking and writing

Although problems with the grammar of verbs may not cause significant problems of comprehension, they lead to mistakes in speaking and writing. Some examples of these mistakes are given below – they are dealt with in more detail as appropriate in the *Typical difficulties for learners* sections of Chapters 9–18.

State verbs

Learners may use state verbs in tenses where they are not normally used.

    * *I'm knowing this song.*   * *This fish is tasting funny.*

Questions

Learners may leave out auxiliary verbs which are necessary in questions, and/or they may forget to change the order of the subject and the auxiliary verb.

    * *You like music?*   * *Where you're going?*

Question and negative forms of be

Learners sometimes need to spend a lot of time noticing and practising these (very irregular) forms before they are confident in using them correctly. They may over-generalise the use of *do/does/did*.

    * *Did you be here?*   * *I didn't be . . .*

Irregular forms

Where an irregular verb has a past participle form which is different from the past tense form, learners may mix them up and use one in place of the other.

* *She has went to Germany.*   * *I woken up early this morning.*

Verb types

Learners may use object verbs as if they were no-object verbs.

* *She saw the film but didn't like.*

They may also do the opposite. *Talk* is normally a no-object verb, but in the following the learner has used it as a two-object verb (e.g. *I told my brother the news*).

* *I talked my brother the problems.*

8.6. Consolidation exercises (see pp. 445–447 for possible answers)

Language in context (see pp. 445–446)

Read the following text and then answer the questions:

> I don't watch much telly – mostly *Neighbours* and *Newsnight*, neither being at meal times, and *Men Behaving Badly* which I laugh at too much to be eating. I don't cook for myself and, because I absolutely hate supermarkets, don't shop. But I have been known to fill a plate with toast and marmite, tomatoes and bits of fruit and cheese, and sit down in front of the television.

a Which words in the text are verbs?
b Which verbs are main verbs?
c Which of these verbs describes a state rather than an event?
d Which auxiliary verbs are components of a tense or passive form?
e Which auxiliary verbs are introduced to make a question or negative statement?
f Which verbs are infinitives?
g Are the following verbs used as object verbs or no-object verbs in this context: *watch, cook, hate, shop*?

Pronunciation (see p. 446)

Study the following regular past simple forms:

fitted	looked
smoothed	printed
faded	washed
puffed	tapped
purred	hated

a Sort them into two groups – those which are one-syllable words and those which are two-syllable words.

b What do the infinitives of the two-syllable words have in common?

c Which one-syllable words end in /t/ and which ones end in /d/?

d What determines whether the words end in /t/ or /d/?

Spelling (see p. 447)

The following are spelling mistakes made by learners of English. In each case speculate about the cause of the mistake:

cryed offerred peelled staied refered

Similarity in form (see p. 447)

Study the following lists of irregular verbs. Match each verb in the top line with one verb in the bottom line. The two items in each pair should be similar in terms of how the infinitive changes to make the past tense and participle forms. For example, *become* and *run* form a pair because their past tense forms involve a simple change of vowel and the past participle is the same as the infinitive.

become   drive   begin   teach   bend   sleep   broadcast

mean   cut   catch   drink   *run*   burn   freeze

PART B

More about verbs and related forms

Introduction to Part B

English language courses generally pay a great deal of attention to different forms of verbs and people often argue that this attention is excessive. However, as teachers we still need to know and understand the full range of forms and uses.

In Chapters 9–18 we look at verbs under a variety of guises:

	Examples	Chapter
Multiword verbs:	*pick up; look after; work through; put up with*	9
Multiword verbal expressions:	*make a noise; take a holiday; have a meal*	9
Modal verbs:	*can; may; must; have to*	10
Infinitive forms:	*(to) be; (to) go; (to) speak*	11
-ing forms:	*being; going; speaking*	11
The present:	*I eat; I am eating; I have been eating*	12
The future:	*I'll eat; I'm going to eat; I'll have eaten*	13
The past:	*I have eaten; I ate; I was eating; I used to eat*	14–16
Reported speech:	*He said he had eaten; He urged me to eat*	17
Conditional sentences:	*If he comes, I'll leave; I would leave if he were to come*	18

The present perfect tense causes problems to many learners because we use it both to refer to events that translate into present tenses in other languages (e.g. *I've been here for three days*) as well as to events that translate into past tenses (e.g. *I've been here before*). In this book we consider these two uses of the present perfect respectively in Chapters 12 and 14.

Tense and aspect

The term 'tense' is sometimes used to refer only to the present simple (e.g. *I eat*) and past simple (e.g. *I ate*). This book follows most modern coursebooks in using the term more generally to refer to the large variety of forms we use to refer to different aspects of time.

Form	Tense
I am eating.	Present continuous
I am going to eat.	'Going to' future
I'll have been eating.	Future perfect continuous
I had been eating.	Past perfect continuous

The term 'aspect' is sometimes used in a technical sense to refer to:

• events viewed retrospectively
  have / had / will have etc. + past participle (Perfect aspect)
  e.g. *I have seen him.*

• events viewed as being in progress
  be / will be etc. + *–ing* form (Continuous or Progressive aspect)
  e.g. *I am eating.*

9 Multiword verbs and multiword verbal expressions

call on   put up with
mess about   take over
give a hand   make progress

9.1 Key considerations

Learners often identify multiword verbs as one of the most important and difficult features of English.

They often fail to understand the meaning of multiword verbs and multiword verbal expressions.

They often avoid using multiword verbs and multiword verbal expressions. For some learners this may be a thoroughly reasonable 'coping strategy' that we should respect; other learners may welcome help and encouragement to use what they have learned.

Some learners find it helpful to analyse the form of multiword verbs and multiword verbal expressions, and to classify them under 'types'. Others prefer to learn them as individual items of vocabulary.

9.2 Multiword verbs

What are multiword verbs?

Multiword verbs are made up of a verb (e.g. *come, get, give, look, take*) and one or more particles. Particles are words that we use as adverbs and/or prepositions in other contexts (e.g. *away, back, off, on, out*).

> ***come to***: I didn't **come to** until several hours after the operation.
>
> ***put up with***: I couldn't **put up with** the noise any longer.

One verb may combine with different particles to give multiword verbs with different meanings (e.g. *break away*; *break in*; *break down*). Other verbs combine only with one particle and generally have only one meaning (e.g. *log on*; *nip off*). One multiword verb may have more than one meaning (e.g. *The man broke down under police interrogation* or *I broke the chapter down into smaller units*). The meaning of a multiword verb is not the same as the independent meaning of the verb and particle(s), e.g. *come to* ('regain consciousness') is not about *coming* or *to* (see *Literalness* pp. 111–112).

In terms of what they do and where they come in sentences, multiword verbs are no different from other main verbs with one exception, which we look at under Type 3 verbs.

Some examples of multiword verbs in context

The text which follows is a transcription of someone telling a story about an unsuccessful attempt to hitch-hike from London to Scotland. Some of the expressions he uses are colloquial English. The multiword verbs are printed in italics:

> We *set out* really early, before it was light, and we got *picked up* real easy and taken to the main road. Well, that was that. No one *came along* for hours. And then, in the end, this bloke *rolled up* in a big car. He looked at us, *slowed down*, stopped, we *got in*, and *off* we *went*. Only he *doubled back* and took us in the opposite direction to where we wanted to go – we were *heading towards* London. Well anyway, this joker hated hitch hikers and just took them off their routes for a laugh. Eventually he *dropped* us *off* somewhere in North London. After that, we *packed* it *in*. We had a bite to eat and then my mate, he *rang up* his Dad and got his Dad to *come down* and rescue us. Ever since then I've got this real thing against blokes in big cars. I nearly bought one once but I couldn't *go through with* it in the end.

Main types of multiword verb

Learners are often taught that there are four 'types' of multiword verb:

Type 1 No object (intransitive) i.e. they don't take a direct object

> We **got up** early.   The plane **took off**.

These type 1 verbs appear in the text above: *set out*; *come along*; *roll up*; *slow down*; *get in*; *go off*; *double back*; *come down*.

Type 2 Object (transitive) inseparable i.e. they need a direct object and this *can't* go between the verb and the particle

> She never asks me to **look after** her children. (NOT * . . . *never asks me to* **look** *her children* **after**.)

This type 2 verb appears in the text above: *head towards*.

Type 3 Object (transitive) separable i.e. they need a direct object and this *can* go between the verb and the particle

> Can you **put** my parents **up** if they come?
> Don't **bring** these problems **up** at the meeting.

We can also put the object after the particle, e.g. *put up my parents*; *bring up these problems*. However, if the object is a pronoun we have to put it between the verb and the particle, e.g. *put them up*; *bring them up*. (NOT * *put up them*; *bring up them*.)

These type 3 verbs appear in the text on page 109: *pick up* (in a passive construction); *drop off*; *pack in*.

Type 4 Object (transitive) with two particles (the particles are inseparable)

> *You should **look up to** teachers*. (NOT * . . . ***look up** teachers **to**.*)

This type 4 verb appears in the text on page 109: *go through with*.

Note: Teachers as well as learners generally find this degree of analysis sufficient for all practical purposes. However, sometimes multiword verbs are also known as and divided into *phrasal* and *prepositional* verbs, and the particles are described as *adverbs* or as *prepositions*. In this case types 1 and 3 multiword verbs are known as phrasal verbs and their particles are classified as adverbs. Type 2 multiword verbs are known as prepositional verbs and their particles are classified as prepositions. Type 4 multiword verbs are known as phrasal-prepositional verbs. The first particle is classified as an adverb and the second as a preposition.

Other types of multiword verbs

Not all multiword verbs fit neatly into one of these four categories.

Some verbs and particles have to be separated by an object, even if this is not a pronoun.

> He *knocked* his children *about* (NOT * He knocked about his children).

The object of some multiword verbs can only be *it*. We can't use other nouns, expressions or pronouns.

> *We both sulked for ages but in the end we **had it out** and now we've **made it up**.*

Clauses which end in a particle

Some people don't like to 'end sentences with prepositions' (or/and multiword verb particles) and they try to avoid doing so, particularly in written English.

In fact most people do end clauses with particles in written as well as in spoken English. This is practically unavoidable in the case of type 1 and type 3 verbs.

> Type 1: *The noise **died down**.*

> Type 3: *Her grandmother **brought** her **up**.*

It is also particularly common in these cases:

> Passive constructions: *A solution to the problem still hasn't been **worked out**.*

> Relative clauses: *That's the solution he's **come up with**.*

> Infinitive clauses: *There's a lot left to **eat up**.*

The difference between multiword verbs and other verbs followed by an adverb or preposition

In multiword verbs the verb and particle(s) function as inseparable parts of a single unit of meaning. In the case of '*He made up a story*' it would be nonsense to ask and answer questions about the individual components of the multiword verb:

What did he do?	*He made*
In which direction?	*up*
Up what?	*a story.*

In a straightforward combination of verb + preposition or adverb (e.g. *He ran up the stairs*) we can ask and answer these questions:

What did he do?	*He ran*
In which direction?	*up*
Up what?	*the stairs.*

Note: The same combination of two words may sometimes be a multiword verb and sometimes not:

> *He **looked up** the meaning in the dictionary*: **look up** *is a multiword verb.*

> *He **looked up** and saw her smiling at him*: **up** *is an adverb saying where he looked.*

Literalness

By definition, the meaning of multiword verbs is not completely literal. However, some are more literal than others, e.g. *eat up*; *move away*; *switch off*.

In these cases, learners can sometimes work out their meaning by looking carefully at the meaning of the verb (e.g. *The car really eats up petrol*) or of the particle (*up*, for example, can often suggest completeness, as in *catch up*; *clear up* etc.).

At the other end of the spectrum are multiword verbs whose meaning is apparently completely opaque.

> *The plane **took off**. She **gave up** smoking.*

Learners can sometimes work out the meaning of these items from the context they're used in, but they are also sometimes misled by their knowledge of what the verbs or particles mean on their own or in other contexts (see 9.5 *Comprehension*).

9.3 Multiword verbal expressions

What are multiword verbal expressions?

Multiword verbal expressions are composed of a verb and at least one other word. This is usually a noun (*have **dinner***) and may also involve the use of an article (*make **a** meal*) or an adjective (*do **good***). Some expressions can/must be followed by an infinitive (*get something **to drink***) or a phrase beginning with a preposition (*put the blame **on someone***).

The verbs in multiword expressions are characteristically 'empty' or 'delexicalised', i.e. they contribute little or no meaning to the expression.

The following verbs often occur in multiword verbal expressions: *do, get, give, have, make, put, set, take.*

> *do the cleaning; give rise (to); have a laugh; take a chance*

Many of these expressions are generally thought of as idioms, and some of them are more 'fixed' than others. For example, we can't always introduce adjectives or adverbs into the expressions, or alter whether the noun is singular or plural. Here, in italics, are some examples of multiword verbal expressions:

Dear Martin

We're having a brilliant *time*[1] here in Malta – I can't tell you how glad I am you persuaded us to make the *effort*[2] to get away. I really feel we are having a good *break*[3] at last and I'm sure we'll both be better for it when we get back.

I hope Julio is giving you a *hand*[4] with the garden. I tried to set him a good *example*[5] of what to do!

With love

Tom

(1) *have a . . . time*: This expression requires an adjective which expresses a subjective judgement such as *good, wonderful, amazing* or *bad, terrible, dreadful*.

(2) *make an/the effort*: This expression is always singular (never * *make effort* or * *make two efforts*) and is usually followed by an infinitive (*to do something*).

(3) *have a break*: This expression doesn't require an adjective but we can use one which is subjective (*a good break*) or descriptive (*a long break*).

(4) *give someone a hand*: This expression requires an object (*you, someone* etc.), which always immediately follows the verb. We can't use an adjective before *a hand* (NOT * *he gave me a useful hand*).

(5) *set an example*: This expression doesn't require an adjective but we can use one, which is usually subjective (*a bad example*). We can choose whether or not to use an object (*you, someone* etc.) before *example*, and can follow the expression with *of . . .* (. . . *example of what to do*).

Literalness

In many multiword verbal expressions, it is the words following the verb that carry the meaning of the expression (e.g. In *I had a bath* and *I did the shopping* it is *bath* and *shopping* which contribute meaning rather than *I had* or *I did*).

In many cases, although the verbs are 'empty' or 'delexicalised', they do express something of their original meaning, for example, the expressions with *do* often have a sense of action and the expressions with *give* often have a sense of contributing something.

In other words, many multiword verbal expressions are fairly literal, and in context don't generally present learners with a problem.

The meaning of other expressions may on the other hand be more opaque. Sometimes the meaning of what follows the verb is metaphorical, (e.g. *make a splash, give ground (to)*) but sometimes there are no obvious associations with the literal meaning of the word at all (e.g. *have a go, make do (with)*).

9.4 Formality

Learners sometimes believe that they should use a multiword verb or verbal expression only in a 'colloquial' context. This is occasionally true, for example: *He pissed me off; We chilled out.* (*Piss off* and many other expressions with *off* can be offensive.)

Some multiword verbs and verbal expressions have a one-word 'equivalent', often with a Latin root, e.g. *get off* (alight); *give in* (concede); *put an end to* (finish).

Learners sometimes have the impression that the multiword form is colloquial and the single-word form is 'neutral'. However, it is more often the case that the multiword form is neutral, and the one-word equivalent is either exaggeratedly formal (*dine* – have dinner; *extinguish* – put out) or used in fixed expressions (*concede defeat; rise and shine*).

Other multiword forms have no equivalent (e.g. *boil down to, set a precedent*) and so we have to use them even in very formal written registers).

*The recommendation, thus, essentially **boils down to** two points, neither of which **sets a precedent** that we would wish to avoid.*

9.5 Typical difficulties for learners

Comprehension

Not recognising the multiword form

This problem is particularly severe when we can't work out the meaning of the item from the individual words that make it up. Learners may assume that the words each contribute meaning independently.

She looked up the road to find out where they lived. (The learner may understand *look up* to refer to looking in a particular direction.)

She was the first person to recognise his talent and to give him a break.
(The learner may understand *break* to mean time off.)

Being misled by meanings they already know

Many multiword forms have two or more meanings, and learners may be misled by recognising a form and assuming that it has the meaning that they already know. For example, the learner who knows *come round* only to mean 'visit' may be misled in interpreting the meaning of *After she had lain on the ground for some minutes she came round . . .*

Recognising the verb but not the particle

This is particularly a problem where the verb and particle of a multiword verb may be separated by several words in a sentence.

> *Can you please drop the boxes of glass and china off?*

Even if the learner knows *drop off*, her attention may be caught by *drop* and *glass* and *china*, and she may miss the final *off*, which crucially affects the meaning of the sentence.

Speaking and writing

Leaving out particles and prepositions

This is a very common mistake, perhaps because the particles in some multiword verbs appear to have no intrinsic meaning:

> * *I want to polish my English.*

It is particularly common for learners to leave out:

- the second particle of multiword verbs with two particles (* *I look forward your visit*).
- prepositions that should follow verbal expressions (* *She took care me*).

Choosing the wrong particle

When the particle does contribute to the meaning, learners may choose one with a roughly similar meaning to the correct one.

> * *Let's put over the meeting till tomorrow.* (put **off**)
> * *He made up he was ill.* (made **out**)

Using an unnecessary particle

Learners sometimes create a multiword verb where a simple verb is needed.

* *As a courtesy to other passengers, please wipe off the wash basin after use.*

Word order

Some learners instinctively avoid separating the verb and particle in type 3 multiword verbs, and they may avoid doing this even when the direct object is a pronoun.

* *We don't have room to put up you.*
* *It isn't completely true but I didn't make up it all.*

Avoidance

Learners may prefer using single-word verbs to multiword verbs and verbal expressions, even when the single word seems odd or archaic. This is not, however, necessarily technically incorrect.

(*) *I prefer bathing to showering.*   (*) *Have you lunched yet?*

Learners who speak a Latin-based language may be tempted to use words that resemble words in their own language in place of multiword forms, e.g. *pacify* instead of 'calm down', *elevate* instead of 'lift up', *mount* instead of 'get on(to)'.

Over-using multiword forms

Many of the more idiomatic multiword forms have very restricted connotations, and adventurous language learners may miss these:

* *Excuse me, waiter. Could I please cough up now?* (*cough up* normally expresses unwillingness and is extremely colloquial.)
* *I'll lurk about here till you get back.* (*lurk about* suggests some evil or immoral intention.)

Choosing the verb in multiword verbal expressions

There is some overlap in the general meanings of the verbs most often used in multiword verbal expressions. Sometimes this means that we have an element of choice, e.g. *have a bath* or *take a bath*; *lay the table* or *set the table*. More often though, only one verb is possible.

* *He did a mistake.* (***made** a mistake*)
* *I took a long sleep in the train on the way down.* (***had** a sleep*)

Choosing the article in multiword verbal expressions

In some expressions we choose between *a* and *the* according to context (*I made **a** mess; I made **the** mess in your room*). However, in some expressions the use of *a* and *the* (or of no article at all) is a fixed part of that expression. This may seem arbitrary to the learner and may be difficult to remember.

* *I'm going to have shower. (have **a** shower)*
* *Couldn't you please make the exception this time? (make **an** exception)*

9.6 Consolidation exercises (see pp. 448–451 for possible answers)

Learners' English (see pp. 448–449)

The following was written by an intermediate learner of English attending a language 'phrasal verbs and idioms' class. He used a dictionary.

> I went out my wife for many years before we married because we had to save our money to pay the wedding expense and to set our new home. So when we married we were no longer young and we knew each other very well. I think that is the secret of we get on happily together, even now, and that we seldom have argument, or if we have arguments we make them up rapidly.
>
> Now we have three strapping children and seven grandchildren and have set them up all on life's highway. For many years we were very busy with our children but now we compensate the lost time by enjoying the life together. We expect many more happy years together. Don't you think this is a nice story? I didn't fabricate!

a Identify each instance where the student has used, tried to use or has neglected to use a multiword verb or multiword verbal expression.

b In each case comment on the student's use and speculate about the reasons for any non-standard use.

Looking at examples (see p. 449)

Look at this list:

(i)	She passed away.	(vi)	She ran off.
(ii)	She walked away.	(vii)	She made off.
(iii)	She had a look at it.	(viii)	They ran off together (i.e. eloped).
(iv)	She had a go at it.	(ix)	She dropped in on him.
(v)	She reached out to it.	(x)	She put up with him.

a Which of these sentences contain multiword verbs or multiword verbal expressions?

b Comment on each sentence, explaining why you have (or haven't) classified it as containing a multiword verb or multiword verbal expression.

c Which types do the multiword verbs belong to?

Language in context (see pp. 450–451)

The passage which follows is from a book about linguistics. It introduces three theories of how languages began. Read the passage and then answer the questions which follow:

> Most people . . . are quite puzzled about how languages might *come into being* (1). When they think about language birth, their thoughts are *led* inevitably *to* (2) the fascinating and unsolved problem of the ultimate origin of language. As we noted in the last chapter, there seems to be no evidence either to support or refute the various hypotheses *put forward* (3) over the past hundred years. If we were to choose, there seems to be no reason to prefer the 'ding-dong' theory – which claimed that the earliest words were imitations of natural sounds such as bang! cuckoo, splash! moo – over the 'pooh-pooh' theory which suggested that language arose from cries and gasps of emotion. There is also the 'yo-he-ho' theory which proposed that language was ultimately *based on* (4) communal effort, with essential instructions such as Heave! Haul! being the first words spoken, as well as numerous other speculative ideas. We shall not therefore discuss this topic any further, but *look at* (5) a more concrete and interesting type of language birth, how a new language can *come into existence* (6) in this day and age.

a Is the italicised item a multiword verb, a multiword verbal expression or simply a combination of words whose meaning is literal?

b If the item is a multiword verb, which type does it belong to?

c Could the item be replaced by a one-word verb? How might this influence the meaning or effect of that clause or sentence?

10 Modal verbs

can   may   need
should   ought to
have to   be able to

10.1 Key considerations

Learners often consider modal verbs to be a particularly 'problematic' area of English grammar. They have problems

- in choosing when to use them.
- in choosing which ones to use.
- in constructing questions and negative statements involving modal verbs.

At lower levels, learners often prefer to concentrate on only one meaning or function of a particular modal verb at one time. They sometimes find it confusing that one modal verb may have several meanings or functions.

Not all grammars and textbooks agree about whether some forms (e.g. *have to*; *had better*) are modal verbs or not. If we define modal verbs for our students, we need to bear in mind that they may come across alternative definitions.

10.2 What are modal verbs?

Modal verbs belong to the larger category of auxiliary verbs (i.e. we don't use them on their own; we have to use them in conjunction with another (main) verb – see p. 99) and are sometimes called 'modal auxiliaries'.

What do they do?

We use modal verbs to make an assessment, judgement or interpretation of what we are speaking or writing about, or to express our attitude to this.

> *She **can** swim.* (ability)
>
> *You **ought** to be more polite.* (obligation)
>
> *You **must** try to stand up and walk.* (necessity)
>
> *It **could** rain tomorrow.* (possibility)
>
> *The family **should** be home soon.* (logical deduction)
>
> *They **will** try to do things before they have learnt how to.* (disapproval)

Course materials usually also link modal verbs to particular communicative functions.

requesting	***Can*** *you please give me a hand?* ***Would*** *you like to open the window?*
offering	***May*** *I help you?* ***Would*** *you like another biscuit?*
asking for or granting permission	A: *Please **can** I take tomorrow off?* B: *I'm afraid you **can't**.*
advising	*You **ought to/should/had better** stay in bed.*
suggesting	*You **could** buy a smaller one.*
inviting	***Would*** *you like to join us?*

What do they look like?

For teaching purposes, a number of verbs and expressions are grouped together as modal verbs because they have a broadly similar meaning or function. In fact, the form of these verbs varies, and it is helpful to consider modal verbs under the following broad headings:

- 'pure' modal verbs
  *I **can** swim.*   *They **may** come.*

These all have the same formal characteristics.

- semi-modal verbs.
  *I **ought to** go now.*   *We **have to** arrive by 6.00.*   *Will you **be able to** help us tomorrow?*

These forms are very closely related to 'pure' modal verbs in terms of meaning but do not share all or any of their formal characteristics.

We look at 'pure' modal verbs in 10.3 and semi-modal verbs in 10.4. In the rest of this chapter we consider them together unless otherwise specified.

Where do they come in sentences?

Modal verbs come immediately before the main verb in affirmative and negative statements (e.g. *can do*; *shouldn't matter*). In questions, modal verbs come before the subject (e.g. *May I go?*).

10.3 'Pure' modal verbs

Formal characteristics of modal verbs

Can, could, may, might, must, shall, should, will, and *would* are 'pure' modal verbs. They:

- are not inflected in the third person, e.g. *He must go* NOT * *He musts go.*
- are followed by the 'bare infinitive', e.g. *I must go* NOT * *I must to go.*
- are negated by the addition of '*n't*' or '*not*', e.g. *I can't; I cannot* NOT * *I don't can.*
- are inverted with the subject to form a question, e.g. *Should I do it?*
- have no past form (but see also 10.7 below), e.g. NOT * *I musted go.*

See page 406 for factors affecting how we pronounce modal verbs.

Need *and* dare

We can use both *need* and *dare* as modal verbs – we generally use *need* as a modal verb when we are in a position of authority and able to give permission or remove obligation. We tend to use it in negative statements.

> *She **needn't** bring the files as long as she can remember the main details.*

We use *dare* as a modal verb, primarily only in fossilised expressions (e.g. *I dare say; How dare you . . .?*)

However, we also use *need* and *dare* as main verbs (i.e. not modal).

> *She needed to explain the circumstances.   I didn't dare speak.*

10.4 'Semi-modal' verbs

Ought

Ought is similar to the pure modal verbs, except that we use the full infinitive (i.e. with *to*) after it rather than the bare infinitive.

> *You oughtn't to cook vegetables so long.*

We generally include ***to*** when we miss out repetition of the main verb.

> *I don't really want to go into work tomorrow but I ought **to**.* NOT * *. . . but I ought.*

However, we leave out ***to*** in 'question tags'.

> *We ought to pack up soon, oughtn't we?* NOT * *. . . oughtn't we to?*

Some people avoid using *ought* in questions and negative statements, preferring instead to use *should*. Some people even use *should* in question tags which follow *ought*, although we would not teach this.

> *We ought to think about what we are doing tomorrow, shouldn't we?*

Other people use *did* to construct questions and question tags (and, occasionally, also to construct negative forms).

> (*) *Did we ought to be leaving soon?*　　(*) *We oughtn't to open it, did we?*

We would not teach this.

Had better

Had better is similar to pure modal verbs except that it consists of two words, and we form the negative in a different way.

We generally use *had better* to give advice.

> *You'd better check that the doors are all locked.*

The negative form of *had better* is *had better not* (NOT * *hadn't better*).

> *You'd better not go home till the fog clears.*

Many people avoid *had better* in question forms, preferring to use, for example, *should*. However, if we do use *had better* in a question form, we place the subject after *had* (or *hadn't*).

> ***Hadn't you better** wear something warmer?*

Some people miss out the auxiliary *had*, particularly in speaking. Learners may be penalised for doing this in examinations.

Have (got) to

Have (got) to is modal in meaning, but not in form.

We use *have to* to express necessity or obligation.

> *They'll **have to** take the whole course again.*

We use the auxiliary *do* or *did* in questions and negative statements.

> ***Do** you have to do that?*　　*They **didn't have to** check in.*

In spoken English and in informal written English, many people use *have got to* as an alternative to *have to*.

***Haven't they got** to scrub the wall down before they begin painting it?*
(***Don't they have to** . . . ?*)

We use *have got to* mainly in the present tense, but it is possible to use it
in the past tense.

*They thought **they'd got to** sign the contract right there and then. (. . .*
*thought they **had to** . . .)*

In British English, the answer to *Have you got to . . . ?* is usually *Yes, I*
have/No, I haven't. In American English it is usually *Yes, I do/No, I don't.*

Be able to

Be able to is modal in meaning, but not in form.

We use *be able to* to express ability.

*I'm sorry, he**'s not able to** come to the phone just at the moment.*

Have to, be able to, *tense and use after other modal verbs*

'Pure' modal verbs have no tense forms, and we generally use them to
refer only to the present or the future.

We can use *have to* and *be able to*, on the other hand, in the full range of
tense forms.

*She**'ll have to** learn to drive if she moves to the country.*
*I wish I**'d been able to** persuade them to stay here longer.*

We can also use *have to* and *be able to* after other modal verbs.

*We **might have to** help.*   *They **ought to be able to** repair it.*

10.5 Multiple meanings

One of the biggest sources of difficulty for learners is that most modal
verbs have more than one meaning or function, and that it is usually only
the context which makes clear which of these is intended.

***May** we go now?* (permission)
*I **may** get back late.* (possibility)

*They left hours ago, they **ought to** be home now.* (logical deduction)
*They **ought** to shut up and listen.* (disapproval)

Shall I help? (offering)

Shall we go now? (suggesting)

*Who **shall** I ask to help me?* (asking for advice or suggestions)

Occasionally we use intonation and 'tone of voice' to help us make the meaning clear.

possibility	disapproval
*You **might** talk to him.*	*You MIGHT talk to him.*
*You **might** have talked to him.*	*You MIGHT have talked to him.*

The use of meaning and function 'labels' such as *possibility, permission,* and *requesting* is a helpful way of identifying the different uses of modal verbs for learners. However, in reality, these categories often overlap and the distinctions between them become blurred. For example, in both the uses of *can't* which follow, *impossibility* is implied and underlies the labels which are given:

*He's broken both his arms. Of course, he **can't** swim.* (ability)

*If he isn't a member of the club, I'm afraid he **can't** swim.* (refusing permission)

Impossibility can be the explicit as well as the implicit meaning of *can't*:

*He **can't** swim. There's no water in the pool.*

10.6 Different verbs with similar meaning

Just as one modal verb may express several meanings, a particular meaning or function may be expressed by more than one modal verb:

(future) possibility	advice
*It **may** rain.*	*We **should** go now.*
*It **might** rain.*	*We **ought to** go now.*
*It **could** rain.*	*We**'d better** go now.*

Some people use the modal verbs in each of these columns interchangeably. If they want to express different degrees of probability for example, they use underlining or capital letters when they write, or intonation when they speak.

She may come tomorrow. (quite probable)

She may come tomorrow. (unlikely)

Other people actually choose between, for example, *may, might* and *could* to express different degrees of future probability (they may not conform regarding which ones they choose to express greater or lesser degrees).

Obligation

Must and *have to*

Course materials often teach that *have to* expresses 'external' obligation (obligation which is imposed by regulations, conventions or by somebody else's will) whereas *must* expresses 'internal' obligation (obligation which is imposed by the speaker).

> You **have to** *declare everything in your tax return.* (external obligation)
>
> You **must** *try to get here earlier in future.* (internal obligation imposed by a teacher on a pupil.)

This distinction may provide learners with a useful rule of thumb to help them to choose an acceptable form. However, many people don't make this distinction. Some people rarely use *must* to express any form of obligation, reserving it to express logical deduction (e.g. *It must be later than I thought.*) or advice (e.g. *It's a brilliant film. You must see it.*).

Some learners use *must* to express any degree or kind of obligation. In this case teachers may want to 'ban' it in order to promote some of the alternatives which more often express obligation (e.g. *have to, should, ought to* and *had better*).

Needn't and *don't have (need) to*

Course materials often teach that we use *needn't* to express 'internal' obligation and *don't have (need) to* to express 'external' obligation. This is similar to the 'internal/external obligation' distinction between *must* and *have to* (see above).

> You **needn't** *stay after 6.00.*
>
> (The person who says this has the authority to allow the employee to leave.)
>
> You don't **have (need) to** *clean the tools each time you use them.*
>
> (The person who says this is referring to external conventions or regulations.)

This distinction provides a useful rule of thumb for learners, but in fact many people use only one of them regardless of whether the obligation is 'internal' or 'external'. Other people use them interchangeably.

The meaning of *don't have to* and *don't need to* often overlaps, but some people choose *don't need to* rather than *don't have to* in order to give permission *not* to do something.

> You **don't need to** wait for me.

Needn't have and didn't have (need) to

Course materials often teach that *needn't have* refers to something which took place but was unnecessary, and that *didn't have (need) to* refers to something which was unnecessary and so didn't take place.

> *The flight was delayed for 8 hours so I **needn't have** got up so early.*
>
> *I **didn't need** to go into work and so I spent the morning catching up at home.*

In many varieties of English (e.g. US) *didn't need to* is used in both these contexts.

Mustn't and don't have to

The negative form of *must* and the negative form of *have to* have completely different meanings. *Mustn't* expresses an obligation not to do something. *Don't/doesn't have to* expresses an absence of obligation.

> *You **mustn't** eat anything for 12 hours before the blood test.* (negative obligation)
>
> *Everything is ready so you **don't have** to be here early.* (absence of obligation)

Some people use *haven't to* to express negative obligation, but this is not standard use.

> (*) *You **haven't to** park on double yellow lines at any time.*

Hypothetical meaning

Would

Some course materials teach *would* as a modal verb only in conditional sentences with a clause beginning *if*....

> *I would pay someone to do my cleaning if I could afford to.*

In fact we frequently use *would* without *if.* This is often to

- speculate.
- express hypothetical meaning.
- describe what we are imagining.

*I **would** never consider changing career.*

Could and might

We also use *could* and *might* to express hypothetical meaning. *Could* refers to *ability* and *might* to possibility.

> *I **could** never run a marathon now.*
> *Don't eat. You **might** feel sick again.*

Logical deduction

Will ('ll), must and should

In its weak or contracted form we use *will ('ll)* to express logical deduction when we are 100% certain.

> *Can you answer the phone? It**'ll** be Mum.*

We also use *must* to express 100% certainty (*It **must** be the battery . . .*).

We sometimes teach that we use *will* rather than *must* when our deduction is based on our knowledge of typical or repeated behaviour or performance. However, *will* and *must* are often interchangeable.

Should usually expresses greater uncertainty, e.g. *It should be Mum* (but it might not be).

Could and might

There is little difference between *could* and *might*.

> *Don't eat that. It **could**/**might** be poisonous.*

Can't and mustn't

In most varieties of English, the opposite of *must* to express logical deduction is *can't*.

> *It **must** be six o'clock.*   *It **can't** be five o'clock.*

In some varieties of English (e.g. in parts of Ireland) *mustn't* can be used in place of *can't*.

10.7 Time reference

Past

Could is the only 'pure' modal verb that we can normally use on its own to refer to past time.

Present	Past
*She **can** swim.*	*She **could** already swim when she was six.*

We use *could* to refer to the past only for general abilities. For specific events we have to express this in another way (e.g. She *managed/was able to prise the door open.* NOT * *She could prise the door open.*).

We can use other 'pure' modal verbs (and also *ought to*) to refer to past time by adding *have* + past participle.

> I **must have forgotten** to lock the door.
>
> She **could have found** the note.
>
> You **ought to** have spent the evening resting.

Future

Modal verbs can normally refer to either the present or the future.

> Present   *You **should** try to exercise more control over the children.*
>
> Future   *You **should** really try to visit us next year.*

Sometimes we choose between a 'pure' modal verb and a semi-modal verb that has an explicit future form in order to make a subtle distinction.

> *I can finish the work tomorrow.* (The ability exists now.)
> *I'll be able to finish the work tomorrow.* (Something prevents me from being *able* to finish it now.)

Future arrangements and temporariness

We use modal verbs with a form of *be* and an *-ing* form to express meanings we normally associate with continuous forms of the verb (see pp. 172–174).

Future arrangement	*They **should be recording** another programme tomorrow.*
Temporary activity in progress at a fixed point in time	***Ought** he to **be drinking** so much?*

Reported speech

We generally use *could, might, ought to, should* and *would* in reported speech just as we do in direct speech. *Can* and *may* frequently change in reported speech (*can* ⇒ *could*; *may* ⇒ *might*). We sometimes use *had to* instead of *must*.

See page 222 for examples of modal verbs in direct and reported speech.

10.8 Non-modal meaning

Some modal verbs can also be used to express non-modal meaning.

Will *and* would

See page 162 for the use of *will* to express present meaning, and page 169 for its use to express future meaning. See page 209 for the use of *would* to express past meaning.

We also use *would* to express 'future in the past'.

> *I knew he **would** be late.*

Should

We can use *should* in certain kinds of subordinate clauses, where it has no connotations of obligation or logical deduction.

> *I'm sorry you **should** feel that way.*
> *We brought a blanket just in case you **should** feel cold.*

Should can be used after:

* the conjunctions *in case* and *if*.
* adjectives such as: *anxious (that), concerned(that), delighted(that), disappointed(that), eager(that), excited(that), glad(that), happy(that), pleased(that), sorry(that), thrilled(that), worried(that).*
* verbs such as: *demand(that), insist(that), recommend(that), request(that).*
* nouns such as: *(the) fact (that); (the) idea (that).*

May *and* might

We can use *may* and *might* after *whatever, whoever, wherever* etc.

> *I'll find him wherever he **may (might)** go.* (or *wherever he goes.*)
> *Whoever he **may (might)** be, I'll still tell him off if he parks in front of my house!* (or *Whoever he is.*)

10.9 Other ways of expressing modal meaning

We can express modal meaning (ability, possibility etc.) through a range of adjectives, nouns and adverbs as well as through modal verbs.

adjectives: *It's **possible** that he's just exhausted.* (*He **may** just be exhausted . . .*)

nouns: *There's no **necessity** for anyone to come in tomorrow.* (*No one **has** to come . . .*)

adverbs: ***Perhaps** he can't read and write.* (*He **may** not be able to read and write.*)

Learners of English sometimes rely largely on adjectives, nouns and adverbs to express modal meaning, and avoid using modal verbs. This can seem laboured and unnatural, particularly in spoken English.

10.10 Typical difficulties for learners

Comprehension

In most contexts modal verbs are pronounced in a very weakened form and learners may fail to hear or identify them. This doesn't always stop the learner from understanding the essential message, but it may do. For example, if the learner doesn't hear *can* in the following, she may interpret the statement as a promise rather than as an offer: *I can collect the children from school for you.*

A particular problem is sometimes posed by the use of *should* to give advice. *If I were you, I should . . .* is often abbreviated to *I should . . .* and learners may understand an offer or promise where what is intended is advice, e.g. *I should ask your landlady to lend you an alarm clock.*

Speaking and writing

Avoidance

Many learners find other ways of expressing what they want to say, even when they understand the meaning of modal verbs and can use them appropriately and accurately in controlled exercises.

If the verb is in an appropriate tense, the result may be acceptable.

It is possible that it'll rain tomorrow.   It is possible that they are back home already.

However, if the learner frequently uses constructions like this in place of modal verbs, the style will seem odd, and if an incorrect tense is used, unacceptable.

> * It is possible that it rains tomorrow.   * It is likely that he comes tomorrow.

This problem is common among speakers of Latin-based languages, where a special form of the verb (subjunctive) is sometimes used in equivalent contexts.

Learners sometimes use constructions to express modal meaning which are grammatically possible but not used.

> * I am very pleased that I had the possibility to come here.

Using the full infinitive

Learners often use full infinitives after 'pure' modal verbs instead of bare infinitives. We tend to notice mistakes like this, but they generally don't lead to confusion or breakdown in communication. They may be caused by over-generalisation from the many other instances in which the infinitive needs to be accompanied by *to* (e.g. *I want to go*).

> * You must to do it.   * I can't to swim.

Question and negative forms

Learners may over-generalise the rules for forming questions and negative statements which involve adding *do* or *did*.

> * Do you can swim?   * She doesn't must finish it.

Different forms with very similar meanings

Examples are:

> *have to/must*   *may/might/could*
> *needn't/don't need to/don't have to*   *can/be able to*

Typically, learners adopt one form and over-use it in cases where it would be more natural to vary the use for stylistic reasons (e.g. they may use *may* to express probability, and never use *might/can/could* in contexts where they would be acceptable alternatives).

Pronunciation

Learners may over-emphasise modal verbs in contexts where they would normally not be stressed. This may give the impression that they are contradicting something that has already been said and can lead to people misinterpreting their attitude.

In many contexts stress is the most important feature we use to distinguish between *can* (generally not stressed) and *can't* (generally stressed). If learners inappropriately stress *can*, people may understand that they have said *can't*.

10.11 Consolidation exercises (see pp. 451–453 for possible answers)

Forms and meanings (see p. 451)

Match each of the modal verbs in the utterances on the left to one of the meanings and functions listed on the right:

(i) He has hurt his foot but he *can* still swim.	**a** ability
(ii) *Can* you please pass that corkscrew over here?	**b** obligation
(iii) *May* I smoke in here?	**c** necessity
(iv) A: She's very late.	**d** possibility
B: She *may* come tomorrow.	**e** logical deduction
(v) A: There's a woman outside who wants	**f** requesting
to speak to you.	**g** offering
B: She *can* come tomorrow.	**h** granting or asking
(vi) A: The phone's ringing.	for permission
B: I'll take it – it*'ll* be John.	**i** advising
(vii) A: I'll never get the lunch finished in time.	**j** suggesting
B: *Shall* I prepare the vegetables for you?	
(viii) A: I didn't recognise the children at all.	
B: Well, they *must have* grown a lot.	
(ix) A: I like plays with plenty of action.	
B: Then you *must* see 'Macbeth'.	

Comparing exercises (see p. 451)

Regulations (for example, driving regulations) are sometimes used for presenting or practising *must* or *have to*. Look at the following two texts and consider which of them is more useful and appropriate for this purpose.

> i) In Britain you have to drive on the left hand side of the road. You have to give way to traffic coming from the right at roundabouts and when you go from a minor road to a major one.

> ii) In Britain you must drive on the left hand side of the road. You must give way to traffic coming from the right at roundabouts and when you go from a minor road to a major one.

Differences in meaning (see pp. 451–452)

a Comment on the difference (if any) between the sentences in the following groups:

(i)   You needn't bring it tomorrow.

(ii)   You don't have to bring it tomorrow.

(iii)   You don't need to bring it tomorrow.

(iv)   She didn't need to bring it.

(v)   She needn't have brought it.

(vi)   I'm afraid I may be late tonight.

(vii)   I'm afraid I might be late tonight.

(viii) I'm afraid I could be late tonight.

b *You might have visited him* can mean

(i)   it is possible that you visited him (I don't know).

(ii)   you didn't visit him but I think you should have done.

Context sometimes makes it clear which of these is intended but we also use intonation to differentiate between these two meanings.
What is the difference in terms of intonation?

Language in context (see pp. 452–453)

Read through these brief extracts from conversations, newspapers and books and then study them in more detail to answer the questions.

(i) (from a study about pupils in language classes)

> However interesting it may be to have some idea about
> how many learners are attending at one time, it would be
> even more interesting to know why those who are not
> attending have, if only for the moment, switched off.

(ii) (a novelist is speaking to her publisher)

> You haven't even the decency or the courage to tell me direct. You
> could have asked me to come to talk to you at the office, or it
> wouldn't have hurt you to take me out to lunch or dinner to break
> the news. Or are you as mean as you are disloyal and cowardly?
> Perhaps you were afraid that I would disgrace you by howling in
> the soup. I'm a great deal tougher than that, as you will discover.
> Your rejection of *Death on Paradise Island* would still have been
> unfair, unjustified and ungrateful, but at least I could have said
> these things to your face. And now I can't even reach you by
> telephone.

(iii) (a detective is looking at a man found murdered with a toy snake in
       his mouth)

> But what to do about the forcing open of the mouth? Hissing Sid,
> the snake, must have been an inspiration. There it was ready to
> hand. He need waste no time fetching it. All he had to do was wind
> it around Etienne's neck and stuff its head into his mouth.

(iv) (an exchange between a child and her mother)
   A: Do I have to come in?
   B: I've already told you you must.
   A: But does it have to be now?

(v) (from a novel)

> . . . Delia broke in and said, "Can you two stay for dinner? We're having this Chinese dish that's infinitely expandable."
> "Well, I *might* could," Courtney said.

(vi) (John McCarthy describes how he saw his girlfriend on TV while imprisoned)

> We talked over the remaining shots trying to tie the words to the pictures. The fact that the story should be on the news the one night we'd risked a look, was amazing. It had to mean something . . .

a Underline all the modal verbs (including any 'semi-modal' verbs) in the text.

b In each case specify the meaning or function they express.

c Consider what (if any) alternatives might have been used in the same context and how these might have affected the meanings expressed.

11 Infinitive and
–*ing* forms of verbs

> *(to) be   (to) speak*
> *having spoken   speaking*
> *working   (to) be speaking*
> *(to) have spoken*

11.1 Key considerations

There are many different contexts where we have to make a choice between an infinitive or -*ing* form of the verb, and the rules which guide us may seem arbitrary to learners. We need to be wary of focusing on too many of these rules at once; learners usually prefer to have their attention drawn to these, rule by rule over a period of time.

Mistakes in choosing between infinitive and -*ing* forms rarely lead to serious misunderstandings. However, most learners make a lot of mistakes and they are often penalised for these mistakes in examinations.

11.2 Infinitives

What do they look like?

The infinitive is the simplest form of the verb. It is exactly the same as the *base* form that follows *I, you, we* and *they* in the present simple tense of all verbs other than *be* (e.g. *I drink; They believe*). We refer to these verbs as infinitives when they are not part of the tense of a verb.

Sometimes the infinitive follows *to*, and we call this the *full infinitive* or the *infinitive with to*, e.g. *to ask* in *He wanted me to ask a question.*

Throughout this book we follow most course materials in using the term 'infinitive' to refer to this two-word form.

We look at one-word *bare* infinitives in 11.5.

What do they do?

We use infinitives

- to add more information to what is expressed in certain verbs, verb + object combinations, adjectives and nouns, or expressions including these.
- to explain the reason for something or its purpose or function.

- as subjects and complements.
- in certain tense forms.

Where do they come in sentences?

After certain verbs

We can use an infinitive after certain verbs. The following are some common examples:

agree, appear, arrange, attempt, decide, expect, fail, hope, need, offer, promise, refuse, want, wish.

	Verb	**Infinitive**	
I	*wanted*	*to meet*	*him.*
They	*hoped*	*to get*	*back early.*

After certain verb + object combinations

We can use an infinitive after certain verb + object combinations. The following are some common examples:

advise, allow, ask, cause, encourage, forbid, force, instruct, invite, order, permit, persuade, prefer, recommend, remind, require, teach, tell, tempt, warn.

	Verb	**Object**	**Infinitive**	
Who	*asked*	*Valentine*	*to come*	*to the party?*
The police	*required*	*everyone*	*to stay*	*in the room.*

After certain adjectives

We can use an infinitive after certain adjectives. Some of the commonest adjectives in this category are those which describe
- personal feelings or attitude: e.g. *anxious, determined, delighted, eager* etc.
- aspects of possibility, probability, necessity or ability: e.g. *certain, crucial, imperative, likely, possible* etc.

	Adjective	**Infinitive**	
I'm	*sorry*	*to be*	*a nuisance.*
Is it	*necessary*	*to make*	*so much noise?*

We sometimes use these adjectives with a phrase beginning *for*.

> *Is it possible for everyone?*

We also use an infinitive after these phrases.

> *Is it possible for everyone **to be** here early tomorrow?*

After *too* + adjective/*much* or *many* + noun

We use an infinitive after *too* + adjective, *too* + *much*/*many* + noun.

> *I'm too old **to learn** new tricks.*
> *There's too much information **to digest**.*

After adjective + *enough* or *enough* (+ noun)

We use an infinitive after adjective + *enough*, *enough* (+ noun).

> *I'm fit enough **to play**.*
> *Have you got enough (money) **to get** home?*

After certain nouns and noun expressions

We can use infinitives after nouns which express something about

- personal feelings or attitude: e.g. *desire, wish* etc.
- aspects of possibility, necessity and ability: e.g. *ability, capability, possibility, need* etc.

	Noun	Infinitive	
I have no	*desire*	***to hurt***	*you.*
There's a great	*need*	***to improve***	*our service.*

We also use infinitives after certain other nouns.

> *He made an attempt **to escape**.*

The nouns we follow with infinitives are restricted in number, and often we follow them with infinitives only in set expressions (e.g. *I have no wish to . . .; make an attempt to . . ..*). We often only teach this use of infinitives idiomatically, in these expressions.

After a direct object

The direct objects in the examples which follow are: *the drill, something* and *a more substantial table.* (See p. 256 for more information about direct objects.)

We use infinitives to explain the reason for something, or to answer the question *Why?*.

> *He borrowed the drill **to put** up more shelves.*

In this case we can also use *in order to*, e.g. *in order to put up more shelves.*

We also use the infinitive to explain the purpose or function of something.

> *I think it must be something **to eat**.*
> *I need a more substantial table **to work** at.*

When we define something's intrinsic function, we often use *for . . .-ing* instead of an infinitive.

> *A corkscrew is a thing **for opening** wine bottles.*

After 'question words' in indirect questions

We often use infinitives after question words such as *how, what, when, where, who, which, why, whether.*

> *I don't know how **to respond**.*
> *She hasn't decided whether **to stay** in or not.*

We only use the infinitive after question words when the main verb and the verb in the infinitive have the same subject. We can say *I don't know how to respond* because *I* am the person who will respond. We can't say: * *I don't know how you to respond.*

We also use the infinitive in expressions which *imply* a question word.

> *I don't know **the way** to respond.* (I don't know how to respond.)
> *I don't know **the right person** to ask.* (I don't know who to ask.)

See page 344 for more information about indirect questions.

Subjects and complements

We can use an infinitive as the subject of a clause when it refers to an activity.

> ***To eat** would be stupid if you are still planning to swim.*
> ***To travel** hopefully is better than to arrive.*

Although this use is perfectly correct, we often prefer not to begin sentences with an infinitive, particularly in more casual, spoken contexts.

We frequently begin the sentence with *it* instead. In this case the infinitive is part of the complement.

> ***It*** *would be stupid* ***to drink*** *anything if you are planning to drive home.*

We use an infinitive as a complement in expressions like the following:

> *Your best bet is* ***to wait***.

We can also use an infinitive as a complement in pseudo-cleft sentences.

> *What you need is* ***to relax***.

(See p. 255 for more information about subjects, p. 260 for more information about complements and p. 279 for more information about pseudo-cleft sentences.)

After an auxiliary verb in tense forms

We generally refer to the *'going to* future' (*He's going to cry*) as though *to* were attached to *going*. We also refer to *'used to* for past habits and states' (*I used to have a lot of dreams*) as though *to* were attached to *used*.

In both cases, we can also think of the verb that follows *going* or *used* as an infinitive.

> *I'm going* ***to see*** *her tomorrow.*
> *Doctors used* ***to make*** *more home calls.*

11.3 *-ing* forms

What do they look like?

–ing forms are words that end in *–ing* like *drinking, eating, laughing.*

We look at the spelling of these words on page 410.

What do they do?

We use *-ing* forms:

- to add information to what is expressed in certain verbs and verb + object combinations.
- when we want to use a verb after a preposition.
- as subjects and complements.
- to list activities.

- to add information to what is expressed in a clause.
- in continuous tenses.

Where do they come in sentences?

After certain verbs

We can use an *-ing* form after certain verbs. The following are some common examples:

> *avoid, bear, consider, deny, detest, dislike, endure, enjoy, imagine, involve, mention, mind, miss, practise, resent, risk, postpone, stand.*

> *He **enjoys looking** around antique shops.*
> *The journey **involves changing** trains several times.*

We can also use an *-ing* form after many multiword verbs, e.g. *give up; look forward to; put off; put up with.*

> *I **look forward to hearing** from you.*

After certain verb + object combinations

We sometimes use an object between the verb and the *-ing* form.

> *Do you mind **me smoking**?*

In informal speech, as in these examples, we use words and expressions like *me, him, Mike, the team*. In more formal contexts (for example, academic writing) we sometimes choose *possessive* forms before the *-ing* form – words and expressions like *my, his, Mike's, the team's.*

> *No one minded the ambassador**'s** request**ing** a state reception.*

After prepositions

When we use a verb after a preposition, this has to be an *-ing* form.

> *Is she still interested **in dancing**?*
> ***On coming** into the room, she immediately noticed the uneasy atmosphere.*

Subjects and complements

We usually use an *-ing* form when we want to make an activity the subject of a clause.

> ***Grumbling** is a waste of time.*   ***Lying** is sure to get you into trouble.*

This is more common than use of an infinitive (see p. 139).

We can also use an *-ing* form as a complement in pseudo-cleft sentences.

> *What really gets on my nerves is **singing** out of tune.*

We look at subjects and complements in more detail in Chapter 19, and at pseudo-cleft sentences in Chapter 20.

Items in lists of activities

The following example is taken from a list of school regulations:

The following are completely forbidden on school premises:

- **spitting**
- **pushing and shoving**
- **running in the corridors**
- **shouting**

Additional information

We often use an *-ing* form to add different kinds of information to the information in a main clause.

> *He walked out of the room **smiling**.*
> *He made his fortune **playing** bridge.*

These *-ing* forms constitute or partly constitute non-finite *participle* clauses. We look at these in more detail in Chapter 27.

Continuous forms

We use an *-ing* form together with some form of the verb *to be* (e.g. *am, is, were, have been* etc.) in constructing continuous or 'progressive' tense forms such as the present continuous, future continuous or past continuous.

> *I have been **trying** to learn Japanese for over three years.*

In formal contexts (particularly written) we often 'reduce' the form of continuous tenses by leaving out the subject of the clause and the form of the verb *to be*.

> (Printed notice in a hospital ward)
> *Wear protective clothing when* [you are] ***emptying*** *bins.*

Gerunds and present participles

For most practical purposes we consider *-ing* forms of the verb as one grammatical class. However, they are sometimes considered as two separate classes (different in function but not in form): *gerunds* and *present participles.*

Where the *-ing* form can be replaced in the sentence by a noun it is a gerund.

Gerunds	**Nouns**
*He likes **singing.***	*He likes **music.***
***Walking** is good for you.*	***Exercise** is good for you.*

Where the *-ing* form is part of the verb or functions like a verb it is a present participle.

*Are you still **working**?*   *I saw him **dancing**.*

-ing *forms that aren't verbs*

Some words that end in *-ing* are not forms of the verb at all.

An ***interesting** experience; a **distressing** encounter.* (adjectives)

*A **meeting**; a **warning**.* (nouns)

The same word can sometimes be the *-ing* form of a verb and sometimes an adjective or noun.

*What are those sheets **covering**?* (verb)

*A light **covering** of snow.* (noun)

11.4 Choosing between infinitive and *-ing* forms

Open choice

In a small number of cases (for example, after *begin* and *start*) it makes no difference whether we choose an infinitive or an *-ing* form.

*It began/started **raining/to rain** just as we were leaving.*

Hypothetical and factual statements

When we can choose between an infinitive and an *-ing* form, we sometimes choose the infinitive in order to stress that something is more speculative or hypothetical. We choose an *-ing* form more to describe what actually happens or has happened.

> *It's bad for you **to do** exercise straight after a meal.* (So, if you were thinking about doing some exercise, perhaps you shouldn't.)
>
> ***Doing** exercise straight after a meal is bad for you.* (Statement of fact.)

After certain verbs

Try

After *try* we use:

- an infinitive to suggest some kind of effort or difficulty involved in an action.
  *They tried **to persuade** their daughter not to smoke.*
- an *-ing* form to make suggestions.
  *Try **drinking** camomile tea just before you go to bed.*

Stop, remember, forget, regret and go on

After a number of verbs we choose:

- infinitives to look forward.
- *-ing* forms to look at the present or past.

stop + infinitive	*I stopped to stretch my legs.* (I stopped (walking) and then stretched my legs – that was why I stopped.)
stop + *-ing*	*I stopped smoking.* (I smoked until I stopped.)
remember/forget + infinitive	*Remember/Don't forget to pick up your dry-cleaning.* (i.e. remember something which should happen subsequently.)
remember/forget + *-ing*	*I can remember/never forget going to my great-grandmother's.* (i.e. remember/forget an event from further back in the past.)
regret + *infinitive*	*I regret to inform you that your presence is no longer required . . .* (I am about to inform you.)
regret + *-ing*	*I don't regret getting married.* (i.e. my marriage which took place in the past.)
go on + infinitive	*After he left university he went on to become one of the world's top medical researchers.* (This is what happened next.)

go on + -ing   *He went on playing tennis long after the doctors had told him to stop.*
(He continued an activity that he had started previously.)

Love, *like* and *hate*

After *love, like* and *hate* in British English we generally use an *-ing* form, while in American English the infinitive is equally common.

> *I like dancing.* (British and American)
>
> *I like to dance.* (American)

In British English we can also use an infinitive after *love, like* and *hate* to refer to actions which happen only occasionally.

> *I hate **to interrupt** your class, but there's a call for you.*
>
> *I love **to find** myself completely alone in some vast gothic building.*

We use an infinitive after would *('d) like, love* and *hate.*

> *I'd like **to leave**.*

Allow, *permit, advise, forbid*

We use an *-ing* form after these verbs on their own.

> *They didn't allow **eating** in the laboratories.*

However, if we specify an object or use a passive form, we use a full infinitive form instead.

> *They didn't allow anyone **to eat** in the laboratories.*
>
> *We weren't allowed **to eat** in the laboratories.*

11.5 Bare infinitives

What do they look like?

Bare infinitives are one-word infinitive forms such as *be, do, give, ask.*

> *He made me ask a question.*

What do they do?

We use bare infinitives:

- in some tense forms.

- after certain verb + object combinations.
- in a number of expressions for giving advice, making suggestions, requesting, inviting or giving orders.

Where do they come in sentences?

Tense forms and after auxiliary verbs

We use a bare infinitive in the question and negative forms of simple present and past tenses after the auxiliaries *do, does*, and *did*.

> *Do you **love** me?*   *They didn't **like** the film.*

We also use a bare infinitive after 'pure' modal verbs.

> *He can **swim**.*   *Why shouldn't people **protest**?*

After verb + object combinations

Make and let

We use a bare infinitive after *make* and *let*.

> *We **made** the children **clean** up the mess.*
> *We didn't **let** them **go** out of the house.*

'Inert perception' verbs

We can use a bare infinitive after many 'verbs of inert perception', e.g. *hear, see, perceive, notice, sense*.

> *Did you **hear** a child **scream**?*

(We can also use the *-ing* form – see p. 147 for the difference between these.)

In passive constructions we have to use the full infinitive form of these verbs.

> *The children **were made to wash** the walls* . . .
> *Something **was** dimly **perceived to move*** . . .

After *why. . .?* and *why not. . .?*

We can use the bare infinitive with *Why . . .?* to question or cast doubt on someone's intention or suggestion. The reason for questioning this is frequently introduced with *when . . . .*

> *Why **tell** her the bad news when she doesn't need to know?*

We use _Why not . . .?_ to make suggestions.

> **_Why not try_** _phoning again?_

Some learners find it helpful to think of _Why not . . .?_ as an abbreviation of _Why don't you . . .?_

After _try and, come and_ and _go and_

When we make suggestions or give advice we often use _try and_ with the bare infinitive as an alternative to _try + -ing._

> _Why don't you_ **_try and get_** _here early if you can?_

We also use _and_ with the bare infinitive after _come_ and _go_ in suggestions, orders, requests, and invitations.

> **_Come and sit_** _down._
>
> _Could you_ **_go and see_** _who's at the door?_

In American English _and_ can be left out after _come_ and _go_ (_Come sit . . .;_ _Go see . . ._).

11.6 Choosing between bare infinitives and _-ing_ forms

After verbs of inert perception + object

Momentary and extended actions

We sometimes use an infinitive to describe a momentary action, and an _-ing_ form for a more extended action.

momentary action	extended action
I heard something **snap**.	_I heard someone_ **groaning**.

Completed events and actions in progress

We can also use the bare infinitive to describe something which has been completed while we use the _-ing_ form to show that something has started or is in progress.

completed event	action in progress
I saw Olivier **perform** _'Othello'._	_I saw the children_ **leaving** _school._

11.7 Complex infinitive and *-ing* forms

In addition to the straightforward infinitive and *-ing* forms (e.g. *to speak*; *speak*; *speaking*), there are perfect, negative and passive infinitive and *-ing* forms, and also a continuous infinitive form.

Perfect infinitive forms	Perfect -ing forms
(*to*) *have* + past participle	*having* + past participle
*I am sorry **to have kept** you waiting.* *I may **have forgotten** my wallet.*	*She can't remember **having travelled** in Europe at all.*

Negative infinitive forms	Negative -ing forms
not + infinitive	*not* + *-ing* form
*It is quite common **not to understand** everything in lectures.*	***Not understanding** all the details is quite normal in the beginning.*

Passive infinitive forms	Passive -ing forms
(*to*) *be* + past participle	*being* + past participle
*I want **to be treated** with more consideration.* *How can people let their children **be used** in TV commercials?*	*I like **being treated** with respect.*

Continuous infinitive forms
(*to*) *be* + *-ing* form
*I seem **to be getting** more headaches recently.*

Perfect forms emphasise that something happened before something else.

We use continuous forms to emphasise the temporariness of what we are describing.

These forms can also be combined. For example an infinitive form can be both perfect and continuous (*to*) *have* + *been* + *-ing* form), or both negative and passive (*not* + (*to*) *be* + past participle).

> *He could **have been working** outside.*
>
> *Someone gave the order that the prisoners were **not to be shot**.*

11.8 Typical difficulties for learners

Comprehension

In context, learners usually understand what a speaker or writer intends, even where they are unaware of how choosing between infinitive and *-ing* forms can make a difference to meaning.

Speaking and writing

If learners make mistakes in speaking or writing, there is more room for misunderstanding, but this is still rare. Mistakes may, however, distract listeners and readers from what the learner wants to say.

Words which should be followed by an infinitive

Learners sometimes use an *-ing* form after a verb, adjective or noun which has to be followed by an infinitive.

> * *She allowed me going.*
> * *I didn't expect being in the final of the competition.*

Purpose and function

In some European languages (e.g. French and Italian), purpose and function can be expressed by a preposition followed by an infinitive. Speakers of these languages sometimes try to use similar structures in English..

> * *I left the documents at work for (to) look at later.*

Over-using infinitives

They sometimes use an object + infinitive combination instead of a clause.

> * *They suggested me to go there.*

Avoiding infinitives

They sometimes use a clause instead of an object + infinitive combination.

> * *I want that you open your books at page 11. (I want you to open . . .)*

Words which should be followed by an -ing *form*

Learners sometimes use an infinitive after a verb, adjective or noun which has to be followed by an *-ing* form.

> * *There was nothing I could do so I stopped to worry about it.*

They sometimes use an infinitive after a preposition.

> * *I'm interested in to go shopping.*

Over-using -ing *forms*

Learners sometimes use *-ing* forms which are correct but which we don't naturally or commonly use.

> (*) *I am sorry for being late.* (*I am sorry I am late.*)
>
> (*) *I am glad I had the possibility of travelling to Europe.* (. . . *glad I was able to travel . . .*)

Learners may over-use 'reduced' continuous forms. For example, the sentences below were spoken by advanced learners. They are 'correct' but unnatural. It is more natural to include a subject and full continuous form.

> *People are stupid to drive while using mobile phones.* (. . . *while **they're** using mobile phones.*)
>
> *Try to keep your mouth closed when eating.* (. . . *when **you're** eating.*)

Words which should be followed by a bare infinitive

Learners sometimes use a full infinitive where a bare infinitive is needed.

> * *Did you hear him to come home last night?*

11.9 Consolidation exercises
(see pp. 453–456 for possible answers)

Differences in meaning (see pp. 453–454)

Comment on any differences in meaning between the sentences in the following groups:

(i) She went out smoking.
     She went out to smoke.

(ii) Being drunk at work isn't a crime.
      To be drunk at work isn't a crime.

(iii) I like to have a run at the weekend.
      I like having a run at the weekend.
      I'd like to have a run at the weekend.
      I'd like having a run at the weekend.

Acceptability (see p. 454)

Study the following sentences:

(i)   Both parties are committed to reduce taxes.

(ii)   I want him working a lot harder than he is now.

(iii) I'd appreciate you to knock before you come in.

(iv)   I'm too tired for going out tonight.

a Which ones (if any) do you consider not to be examples of standard English?

b What features make these 'non-standard'?

Language in context

1 (see p. 455)

The following extract is from an article about different conventions, attitudes and behaviours in different cultures. Read the text and answer the questions which follow it:

The situation is quite different in the Mediterranean region and	1
in the Middle East, where it would be considered highly unusual,	2
even rude, to get down to business right away. This may be	3
viewed as a waste of time to people from other cultures, but in	4
the Mediterranean and Arab cultures drinking coffee and	5
engaging in small talk are essential components to developing	6
good working relationships with people before getting down to	7
business.	8
Such cultural differences exist due to many factors: climate	9
and weather, religion, agricultural practices, attitudes towards	10
material and technological advancement, traditions from	11
unknown origins and so forth. To suggest that one time system is	12
better than any other is misleading, and culturally insensitive. It	13
is more important to acknowledge that such cultural differences	14
exist, and that the awareness of such differences can be a	15
valuable tool both in business and in daily interactions in the	16
second language.	17

a Identify all infinitive and *-ing* forms.

b In each instance account for the form that has been chosen.

Example: The first instance is *be* (line 2). The bare infinitive is used here because it follows a modal verb (*would*).

2 (see p. 456)

The text which follows discusses Guy Fawkes Night, which is celebrated in Britain with fireworks and parties for children. Some of the verbs in the text have been modified and three possibilities are provided. Read the text and then answer the questions.

Guy Fawkes Night makes me *think/to think/thinking (1)* principally of three things: the dangerous thrill of *handle/to handle/handling (2)* fireworks, the shocking expense of *buy/to buy/buying (3)* them, and the burning question of what *cook/to cook/cooking (4)*. This is an occasion when young and old take their evening meal together. *Accommodate/To accommodate/Accommodating (5)* both tastes can be tricky, since young eaters don't appreciate the bold flavours beloved of their palate-hardened elders.

There are three ways of dealing with the problem. One is *find/to find/finding (6)* a bland menu that children eat happily and grown-ups grudgingly. The second *is cook/to cook/cooking (7)* whatever you feel like *eat/to eat/eating (8)* and *let/to let/letting (9)* the children *fend/to fend/fending (10)* for themselves. The third solution is a compromise approach, and its central tenet is *make/to make/making (11)* spiciness an optional extra.

a Choose the 'best' form of the verb.

b In each case give reasons for the choice you have made.

12 The present, including uses of the present perfect

lose speaks do they work?
does she understand?
is sleeping   has lived
has been wearing   'll go

12.1 Key considerations

Many learners are confused by the number of tense forms we use for expressing present time in English – in choosing the appropriate form we are obliged to make distinctions that many learners find unfamiliar and unclear. They often like teachers to introduce or draw attention to the different uses of the different forms separately and with clear rules of thumb for using them. Subsequently, learners usually like to focus on examples of how we choose and use these tenses in real conversation and text.

Most learners find the forms of the present simple that we use to ask questions and make negative statements particularly complex. They often continue to make mistakes long after they have understood the relevant rules. It is unrealistic to expect learners to 'get the form of the present simple right' before they study other tense forms.

Many learners find it difficult to think of the present perfect as a form that can refer to present time in some contexts, and past time in others. This is a particular problem for speakers of many European languages whose first language has a similar form which is always used to refer to past time.

12.2 Present simple

Form

In looking at the form of the present simple tense we need to make a distinction between verbs used with a third person singular subject (e.g. *he, she, it, Barbara, a book* etc.) and verbs with other subjects (e.g. *I, you, Lauren and Jack, the books* etc.).

Verbs with third person singular subjects:

	Question word	*does* or *doesn't*	Subject	*does not* or *doesn't*	base form	base form + *s*	
Affirmative:			*The race*			*starts*	in Paris.
Question:	*Why*	*Does* / *doesn't*	*this machine* / *this machine*		*make* / *make*		*a noise?* / *a noise?*
Negative:			*She*	*doesn't*	*get up*		*early.*

The -*s* or -*es* that we add to the base form is often called 'the third person *s*'.

See pages 406–407 for pronunciation rules and page 412 for spelling rules related to this.

Verbs with other subjects:

	Question word	*do* or *don't*	Subject	*do not or don't*	base form	
Affirmative:			*Trees*		*lose*	*their leaves in autumn.*
Question:	*Why*	*Do* / *don't*	*you* / *you*		*want* / *want*	*to eat?* / *to eat?*
Negative:			*I*	*don't*	*believe*	*you.*

When do we use the present simple?

Main use: general actions, events and states

We use the present simple to describe general actions, events and states when we have no reason to think of them as being in any way temporary or limited in time.

For teaching purposes we sometimes break this use down into 'repeated events' and 'general facts':

repeated events

Example: *I get up early.*

We can show this use diagrammatically:

I get up early

We often use adverbs of frequency (e.g. *always, usually* etc.) and expressions of repeated time (e.g. *on Tuesdays, in the summer, twice a year* etc.) with this use of the present simple. We also often focus on 'habitual behaviour' in presenting this use to learners.

General facts

Examples: Ice melts at O°.
I live in London.

We can show this use diagrammatically:

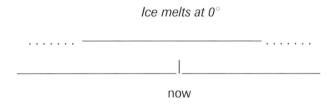

Ice melts at 0°

We often focus on 'timeless facts' in presenting this use to learners.

In special circumstances we can also use the present simple to describe temporary states and actions. We look at examples of this below.

Other uses

State verbs

We use the present simple with certain verbs to refer to states, even when we think of them as being temporary. These include verbs grouped under the following topics:

existence	*be, exist*
mental states	*believe, doubt, know, realise, recognise, suppose, think, understand*
wants and likes	*want, like, love, hate, need, prefer*
possession	*belong, have*, possess, own*
senses	*feel, smell, taste*
appearance	*appear, look, seem*

Example: *I don't understand.*

* We use *have/has got* as a very common alternative to *have/has* to express possession and a range of related meanings such as family relationships, ailments, physical characteristics, e.g. *I haven't got any sisters. Have you got a headache?* Although the form of this expression is not the present simple, the meaning is the same as *have/has.* Some people try to avoid *have/has got*, particularly in formal written English.

Perception verbs

We sometimes find perception verbs (e.g. *hear, see*) listed with state verbs. However, we tend to use *can* and *can't* with these perception verbs more often than the present simple.

> *Can you hear anything?*

Running commentary

Sports commentators use the present simple (as well, sometimes, as the present continuous) in 'running commentaries' on broadcast sports events. The present simple saves time when the action is fast.

> *Chang serves to Sampras and runs to the net.*

It's rare that we need to teach this use, although we sometimes need to be able to explain it.

Past narrative

In exceptional circumstances we can also use the present simple to refer to past time.

We sometimes use this tense instead of the past simple to create a sense of immediacy in certain kinds of informal, spoken narrative such as comic and dramatic story-telling (e.g. *So this man walks into a bar and takes out a gun . . .*).

Verbs which change things

We also use the present simple in making pronouncements which actually change something. This involves a restricted number of verbs (e.g. *arrest, baptise, declare, pronounce*) known as *performative* verbs.

> *I pronounce you man and wife.*   *I declare the fete open.*

We generally have to have some special authority (e.g. to be a member of the police or the clergy) to perform these actions. Teaching learners to use these verbs is probably very low on our list of priorities, but we may need to explain why this tense is used.

12.3 Present continuous

This tense is also called the *present progressive.*

Form

We form the present continuous with a present tense form of *to be* (*am, 'm, is, 's,* or *are, 're*), and an *-ing* verb form:

	Question word	am/is/ are	Subject	am/is/ are	not or + n't	-ing form	
Affirmative:			People	are		beginning	to leave.
Question:	(Where)	are	they			going?	
Negative:			She		isn't	making	a noise.

See page 410 for spelling rules concerning the *-ing* form of verbs.

When do we use the present continuous?

Main use: temporary events and actions

We generally use the present continuous to refer to something temporary which has begun and has not finished, something which is completable and is in the process of being completed. What is important is that the action or event is taking place for a limited period of time which includes the moment of speaking. Events can be constant, but they can also be repeated or intermittent, and not necessarily happening at the moment of speaking.

We can show these uses diagrammatically:

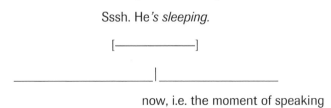

Sssh. He *'s sleeping.*

[————————]

_____|_____

now, i.e. the moment of speaking

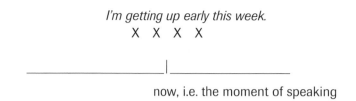

I'm getting up early this week.

X   X   X   X

now, i.e. the moment of speaking

Other uses

Changing and developing states

When we describe changing or developing states (e.g. using verbs like *become, decline, decrease, develop, expand, get, grow* etc.) we use the present continuous even though we don't necessarily think of the process as being temporary.

> *Moral standards **are declining**.*

Habitual action

We normally use the present simple to refer to things we do on a regular basis. However with certain time expressions (e.g. *all the time, always, constantly, continually, forever*) we can also use the present continuous.

> *They're forever **asking** me to visit them.*

We use the present continuous in this way to stress the repetitiveness of an action and sometimes (but not necessarily) to express our irritation with this.

State verbs

Although we give learners the rule of thumb that we can't use state verbs (see p. 95) in the present continuous, in reality we sometimes use verbs that express likes, wants, mental states, senses and appearance in this tense in order to give special emphasis to the temporariness of the state.

> ***Are** you **wanting** another drink?* (addressing a friend with an empty glass)
>
> *Sssh, I'm **thinking** what I want to say.*

'Things happening now'

Learners are sometimes taught that we use the present continuous for 'things happening now', and they may even get into the habit of tagging *now* onto every expression which contains the present continuous (e.g. *She's having lunch **now***).

The 'happening now' rule of thumb is not very helpful. In the first place we also use the present continuous to refer to future time (see p. 168). In the second place we can use lots of other tenses to refer to what is happening now (e.g. *He's been talking for the last ten minutes*; *She understands*), and indeed we often use other tenses with the adverb *now* (*Now she understands*; *She's arrived now*). Most importantly, however, this rule of thumb doesn't describe the main and real reasons we choose to use this tense to talk about the present.

Tagging the adverb onto expressions which use the present continuous can also be counter-productive. Many languages rely entirely on adverbs to express that an action is temporary, and it is a problem for many learners to get used to using a verb form (i.e. continuous aspect) to express this in English. If we actively encourage learners to use *now* where it isn't necessary, this may encourage them to rely on adverbs rather than choosing appropriate tense forms.

12.4 Present perfect continuous

Form

We form the present perfect continuous with *has* (*'s*) or *have* (*'ve*) followed by *been* and an *-ing* verb form:

	Question word	*have/ has*	Subject	*have/ has*	*not* or *+n't*	*been* + *-ing* form	
Affirmative:			*She*	*has*		*been wearing*	*glasses for years.*
Question:	*(How long)*	*have*	*you*			*been driving?*	
Negative:			*I*	*haven't*		*been learning*	*Thai for long.*

When do we use the present perfect continuous?

We use the present perfect continuous when we measure the duration so far of a present action or to specify when it began. We use the present perfect continuous in conjunction with an expression beginning with the preposition *for* or *since*, or with the question *How long . . .?*, or when one of these expressions is implied.

> *We've been driving for hours.*
>
> *How long have you been trying to contact me?*

We can show this use diagrammatically:

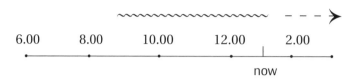

We've been driving for hours.

We compare use of the present perfect continuous and simple to refer to present time on page 162.

12.5 Present perfect simple

Form

We form the present perfect simple with *has* (*'s*) or *have* (*'ve*) followed by the main verb in a past participle form:

	Question word	*have/ has*	Subject	*have/ has*	*not* or +*n't*	past participle	
Affirmative:			*She*	*has*		*known*	*about it for weeks.*
Question:	*(How long)*	*have*	*they*			*worked*	*here?*
Negative:			*They*		*haven't*	*lived*	*in Shanghai for long.*

Past participles may be regular (e.g. *lived*) or irregular (e.g. *known*).

See pages 99–101 for more information about regular and irregular past participles.

When do we use the present perfect simple instead of the present perfect continuous?

Open choice

Like the present perfect continuous, we can use the present perfect simple when we specify the beginning of a present action or when we measure its duration so far. Like the present perfect continuous, we often use the present perfect simple in conjunction with the prepositions *for* and *since* or the question *How long . . .?*.

In describing general (biographical) facts we can choose either form.

    He's smoked/been smoking since he was in the army.

Duration

Sometimes we choose the simple rather than the continuous form to emphasise that something isn't short-term.

simple: *I've worked here most of my life.*   (i.e. long-term)

continuous: *I've been working here for just a few days.* (i.e. short-term)

Repetition

We can choose the continuous form to stress that something is repeated.

continuous: *I've been using the swimming pool since* (i.e. repeated)
                 we moved into the district.

simple: *I've used the swimming pool since we* (i.e. on one or
              moved into the district.   two occasions)

State verbs

On page 96 there is a list of types of verbs we generally avoid using in the present continuous tense. We also tend to avoid these in the present perfect continuous, particularly those describing existence, mental states and possession.

I've known about the inspection for weeks. NOT * *I've been knowing . . .*

However, we are less strict about avoiding these verbs when we use the present perfect continuous, particularly those which describe wants and likes.

I've been wanting to have an opportunity to talk to you for a few days.

After 'the first (second etc.) time'

We use the present perfect simple after this expression when we refer to an event in the present (or the future).

Is this the first time she has flown?

Summary of differences

The table below summarises these differences between how we use the present perfect continuous and simple to express present meaning:

	Present perfect continuous	simple
Expresses duration until now.	✓	✓
Frequently used with expressions beginning *for . . .*, *since . . .* or *How long . . .?*.	✓	✓
Emphasises that something is short-lived.	✓	
Emphasises that something is repeated.	✓	
Suggests a limited number of occasions.		✓
Not used with state verbs	(✓)	
After 'the first (second etc.) time'		✓

12.6 *Will* (*'ll*) + bare infinitive

We sometimes use *will* (*'ll*) + bare infinitive to express repeated and typical actions. This use is very clearly illustrated in the text which follows. A young actor is being interviewed about his lifestyle. (A Harley-Davidson is a kind of motorbike.)

> "When I get a day off, which is very rare, I'll *take* my Harley-Davidson out. I'll *ride* up the coast and have fun, or visit my parents. I live very close to Malibu now and they live ten minutes from me – close enough to visit whenever I want to and far enough away not to see them every day. At the weekends, friends *will come* over and we'll *play* basketball. Most of them are producers and writers; I don't hang out with many actors and actresses."

We may choose not to teach learners to use *will* in this way, but the use is common and we need to be prepared to help learners when they come across it. Course materials often ignore this use but teach the equivalent *would* to express repeated and typical actions in the past.

12.7 Typical difficulties for learners

Comprehension

Learners generally have far more difficulty in using present tenses correctly than in understanding them. Even if they don't know or are unclear about the difference in meaning between different tenses, in most cases there is plenty of information in the context to help them understand whether, for example, an action is temporary or not.

Form and meaning

What can be misleading for learners is coming across forms used with present meaning, that they associate with other time periods. In particular, they may assume that *will* refers to the future and that the present perfect refers to the past in instances where this is not the case.

How long . . . ?

The expression *how long* includes no explicit reference to time, and learners may fail to understand the following question:

How long have you been living here?

We often compress all the syllables before and after *long* in normal, casual speech, and this can make it even more difficult for learners to understand the question.

Speaking and writing

Choosing between present simple and continuous

When learners choose the wrong tense their meaning is still usually clear. However, the mistakes are sometimes very noticeable.

It is more common for learners to use the present simple when the present continuous is appropriate than vice versa. This may be the result of a tendency for learners to simplify and standardise. For some learners it may also be because their own language indicates the temporariness of something only in special cases.

* What do you do with my handbag?

When learners use the present continuous in place of the present simple, this is often with verbs that can't normally be used in a continuous form.

* I'm not believing you.   * Are you hearing any noise?

Leaving off the 'third person s'

Many learners forget the 'third person *s*' even when they have reached a high level of accuracy and general competence in the language.

* My father smoke too much.   * She believe I lied to her.

Question and negative forms of the present simple

Many learners need a lot of practice before using the rules for making questions and negative statements accurately.

Sometimes they may over-generalise the 'third person *s*' rule.

* *Does he likes classical music?*

They may also simply leave out the auxiliary (this is particularly common after question words such as *how, when, where, who* etc.).

* *What you want?*   * *He not speak French?*

Choosing between present and present perfect

It is very common for learners to use the present simple or continuous instead of the present perfect with *How long . . .?, for* and *since*.

* *I am waiting for you since 6.00.*   * *I stay in London since Saturday.*

Many learners find this use instinctively logical and 'correct', and continue making this kind of mistake long after they have learned the correct rule.

This problem can lead to serious misunderstanding when the present continuous is used with *How long . . . ?* or *for . . .* in place of the present perfect continuous, because the sentences may be structurally correct, but express something the learner doesn't intend. Learners may say the following, meaning 'until now' but people may understand that 'two weeks' is the total length of the stay: *We're staying in London for two weeks.*

How long . . . ?

Because the expression *how long* includes no explicit reference to time, learners may adapt it to make it more explicit.

* *How long time have you been living here?*

They may also avoid it altogether, opting for a simpler but less idiomatic form such as *When did you start living here?*

The first (second etc.) time

Learners may choose a tense that they consider more logical than the normal present perfect.

(*) *It is the first time I am travelling by plane.*

Native speakers also vary the tenses after *the first time*, but teachers may choose to treat this as a mistake so that learners become familiar with the *standard* form (which some examinations may demand).

Over-use of present perfect forms

Learners may pay so much attention to using the present perfect instead of the present when they use expressions beginning with *for*, *since* or *How long . . .?*, that they begin to over-associate the present perfect with these expressions and use this tense even when it is not appropriate.

> * *I have been living there for a long time when the war started.*
> (instead of *I had been living . . .*)

Mistakes of this kind may go unnoticed when the time (e.g. *when the war started*) is not specified, and this can lead to serious misunderstanding. For example, if a retired person says the following, people will understand that they are still working: * *I have been working as a police inspector for many years.*

12.8 Consolidation exercises
(see pp. 456–458 for possible answers)

Differences in meaning (see pp. 456–457)

Explain the differences in meaning between the sentences in each of the following groups, referring where appropriate to contexts in which one or other might be preferred:

(i)   She smokes. / She's smoking.

(ii)   Are you wanting to go home? / Do you want to go home?

(iii) Are you liking the concert? / Do you like the concert?

(iv)   How long are you staying here? / How long have you been staying here?

(v)   I've lived here for 60 years. / I've been living here for 60 years.

(vi)   She always brings me flowers. / She's always bringing me flowers.

(vii) He's got a bath. / He has a bath. / He's having a bath.

Language in context (see pp. 457–458)

The following is part of an interview with Judy Bennett. She and her husband Charles both act in a popular soap opera called 'The Archers'. Read the text and answer the questions that follow.

There is no set pattern to our days. Whichever one of *us is not working (1)* does the housework and cooking. Charles *does (2)* his own washing and if I'm working, he *'ll do (3)* mine, too. He quite enjoys it; we have always done things that way. He does the flowers too. I *like (4)* flower arranging, but I can't do it and Charles is quite critical, so I don't try it now. I like weeding and reading – I'm never without a book, especially on my journeys to Birmingham!

What we do in the evenings depends on Jane. She *gets (5)* home from school between 4 p.m. and 6 p.m. I like watching soaps on television. Well, you have to keep up with the opposition! We also listen to 'The Archers' from time to time - we *don't always know (6)* what *is happening (7)* if we've not been in a few episodes.

a   Identify the tense of each of the verbs which is printed in italics in the text. In each case account for the choice of tense.

b   Look at the following words or expressions: *always; never; from time to time; now*. What tense or tenses do you generally associate them with? Check which tenses these words or expressions are used with in the text. Explain any examples of 'untypical' use.

c   The following sentences are from another part of the text above. For each sentence decide which of the two tenses is appropriate and justify your choice:

(i)   If Charles and I *record/are recording* 'The Archers' there is no "typical" day.

(ii) Our home in London *has/is having* a pool, so I *swim/am swimming* regularly.

(iii) I *'ve been/am* in the show for 22 years now.

13 The future

13.1 Key considerations

Some languages have a single 'future tense', whereas English uses a lot of different verb forms to refer to future time (e.g. *will, going to, will be . . . -ing*). Learners often find it bewildering to have to choose an appropriate form from so many, and in general, choosing forms is more problematic than constructing them.

Most learners want rules of thumb to help them choose appropriate forms, but these rules of thumb are also sometimes problematic:

- Some of these rules of thumb depend on apparently 'fuzzy' distinctions (for example the difference between an 'arrangement' and a 'plan'; between a prediction which is based on present or past evidence and one which is not).
- More than in most areas of grammar, the rules of thumb for choosing between future tenses are approximate. These rules of thumb are based on the meaning we want to express. However, in making choices we are also influenced by personal preferences and stylistic factors. Most real texts and transcriptions of speech which include future tenses include choices not accounted for by the rules of thumb.

In the early stages of learning, teachers and materials often concentrate on one future form, and encourage learners to use this as though it were a general 'future tense'. Usually this form is *going to*.

In 13.2–10 we look at the most common future tenses, and consider the meanings as though they were clear and separate. These definitions of meaning are the ones we usually give to learners. In 13.11 we explore some of the other factors that influence our choice of tenses.

We look at the different future tenses in roughly the order they occur in most courses. We concentrate on meaning much more than on form but there are cross-references to the pages that deal with form in more detail.

13.2 'Going to'

Form

We generally refer to this form as the 'going to' future, and teach it as *be + going to* + bare infinitive. It is also logical to think of this as the present continuous form of *go* + the full infinitive:

	Question word	am/is/ are	Subject	am/is/ are or 'm/'s/ 're	not or n't	going to	bare infinitive	
Affirmative:			*I*	*'m*		*going to*	*have*	*a wash.*
Question:	*(When)*	*are*	*they*			*going to*	*leave?*	
Negative:			*We*		*aren't*	*going to*	*make*	*a fuss.*

When do we use 'going to'?

Going to has two main uses:

- planned future events (i.e. the intention is *premeditated*).
  We're going to spend a few days with my Mother.
- predictions based on present or past evidence.
  It's going to rain.

We often teach these two uses quite separately. In fact they are closely related since both of them have a basis in present or past evidence (in the one case this is a decision we have made about our own actions and in the other it is something that helps us to predict external actions or events).

13.3 Present continuous

Form

We look at the form of this tense on page 157.

When do we use the present continuous?

Arrangements

We use the present continuous to refer to the future when arrangements have been made (for example, we have made a booking, bought tickets, or someone is expecting us to do something or be somewhere at a particular time), and we often refer to this use as the 'arranged future'. We usually specify a future time such as *next week, at Christmas* etc. unless it is already clear that we are referring to the future rather than the present.

> *Nobody's **working** on Monday the 5th.*

Go and come

Some people don't like to say or write *going to go* and *going to come,* and they use *going* and *coming* instead. In this case the events may only be planned and not necessarily 'arranged'.

> *I'm **coming** (**going**) home early on Friday.*

13.4 Will ('ll; won't)

Form

We use these forms with the bare infinitive of the main verb.

Subject	Will ('ll; won't)	bare infinitive	
I	*'ll*	*go*	*soon.*
I	*won't*	*let*	*the children bother you.*

We form questions by inverting the position of *will* (*'ll; won't*) and the subject.

> *Will you wait?*

We tend to choose the full form *will* when we are writing or speaking formally, and often in informal speech after nouns and noun phrases (as opposed to pronouns). In informal speaking and writing we use *'ll* after:

* pronouns in affirmative sentences (e.g. *she'll; we'll*).
* question words (e.g. *when'll; who'll*).

If students choose the full form *will* when they're speaking, we need to be careful that that they don't stress it as this can suggest a degree of obstinate insistence.

'll not (e.g. *I'm afraid I'll not be there*) rather than *won't* is the standard negative form in some regions of the United Kingdom.

When do we use Will ('ll; won't)*?*

Just as we generally teach that we choose *going to* to refer to planned future events and predictions based on present or past evidence, we generally teach that we choose *will* or *'ll*:

- for UNplanned future events.
- to make predictions that aren't based on present or past evidence.

We often teach unplanned events in the context of making decisions or offers spontaneously (i.e. the intention is UNpremeditated).

> *I'll do that for you.*

We often teach predictions that aren't based on present or past evidence as

- guesses based on characteristic behaviour.
  I bet he'll bring his mother.
- assertions of faith about the future.
  We'll never lose an election in this constituency.

13.5 *Shall (shan't)*

Form

After *I* and *we*, we can choose between *will* and *shall*, and *won't* and *shan't*. We use *shall* and *shan't* with the bare infinitive in exactly the same way as we use *will* (*'ll; won't*).

Subject	*Shall (shan't)*	bare infinitive	
I	*shall*	*go*	*soon.*
I	*shan't*	*let*	*the children bother you.*

The question form places *shall/shan't* before the subject.

> *Shall we go?*

Shall is usually pronounced as a weak form (/ʃəl/).

When do we use shall (shan't)*?*

Some people consistently choose *shall* and *shan't* in preference to *will* and *won't* after *I* and *we*. Other people never use these forms. Modern teaching materials tend to ignore this use of *shall* altogether. Some older materials misleadingly teach that *shall* and *shan't* are the only correct forms to use after *I* and *we*.

In question forms we generally use *shall* only to make offers and suggestions.

13.6 Present simple

Form

We look at the form of this tense on pages 153–154.

When do we use the present simple?

Timetables and programmes

We use the present simple to anticipate things on the basis of a timetable or programme, often when we are referring to itineraries and travel arrangements, or entertainments and planned public events.

> *The next train **leaves** at 6.30.*
> ***Does** the play **start** at 8.00 or 8.15?*

When we use the present simple to refer to the future, we usually specify precise times and often use the following verbs:

> *come arrive start (begin) go leave (depart) finish (end)*

People sometimes argue that we use the present simple in this way because we see these events as being factually certain.

After time conjunctions

After conjunctions of time (e.g. *after; as soon as; before; by the time; if; till; when; while; unless; until*) we don't use future tenses. Instead we use a present tense to refer to the future. This is often the present simple but, according to what we want to express, we can also use the present continuous or the present perfect.

> present simple: *I'll get back to you when he **arrives**.*
> present continuous: *I'll ask her to phone you as soon as she**'s feeling** better.*
> present perfect: *I shan't speak to you until you**'ve apologised**.*

13.7 *Am/is/are* + infinitive

Form

The form of this is very simple:

Subject	*am/is/are*	infinitive
He	isn't	to leave.

When do we use am/is/are + *infinitive?*

We use *am/is/are* + infinitive for events (activities or states) we see as being in some sense inevitable. Often they have been determined by some external and, perhaps, official body and so an element of obligation is also implied.

> *The whole cast is to assemble on stage after the performance.*
> (i.e. this has been determined by the director.)

13.8 Continuous, perfect and perfect continuous forms of future tenses

Course materials often focus on the continuous, perfect and perfect continuous forms of *will* and *'ll*, and ignore the fact that we also use continuous, perfect and perfect continuous forms of *shall* and *going to*.

The continuous form of future tenses

Formation

We replace the bare infinitive (main verb) with *be + -ing* to form the continuous form of future tenses:

Subject	*will/shall/ be going to*	*be -ing* form	
I	'll	be having	dinner.
Dorothy	is going to	be working	late.
We	shan't	be needing	you any more.

When do we use the continuous form of future tenses?

This form has two distinct uses:

- future events in progress.
- future as a matter of course.

Future events in progress

We use future continuous forms to refer to something that is predicted or programmed to begin before a particular point in the future (and, possibly, to continue after this time), e.g. *I'll be working then.*

Future as a matter of course

We also use future continuous forms as a very neutral way of referring to the future, when we want to avoid suggesting anything about intention, arrangement, prediction or willingness, e.g. *They'll be bringing the children.*

We often teach this use of future continuous forms in the following contexts:

- reassuring people that we are not putting ourselves (or someone else) out.
  She'll be going there anyway.
- sounding out plans before making a request or an offer
  Will you be using your car?

The perfect form of future tenses

Formation

We replace the bare infinitive (main verb) with *have* + a past participle:

Subject	will/shall/ be going to	have + past participle	
Nobody She	's going to won't	have prepared. have arrived	before you.

When do we use the perfect form of future tenses?

We use future perfect forms to view things from a particular point in the future as already having taken place or as having been completed.

We frequently use these forms with expressions beginning *by . . .* or *before . . .*

>*She will have finished work by 6.00.*

See also 'state verbs' in 13.9.

The perfect continuous form of future tenses

Formation

We replace the bare infinitive (main verb) with *have been* + an *-ing* form:

Subject	will/shall/ be going to	have been + -ing form of the verb
He	*'ll*	*have been living in Ghana for 40 years next July.*

When do we use the perfect continuous form of future tenses?

We generally teach that we use future perfect continuous forms to view things from a particular point in the future when we are interested in how long they have been happening. We generally use these forms with expressions that begin with *for . . . .*

>*She'll **have been working** there for over twenty-five years when she retires.*

13.9 State verbs in future tenses

We normally avoid using state verbs (see p. 95), especially *be*, in continuous forms. When we use a state verb to express something that we normally associate with continuous tenses (e.g. 'future as a matter of course'), we use a simple form instead.

> ***Will** you **be** at home tonight?* NOT * *Will you be being . . .?*
>
> *He**'ll have known** her for two years when they get married.*
> NOT * *He'll have been knowing her . . .*

13.10 Other factors in choosing future tenses

Course materials generally teach that we choose between future tenses on the basis of meaning – whether or not, for example, something is:

- arranged.
- premeditated.
- predicted on the basis of present evidence.
- part of a regular itinerary.
- a state or an event.

For learners who want dependable rules of thumb to help them avoid mistakes when they speak and write, this focus on meaning may be the best policy. However, we also need to be aware that we take on board all kinds of other factors in choosing between future tenses. In particular, we often use *will* or *will be . . . -ing* for predictions based on present or past evidence – when the rules of thumb we teach suggest we should use *going to.*

Below we look at some of these factors and at examples to illustrate them. Many of the examples can be attributed to more than one of the factors (e.g. both formality and type of text). Italics have been added to highlight the future tense forms:

- **Personal preference** This example is from a letter from a publisher to an author. The first use of *shall* is unusual.

```
Jeanne shall be answering your letter herself and I shall
shortly be arranging for someone to read the reworked
chapters.
```

- **Variety** We often vary the tenses we use simply in order to avoid repetition – particularly of *going to.* In the first example a child is talking.

  In the morning I*'m going to go* swimming. Then I*'ll come* back and I*'ll get* my sweets from the sweet shop. And then on Sunday in the morning we*'re going to go* to church . . .

  In this example a TV sports journalist looks forward to the summer.

  It's *going to be* a hectic time, as Wimbledon starts only three days later, where I think everyone *will watch* to see if Pete Sampras and Steffi Graf can repeat their success of last year. . . . We*'ll be providing* our usual comprehensive coverage from the 133rd Open championship in July . . .

  In this example the speaker is talking to a TV audience about gardening. He freely mixes contracted and uncontracted forms.

  I*'ll mix* it with some compost, and then I *shall plunge* the pots in a bucket of water, then I *shall fill* the hole till the water stops running out, and then lug it so it gets a good go, and then it*'ll have* to take its chances.

- **Formality** We often use *will* or *shall* rather than *going to* to express *plans* when we use language formally – particularly when we write.

  The first example comes from a political manifesto.

  We *will abolish* the right of the hereditary peers to vote in the House of Lords. We *will reform* the House of Commons. We *will make* sure the quangos that spend vast sums of taxpayers' money are put under public scrutiny . . .

  The second example was spoken during a job interview.

  As we said in the letter we sent you, we *will let* you know our final decision before the end of next week.

- **Type of text** *Will* is widely used in weather forecasts to make predictions based on present evidence.

  Rain *will spread* from the southwest. Tomorrow *will be* cloudy with scattered showers. The rain *will fall* mostly over coastal areas.

  Shall (and also *will*) is used in books and articles to anticipate and introduce the content.

> In this chapter I *shall be looking* particularly at the problems which arise when . . .

In this chapter I *shall describe* the parameters for a culture-sensitive approach: in Chapter 11 I *shall exemplify* the process . . . and in Chapter 13 I *shall discuss* appropriate curriculum . . .

- **Sentence structure** We frequently choose *will* rather than *going to* in complex constructions such as subordinate clauses (first example) and continuous or perfect forms of the verb (second example).

  He said he'll phone later.

  We'll be finishing at about three o'clock.

13.11 Typical difficulties for learners

Comprehension

Learners generally have far more difficulty in using future tenses correctly than in understanding them. Even if they don't know or are unclear about the difference in meaning between different tenses, in most cases there is plenty of information in the context to help them understand whether, for example, an action is premeditated or not.

Speaking and writing

The biggest problem that most learners face is that of choosing the tense which is most appropriate for expressing what they want to say. However, some learners still have problems with the form of the tenses they choose.

Choosing tenses

Over-generalising and simplifying

Learners often choose one tense to express future time in English and use it whenever they refer to the future. They sometimes choose the first form they learn or the one that is most similar to the way they express future time in their own language.

Learners often adopt *will* as their all-purpose future tense.

(*) *Will you go out this weekend?*
(instead of *Are you going out . . .?* or *Are you going to go out . . .?*)

(*) *I'm sorry I can't stay late. I'll play squash tonight.*
(instead of *I'm playing . . .*)

Other learners over-use 'going to'.

> A: *I'm afraid she isn't here this week.*
>
> B: *Don't worry, (*) I'm going to phone him tomorrow then.*
> (instead of *I'll phone him . . .*)

Mistakes like these are not always systematic. Some learners mix up the rules or simply forget them under the pressure of communicating. Other learners consciously or unconsciously use inappropriate rules, for example using *going to* as a 'near' future tense and *will* to refer to a more distant future.

Many learners avoid the complex continuous, perfect and perfect/ continuous forms. Both the meaning and the form of these constructions may seem dauntingly and unnecessarily complicated.

Time conjunctions

Learners often use a future tense instead of a present tense after time conjunctions.

> * *We'll call you as soon as he'll get here.*

The learner may be applying rules from her own language and/or over-generalising from the use of *'ll*. This use seems logical and learners often feel this is right even when they have learned the correct rules.

Native speakers sometimes use future tenses after time conjunctions, but students may be penalised if they do this in exams.

Present tenses

Learners sometimes over-use present tenses to refer to the future. In the text which follows, there are additional mistakes of vocabulary (e.g. *enjoy*).

Tomorrow I go **1** on a trip to Salisbury and Stonehenge. We enjoy **2** the whole day by bus. I hope it isn't **3** rain.

(Corrections: *1 I'm going; 2 We're going to enjoy; 3 I hope it won't rain.*)

Some learners who generally choose tenses appropriately may also over-use present tenses, even in a very systematic way. For example advanced learners may consistently choose the present simple to express a spontaneous (i.e. unplanned or 'unpremeditated') decision, perhaps because they use a similar tense for this purpose in their own language.

*A: There's someone at the door. — B: OK. * I get it!*

Form

Using auxiliary verbs

Learners sometimes miss out auxiliary verbs.

* What you going to do?   * Will you staying here?

They also sometimes use infinitives as auxiliaries instead of *-ing* forms and vice versa.

* The family is go get into the car.   * It'll getting colder this evening.

They may also add unnecessary auxiliaries.

* With music on the Internet, we will don't need to buy CDs any more.

Infinitives

Learners may also be unsure when to use a bare or full infinitive.

* I shall to see her again next week.

Word order

Word order can also cause problems, particularly in question forms.

* When you will come back?   * Why you won't come with me?

13.12 Consolidation exercises
(see pp. 459–462 for possible answers)

Form and meaning (see p. 459)

Match each of the future forms used in the texts with an appropriate rule of thumb from the list below:

From a programme accompanying a series of concerts
I hope you *will enjoy (1)* this year's season as much as the last.

From a political biography
I believe that the Conservative government of the 1980s *will be seen (2)* by future historians as the most successful British government of the 20th century.

From a programme accompanying a series of concerts

... Ivor Bolton *brings (3)* the St James's Players from St James's, Piccadilly.

From a local newspaper

A lighthouse built over two centuries ago to guide ships into the Mersey *is to enjoy (4)* a new lease of life as a tourist attraction ...

From an advertisement for a concert of classical piano music

Renowned as a world authority on the music of Liszt, Leslie Howard is recording Liszt's entire piano works. This project *will have taken (5)* fifteen years to complete and amount to some eighty Hyperion compact discs.

A teacher talking to a visitor to his class

T: Well, at the moment they're writing scripted dialogues that they'*re going to use (6)* later for a role-play.
V: And what roles *are* they *going to play (7)*?
T: Well, they'*re* all *going to play (8)* imaginary roles ... well, it looks like they're finished so I'*ll* just *go (9)* back over to them ...

a An unplanned future event (decision taken at the time of speaking).

b An inevitable event 'determined' by someone.

c A planned event (decision already taken – 'premeditated intention')

d We see something as finishing before a point in the future.

e A prediction or assertion not based on present or past evidence.

f Something which is part of a fixed programme of planned public events.

Language in context

1 (see pp. 459–461)

The first text that follows is a transcript of someone talking about his forthcoming weekend away with two friends. Two of the three men are interested in football. The second text is from a newspaper. The report looks forward to a visit to London by the ex-Soviet leader Mikhail Gorbachev. Read these texts, examine the ways in which future time is expressed in them and answer the questions.

A: Next week you're *going (1)* away, aren't you?

B: Well, three of us *are going (2)* up to the Lake District for six days' freedom . . . there'*ll be (3)* no restrictions on the time that we *do (4)* things, how much we eat and drink. We'*ll be leaving (5)* some time on Saturday afternoon and, I guess, getting to the Lake District about 8 or 9 o'clock at night. Two of us *will want (6)* to listen to the outcome of Saturday's football matches, and one of us won't. So that'*ll be (7)* an interesting dynamic. It's the first time the three of us have been away together.

The Congress of People's deputies never saw anything like it. Former Soviet leader Mikhail Gorbachev *is coming (8)* to London for the first time since he was deposed – and *will be answering (9)* questions from ordinary members of the public. At the beginning of December he *arrives (10)* for a short lecture tour the highlight of which *is (11)* an evening at Westminster Central Hall in front of an audience of more than 2,000.

Unlike events on the rest of the tour, that evening – on 7 December – *will be (12)* no ordinary lecture. Ticket buyers *will be asked (13)* for questions which will then be put to Mr Gorbachev and a panel . . .

a Name the forms which have been highlighted.

b Speculate as to why these choices have been made. (Refer to the context in which these forms are used and consider the full range of factors that influence our choice of future tenses.)

c Consider what alternative forms might have been used and in what ways this might have affected meaning or emphasis.

2 (see pp. 461–462)

The first text that follows is a transcription of a boy (A) and his mother (B) telling a visitor their plans for the following weekend. A is going away with his father (C). B is going away with her other son (D) and a friend (E). In the second text a nine-year-old child is talking about his future. Some of the verbs have been written in their infinitive form. In each case:

a Use the context to help you guess what future form was originally used.

b What alternatives to this might be possible?

c How might choosing between different possible alternatives influence meaning and emphasis?

> A: We *go* **(1)** camping. We *go* **(2)** on the River Thames.

> B: Friday *be* **(3)** spent getting A and C ready to go off, and then on Saturday D and I *go* **(4)** down to Wokingham on the train for the weekend, which *be* **(5)** very exciting. And I'm sure E *have* **(6)** some plans in mind. I expect we *do* **(7)** some exploring, and I know that E and I *talk* **(8)** a bit about these Open University courses.

> I'm not *get* **(9)** married. I *live* **(10)** in Manchester, Leeds or Blackburn. I *be* **(11)** a policeman, a life-saver or a fireman. Or I *be* **(12)** a star football player.

14 The past: past simple, present perfect simple and present perfect continuous

spoke   loved
didn't dream   Did you go?
has spoken   have loved
haven't dreamed

14.1 Key considerations

The biggest difficulty for many learners is knowing when to use the present perfect as opposed to the past simple. Choosing between the present perfect simple and continuous can also pose problems. Learners usually welcome:

- clear rules of thumb to help them choose one form or the other (particularly at lower levels).
- opportunities to explore how these tenses are used in real conversations and texts (particularly at higher levels).

Learners also often have difficulty mastering the forms of the past simple. In particular, they often need opportunities to study and practise

- question and negative forms.
- irregular past tense forms.
- the spelling of regular past tense forms.

Learners often find the form of the present perfect relatively straightforward. However, they may still need opportunities to study and practise irregular past participle forms.

14.2 Past simple

Form

Verbs other than *to be*

	Question word	*Did*	Subject	*Did not* or *didn't*	past tense form	base form
Affirmative:			He They		waited. spoke.	
Question:	(When)	did	you			ring?
Negative:			I	didn't		understand.

See pages 99–101 for information about regular and irregular past simple verb forms.

To be

To be is different from all other verbs in having two forms of the past simple:

I / She / He / It   was
We / You / They   were

and from other non-modal verbs in forming questions and negatives without *did*:

	Question word	Subject	*was/were*	+ *not* or + *n't*	Subject	Complement
Affirmative:		The train	was			late.
Question:	Where		were		the knives?	
Negative:		We		weren't		alone.

When do we use the past simple?

Finished periods of time

The past simple is one of the tenses we use to refer to completed events, states or actions. We choose the past simple when we consider that the event, state or action took place within a finished period of time.

We often use an expression such as *last week, at the weekend, in 1972, 3 years ago*, or *when we were on holiday* to make it clear that the period of time is finished. Sometimes, however, this completed period of time is only implied:

> *Shakespeare wrote over 30 plays.* (i.e. during his life. We know that he's dead).
>
> *Did you go to the party?* (on Saturday.)

Sometimes the 'finished period of time' is not only implied, it is also entirely subjective. The following example appears to contradict the rule about finished periods of time as *today* by definition is UNfinished. However, the speaker thinks of *today* (perhaps the *working* day) as over:

> *I saw Harry in the office today.*

Precise detail

We also use the past simple when we provide precise circumstantial detail about an event (e.g. we can say *I've had my appendix out* but we have to use the past simple as soon as we specify, for example, *where* or *how* – we don't say * *I've had my appendix out in Warsaw* but *I had my appendix out in Warsaw*). Newspaper reports often introduce a description of an event using the present perfect simple but then 'drift' into the past simple as more detail accumulates.

Time anchor

In telling stories and describing what happened in the past we use the past simple as a 'time anchor' – to establish the key 'time frame' of events. We also use the past simple to describe the key events that move the story forward. We use other tenses (notably the past perfect and past continuous) to show the relationship of other events to this 'time frame'. In the early stages of teaching past tenses, teachers often focus exclusively on the use of the past simple for events within a finished period of time, leaving its use in narrative until later. See pages 188–189 and 197 for a more detailed description and illustration of this.

Different kinds of events

Some languages use different tenses for different kinds of past events (e.g. 'momentary' as opposed to 'extended over a period of time' or 'repeated'). In English we can use the past simple for many kinds of event.

The following paragraph is taken from an article about the French film director Jean Renoir, who died in 1979:

Renoir's richest period, when he *made* (**1**) his most imperishable films, was in the 1930s and *ended* (**2**) abruptly with the Second World War, most of which he *spent* (**3**) in Hollywood making movies for 20th Century-Fox.

1 things which are repeated over a period of time

2 single, momentary events

3 things which are extended over a period of time

14.3 Present perfect simple

Form

We form the present perfect simple with *has* (*'s*) or *have* (*'ve*) followed by the main verb in a past participle form:

	Question word	*have/ has*	Subject	*have/ has*	*not* or + *n't*	past participle	
Affirmative:			*She*	*has*		*passed*	*her test.*
Question:	*(What)*	*Have*	*you*			*eaten?*	
Negative:			*She*		*hasn't*	*finished*	*school.*

See pages 100–101 for information about the form of past participles.

When do we use the present perfect simple?

Unfinished periods of time

We use the present perfect simple to refer to completed events, states or actions in the past which took place within a period of time which is

UNfinished. Sometimes we use expressions like *today* or *this year* to specify this unfinished period of time.

> *I've had two accidents this week.*

Often it is just implied.

> *I've never been outside Europe.* (The period of the person's life is an implied unfinished period of time.)

In American English the past simple may be used in place of the present perfect simple in these instances.

Rules of thumb

Course materials often explain when we use the present perfect simple with one or more rules of thumb. However, we need to be very wary of simplifications such as these:

We use the present perfect simple:

- for a more recent past than that expressed by the past simple.

  This is simply wrong (e.g. *I've lived through two world wars* is clearly not 'more recent' than *I saw him a minute ago*).
- for events which have present relevance or a connection with now.

  This is very vague and we can argue that everything we express has present relevance regardless of the tense we choose (why else would we be saying or writing it?).
- with adverbs such as *just, already, yet, ever* and *before*.

  This is misleading because we use these adverbs with a variety of tenses.
- in contexts such as news reports or personal biographies.

  This is unhelpful since, depending on whether a finished period of time is or isn't mentioned or understood, other tenses are also used in these contexts.
- to refer to completed events, states or actions 'when no past time is specified'.

  This rule of thumb may help some learners to make appropriate choices, but still ignores the key factor (unfinished time period).

We occasionally choose to use the present perfect simple with expressions of finished time (e.g. *I've seen him yesterday*) because, despite the adverb *yesterday*, we *feel* that the event is within a present time period. However, it would be confusing to draw learners' attention to examples like this.

14.4 Past simple contrasted with present perfect simple

News reports and biographies provide a useful source of material for teachers who want their students to analyse how these two tenses are used. For example, in the short text which follows, the use of the past simple followed by the present perfect makes the distinction clear:

> Christian Barnard, 73, was born in Cape Province, South Africa. He performed (**1**) the first human heart transplant operation in 1967, and the first double heart transplant seven years later. Now retired, he has homes in Cape Town and Cape Province. As well as his many medical publications, he has written (**2**) three novels.

1 Past simple: This is clearly qualified by *in 1967* – a finished period of time.

2 Present perfect simple: No time is specified – we understand that this is during his life and that he is still alive.

We can express this difference diagrammatically:

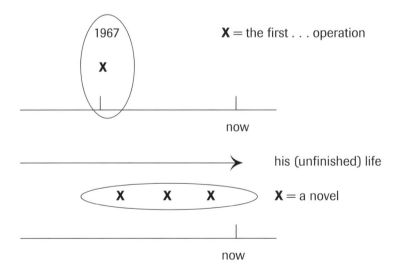

Some key differences between these two tenses (and their similarity) are summarised in the following chart:

	Past simple	Present perfect simple
Finished events	✓	✓
Events in a finished period of time	✓	
Events in an unfinished period of time		✓
General biographical details about a living person		✓
General biographical details about someone who is dead	✓	
Generally used in telling stories	✓	

14.5 Present perfect continuous

Form

We form the present perfect continuous with *has* (*'s*) or *have* (*'ve*) followed by *been* and an *-ing* form:

	Question word	*have/ has*	Subject	*have/ has*	*not* or + *n't*	been + *-ing* form	
Affirmative:			*It*	*has*		*been raining.*	
Question:	*(Why)*	*have*	*you*			*been crying?*	
Negative:			*They*		*haven't*	*been paying*	*attention.*

When do we use the present perfect continuous?

We use the present perfect continuous to refer to an activity which took place over a period of time and, usually, has recently stopped.

> *Your telephone has been ringing* (This continued for some time. It is now silent).

> *It has been raining* (The sky is now clear but the ground is wet).

The activity may be constant or repeated (e.g. *It has been raining* may describe an extended, single period of rain or a series of short showers).

14.6 Present perfect simple and continuous contrasted

The present perfect simple may describe something which has only recently finished, but this is not necessarily the case.

> *I've read 'Crime and Punishment'* (I read it when I was at school).

We use the present perfect continuous to describe an activity recently stopped.

> *I've been reading 'Crime and Punishment'.*

The present perfect simple may describe something which is repeated or extended, but this is not necessarily the case.

> *Your wife has rung.* (She may have rung just once, and only briefly.)

When we use the present perfect continuous, we understand that the event is repeated or extended.

> *Your wife has been ringing.*

Because of the recentness of events described by the present perfect continuous, we don't use it to describe general biographical, historical or circumstantial detail.

Summary of key differences between these two tenses:

	Present perfect simple	Present perfect continuous
Finished events	✓	✓
Events located in an unfinished period of time	✓	
Events which may be part of general biographical, historical or circumstantial detail	✓	
Events which have only very recently finished	?	✓
Events which took place over an extended period of time	?	✓

14.7 Typical difficulties for learners

Comprehension

Misunderstanding is unlikely to result from uncertainty about the differences between these tenses.

Speaking and writing

Choosing between tenses

It takes a long time and a lot of exposure to English for many learners to be clear when to use the present perfect and when to use the past simple. Even when they are clear, they may continue to make mistakes under the pressure to communicate.

Some learners find choosing between the past simple and the present perfect difficult because their own language doesn't make this kind of distinction. Speakers of some European languages may be misled by the fact that their own languages have tenses which are similar in form, but which are used quite differently.

Past simple and present perfect simple

The most noticeable mistakes are often those in which learners use the present perfect simple in place of the past simple.

> * *Has she been there last year?*
> * *When I was 9 we have moved to a large house.*

Learners also sometimes use the past simple in place of the present perfect simple. This is generally considered incorrect in British English although it is correct in American English.

> (*) *I already did it.*   (*) *Did you have dinner yet?*

Past simple and present perfect continuous

Learners may also use the past simple in place of the present perfect continuous, for example using the following to express irritation:

> * *You drank!* (instead of *You've been drinking!*)
> * *I waited for you!* (instead of *I've been waiting for you!*)

This use of the past simple can conceal or confuse the speaker's intention since the meanings of the two tense forms are significantly different.

Simplification

Under the pressure of on-the-spot communication, learners may simplify grammar and leave words out. This happens frequently in all question forms, particularly after question words (*what, when* etc.), perhaps because these already show that the sentence is a question. It also happens particularly in negative questions (see the second example below), perhaps because they include so many grammatical elements (tense, question form and negative).

> * *What you have brought us?*   * *Why you didn't tell us before?*

Learners whose first language indicates questions only by punctuation or intonation are especially likely to make mistakes like this.

Learners sometimes simplify grammar in affirmative sentences as well as in questions. They may leave out an auxiliary verb in contexts where they should use two together:

> * *He has living there.*

Regular and irregular forms

There are several reasons why learners may make mistakes in the use of regular and irregular forms. They may:

- (consciously or unconsciously) have learnt the wrong form of a particular verb.
- be guessing the form because they don't know what it is.
- over-generalise rules (for example, ignoring irregular forms or using past forms in questions or infinitives).

These reasons are often not immediately clear, and we need to talk to the students about particular mistakes in order to learn the precise causes. Typical examples are:

> * *I've speaked about it.*   * *Did you wrote to him yesterday?*
>
> * *I dranked two glasses.*   * *Do you ate everything?*
>
> * *Have they took the rubbish away?* * *I wanted to told you about it myself.*

Pronunciation

Many learners 'over-pronounce' the regular past tense ending.

> *loved* (*/lʌvəd/); *picked* (*/pɪkəd /); *dropped* (*/dropəd /)

This may be:

- because they find the combination of consonants difficult to pronounce without a vowel to separate them.
- because they haven't learned the appropriate pronunciation rules.
- because they are influenced by adjectives they know like *wicked* (/wɪkɪd/).

14.8 Consolidation exercises (see pp. 462–464 for possible answers)

Language in context

1 (see pp. 462–463)

Read the following text, which provides biographical information about the editor of the published diaries of Kenneth Williams, a popular British entertainer who died in 1988. Some of the verb forms are printed in italics:

> Russell Davies, editor of <u>The Kenneth Williams Diaries</u>, *became* *(1)* a freelance writer and broadcaster soon after leaving Cambridge University in 1969. He *has been (2)* a film and television critic of the Observer and television critic of the Sunday Times, and lately *has been writing (3)* a column about sport for the Sunday Telegraph. For television and radio, he *has presented (4)* many literary and political features, a history of radio comedy, more than fifty editions of 'What the Papers Say', sundry jazz documentaries (some of them watched by Kenneth Williams); but in spite of his involvement with Light Entertainment, particularly in radio, he never quite *collided (5)* with Williams himself – except in print.

   a In each case explain the choice of tense. (Make specific reference to the contexts in which they occur.)

   b Consider whether any other tense might be acceptable in the same context. What difference (if any) might this make to meaning?

2 (see p. 463)

Read the following extracts from various sources. Some of the verbs are provided only in their infinitive form:

From a letter to an author

> We meet **(1)** last year when you come **(2)** to the school to give a talk.

From the beginning of a conversation

So what *happen* **(3)** since the last time we *meet* **(4)** then?

TV presenter talking about eating his favourite evening meal

The garlic makes it pretty pungent, so the BBC make-up ladies in the mornings can always tell when I *eat* **(5)** it.

A critic talking about a piece of music played at a piano competition

I *hear* **(6)** it twice already yesterday.

Letter sent by author

> I talk **(7)** about the lexical approach in a seminar about three months ago.

  a Study the numbered verbs and decide in each instance which tense was used in the original text: past simple, present perfect simple or present perfect continuous.

  b Consider whether any other tense form might be acceptable in the same context. What difference (if any) might this make to meaning?

Learners' English (see pp. 463–464)

Study the following sentences, all of which were spoken by learners. Each sentence contains forms that some teachers would consider to be a mistake.

  (i)   Shakespeare has written over 30 plays.
  (ii)   Hi. Sorry I didn't call you earlier but I just got home.
  (iii) Did you ever go to Ravello in Italy ?
  (iv)   My bike works now. I've mended it last week.

 a Identify and explain the 'incorrect' forms.

 b Which of these forms might be used by native speakers?

 c A student asks you to 'correct every mistake'. Which of these would you correct?

15 The past: past perfect simple, past continuous and past perfect continuous

> *had lived* *was waiting*
> *had been supposing*
> *had you thought?*
> *wasn't expecting*

15.1 Key considerations

We generally teach past tenses initially from the point of view of a sequence of events, i.e. we choose between different tenses according to when the events take place in relation to some fixed time or event in the past. We also sometimes show how we can choose the past perfect simple and the past continuous according to their narrative function, and some learners find this is easier to understand and use as a rule of thumb. Narratives also provide a valuable opportunity for learners to practise these tenses.

When our students are studying a tense for the first time, we usually focus on what makes this tense different from others. We want to help our learners make confident choices, and so we often teach rules of thumb which suggest that in any context there is one correct – or at least 'best' – choice, even though there are sometimes two, equal possibilities.

Many other European languages have a form which is similar to the past perfect simple in English and is used in similar circumstances. Speakers of these languages generally find it easy to understand and use this tense.

15.2 Past perfect simple

Form

We form the past perfect simple with *had* followed by the main verb in a past participle form:

	Question word	*had*	Subject	*had*	*not* or *+n't*	past participle
Affirmative:			*Everyone*	*had*		*spoken.*
Question:	*(Why)*	*had*	*they*			*left?*
Negative:			*They*		*hadn't*	*eaten.*

See pages 100–101 for information about past participle forms.

When do we use the past perfect simple?

Sequence of events

We use the past perfect simple when we want to draw attention to the fact that something took place and finished before something else in the past.

We often use the past perfect simple in clauses connected by a conjunction (e.g. *when, and, that, because, so*) to a clause containing a verb in the simple past.

> *I knew (that) I **had seen** her somewhere before.*
> *It **had stopped** raining so they didn't bother to put the car away.*

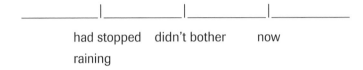

We use the past perfect simple to avoid confusion or ambiguity. We don't use it simply because one event came before another, but in order to clarify the order of events. So, for example, we use the tense more frequently with the conjunction *when* than *before* or *after*:

> *They **had finished** eating when I got there.* (Only the two tenses make the sequence of events clear.)
> *They **finished** eating before I got there.* (The conjunction *before* makes the sequence of events clear, and so we can use the simple past (rather than the past perfect) for the earlier of the events.)

Very often, context provides *some* information about the sequence of events. In this case choosing between simple past and past perfect involves making subtle judgements about how much information is needed, and we generally prefer to provide too much rather than to risk misunderstanding.

State verbs

We use the past perfect simple instead of the past perfect continuous (see p. 200) if the verbs belong to the group that we avoid using in continuous forms (see pp. 95–96 for more information about these).

> *I **had understood** that she was dissatisfied for a long time before she said anything.*

Narrative

When we tell a story or describe a sequence of events we generally use the past simple to establish the main facts and to move the story forward if we describe events in the order they happened.

We use the past perfect to describe the background – to introduce the events that happened before the main narrative and have some bearing on it. We often use it to show that a character is recollecting something that happened previously.

The following is the beginning of a chapter in a novel. The novel describes an imaginary republican take-over in Britain, in which the Royal Family are forced to move from Buckingham Palace to a council housing estate. They are given houses in a street called Hellebore Close. The text below explores the use of tenses in this passage.

> The street sign at the entrance to the Close had lost five black metal letters. HELL . . . CLOSE it now said, illuminated by the light of a flickering street lamp.

> The Queen thought, 'Yes, it is Hell, it must be, because I've never seen anything like it in the whole of my waking life.'

> She had visited many council estates – had opened community centres, had driven through the bunting and the cheering crowds, alighted from the car, walked on red carpets, been given a red posy by a two-year-old in a 'Mothercare' party frock, been greeted by tongue-tied dignitaries, pulled a cord, revealed a plaque, signed the visitor's book.

The past perfect (*had lost*) is used in the first sentence to set the scene – to establish something which happened before the key event, and which had some bearing on the key event. By beginning with this 'scene-setting', the author also establishes a sense of expectation.

The second sentence of the first paragraph and the whole second paragraph establish (implicitly) the main point of reference in this narrative i.e. the 'key event', the arrival of the Queen.

The past perfect (*had visited, had opened* etc.) is used in the third paragraph to establish that the events described are again further in the past. The auxiliary verb *had* is used three times in the list of events and then left out before the other past participles (*alighted* etc.) since it is clear that these events are all in this 'past perfect sequence'.

15.3 Past continuous

Form

We form the past continuous with *was* or *were* followed by the main verb in an *-ing* form:

	Question word	*was/ were*	Subject	*was/ were*	*not* or *+ n't*	*-ing* form
Affirmative:			*They*	*were*		*dancing.*
Question:	*(Why)*	*was*	*she*			*talking?*
Negative:			*I*		*wasn't*	*concentrating.*

See page 410 for the spelling rules for forming the *-ing* form of the verb.

When do we use the past continuous?

Sequence of events

We use the past continuous to describe something which began before a particular point in the past and is still in progress at that point. The action may continue after that point.

> I *was* still *working* at 6 o'clock (and I continued working after that point).
>
> He *was using* the vacuum cleaner and so he just didn't hear the doorbell ring (and continued using the vacuum cleaner after the doorbell rang).

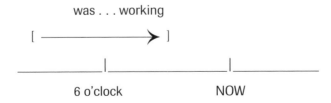

We can also use the past continuous when the action stopped at the key point in the past.

> He *was working* at his computer when the power cut occurred.

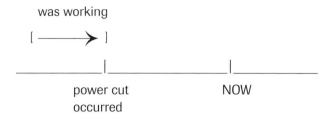

This use is sometimes called the 'interrupted past continuous'. We use the simple past to describe the action which 'interrupted' the past continuous action.

'Complete' periods of time

We sometimes use the past continuous to describe events that extend across 'complete' periods of time (e.g. *all day; the whole lesson; every minute of the journey*).

> We ***were slaving*** *away from morn to night.*

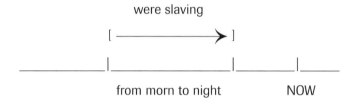

This choice of the past continuous rather than the past simple emphasises that the activity was happening at every moment during the specified period.

Narrative

In narrative, the past continuous is often used to 'set the scene' for events which are taking place. In the following extracts from a novel the author uses the past continuous to establish the background against which the key events happen:

> Mona *was washing* dishes with a vengeance when Mrs Madrigal walked into the kitchen.

> Mona *was beginning* her second half liter of wine when Mrs Madrigal arrived at the Savoy-Tivoli.

15.4 Past perfect continuous

Form

We form the past perfect continuous with *had* followed by *been* and the main verb in an *-ing* form:

	Question word	*had/ 'd*	Subject	*had/ 'd*	*not* or *+ n't*	*been + -ing* form	
Affirmative:			*They*	*had*		*been losing*	*a lot of money.*
Question:	*What*	*had*	*you*			*been doing?*	
Negative:			*I*	*hadn't*		*been working*	*for long.*

When do we use the past perfect continuous?

Sequence of events

We use the past perfect continuous when we are concerned with an extended or repeated event or activity which took place before a particular point in the past.

Sometimes this event or activity stops at the specified point of time.

> *He'd been driving without a break for several hours when the accident happened.*

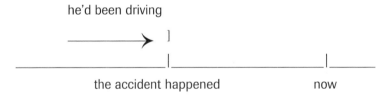

Sometimes this event or activity continues beyond the specified point of time.

> *The family had been living in the house for years before they noticed the bulge in the wall.*

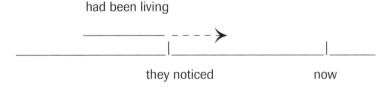

Sometimes this event or activity has recently finished before the specified point of time.

*His eyes were red. I could tell **he'd been crying**.*

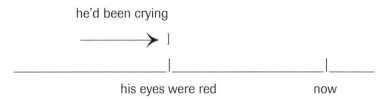

As in the first and second of the three examples above, we often use the past perfect continuous with expressions beginning *for* or *since* to measure how long something lasted until a particular point.

15.5 Comparing 'new' and familiar tenses

Some learners find it helpful to compare the tenses they learn with similar tenses that they already know.

The 'new' tense	A familiar tense
Past continuous [--------] _____|_____|____ Key point now in the past	**Present continuous** [----------] _____|_____ now

Past perfect simple
 	
  X   ___|_____|____
Key point   now
in the past
	Present perfect simple
	
	  X |_____
	now

Past perfect continuous ———→] _____|_____|____ Key point now in the past	**Present perfect continuous** ———→] _____|_____ now

15.6 Choosing between tenses

Crucial choices

Choosing between past continuous or past perfect continuous forms can make a particularly crucial difference to the meaning we express. In the first of the examples below the speaker's mother is still living in the house at the time of the visit. In the second example we understand that she is now living somewhere else.

> *We called at the house where my mother **was living** and left some flowers for her there.*
>
> *We called at the house where my mother **had been living** to see if the new people had received any mail for her.*

Open choice

Sometimes it is possible to choose more than one tense, and this choice makes no perceptible difference to meaning. In the following extracts, each author chooses a different tense. We can only speculate about whether the authors wanted to achieve particular effects of style or emphasis through their respective choice, or whether their choice was unconscious or arbitrary. What is clear is that either tense is possible in either context.

Past continuous or past perfect continuous?

Past continuous

Auntie Du and the servants all laughed loudly, recounting at least ten times where they *were sitting* or standing when the sirens came.

Past perfect continuous

The voices he could hear were . . . simply the indignant residents of the neighbourhood who *had been cooking* or watching television or reading when the lights went out.

Past simple or past perfect simple?

> Two days after he had returned from Germany, Britten began to compose a new song-cycle for Pears, with piano accompaniment.

Two days after he returned (past simple) is also possible here as the order of events is completely clear.

Past perfect simple or continuous?

> I had hoped to catch an early-morning bus to Stonehenge with a view to proceeding on to Avebury for the afternoon, but this, I apprehended, was an impossibility.

I had been hoping (past perfect continuous) is also possible here. However, the context makes it clear that the writer continued hoping up until a particular moment (*I apprehended*), and so it isn't necessary to convey this in the grammar.

15.7 Typical difficulties for learners

Comprehension

Learners may have some problems in understanding the differences between these tenses, but these rarely lead to serious misunderstanding since the distinctions are often unimportant and already clear in the context.

The greatest source of potential misunderstanding is in sentences like the following:

> *He left when I got there/He'd left when I got there.*
> *I knew he liked me/I knew he'd liked me.*

Here, the learner has to:

- recognise the significance of the tense choice (simultaneous events or in sequence).
- hear the (barely perceptible) difference between *he left/liked* and *he'd left/liked*.

Native speakers are often unsure whether they've heard the past simple or past perfect, and may ask a question to check this.

Speaking and writing

Simplifying the form

Learners may use a bare infinitive instead of the *-ing* form or instead of the past participle.

> * *I was do my homework when he came to see me last night.*

> * *I didn't believe that I had pass my examinations.*

Or, they may leave out an auxiliary verb.

> * *I trying to open the carriage door when the train started.*

> * *The army had preparing for the attack.*

Or, in asking questions, they may fail to make necessary changes to the order of words. This is particularly common if the question contains a question word (*What, when, why* etc.) or a negative form. The following example contains both these features:

> * *Why he hadn't been living there?*

Having learnt the use of *did* and *didn't* to ask questions and make negative statements in the past simple, learners may inappropriately extend this to other tenses.

> * *The survivors didn't had eaten anything for days when they were finally rescued.*

Avoidance

Learners often avoid what they feel they don't properly know yet. Particularly in speaking, learners may 'play safe' by avoiding the more complex past tenses. For example, they may use the past simple to make any reference to past time.

> * *Yesterday I got up early because I went to the antiques market. When I got to the market it already opened.*

Mistakes like this may also be the result of not knowing the appropriate forms, or may be due to 'forgetting' them under the pressure of communicating.

Over-use

They may also over-use a form because they have learnt a rule which is incomplete or inaccurate. This learner seems to have grasped that we use the past perfect simple for actions that are 'further back in the past', but isn't yet aware of the other factors which make us choose this tense.

> * *I had graduated from university and then I had joined the army. I started working several years later.*

Mis-use

In the following example, it is difficult know whether the learner is avoiding the past perfect continuous or is making a 'slip' in the process of composing the sentence. Mistakes like this are particularly common when learners use phrases with *for* and *since*. This may be because they have previously made an effort to associate *for* and *since* with present perfect rather than present simple or continuous forms.

> * *She has been living in England for a long time but she still didn't speak English.*

15.8 Consolidation exercises (see pp. 464–468 for possible answers)

Differences in meaning (see pp. 464–465)

Explain the differences in meaning between the sentences in these groups:

(i)   I left when he arrived.

(ii)   I had left when he arrived.

(iii)   I was leaving when he arrived.

(iv)   She pointed out he spoke English.

(v)   She pointed out he had spoken English.

(vi)   She pointed out he was speaking English.

(vii)   She'd been painting the room when she was taken into hospital.

(viii) She'd painted the room when she was taken into hospital.

(ix)   She was painting the room when she was taken into hospital.

Learners' English (see p. 465)

The following were written by learners of English.

> (i)   I travelled in a coach to Ankara. A car on the outside lost control and pushed us off the road.

(ii)   I had got up and then I had washed. Then I had put on my clothes and I left home.

(iii) We used to stay with friends in Kabul for two years when we came to Britain and got asylum.

a What is strange about the use of tenses in each extract?

b Why do you think the learners may have expressed themselves in this way?

c What general rule of thumb would you want to give to each learner?

Language in context

1 (see pp. 466–467)

Read the following extracts, in which some of the verbs have been printed in italics. Answer the questions about the verbs:

(i) This is from a newspaper article about the ending of Prohibition (the banning of alcoholic drinks) in the United States

It was the end of a startling social experiment which *had begun (1)* at midnight on January 17, 1920 – when constitutional prohibition *made (2)* America 'dry'.

But less than two years later, the experiment *had* patently *failed (3)* and Americans were busy paralysing, blinding and killing themselves with huge quantities of bootleg [i.e. illegal] liquor.

Gangsters *were making (4)* millions from the licensing trade and the most inoffensive citizen regularly *defied (5)* the law in order to get a little of what he fancied.

(ii) This is from a TV programme about the war poet, Siegfried Sassoon

He was one of the people whom the war rescued in the sense that it gave his life meaning. He *had been dreaming (6)* in the garden at home, writing poems, having them privately printed, and it *had been (7)* a very drifting, purposeless kind of life. It didn't satisfy him and he didn't know what to do about it.

(iii) In this extract from a novel, a woman wakes up after dreaming about her husband, who is a doctor

She woke up still squinting against the sunlight that *had flashed* **(8)** off his glasses. He *had been wearing* **(9)** a stethoscope, she recalled, looped across the back of his neck like a shaving towel. He *hadn't worn* **(10)** a stethoscope since the first week he came to work for her father. It was a new-young-doctor thing to do, really.

(iv) This is from a newspaper article about John McCarthy, a political hostage

John McCarthy *was working* **(11)** as a journalist in Beirut when he was seized on his way to the airport to leave.

a What is the tense?

b What reasons are there for choosing this tense in this context?

c What other tense(s) might also be possible here? How might these affect meaning?

2 (see pp. 467–468)

Read the following extracts, in which some of the verbs are provided only in their infinitive form. Study these and consider the question below.

(i) From an interview with a popular British entertainer

My most memorable Christmas has to be 1970, when my eldest son, Robert, was 6 months old and I *play* **(1)** Aladdin in panto at the London Palladium. We *wake* **(2)** up on Christmas Day to find it *snow* **(3)** during the night. In the middle of the lawn was a single rose, which my husband Bobby *put* **(4)** there. The day was perfect from then on.

(ii) From a novel

I met this same man Lin for the first time twenty years later, when I already *live* **(5)** in the United States for five years.

(iii) From a novel

> . . . it was Drosoula who died first, perfectly upright in her rocking chair, so quietly that it seemed she *apologise (6)* for having lived at all. She was an indomitable woman who *live (7)* a few short years of happiness with a husband that she *love (8)*, a woman who *disown (9)* her own son as a matter of principle, and lived out her days in ungrudging service to those who had adopted her by apparent accident, even earning them their daily bread.

a What tense do you think was used in the original text?

b Might any other tense form be acceptable in the same context? What difference (if any) might this make to the meaning?

16 The past: *used to* and *would*

used to live   would visit

16.1 Key considerations

Most learners find it relatively easy to understand the meaning of *used to* and to use it in affirmative sentences. They may have more difficulty in constructing questions and negative statements.

Many learners are confused that we use *would* to refer to the past. They are usually familiar with other uses of *would*.

Many learners avoid using *would* and *used to* to refer to the past even when they are confident about how to do this. We may need to prompt and encourage them to use these forms – for example when they are writing about people or places, describing them now and in the past.

16.2 Form

used to

Although we refer to this form as *used to* it makes sense to analyse the grammar as *used* + infinitive.

	Question word	*Did*	Subject	*Did not* or *didn't*	*never*	*used*	*use*	infinitive	
Affirmative:			They			used		to live	locally.
Question:	*(What)*	did	you				use	to smoke?	
Negative:			I	didn't				use	to drink.
			I		never	used		to believe	in ghosts.

Although question and negative forms are given in the table, some people avoid using them. As the table shows, *never used to* is an alternative to *didn't use to*.

would

There is no difference between the form of *would* when it refers to the past and its form as a modal verb. Some people avoid using the negative and question forms of *would* to refer to the past.

16.3 Meaning

Common features

We use *used to* and *would* as alternatives to the simple past in describing habits and repeated actions which took place over a period of time (and which often then ceased).

> When we were children we **used to spend** our dinner money on pasties and cakes.
>
> We **would** feel sick in the afternoons.

Used to and *would* emphasise both remoteness and duration. Once we have used one of these auxiliary verbs to establish this, or if the context makes this clear, we often then vary our choice and also use the simple past. There are no contexts in which we absolutely have to use *used to* or *would* but it appears odd both to over-use and, conversely, to completely neglect these forms in any extended description.

Differences

Repeated actions and states

We use both forms to describe repeated actions but we use only *used to* to describe extended past states. In the following examples we could not use *would*:

> We **used to live** in the town centre.
>
> There **used to be** three cinemas in the High Street.

We can use *would* (as well as *used to*) to describe repeated states which are temporary and related to a particular context, even if they continue over an extended period of time.

> She **would** usually **be** hungry when she got home from school.
>
> When the local children spoke I **wouldn't understand** anything.

We also use *used to* to describe past states.

The chart shows the difference:

	used to	*would*
actions	✓	✓
temporary/repeated states	✓	✓
permanent states	✓	–

Time reference and new topics

We can introduce a new topic using *used to*, and we don't need to specify a particular time. We usually use *would* only when a time and topic have been established, so the speaker of the following example could not have used *would buy*:

> *I used to buy that stuff but it's a waste of money, you know.*
> (One customer to another customer in a supermarket)

Individual variation

There is quite a lot of individual variation in how we use these forms – some people prefer one or the other; some people tend to use one or both of them a lot; other people seem to use them less. Some choose *would* to convey psychological 'remoteness', often suggesting a feeling of nostalgia or longing. Other people use *used to* more when they want to emphasise the repetitive aspect of a regular activity.

Frequency adverbs

We use *would* a lot with 'frequency adverbs' (*always, usually, sometimes* etc.).

16.4 Pronunciation

Used to and (*didn't*) *use to* are normally pronounced in precisely the same way – /juːstə/. This pronunciation is different from that of the verb *to use* (/juːz/) even though the spelling is the same.

Would is often pronounced /d/ or /wʊ/.

We usually don't stress either *used to* or *would*.

16.5 Teaching considerations

Learners who are familiar with the use of *will* to describe typical or repeated actions (see Chapter 12.6) may find it helpful to think of this use of *would* as a past form of *will*.

We often teach *used to* at an elementary or early intermediate level, introducing it as a way of talking about discontinued past habits. We usually teach the use of *would* (to refer to past events) at a much later stage.

16.6 Typical difficulties for learners

Comprehension

Used to

Many learners understand this form to refer to habitual activity in the *present*, perhaps because they have come across and remembered *be + used + -ing* (e.g. *I'm used to getting up early*), or because the two forms have been taught together and they forget which is which.

Would

Learners often know *would* as a modal verb which expresses hypothetical meaning (e.g. *I would be happier in another job*), and may understand this meaning instead of its reference to the past.

They may also simply fail to hear *would*, for example understanding *I go* when someone has said *I'd go*.

Speaking and writing

These forms present little difficulty to learners in terms either of meaning or form. However, what learners often do find difficult is knowing when to use them.

Avoidance

Many learners avoid using *would* altogether to refer to past time. They may also neglect opportunities to use *used to*. As in the following piece of writing, learners often simply choose other ways of expressing past time:

We lived in a small house on a modern housing estate, but we had a garden. I grew anemones and a yellow flower – I don't remember the name. My mother often wanted to pick the yellow flowers and she wanted to put them in vases in the house but I didn't permit her to do this. Sometimes I bought her flowers from the florist's so that she didn't ask me to let her pick my flowers.

Over-use

The following is an extract from a learner's homework, written after a lesson which focused on *used to*. The repetition of *used to* seems unnatural.

I used to have long hair and I used to wear glasses and I used to ride my bicycle to school. I used to like watching television and I used to play basketball in the park.

Present habitual activity

Learners may assume that *use to* is a present form of *used to*..

*I *used to take the bus but now I use to come to work by bike.*

Spanish-speaking learners of English in particular sometimes use *used to* in place of the simple present. This can lead to significant misunderstandings.

* *I used to speak Spanish at home.* (Correct sentence: *I speak Spanish at home.*)

Spelling

Learners sometimes make mistakes in the spelling of *used to*:

* *I use to like chocolate.*   * *Did you used to eat meat?*

These mistakes are also common among native speakers.

16.7 Consolidation exercises
(see pp. 469–470 for possible answers)

Learners' English (see p. 469)

Look back at the two examples of learners' writing on pp 000. Re-write these so that the use of tenses is more natural. If possible, compare your version of this with someone else's.

Language in context

1 (see pp. 469–470)

The following text is part of an interview with the musician Rick Parfitt who is reminiscing about his childhood. Study the verbs which are printed in italics. In each case answer the questions below.

We *had (1)* woods out the back, a cricket field and a football field within three minutes' walk. We *had (2)* bows and arrows, which we *cut (3)* ourselves and sharpened; we all had knives and catapults. We were out till all hours, playing football, commandos, playing with trolleys you'*d steer (4)* with ropes, playing with roller-skates with metal wheels . . . I challenge anyone to say he had a better childhood than mine.

My dad *used to take (5)* me down to Woking Working Man's Club and encourage me to take that guitar, because in those days people just *used to get up (6)* and give a song.

a What form is used?

b Could an alternative form be used? What? How might this alter the meaning expressed or the effect created?

2 (see p. 470)

Read the following extracts. Some of the verbs have been printed in their infinitive form.

(i) The narrator of a novel is describing a woman he is obsessed with.

When she was home from her boarding-school I *see (1)* her almost every day sometimes, because their house *be (2)* right opposite the Town hall Annexe. She and her younger sister *go (3)* in and out quite a lot, often with young men, which of course I didn't like. When I *have (4)* a free moment from the files and ledgers I *stand (5)* by the window and *look (6)* down over the road over the frosting and sometimes I *see (7)* her.

(ii) A character in a novel thinks about her father, who has recently died.

On impulse she went to the hall cupboard for her warm winter coat then, putting out the light, opened the window and stepped outside on to the balcony . . . This was how her father had stood night after night before going to bed. She *be (8)* busy in the kitchen after dinner and *come (9)* into the sitting room to find it in darkness except for the one low lamp, and *see (10)* the dark shadow of that one silent motionless figure standing there looking out over the river.

a Try to work out what verb form would have been used in the original.

b Give reasons for this or explain what alternatives would be possible. How might these alter the meaning expressed or the effect created?

17 Reported and direct speech

Helen said she might see you today.
"It's possible I'll see Mary tomorrow"

17.1 Key considerations

Direct speech is what people actually say, e.g. *I'm tired.* Reported speech (also called indirect speech) is how we later report this, making changes to the words the speaker originally used, e.g. *She said (that) she was tired.*

In order to make these changes appropriately, learners need to consider the context in which they are reporting (e.g. who they are speaking to, whether this person knows the person who said the original and whether what was said is still true). They also need to know a number of reporting verbs such as *say, tell, explain* and *suggest*, and they must be able to construct the clauses that follow these verbs. In order to find the 'correct' answer in certain kinds of test and examinations, learners also sometimes need to know a number of formulaic 'rules'.

We use the term 'reported speech' to include reports of what was written as well as spoken.

17.2 Reported speech

What is reported speech?

Traditional practice exercises and tests ask learners to change sentences like those in the left-hand column into ones like those in the right-hand column (and sometimes even vice-versa):

Direct speech	Reported speech
She said, "We live in London".	She said (that) they lived in London.
She said, "John phoned me last night".	She said (that) John had phoned her the night before.

Often no context is provided in such exercises and tests, and little guidance is given for choosing between 'direct' and 'reported' speech. In fact, the two are rarely interchangeable – in reality we almost never use reported speech to convey exactly what someone has said. If we are interested in what was said exactly, we generally use direct speech.

Direct speech

Direct speech conveys exactly what someone has said, often

- to dramatise.
- to create a sense of immediacy.
- because the precise words used were in some way important (for example funny or strange).

It is found in newspaper reports, fiction, and oral narratives.

> *"I feel angry and empty in my stomach and I cannot get on the wavelength of someone who comes and does something like this,"* he said. *"We are working with the police and will give them any help we can to apprehend whoever was involved in this."*

Reported speech

We use reported speech when we are interested not in the words that someone has chosen, but in the essential information they conveyed. We often use far fewer words to report this than were originally spoken.

Reported speech is found in newspaper reports, fiction, talking or writing about conversation, reports, articles or speeches we have heard or read.

> . . . managing director Michael Chambers said *services were bound to be affected.*

> At the end of her first week Mrs Crealey had asked *if she was happy* and Mandy had replied *that there were worse jobs* . . .

Choosing reporting verbs

Neutral verbs: *Say* and *tell*

The most neutral and most common verbs we use to introduce what we are reporting are *say* and *tell*, and choosing between these verbs often poses a problem to learners. *Say* is never followed by an indirect object (e.g. *him, us, them, my sister*), whereas we have to use an indirect object after *tell.*

We choose *say* when the person who was spoken to is unimportant or already known. We choose *tell* when we wish to draw attention specifically to the person who is being addressed.

   He said (that) he was ill.   *He told me (that) he was ill.*

We follow *say* with a *that* clause (e.g. (*that*) *he was ill*) whereas we can follow *tell* + indirect object with a variety of clause types and with a noun phrase.

	Clause type
He told me (**that**) **he was ill**.	*that*
He told me **where he was.**	question word
He told me **to go.**	infinitive
He told me **where to go.**	question word + infinitive
He told me **a lie.**	noun phrase

We often introduce a report with *tell* to make clear who was spoken to. We don't subsequently need to repeat this, and so we continue using *say*.

Topic verbs

We use topic or 'summarising' reporting verbs such as *discuss* or *talk about* to report the topic rather than the detail of conversation or text. We follow these verbs with a noun phrase, a question-word clause or a question-word infinitive clause, not a *that* clause.

We talked about	*the news.*	(noun phrase)
	when the project had started.	(question-word clause)
	when to arrive.	(question-word infinitive clause)

NOT * *We discussed/talked about that she was ill.*

Non-attitude verbs

These verbs comment on the function of what is said, but don't involve a judgement about the attitude behind it:

   add   answer   ask   explain   reply   mention

We generally only choose these verbs (in preference, for example, to *say*) when the additional information they provide is important. For example, we are unlikely to choose the verb *answer* if the context makes it clear that something is the answer to a question.

Attitude and interpretation verbs

When we report what someone has said, we often make some kind of interpretation or judgement about this, and we choose our reporting verbs accordingly. For example, we can:

- cast doubt on the truth of what someone said.
  *She **claimed** she'd been asleep when it took place.*
- say something about the speaker's attitude.
  *Are you **complaining** that I don't pay enough attention?*
- say something about the speaker's intention.
  *They **warned** us this might happen.*

These are some of the verbs we use in this way:

> *accuse allege beg blame claim complain confirm demand deny*
>
> *insinuate insist recommend suggest threaten warn*

We often choose one of these verbs to establish our attitude and then, although this attitude is still relevant, we use more neutral verbs.

Other verbs and expressions

We sometimes also report what people have said by using verbs and expressions that are not primarily used for reporting.

> *The caretaker **wanted to know** what time we're leaving.*
>
> *Yesterday they **thought** it was a good idea.*

Clauses that can follow reporting verbs

Learners need to know whether an indirect object is required, is optional or is impossible after the verb, and what kinds of clause can (and cannot) follow the reporting verbs they choose. Good dictionaries such as the *Cambridge International Dictionary of English* provide this information. Learning (and practising) these is often as important as learning the meanings of the verbs.

The choices include:

- *that* noun clause: I insisted *that we couldn't go.*
- question-word noun clause: They explained *where to put it.*
- infinitive clause: They claimed *to believe it.*

- question-word infinitive clause: I asked (him) *what to buy her.*
- *-ing* clause: Didn't I suggest *tying back the roses?*
- preposition + *-ing* clause: Are you accusing me *of lying?*
- (*that*) + subject + bare infinitive:I recommended *she call back later.*

Choosing tense forms

Tests and examinations sometimes require learners to 'convert' direct speech to reported speech, mechanically changing the tense of any verbs which follow a past tense 'reporting verb' according to a set of formulaic 'back shift' rules (see pp. 221–222).

In fact, in any narrative we usually establish a particular time in the past – a key, 'anchoring' time reference when something crucial happened (see also p. 185). We then use other tenses such as past perfect, past continuous and past perfect continuous to clarify when other events happened in relation to this. In reported speech, this 'anchoring time' is the time of reporting (i.e. as expressed by the reporting verb). Looked at like this, there is nothing particularly 'special' about the tenses in reported speech. For many learners it makes more sense to think of tenses in this way than according to a set of rules for converting the tenses that were actually used at the time into 'reported' forms. We can, for example, explain the choice of tenses in the following without referring to 'reported speech':

> She *said (1)* that her daughter *was working (2)* somewhere in the garden and *couldn't (3)* come to the telephone. She also said that she *had given (4)* her daughter my three previous messages.

1 Past simple: the key point in the past in relation to which the time of other events is defined.
2 Past continuous: a temporary event which began before *1* and was still taking place at the time of *1.*
3 Past form of modal verb: the time is the same as *1.*
4 Past perfect: events which had taken place before *1.*

Choosing between present and past

Mechanical conversion exercises and tests often require learners to change the tense of verbs that come after the reporting verb. We may often choose to make these changes, but in fact when we want to make clear that circumstances have not changed since the original statement or question, we use a present rather than a past tense.

> *"I am tired"* ⇒ *He told me that he **is** tired.*

Choosing between past simple and past perfect

Sometimes, a sequence of events may be so clear in the context that we don't need to make this additionally clear in the tenses we choose. For example, the following is from a report of the victim of a mugging describing how he was attacked. The past simple tense is used both for the reporting verb *said* and for the much earlier events *was hit* and *were tied* (*had been hit . . .* and *had been tied . . .* are possible but unnecessary alternatives):

```
He said he was hit over the head with a hefty object and
struck fairly smartly between the legs, while his hands
were tied behind his back with telephone wire.
```

'Transformation rules'

So what of the 'rules' for converting direct to indirect speech? Some learners find these a muddling addition to the basis on which they normally choose appropriate tense forms, but others may find them helpful, either on their own or in addition to focusing on using tenses to make clear the order in which things happened. If the materials they use (including tests they take) require them mechanically to 'convert' sentences out of context, then they will probably have to know and rely on the following 'rules' for converting direct to indirect speech:

Characteristic changes in tense forms:		
Present changes to past:	*I don't eat meat.*	⇒ *She said she **didn't** eat meat.*
Auxiliary verbs in the present also change to the past:	*I'm afraid they're working and don't want to stop.*	⇒ *She said they **were** working and **didn't** want to stop.*
	I've never travelled outside the US.*	⇒ *She said she **had** never travelled outside the US.*
	* This rule is sometimes also expressed as present perfect changes to past perfect.	
Past simple changes to past perfect:	*I saw her.*	⇒ *He said he **had seen** her.*

Auxiliary verbs in the past also change to the past perfect:	*I was looking for Julie.*	⇒ *He said he **had been** looking for his sister.*
The following modal verbs often change: *can, may, must*:	*I can see them.* *We may go there later.* *I must leave.*	⇒ *She said she **could** see them.* ⇒ *She said they **might** go there later.* ⇒ *She said she **had to** leave.*
The auxiliary verbs in future forms change from present to past:	*I'll see you.* *I'm going to be back tomorrow.*	⇒ *He said he **would** see me.* ⇒ *He said she **was** going to be back the next day.*

Forms that don't need to change:		
Verbs already in the past perfect:	*We'd finished our work.*	⇒ *He said they **had finished** their work.*
The following modal verbs: *could, might, ought, should, would*:	*You should eat more.* ⇒ *I couldn't eat anything.* ⇒	*She said I **should** eat more.* *She said she **couldn't** eat anything.*

Choosing expressions of time and place, names, pronouns and possessive adjectives

The changes that take place to expressions of time and place (e.g. *now, here*), names, pronouns (e.g. *I, we, you*) and possessive adjectives (e.g. *my, our, your*) depend on when and where the reporting is taking place, and how the people involved in the reporting were or weren't involved in the original conversation. In reality a word like 'here' or 'she' may be interpreted in an infinite number of ways in reporting.

Direct speech

"One day you'll understand why we worry about you now".

Report A:

*My parents always told **me** that one day **I** would understand why **they** worried about **me** in **those** days.*

Report B:

*Mary's Mum told **her** the other day that **she** would understand one day why **they** worry about **her** at the moment.*

The following are only broad generalisations, more useful in mechanical 'conversion exercises' than in realistic communication:

Some common changes in expressions of time and place:

here	⇒	*there*	*now*	⇒	*then*
this	⇒	*that*	*today*	⇒	*that day*
these	⇒	*those*	*yesterday*	⇒	*the day before*
come	⇒	*go*	*tomorrow*	⇒	*the next day*
bring	⇒	*take*	*this week*	⇒	*that week*
			this month	⇒	*that month*

Some common changes in names, pronouns and possessive adjectives:

I	⇒	*he or she*
me	⇒	*him or her*
my	⇒	*his or her*
we	⇒	*they*

We also often use names instead of pronouns when we report.

I can't stand her ⇒ *She said she couldn't stand **Pat**.*

Word order

When we report questions, the word order is generally the same as that of statements (*I could . . .*, *I had . . .*, rather than *could I . . .* or *did I have . . .*).

"*Do you have the time, please?*" ⇒ *Someone asked me if **I had the time**.*

"*Where are we going at the weekend?*" ⇒ *I asked you where **we are going** at the weekend.*

17.3 Direct speech

What is direct speech?

When we report what someone has said, retaining the original pronouns and verb forms, we call this 'direct speech'.

He asked me, "What are you doing?" and I said, "Nothing".

When do we use direct speech?

Written language

Fiction

Dialogue is the flesh and blood of most fiction. It is used to dramatise interaction between the characters, and usually plays a key role in developing and establishing their personalities, their relationships and in moving the plot forward.

> 'Are you going to forgive me, Helen?' he resumed, more humbly.
>
> 'Are you penitent?' I replied, stepping up to him and smiling in his face.
>
> 'Heart-broken!' he answered, with a rueful countenance . . .
>
> 'Then you won't go to London, Arthur?' I said, when the first transport of tears and kisses had subsided.
>
> 'No, love, – unless you will go with me.'

Reported speech is rare in fiction, and when it occurs it usually introduces stretches of dialogue (direct speech) or helps to link together more vivid episodes.

News

Newspaper reports typically use both reported and direct speech, often alternating between them. The following is part of a newspaper report recounting how a man was attacked by strangers as he arrived home. Reported speech (*He said he was hit . . .*) is used to establish the bare facts, and snatches of direct speech are used to add the colourful details:

> He told the court: "I was punched across my nose and my head. It was known that I had a safe. I took them to it."
>
> He said he was hit over the head with a "hefty object" and struck "fairly smartly" between the legs, while his hands were tied behind his back with telephone wire.
>
> He added: "I was dragged inside and my head was put in a large copper urn."

Conversation

In very informal conversation we also use a lot of direct speech. We sometimes describe long conversations in this way, almost to the point of re-enacting them.

> *I said, 'Where are you going?', and he said, 'Why don't you come with me?',*
> *and I said, 'Because I still don't know where you're going', and he said,*
> *'Oh, come on babe'.*

As in this example, we generally use (and keep repeating) the same reporting verb: *said*. Learners may also come across common, very informal equivalents to *said* (which we would very rarely need to teach). These include:

- *says*:
  I says, 'Don't you ask me no questions about it, please. You'll take it –
  won't you?'
  He says: 'Well I'm puzzled. Is something the matter?'

- *goes* (also *go*; *went*):
  Fraser goes, 'Why don't we stay up and watch the film?' and his Mum
  goes, 'You've got to get up early tomorrow', so we all goes, 'O.K.'.

- *am* (*is, was, were*) *like*:
  I'm like, 'What's the matter?', and he's like 'Mind your own business'.

See pages 413–414 for rules for punctuating direct speech.

17.4 Typical difficulties for learners

Comprehension

Learners are sometimes confused by the tense and pronoun changes that can occur in reported speech, particularly if their first language doesn't involve making similar or parallel changes. For example, they may understand *Mary said she was ill* to mean that she was ill prior to saying this, and they may understand *Mary said I was wrong* to mean that Mary was talking about herself.

Speaking and writing

Many mistakes in using reported speech may be caused by learners who have practised reported speech through unnaturally literal transformation exercises. Mistakes tend to occur when learners are thinking about the forms of the language rather than focusing on what they want to convey.

Reporting verbs: clauses that follow

Learners need not only to understand the meaning of the verbs they use, but they also need to know the construction of the clause which follows each verb.

> * *She said me she had to go.*   * *She explained me how to do it.*
> * *She suggested me to go.*   * *She told she was ill.*

Learners often consider this to be the biggest problem with reported speech.

Reporting verbs: different kinds of verb

Learners need to know which verbs we use for reporting the content of what someone has said, and which ones we generally use to refer to what they said.

> (*) *He asked her where she came from and she answered that she came from Greece.*

Here the learner's use of *answered* is unidiomatic. Generally the function of answering is already clear from the context, and so *answered* provides unnecessary information. We are more likely to say *she said that she came from Greece* and to use *answer* in contexts like *I asked her if she was happy but she didn't answer.*

Reporting verbs: over-use

Learners sometimes repeat verbs (particularly *said*) when either no verb is necessary, or when other verbs would be appropriate to summarise and interpret what was said. This happens when learners are asked to convert stretches of conversation into prose.

> (*) *She **asked** Robert if he wanted something alcoholic to drink and he **said** that he didn't. He **said** that he would prefer a cup of coffee and she **said** that would be fine. He **said** thank you.*

Tense and expressions of time

Learners sometimes think of and repeat what was originally said when this is no longer true at the time of reporting.

> * *She said she**'ll** come tomorrow so I waited in all day.*
> * *She said she was busy **now** but I'm surprised she didn't come later.*

Word order

In many languages there is no difference between the order of words in statements and in questions. Learners who have worked hard to remember and use correct word order in English questions may over-use this, in particular when they report them.

(*) *She asked him did he like the music.*

(*) *They wanted to know were there any more people to come.*

(*) *He wondered why were they so late.*

Native speakers sometimes speak (and even write) like this, but learners may be penalised for this in examinations.

17.5 Consolidation exercises
(see pp. 471–473 for possible answers)

Language in context

1 (see p. 471)

Read the transcriptions on the left of two people speaking. The first person is talking on the radio about what he likes about life in the West Indies. The second is explaining on TV how we need to look after young plants. Next to each is a transcription of someone telling another person about a section of the programme they missed.

Original account	*Reported account*
The thing I like about living in the West Indies is that at 8.00 in the evening one can sit on somebody's veranda with a large scotch and soda, and one can sit with short-sleeved shirt, and not worry about the fact that it might get cold a little later. That really is the essence of the beauty of living in the Caribbean. So I shan't miss suits. I find them rather tedious.	"He was saying that the one thing that he liked about being in the Caribbean was that he could sit in a short-sleeved shirt late in the evening and not worry about being cold."
It's a bit like having a baby. When it's small, you've got to really look after it, you've got to keep it warm and protected. But then as it grows bigger, it's able to throw off the odd cold or flu and grow into a healthy adult. And we do the same with our plants. We have to protect them	"He said when they are very young they have to be treated like babies, and take great care of them. You know, babies have to be treated very carefully when they are very young. I know he said like babies easily get the flu.

while they're young, keep them warm and sheltered so they can grow on into really good plants.

And then you can put the plants out more easily when they get a bit older."

a In general terms, what information does each 'reporter' focus on/ summarise/leave out?

b Are the reporters concerned more with interpreting what was said or with reporting factually?

c Do the reporters change the tenses that were used in the original?

2 (see p. 472)

The following is from an interview with the writer, Quentin Crisp, in which he explains how he came to publish his first book. He uses both reported and direct speech in this extract.

I first met Mr Carroll on the telephone. I had spoken words on the radio about my life, on the Third Programme, for Philip O'Connor. A publisher, Mr Kimber, telephoned me and said I should write a book.

He said that if I wrote a 2,000 word synopsis of my life story he would let me know whether he would give me a contract.

When he read my 2,000 words he fainted dead away and said he could never publish such a book, it was too scandalous. I was describing all this to the art masters at Maidstone College, and a man called Citizen Kaine, Bob Kaine, said, "I have my spies and I will put them out." And he came back with the name Donald Carroll. He said that if I gave him the 2,000 words that had frightened Mr Kimber and a transcript of what I had said on the radio, and photographs of myself, he would undertake to sell the book. I telephoned Mr Carroll and he said, "You'd better come and see me." So I crossed the river from Chelsea to Putney.

a Identify the reported speech.

b Identify the direct speech.

c Why do you think the speaker chooses direct speech at specific points in the account?

3 (see p. 472)

The two extracts below both contain a lot of reporting of conversation. Both use 'common' reporting verbs (e.g. *said*) as well as verbs which we don't necessarily think of primarily as reporting verbs.

(i) This is from a book about teaching. The author describes a conversation he had with a successful teacher.

> I asked why the students seemed so willing to communicate and take part in informal discussion (he had also said that they were used to writing in class and working in groups) when other lecturers said that local students would never 'accept' this. He seemed surprised at the question. He didn't think his students were very different from those in other faculties or universities.

(ii) This is from an account of a visit by the then Soviet leader to the Vatican.

> After their private session, Mr Gorbachev introduced his wife Raisa and members of his suite including the Foreign minister Mr Eduard Shevardnadze to the pontiff. And, as expected, he announced that he had invited the Pope to visit the Soviet Union. John Paul was guarded in his reply. He thanked the Soviet leader for the invitation, but said his visit would have to depend upon developments inside the Soviet Union.

a Make a list of the reporting verbs used in each (e.g. the first is *asked*).

b Comment on the degree to which the two reports appear to summarise and/or interpret the original conversation.

4 (see p. 473)

The exercises that follow were designed by different teachers to help late intermediate learners with reported speech. Read them and answer the questions.

(i) Put the following sentences into reported speech. Begin each *He asked . . .* or *He said . . .*
1. Where do you live?
2. The train usually leaves from here.
3. I suggest you watch the information board.
4. We'll come round tomorrow.

(ii) Think of a particularly memorable or vivid conversation you have seen in a TV show, soap opera or film, or that you have heard on the radio. Summarise in English what they said in c100–130 words.

(iii) Read the following request and the two ways it is reported. Tina, the boss, spoke to Irving's secretary:

"Can you please tell Irving that I want him to bring me the report as soon as he gets back?"

(i) The boss wants you to take the report to her right away.

(ii) The boss asked me to tell you she wanted you to take her the report as soon as you got back.
   a) What is the difference between the two ways of reporting?
   b) Which is more natural?

a What is the aim of each exercise?

b How useful do you think each of them is?

18 Conditional sentences

Will he come if I shout?
Would you have enough time?
I'd have been upset if I hadn't known.
She purrs if you stroke her.

18.1 Key considerations

Course materials generally present four basic types of conditional sentence. In this chapter we look at each of these types, but within each type we explore a range of possible forms, some of which may be neglected or ignored in popular materials. Finally, we look at some general variants on conditional forms.

Some European languages have special conditional tenses – forms of the verb that are used primarily or only in conditional sentences. This is not true in English, and some people argue that it is misleading to think of conditional structures as being special.

Some learners find it difficult to remember the grammar of long conditional sentences with two clauses. We can help them by teaching and practising one clause at a time, and can provide a lot of opportunities and help for students to 'get their tongues round' the complete sentences.

18.2 What are conditional sentences?

Course materials usually teach that conditional sentences consist of two clauses – a main ('conditional') clause containing a verb in a form with *will* or *would*, and a subordinate clause that is introduced by *if*.

> I'll help you **if you want**; He'd come **if you called**.

What we express in the main clause, depends – or is conditional – on what we express in the subordinate (*if*) clause.

> I'll turn on the heating if it gets colder.

We can usually change the order of clauses in conditional sentences, e.g. we can say *I'll turn on the heating if it gets colder* or *If it gets colder, I'll turn on the heating.*

How we punctuate conditional sentences depends partly on their length and partly on personal preference, but in general we separate the two clauses by a comma if we begin with the *if* clause. We don't use a comma when we begin with the conditional clause.

In casual conversation *if* is often barely pronounced. The vowel disappears entirely, and even /f/ is whispered. A phrase like *If I were you* is pronounced: /faɪwəjuː/.

18.3 Basic forms and closely related variants

Type 1

'Basic' form and meaning

Type 1 conditional sentences are sometimes called the first or future conditional. Both clauses refer to the future, although the verb in the *if* clause is in a present tense. Coursebooks usually teach this at an elementary or intermediate level:

If clause	conditional clause
If + present tense	future tense
If it gets colder tonight,	I'll turn on the heating.

conditional clause	*If* clause
future tense	*if* + present tense
He'll get here early	if he catches the fast train.

We often teach this conditional to express aspects of persuasion such as cajoling and negotiating and for giving warnings and making threats.

Persuasion: *I'll take the children to the party if you collect them from school.*

Warning: *If you try to take a short cut, you'll get lost.*

Threat: *If you poke your brother again, I'll thrash you.*

Other forms

In this section we look at forms of Type 1 conditional sentences that are different from the 'basic' form.

If + present, imperative

We use an imperative rather than a future form of the verb in the conditional clause, for example to give advice or instructions.

If clause	conditional clause
If + present,	imperative
If you go to the supermarket,	*bring back a carton of milk please.*

Other present tenses

We can also use a range of future forms in the conditional clause (see Chapter 13 for a full description and illustration of the options).

> present continuous: *We're **staying** at home on Wednesday if the transport strike goes ahead.*
>
> going to: *They're **going to** take their mother to the old house if she remembers where it is.*

We can use a range of present forms in the *if* clause depending on the meaning we want to express (see Chapter 12 for a full description and illustration of the options).

> present perfect: *If it **hasn't rained** by the weekend, we'll have to water the garden.*
>
> present continuous: *If they're **watching** TV, they won't hear you.*

Should

We sometimes use *should* before the verb in the *if* clause of Type 1 conditional sentences. Often this weakens the possibility, implying *by any chance . . . .*

> *If you should find yourself at a loose end over the holiday, you'll always be welcome at our house.*

We also sometimes use *should* in place of *if,* usually in more formal, written contexts. For example, the following is part of an internal memo distributed to staff in a chain of stores:

> *Should people complain about the quality of any goods, please refer them directly to the customer services department.*

Type 2

'Basic' form and meaning

Coursebooks tend to teach this form at a lower intermediate level.

Type 2 conditional sentences are sometimes called the 'second', 'hypothetical' or 'unreal' conditional. We use them to refer to or speculate about something that is (or that we perceive to be) impossible or 'contrary to fact'.

They can refer to the present or the future.

Time reference	*If* clause	conditional clause
	If + past tense	*would* + bare infinitive
Present:	*If he didn't annoy me so much,*	*I'd spend more time in his office.*
Future:	*If I got an invitation,*	*I'd go there right away.*

Both Type 1 and 2 conditionals can refer to the future. Sometimes teachers tell students that Type 2 is 'less likely' than Type 1, but this explanation distracts them from the real basis for choosing Type 2.

Type 1: *If it gets colder tonight, I'll turn on the heating.* (a real possibility)

Type 2: *If it got colder tonight, I'd turn on the heating.* (viewed as not a real possibility)

In the *if* clause we often use *were* in place of *was* (some people consider that it is incorrect to use *was* after *if*).

I'd be able to find the information if I were at home.

Course materials often introduce Type 2 conditional sentences beginning *If I were you . . .* idiomatically to express advice, separately from Type 2 conditional sentences as a grammatical class.

If I were you, I'd make an appointment to see the doctor.

Other forms

Should

Some people regularly use *should* instead of *would* after *I* and *we*.

*I **shouldn't** get to sleep at all if I lived next to that noise.*

Should is often used in place of *would* in official or commercial correspondence.

*I **should** be grateful for an early response to my letter.*

Were + infinitive

We sometimes use *were* + infinitive instead of a past tense form in the *if* clause of Type 2 conditional sentences. This makes the event seem more hypothetical or the statement more tentative and, therefore, more polite.

*If the river **were to rise** above the height of the flood barrier, there would be absolutely nothing we could do to save the city.*

*If you **were to have** a few minutes free, I'd really appreciate the opportunity to pick your brains.*

Were + subject

When we use *were* in the *if* clause, we can invert *were* and the subject of the clause, and leave out *if* altogether:

Were he really ill, I might feel more sympathetic.

Were you to accept my offer, I'd personally oversee the arrangement.

If + *would*

In American English, *would* is often used in the *if* clause.

I'd eat something if I wouldn't have indigestion.

Type 3

'Basic' form and meaning

Coursebooks tend to teach the following at an upper intermediate level.

If clause	conditional clause
If + past perfect	*would* + *have* + past participle
If we hadn't wasted time,	we wouldn't have missed the train.

conditional clause	*If* clause
would + *have* + past participle	*if* + past perfect
I would have been more sympathetic	if she hadn't accused me of lying.

We use this conditional to speculate about past events, and about how things that happened or didn't happen might have affected other things (e.g. in the second example she accused me of lying and so I wasn't very sympathetic).

We often teach this conditional to express reproach and regret.

If you hadn't driven so fast, you would never have had the accident.

I wouldn't have left my job if I'd known how difficult it is to find another one.

We sometimes use the Type 3 conditional to make excuses (we can consider this use within the overall category of *regret*).

> *If there hadn't been an accident on the motorway I would have been here in really good time for the meeting.*

Type 3 conditional sentences are sometimes called the 'third' or 'past' conditional.

Other forms

had have + past participle

Many native speakers of English use a non-standard variant of the Type 3 conditional. Although it would be inappropriate for learners to learn this, they will often come across it:

If clause	conditional clause
If + *had have* + past participle	*would* + *have* + past participle
If they'd have arrived on time,	*I'd have let them into the examination.*

Had + subject + past participle

We can use *Had* + subject + past participle in Type 3 conditionals in place of *if* + subject + past perfect.

> *Had I known he was ill, I would never have shouted at him.*

Zero conditional sentences

The form of this conditional is:

If clause	conditional clause
If + present tense	present tense
If you want to change money on a Sunday,	*you have to go to one of the big railway stations.*

conditional clause	*If* clause
present tense	*if* + present tense
Most cats purr	*if you tickle them under the chin.*

We use this conditional to express general truths. Learners usually find this use of tenses logical and straightforward. As long as they know the meaning of the word *if*, they will often automatically produce zero conditional sentences accurately and appropriately.

18.4 General variants on conditional sentences

Conjunctions

Conjunctions other than *if*

We can use a range of conjunctions in conditional sentences as well as *if*. These include: *supposing, as long as* (Types 1 & 2); *provided, on condition (that), unless* (all types).

> *Where will you go **supposing** you manage to have a holiday?*
>
> *I would help him **as long as** he asked me nicely.*
>
> *I wouldn't have come round **unless** you'd phoned and asked me to.*

Supposing suggests an act of imagination; *provided, as long as*, and *on condition (that)*, suggest reservation – often it is the speaker who is imposing the condition. We also use *only if* to express similar meaning.

Course materials sometimes teach that *unless* is the same as *if . . . not*. In fact we use it to express a stronger degree of reservation: *I won't come round unless you phone* is closer in meaning to *I'll only come round if you phone* than *I won't come round if you don't phone.*

In case suggests the need to be ready for something (*Take an umbrella in case it rains.*) and is not a conditional conjunction. However, learners often use *in case* as a substitute for *if* (* *You'll get wet in case it rains*).

Leaving out conjunctions

Very informally we sometimes leave out any word or words that directly express conditional meaning. However, it is clear from context that conditional meaning is implied. In these cases we usually link the two clauses with *and* or *or*.

> *Eat anymore of that pudding and you'll burst.* (i.e. *If you eat . . .*)
>
> *Keep still, you little devil, or I'll cut your throat.* (i.e. *If you don't keep still . . ./Unless you keep still . . .*)

If only and *I wish*

Statements beginning with *If only* or *I wish* are closely connected with conditional sentences in that we use a past tense to refer to a hypothetical present event and past perfect to refer to a hypothetical event in the past.

If only (I wish) she paid a little more attention.

If only (I wish) I hadn't agreed to take part.

Verbs in a continuous form

The examples of conditional sentences which appear in course materials often include verbs only in a simple form (*if he comes . . .; if they had worked . . . ; would she eat . . .?*).

In fact, we use a continuous form of the verb if we want to suggest 'continuous meanings' (e.g. to emphasise the temporariness of something). We can use continuous verb forms in both the *if* and the main clauses.

*They'd have noticed the explosion if they **hadn't been making** so much noise.*

*We would **be lying** on the beach if we were still in Brighton.*

Modal verbs

Type 1

We can use *may, might* and *could* in the conditional clause of Type 1 conditional sentences to show that something is a possible consequence (rather than a certain one).

*I **can** bring something to eat if you want.*

*If you listen to me carefully, you **may** learn something useful.*

Types 2 and 3

We can also use *might* and *could* in place of *would* in Type 2 and 3 conditional sentences.

*If you explained a bit more clearly I **might** understand.*

*If we hadn't worked so hard we **could** have missed our deadline.*

Zero conditionals

We can use modal verbs in either or both clauses of a zero conditional.

*If you have a ticket you **can** go through now.*

*You **should** wear glasses if you **can't** see.*

Will *and* would *in* if *clauses*

As a rule we don't use *will* or *would* in the *if* clause of conditional sentences, and we may have to correct mistakes when learners use them inappropriately. It isn't true, however, that *will* and *would* never occur in the *if* clause.

We can use *would (like)* in *if* clauses where the meaning is similar to *want*.

> If you **would** like to sit down, please help yourself to a seat.

We can use *will* in an *if* clause where the meaning is similar to *be prepared to/be willing to*.

> If you**'ll** wait a minute, the doctor will be here to see you.

Will and *would* can suggest perverse and deliberate behaviour (and are then normally stressed). In this case we can use *will* in Type 1 and *would* in Type 2 *if* clauses.

> If you **will** argue with everyone you can't expect to be popular.
> If you **wouldn't** take so much time off, you might earn more.

Single clauses

Teaching materials sometimes give the impression that all conditional sentences have two clauses.

In fact we very frequently use only one clause. Sometimes we use the *if* clause. This is usually when the conditional clause is already understood – for example, in replying to questions.

> A: Are you going on holiday this year?   B: If I win the pools.

More often we use just the conditional clause. In this case, a condition is usually implied.

> I would have appreciated some help. (i.e. if it had been available)

Sometimes the condition is expressed in some other way.

> Do you think the punch would taste better with more fruit juice? (i.e. if it contained more fruit juice)

Mixed conditional sentences

Things we did in the past may have present consequences, and equally these past events may be the result of timeless or present facts. We often refer both to the present and the past in conditional sentences, and we choose the tense of the main verb in each clause accordingly – one clause may be conditional Type 2 and the other may be conditional Type 3.

Past action: You wasted money last week.

Present consequence: We can't afford a good holiday.

If clause (Type 3)	Main clause (Type 2)
If you hadn't wasted so much money last week,	*we'd be able to afford a better holiday.*

Present (general) fact: I am very busy.

Past consequence: I wasn't able to take off any time last week.

If clause (Type 2)	Main clause (Type 3)
If I weren't so busy,	*I could have taken off a few days last week.*

We also mix Type 1 and Type 2 structures. Some people feel we should avoid this.

> *I would probably forgive Salisbury anything as long as they never mess with the Cathedral close.*

18.5 Should we teach 'conditional sentences'?

At present, most course materials teach four basic *types* of conditional sentence. Many learners find this helpful, especially if their own language has equivalent conditional structures. Other learners may find it simpler to learn the features of conditional sentences in other contexts. For example:

- The grammar of Type 1 conditional sentences is the same as that of non-conditional sentences that include a time conjunction. After these conjunctions (e.g. *when, after, before, as soon as, until* etc.), we also use a present tense even though we are referring to future time (see p. 171). We can teach *if* in the context of these other time conjunctions.

- We can teach *would* and *would have* as a modal verb to express hypothetical meaning, and can teach the use of the past and past perfect tenses to refer to an imagined or unreal present or past in the context of expressions beginning with *if*, or the verb *wish*.

Since some people argue strongly that we should avoid using the term *conditional* and that we should avoid the four basic *types*, we can expect to see course materials that reflect their views.

18.6 Typical difficulties for learners

Comprehension

If learners have studied conditional sentences, when they come across them in reading English they generally don't have problems of understanding, although they may still be misled by sentences which don't include *if* or one of the obvious conditional conjunctions such as *as long as* or *supposing*.

In listening, conditional sentences pose much more of a problem. In many languages conditional meaning is signalled by adverbs in the conditional clause or by an expression added to the end of the conditional clause. There may also be very strict rules about the order of clauses. Learners who speak one of these languages (e.g. Chinese) may have difficulty in recognising conditional sentences, particularly if the order of clauses doesn't match the order in their first language.

Also, we frequently pronounce *if* and auxiliary verbs which establish the time reference of the sentences (e.g. *would*; *would have*) so indistinctly that learners may fail to pick them out.

Learners may also be misled by the use of past tenses to refer to present time, and may understand that phrases like *if I spoke Russian . . .* refer to the past.

We sometimes leave out the *if* clause when we are giving advice. Learners of English are sometimes confused by this use.

> A: *I slept badly again last night.*
> B: *I'd make an appointment to see the doctor.*

Learners sometimes understand (wrongly) that sentences that begin *Were he here . . .* or *Had I known . . .* are questions. They may fail to recognise that sentences like this are conditional.

Learners sometimes confuse *if only* with *only if*.

Speaking and writing

Simplifying the grammar

For many learners, the auxiliary verbs we use in constructing conditional sentences (e.g. *If he had seen anything he would have reported it*) have no rationale; they are just a string of words or syllables.

Under the pressure of communicating, some or all of these auxiliaries may be left out.

> * *If you not tell me the news, I not try to contact anyone.*
> (The learner wanted to say *If you hadn't told me about the news, I wouldn't have tried to contact anyone.*)

People who haven't learned conditional forms and are 'guessing the grammar' sometimes produce similar sentences.

'Regularising' the tense structure

Learners often use future tenses to refer to the future, and past tenses to refer to the past in conditional sentences. The following examples were spoken by advanced learners:

> * *If it'll rain tomorrow we're not going to set up the exhibition outside.*

> * *We'd be a lot happier now if we didn't make such a bad investment last year.*

Native speakers also occasionally produce sentences like this.

Over-using would

Some learners become so concerned not to forget *would* that they may use it inappropriately in the *if* clause as well as in the conditional clause. Some learners (e.g. speakers of German) may also be influenced by their first language.

> * *I could help you if I my arm wouldn't be broken.*

Choosing the wrong conjunction

Learners sometimes use *when* or *in case* instead of *if.* Sometimes they may be influenced by their first language. For example, speakers of German sometimes use *when* when they mean *if*, and speakers of Italian, Portuguese, Romanian and Spanish sometimes use *in case.*

> * *Let's stay at home when it rains.*

> * *Don't worry in case you hear a noise during the night.*

In cases like this, people often don't spot the mistake, and they understand something different from what the speaker intended.

Leaving conjunctions out

Often influenced by the grammar of their first language, some learners rely on context alone to make the conditional relationship between clauses clear. They may also rely on adverbs such as *then.*

* *I like someone. I give them a present I visit them.*
(If I like someone, I give them a present when I . . .)
* *Sorry. I listened to you then I didn't take the wrong road.*
(. . . If I had listened to you I wouldn't have . . .)
* *You come any nearer I'll then scream.*
(If you come any nearer, I'll scream.)

Avoidance

It is very common for learners to find ways of expressing themselves which enable them not to use language they find 'difficult'. Often, the conditional Type 3 is particularly daunting, and learners may consciously or unconsciously avoid it.

(*) *I didn't see him so I didn't run away.*
(If I'd seen him, I'd have run away.)

It is easy for us to miss the fact that even very advanced learners regularly avoid using this conditional. Even if learners don't actually make mistakes, we may need to provide structured opportunities for them to practise the forms of conditional sentences.

18.7 Consolidation exercises
(see pp. 473–477 for possible answers)

Review of form (see p. 473)

Write down an example of each of the four basic conditional types and label the form of the main verb in each clause (e.g. *would* + infinitive). Try to do this from memory, but refer back to pages 232–236 if necessary.

Differences in meaning (see pp. 473–474)

Explain the difference in meaning between the sentences in the following pairs:

(i)   Don't forget to take your umbrella in case it rains.
      Don't forget to take your umbrella if it rains.

(ii) They won't phone unless their train has been cancelled.
      They won't phone if their train has been cancelled.

(iii) I'll help you to move house provided it's at the weekend.
      I'll help you to move house if it's at the weekend.

(iv) She'll come in to work tomorrow if we need her.
      She'd come in to work tomorrow if we needed her.

(v) I'd have finished my assignment if I weren't ill.
I'd have finished my assignment if I hadn't been ill.

Form and function (see p. 474)

Consider the list of functions below. Then answer the questions.

(i) giving advice

(ii) negotiating

(iii) reproaching

(iv) describing scientific processes

(v) threatening

(vi) warning

(vii) making excuses

a Which of the four basic conditional types are we most likely to use to express each of these functions?

b Provide an example in each case.

Language in context (see pp. 475–477)

Each of the following texts contains conditional phrases, although not all of them belong to one of the basic conventional four types.

(i) This is from a newspaper report of a demonstration.

'They stopped it turning into an all-out confrontation', another source said. 'Had it done so, we wouldn't have stood a chance.'

(ii) This is from a review of a TV play.

Were he living at this hour, Dennis Potter would certainly . . . have cautioned writer Richard Monks against directing his own work.

(iii) This is from a discussion about a hospital visit.

If the doctors hadn't have been there the nurse could have seen to you.

(iv) This is from a newspaper article about the use of computers in offices.

> Walk into any large office in Britain and you could probably trip over a computer cable.

(v) This is from a novel in which one man is criticising another for the way he treats his mother.

> 'She never calls me at work,' said Michael.
> 'Well, maybe she would, if you wouldn't be so hard on the old gal.'

(vi) This is from a newspaper article about a vote in the French National assembly.

> The Loi Toubon – named after the Culture minister Jacques Toubon – would have banned foreign terms from the French vocabulary, and offenders would have faced fines for using foreign words . . . The law would have reached into every cranny of French life. Building workers would have been required to clear a path with *un bouteur* instead of *un bulldozer*, businessmen would study *mercatique* instead of *le marketing*, and *gomme à macher* would have replaced *le chewing gum*.

(vii) Here the speaker has just returned from a football match.

I'd have stayed longer except that it began to drizzle . . .

(viii) Pope John Paul II's words to President Gorbachev in 1989 are being reported.

> If fundamental ethical values are forgotten, fearful consequences can result and even the greatest of enterprises can end in failure.

(ix) Someone is speaking about some people investigating corruption in his office.

If they're going to be coming down here, they'll be coming through our office first.

(x) This extract from a management handbook looks at what is meant by 'role relations'.

> . . . if any form of social relation, however transitory or spontaneous, came to be regarded as a role relation, the concept will become so general and all-embracing as to lose its value as a tool of social analysis.

(xi) This extract from the same handbook looks at the individual.

> Unless he is subordinating himself to the group in some way the individual is seen as rather a nuisance.

a Identify the conditional phrases.

b Classify these phrases using the four 'types', or explain in what way they don't fit into these four types.

c Explain why the particular forms have been chosen in these contexts.

PART C

Sentence constituents and word order

Introduction to Part C

Whereas the chapters in Parts A and B of this book deal with grammar at the level of the word or short phrases, those in Part C of this book look at longer stretches of language, and are concerned with the function that different words or groups of words can perform in sentences.

In Chapters 19–21 we look at the organisation of different key elements in sentences.

Chapter 19 'Basic principles and patterns' concentrates on the basic sentence, showing how we make up and order the key elements of noun phrase, verb phrase and adverbials. Central to this are the concepts of subject and object. For example:

Subject (noun phrase)	Verb phrase	Object (noun phrase)	Adverbial
Somebody	*broke*	*the window*	*last night.*

Chapter 20 'Major variants' looks in more detail at ways we can vary this basic order. For example:

Adverbial (fronted)	Subject (noun phrase)	Verb phrase	Object (noun phrase)
Last night	*somebody*	*broke*	*the window.*

Chapter 21 'Passive constructions' focuses on a specific case where we change the basic order: passive constructions. For example:

Subject	Verb phrase	Adverbial
The window	*was broken*	*(by someone) last night.*

Chapter 22 'Discourse markers' looks at some of the words and expressions we use to:

- show the logical links between different sentences and parts of sentences.
- 'manage' our participation in conversation.
- influence how our listeners or readers react.
- express our attitude to what we are saying or writing.

For example:

Logical links: *alternatively, firstly, on the other hand*

Expressing attitude: *obviously, unfortunately*

Chapter 23 'Ellipsis and substitution' looks at how we leave out parts of sentences, and sometimes replace them with words or expressions which stand in place of them. In the examples that follow, square brackets show the information that is left out and the word in capital letters stands in for something else:

[ ] *Got a cold?* [Have you]

Mary answered the mail and her secretary [ ] *the faxes.* [answered]

I've got some stamps. Do you want ONE? (i.e. a stamp)

19 Basic principles and patterns

noun phrase   verb phrase
conjunction   subject
direct object   indirect object
complement
adverbial
'dummy' subject

19.1 Key considerations

In this chapter we look at sentence constituents, the basic units such as noun phrases, verb phrases and preposition phrases that make up meaningful language. We look at the kinds of words we choose and combine in order to form these basic constituents, and the order in which we use them. We also look at the different functions these basic constituents play in sentences (for example, subject, object, complement and adverbial).

The terms that grammars use for classifying sentence constituents vary from grammar to grammar, and the descriptions are often very complicated and technical. For fear of confusing learners, teachers may choose to avoid giving technical explanations and analysis, and we may teach these features more in response to specific problems that arise than according to any pre-determined syllabus. Although we don't need to remember the technical terms for describing basic constituents, we need to know and understand how these constituents are formed and how they fit together.

When we look at real language we find that many sentences contain forms other than those we look at in this chapter. Chapters 20 and 21 deal with a number of ways in which we modify the basic principles and patterns, and Chapters 24–29 look at different kinds of subordinate clauses, which often involve some further variation on these.

19.2 What are sentence constituents?

At the simplest level, a sentence constituent is any word or group of words which can be replaced by another word or group of words. This may change the meaning, but the sentence still makes sense.

Constituents		
a	**b**	**c**
Henry	*eats*	*snails.*
No one	*wants to eat*	*snails with garlic and butter.*

We have to consider sentence constituents from two perspectives:

- what they are in terms of the words that make them up.
- the function they perform in sentences.

Some constituents that have the same form can appear in different parts of the sentence with different functions.

Constituents		
a	**b**	**c**
People	*need*	*people.*

Sentences, clauses and constituents

In the written language we recognise sentences because they begin with a capital letter and have a full stop at the end.

However, in speaking it often isn't clear when one sentence starts and another finishes, and even in writing we can often choose whether to leave a long stretch of language as one sentence or to divide it into two or more shorter sentences.

Unlike sentences, clauses can clearly and unambiguously be identified in both speech and writing. Rather than attempting a definition of what a clause is now, we provide examples of different kinds of clause in the rest of this section, and on pages 262–263 we use the terminology that is introduced here to define what a clause is.

Clause a		**Clause b**
I'll see you on Friday	*but*	*all of us will be keeping our fingers crossed.*

We can divide clauses further into constituents (i.e. clause constituents), each of which may consist of one or several words. In the sentence above *but* is also a constituent, but it does not form part of a clause (see *Sentence constituents which don't form part of clauses* below).

In this chapter, we are concerned with only one kind of clause – *main* clauses, which we refer to here simply as 'clauses'.

In section 19.4 we look at different kinds of constituent, how we can form them and what kinds of role they can take in clauses.

Sentence constituents which don't form part of clauses

When we divide sentences into clauses, we find that there are additional constituents that don't form part of the clauses. These may:

• link the clauses together (conjunctions such as *and* or *but*).

• comment on the information in the clauses in some way, or show how they relate to other clauses and sentences (discourse markers such as *of course, firstly* or *however* – see Chapter 22).

19.3 How do we organise information? – basic principles

It would be very difficult to understand stretches of language in which everything was new and important. When we speak and write, we try to judge how much our audience already knows, and we take care to provide a balance between what is new and important, and what is familiar or can be taken for granted.

In understanding, we depend on this familiar information to help us to orientate ourselves to what is new and important and to put this in context. We also depend on the speaker or writer clearly signalling what is and isn't new and important. The order in which we present information in clauses is a crucial factor in how we do this.

The basic ordering principle we use is to put the familiar information at the beginning of the clause, so that our readers or listeners have time to prepare for and orientate themselves towards what follows. This first part of the clause generally tells us 'what the clause is about', and what comes after this is usually the main point, the new or important information. In general, the further this is towards the end of the clause, the more attention we pay to it.

To illustrate this, we can look at some of the clauses in the previous paragraph and divide them into these two parts:

Familiar information to orientate	New and important information
The basic ordering principle we use	*is to put the familiar information at the beginning of the clause*
This first part of the clause	*generally tells us 'what the clause is about'*

Although we can begin clauses with different kinds of constituent, in the 'basic pattern' we consider in this chapter, the first 'orientating' part of a clause is generally the subject. This 'basic pattern' allows different kinds of constituent to come at or towards the end of a clause.

19.4 Types of sentence constituent

Form and function

Depending on whether we are looking at constituents from the perspective of what they are or what they do, we choose different terms, even though they may describe the same thing. For example, a noun phrase may be a subject, object, complement or adverbial depending on its function (and position) in a clause.

Form

Noun phrases

Noun phrases can consist of one word such as a name, pronoun or noun.

One-word noun phrases	
name:	*Angela, Bolivia*
pronoun:	*she, us, that*
noun:	*people, illness, trees*

Complex noun phrases are groups of words connected to and including a main noun (the headword) which here is underlined, e.g. *an <u>illness</u>; an old, rather bent <u>woman</u>*

We often find the following elements in noun phrases (usually in this order):

noun phrase		
Determiner	modifier	noun (headword)
This	*old*	*kettle*

Determiners include articles, quantifiers, numbers, possessive adjectives (e.g. *my, your, their*) and demonstrative adjectives (*this, that, these, those*).

Modifiers may be:

   adjectives, e.g. *old* kettle
   nouns, e.g. *brick* houses
   possessive forms, e.g. *child's* toy
   adverb-adjective combinations, e.g. *carefully painted* screen

Complex noun phrases can include subordinate clauses.

noun phrase	
	subordinate clause
The woman	***I told you about last Thursday.***

They often also include preposition phrases (see p. 255).

noun phrase	
	preposition phrase
The trouble	***with young people***

Verb phrases

Verb phrases can consist of:

	Example
a single-word main verb	*. . . wept.*
a multiword main verb	*. . . stood up.*
one or more auxiliary verbs and a main verb	*. . . has been weeping.* *. . . ought to stand up.*
two main verbs	*. . . want to speak.* *. . . recommend staying.*

Verb phrases may include *not* or *. . .n't,* e.g. *. . . doesn't drink.*

In some grammars the term 'verb phrase' is used in a wider sense to include also any object that follows the verb.

Preposition phrases

Preposition phrases are groups of words that begin with a preposition and contain a noun phrase.

Preposition phrase	
	Noun phrase
on *with*	*the corner* *many additional features*

Preposition phrases may also form part of larger noun phrases.

Noun phrase	
	Preposition phrase
the house *new software*	*on the corner* *with many additional features*

Adjective phrases

Adjective phrases contain an adjective, which may follow one or more adverbs.

   not very old   really quite glamorous

Adverb phrases

Adverb phrases contain an adverb, which may follow one or more other adverbs.

   rather unwisely   only once

Function

Subjects

Subjects usually come immediately before the verb phrase in a clause, and they frequently consist of a noun phrase. They often tell us what the predicate (i.e. everything in the clause that comes after the subject) is about.

subject	predicate
You	*sighed.*
The woman I told you about last Thursday	*has arrived at last.*

Other kinds of subject include infinitive and -*ing* forms of verbs, and certain kinds of clause.

	subject	predicate
infinitive:	*To lose*	*hurts.*
-*ing* form:	*Drinking*	*can kill.*
non-finite clauses:	*How to make money*	*always sells.*
noun clauses:	*Whether or not I made a promise*	*is irrelevant.*

Direct objects and object verbs

Direct objects

Direct objects usually come after the verb phrase and they are normally noun phrases.

Subject	Verb phrase	Direct object
I	*telephoned*	*her.*
I	*telephoned*	*the woman I told you about last Thursday.*

Teaching materials don't usually refer to infinitives, -*ing* forms and noun clauses that follow the verb phrase as direct objects, and in this book we deal with them in other chapters. However, in some academic grammars they are classed as kinds of direct object:

Examples			
Subject	verb phrase		
She	*wanted*	*to leave.*	(See Chapter 11)
She	*likes*	*dancing.*	(See Chapter 11)
Do you	*know*	*whether he's coming?*	(See Chapter 25)

Object verbs

We use direct objects only after certain types of verbs, known as 'object verbs'. Object verbs make a certain amount of sense on their own but we feel that there is 'something missing' if they aren't followed by a direct object – they are obviously incomplete without this additional information.

She made (?).　　*Don't kill (?).*　　*Turner influenced (?).*

Subject	Object verb	Direct object
She	*made*	*a mistake*
Don't	*kill*	*me.*
Turner	*influenced*	*a whole generation of painters.*

Object verbs can have a wide spectrum of meanings. In the examples above the subjects are doing something to the direct object (*make, kill, influence*) but this isn't necessarily the case.

Subject	Object verb	Direct object
He	*underwent*	*treatment.*
She	*heard*	*a noise.*

Object verbs are also sometimes known as *transitive* or *mono-transitive* verbs.

We can normally use object verbs in passive constructions, in which case there is no direct object.

Subject		Object verb
Some vases	*got*	*smashed.*

In Chapter 21 we look at the reasons for using passive constructions and how to form them in more detail.

Complements and complement verbs

Complements

Complements usually tell us something about the subject, e.g. what it *is*; how it *feels* or what it *is like*.

Complements may consist of:

- a noun phrase, e.g. She became *a nicer person*.
- an adjective or adjective phrase, e.g. She grew (very) *old*.
- a preposition phrase, e.g. The children felt *under threat*.
- another clause (usually a question-word noun clause see 25.3), e.g. Our holiday wasn't *what we expected*.

These complements are sometimes also called subject complements because they describe something about the subject of the clause.

Complement verbs

Whereas object verbs usually make a certain amount of sense on their own (e.g. *killed* . . .), complement verbs usually don't (e.g. *was* . . .; *became* . . .). We use complement verbs to connect the subject to the complement in a clause. The grammar requires this but in terms of meaning we could often leave out the most common complement verb *be* altogether. Many languages don't need any verb in clauses like the following:

Subject	Complement verb	Complement
We	are	late.
Siam	is	the old name.

In as much as they do convey meaning, complement verbs usually express something about:

- being, e.g. *be*; uses of *remain; stay*
- seeming, e.g. *seem*; uses of *appear; feel; look; smell; taste*
- becoming, e.g. *become*; uses of *get; grow*

Subject	Complement verb	Complement
She	grew	old.
The children	felt	uneasy.

Complement verbs are sometimes also called *linking, intensive* or *copular* verbs.

Indirect objects and two-object verbs

Indirect objects

Indirect objects usually tell us who (or what) receives something or benefits from something. We only use them when we also use a direct object (this tells us what they receive or benefit from). Indirect objects are usually noun phrases and refer to people.

	Indirect object	Direct object
Give	*me*	*a hand.*
Who brought	*Sheila*	*the flowers?*

Indirect objects may also refer to animals or things that can receive or benefit from something.

	Indirect object	Direct object
Have you fed	*the plants*	*any fertiliser?*
You ought to give	*the windows*	*a good clean.*

As in all the above examples, we can place indirect objects between the verb phrase and the direct object. We can also place them after the direct object, and we do this particularly if they are long. When they come after the direct object, we use *to* or *for* to connect the two objects. We use:

- *to* if they are *receiving* something.
- *for* if they are *benefiting* from some kind of service.

Subject	Verb phrase	Direct object	*to/for*	Indirect object
We	*gave*	*all our money*	*to*	*a ticket tout.*
He	*can't keep*	*a good seat*	*for*	*us.*

Some academic grammars consider these expressions beginning *to* and *for* as adverbials (see pp. 261–262), and it may be simpler if we teach these like other adverbials.

	adverbial
She has told the truth	*to her husband.*
She has told the truth	*on this occasion.*

Two-object verbs

Two-object verbs need to be followed by an indirect object as well as a direct object. Typically, they express some aspect of giving or communicating something to someone or doing some kind of service.

Subject	Two-object verb	Indirect object	Direct object
She	*told*	*her husband*	*the truth.*

Two-object verbs are sometimes also called ditransitive verbs.

Complements and object-complement verbs

Object-complement verbs need to be followed by both a direct object and a complement. These verbs often describe:

- judgements, e.g. *consider, find, imagine, think*
- liking or wanting, e.g. *like, prefer, want*
- ways of naming, changing or making things, e.g. *appoint, baptise, call, declare, elect, make, leave, name*
- ways of stopping things from changing, e.g. *hold, keep*

The object is often (but not necessarily) a person, and the complement usually describes the qualities or status of the object.

Subject	Verb phrase	Direct object	Complement
They	*appointed*	*Ms Jones*	*treasurer.*
She	*made*	*him*	*angry.*

These complements are sometimes called 'object complements' because they describe something about the direct object of the clause.

Object-complement verbs are sometimes also called complex transitive verbs.

Differences between objects and complements

At first glance, the sentences in each of the following pairs seem to have a similar structure:

She	bought	a car.
She	became	a celebrity.

We	gave	him	money.
We	elected	him	captain.

In fact, it quickly becomes apparent that something is different about them if we try to change each of them into passive constructions. We can say:

> *A car was bought* and *Money was given to him*
> but NOT: * *A celebrity was become* or * *Captain was elected to him.*

What comes after *buy* and *give* (*him*) is a direct object, and can be used as the subject of a passive clause. What comes after *become* and *elect* (*him*) is a complement and can't become the subject of a passive clause.

We can distinguish between objects and complements in terms of meaning. In the first sentence, the subject (*She*) and object (*car*) are clearly different entities whereas in the second sentence the subject (*She*) and complement (*celebrity*) refer to the same person. Similarly, in the second pair of sentences, the two objects (*him* and *money*) refer to different entities whereas (*him*) and the complement (*captain*) refer to the same person.

Alternatively, all these cases can be explained by the type of verb. *Buy* is an object verb and *give* a two-object verb. *Become* is a complement verb and *elect* an object-complement verb.

Adverbials

Different grammars use the term 'adverbial' to mean different things. Some grammars use the term to include a wide range of grammatical features including subordinate and non-finite clauses, while others use it for a much more restricted range of features.

In this chapter we use the term in a restricted sense. Adverbials are usually phrases beginning with a preposition, adverb or noun (one-word adverbials are known as adverbs, and we look at these in Chapter 3).

> preposition phrases: *in the back garden.*
> adverb phrases: *often enough.*
> noun phrases: *Sunday lunch time.*

Unlike objects and complements, which are required by particular verbs, adverbials are usually phrases that we choose whether or not to add to a

---

Grammar for English language teachers

clause. They often provide information about how, where or when something is done or takes place.

We can use more than one adverbial together, e.g. *at 8.00 in the park; on Sunday with luck.*

Adverbials can also refer to a whole clause.

Subject	Verb phrase	Complements and objects	Adverbials
I've	*not been feeling*	*well*	*for the past few weeks.*
They	*broke*	*the window*	*on purpose.*

In this chapter we assume that adverbials come at the end of clauses, and we look at alternative positions in Chapter 20 (20.6).

Coordinating conjunctions

There are only three words that mainly function as coordinating conjunctions: *and, but* and *or*. These words can:

* link together parts of constituents and are therefore contained within the constituent.

  *Boys **and** girls come out to play.*   *She's brave **but** sensible.*
* form a link between clauses.

  *I thought it would rain **but** it didn't.*
  *Did I speak to you yesterday **or** did I dream that?*

When we use coordinating conjunctions to form a link between clauses, they are sentence constituents in their own right, separate from the two clauses that they link together.

Sentences which include several main clauses linked together by coordinating conjunctions are typical of the speech and writing of young children, and we need to encourage learners to use more complex grammar, particularly in writing (see Chapters 24–29).

Review of clauses, clause types and the order of sentence constituents

Most clauses consist of a subject and predicate. The subject is what usually comes before the verb phrase and the predicate is everything else.

There are five kinds of predicate (and therefore five types of clause), depending on what constituents they contain. This table shows the five types of predicate (and clause), and the order in which the constituents occur:

Subject	Predicate			
	Verb phrase	Indirect object	Direct object	Complement
She	*likes*		*music.*	
She	*has been*			*rather irritable.*
She	*gave*	*her sister*	*the news.*	
She	*calls*		*her husband*	*'Snootch'.*
She	*sighed.*			

As we have seen, the verb we choose determines what (if any) types of constituent we can use in the predicate. Another way of looking at the five types of predicate is in terms of the types of verb we use in the verb phrase:

Verb type	What has to follow the verb phrase	Example
Object verb	direct object	*She likes music.*
Complement verb	complement	*She has been rather irritable.*
Two-object verb	indirect object (*1*) + direct object (*2*)	*She gave her sister (1) the news (2).*
Object-complement verb	direct object (*1*) + complement (*2*)	*She calls her husband (1) 'Snootch' (2).*
No-object verb	nothing	*She sighed.*

Predicates (and therefore clauses) can also contain an adverbial.

*She gave her sister the news **on Tuesday.***

19.5 Additional factors and related issues

No-object verbs

No-object verbs are not followed by objects or complements. Their meaning is more 'complete' than that of the other verbs we have looked at.

Subject	no-object (multiword) verb
The river	*has dried up.*

No-object verbs are sometimes called 'intransitive verbs'.

Verbs which belong to more than one type

We use a lot of verbs in different ways. For example a verb like *make* is sometimes an object verb and at other times a two-object or object-complement verb.

Verb	Examples	Verb type
make	*He made all the cakes.* *I'll make them a salad.* *They made us prisoners.*	object two-object object-complement
work	*The car isn't working.* *They worked the mine till it was exhausted.*	no-object object
feel	*She felt a pain.* *She felt a fool.*	object complement

Different kinds of pronoun

We normally use the following personal pronouns only as subjects:

I   he   she   we   they

Example: *I live here.*

We use the following personal pronouns as objects and complements:

me   him   her   us   them

Examples: *He sent **me them**. That must **be her**.*

We use *you* and *it* as subject, object and complement.

Imperatives

Sometimes we miss out the subject of a clause altogether.

Open *the door.*   **Don't get up**.

These clauses are imperative, and we understand that *you* is implied (*You open the door*). We sometimes use imperative forms for giving orders, but more often we use them to make suggestions, give advice or to invite. We can use verbs of any type (object verb, complement verb etc.) as an imperative.

'Dummy' subjects: it *and* there

Because English requires verb phrases to have a subject unless they are imperative, we sometimes have to use a 'dummy' – a word which contributes no meaning but is there because the clause would be ungrammatical without it.

It

We use *it* as a dummy in talking about weather and times.

    ***It'*s raining.**   ***It'*s early.**   ***It** got dark.*

We also use *it* as a dummy when we make certain kinds of change to the basic order of sentence constituents, and we look at these cases in pp 278-279.

There

We use *there* (unstressed) followed by a form of *be* (*is, was, have been* etc.) to say that something exists. *Be* is followed by a noun phrase, and this often includes an embedded preposition phrase or relative clause which qualifies it in some way.

There	*be*	noun phrase	
			qualifying expression
There	*are*	*a number of reasons*	*for upgrading your computer.*
There	*has been*	*no doubt*	*in my mind.*

We generally teach this use of *there* in the context of describing places (e.g. *There's a TV next to the window*) at an elementary level. Learners often get confused by the structure as we need to take a lot of factors into account in choosing the words (verbs and determiners) to use, i.e.

- whether the clause is a statement, a question or is negative.
- whether the noun phrase headword is singular, plural or uncountable.
- the tense of *be*.

	There	*be*	Determiner	Headword	
	There	*is*	*a*	*scratch*	*on the table.*
	There	*is*	*some*	*mud*	*on the table.*
	There	*are*	*some*	*scratches*	*on the table.*
Are	*there*		*any*	*scratches*	*on the table?*
	There	*aren't*	*any*	*scratches*	*on the table.*

In spoken English many people simplify the grammar and use *there is* instead of *there are* with plural headwords, and this is increasingly common in the written language. However, few teachers would encourage students to model their English on examples like the following from a newspaper:

(*) *There's only eleven shopping days remaining . . .*

Separated verb phrases

We sometimes place sentence constituents between parts of the verb phrase if this consists of two or more words.

Question forms

	verb phrase			
		subject		
Have	*you*		*been*	*ill?*

See page 274.

Some multiword verbs

		verb phrase		
			object	
We	*'ll put*		*you*	*up.*

See page 108.

Adverbs and adverbials

		verb phrase		
		adverb(ial)		
I	*can*	*hardly*	*believe*	*it.*
I	*have*	*on many occasions*	*offered*	*help.*

What we mean by word order

When we refer loosely to word order, we may mean different things. The examples of learners' mistakes below all show what we generally think of as problems with word order, although in fact the nature of the problem is different in each case.

'Word order' can refer to:

- the order of words within a constituent

  * *I want a teacher very clever.* (1)   * *I have travelling been.* (2)

- the order of constituents within a clause

  * *My grammar very poor is.* (3)   * *I on Sundays work.* (4)

- the order of two or more clauses

  * *I want a to help me pass my exams teacher.* (5)   * *You should until you get the news wait.* (6)

  (1) This is a problem with the order of words in the noun phrase – adjectives and combinations of adverb-adjective need to come before the headword (*teacher*).

  (2) This is a problem with the order of words in the verb phrase – all the auxiliary verbs need to come before the main verb (*travelling*).

  (3) The complement (*very poor*) needs to come after the verb.

  (4) The adverbial (*on Sundays*) usually can't separate the subject and verb in this way.

  (5) The clause (*to help me pass my exams*) has to be placed after the headword (*teacher*) in this complex noun phrase.

  (6) The clause (*until you get the news*) has to come after the verb phrase (*should wait*) and can't separate the auxiliary and main verbs in this way.

19.6 Typical difficulties for learners

Comprehension

The order of words and basic sentence constituents generally creates more problems for learners when they speak and write than in comprehension.

In reading, particularly if they have time to stop and study bits of text that they don't understand, learners can usually work out from context how the words group together and whether a constituent is functioning, for example, as subject or object. Knowledge (explicit and/or unconscious) of the rules for ordering constituents and words within constituents naturally makes the process of comprehension faster and easier.

In listening, learners may be tricked by mis-placed expectations about the order of constituents and words. These expectations may be instinctive, and may operate even when the learner has explicit knowledge of the appropriate rules. For example, learners may struggle to understand sentences in which the indirect object comes before the direct object (e.g. *I showed Mother the baby*; *I passed Mary the salt*), initially understanding *Mother* and *Mary* respectively to be the direct and not the indirect object. Problems like this occur when the learner 'expects' indirect objects either to be introduced by a preposition (e.g. . . . *showed <u>to</u> Mother . . .*; . . . *passed <u>to</u> Mary . . .*) and/or to come in some other position in the sentence (e.g. after the direct object).

Speaking and writing

The greatest problem that many learners have with the basic principles and patterns of sentence constituents, is not one that leads to mistakes. It is that they *over-use* these basic patterns, leading to stretches of language that are correct but over-simple in construction. We consider this problem in more detail in Chapter 29.

Word order within constituents may be more of a problem for learners whose first languages are broadly similar to English, but where there are minor differences in word order (most European languages), than for those whose languages are very significantly different. Mistakes often persist once learners have understood the principles of word order in English, and they are often then able to identify and correct these mistakes themselves when they are pointed out.

The position of subjects

Learners sometimes reverse the order of subjects and no-object verbs. This is particularly common after conjunctions like *when* or *because.*

>   A: *When did you move back to the city?*   B: * *When began* **the war**.

>   A: *Why were they laughing?*   B: * *Because fell down* **his trousers**.

The position of adverbials

We don't usually place adverbials between verbs and their direct objects or dependent infinitive or *-ing* forms. Learners, however, may instinctively place adverbials in this position.

>   * *She opened* **with difficulty** *the door.*   * *I like* **at the weekend** *to play tennis.*

They may also use the adverbial inappropriately *within* the verb phrase.

>   * *We have* **this week** *been trying to contact you.*

The position of direct objects

Learners sometimes place direct objects between auxiliary verbs and main verbs.

>   * *I'm afraid I still haven't* **the book** *finished.*

>   * *I don't know where she has* **the keys** *left.*

Verbs which require or don't require indirect objects

Learners may leave out indirect objects when they use verbs that need to be followed by them. We usually find plenty of examples of this when learners are reporting what someone has said using verbs like *say, tell,* and *explain* (see p. 226).

>   * *She told [ ] she was ill.*

The learner appears to be unaware or to have forgotten that *tell* has to have an indirect object. *Said* would be more appropriate here.

They may also use indirect objects inappropriately.

>   * *She explained* **me** *how to operate the machine.*

We don't normally use an indirect object after *explain,* although we could use *to me* if we particularly wanted to draw attention to the listener. In this case, we would probably say *She explained how to operate the machine to ME.*

Problems within noun phrases

Some learners may place adjectives (or adjective phrases) after the nouns they modify.

> * *We live in a house **very big**.*

We look at problems with the order of adjectives in noun phrases on page 21.

Dummy subjects

Learners often leave out dummy subjects.

> * [] *Was very cloudy yesterday.* [It]
> * [] *Was a noise in the middle of the night.* [There]

They may also use *it* in place of *there* or a form of *have* instead of *there is/ are*.

> * *It is a problem with the TV in my room.*
> * *Have a cockroach in the bathroom.*

19.7 Consolidation exercises
(see pp. 478–481 for possible answers)

Language in context

1 (see p. 478)

    a Underline the verb phrase in each of the sentences which follow.

    b Identify the main verb in each verb phrase.

    c Decide which type the main verb belongs to (e.g. object verb; object-complement verb etc.).

    d Identify the noun phrases.

    e Identify the prepositional phrases.

       (i)   You're sitting on my chair.

       (ii)   Don't call me stupid.

       (iii)   Beth and Albert will put me up for the night.

       (iv)   They've given me the money at last.

2 (see pp. 478–479)

Read the following letter in which the writer is reproaching a friend for having broken a promise.

I didn't doubt you at the time. Your lies seemed really convincing. However, I started thinking about your promise after a while. I must be an idiot. Anyone else would have seen through you at once. Don't try to tell me your lies ever again.

a Identify the subjects of clauses.

b Identify any direct objects.

c Identify any indirect objects.

d Identify any complements.

e Identify any adverbials.

f Identify any imperative forms.

3 (see pp. 479–480)

The following is from a newspaper article about unusual weather conditions in summer.

There were two remarkable outbreaks of thunderstorms in July 1968. June had ended on a fine, hot note, but a cold front drifted eastwards into western Britain early on July 1 and triggered an unusually severe and prolonged series of thunderstorms in the west and north.

Darkness descended in daytime, and there were reports of very large hailstones.

a Divide the text into clauses.

b Divide each clause into its basic constituents and label each of them (subject, adverbial etc.).

Learners' English

1 (see p. 480)

Read the following, which is part of a student's written composition, summarising the plot of a story concerning two friends, James and Peter. Peter has been wrongfully imprisoned.

> James knew very well the character of Peter. James went to
> the prison to talk to the police about the true story. Peter had
> been tricked by an old man that gave him a chicken stolen. He
> discharged Peter.
>
> In the afternoon when Peter came back home, talked about
> the help of James. Peter asked to his wife: "Where's James?"
>
> When was night, received a letter from parents' Peter.
> Explained everything the letter.

a Identify the following problems.

b Correct these problems.

   (i)   An adverbial that is placed between a verb and its direct object.

   (ii)   A noun phrase in which the order of the headword and an adjective have been reversed.

  (iii) Three examples of missing subjects.

  (iv) A subject which has been placed at the end of a clause.

   (v)   Two noun phrases in which the learner has used a possessive form oddly or incorrectly.

  (vi) An object verb used as though it needed an indirect object.

2 (see pp. 480–481)

a Identify any problems the writer of the following text has had with basic sentence constituents and word order.

b Re-write the text in natural and correct English. Keep to simple sentences (without subordinate clauses) and follow the basic principles and patterns of sentence constituents and word order.

> My speciality engineering hydraulic. Engineering hydraulic very
> important new science. Using engineering hydraulic in the future
> will a modern communications system develop my country. Will
> profit everyone. Will construct a glorious future engineering
> hydraulic. Recently expanding this field of science. In the future
> I will with great pleasure give to my country.

20 Major variants

question forms   fronting
spotlighting
pushing information back
position of adverbials
clefting   pseudo-clefting

20.1 Key considerations

Learners who have problems with the basic patterns for ordering words and sentence constituents often want to develop a good command of these before they begin to try using most of the possible variants. However, if they are hearing and seeing natural English, they inevitably come across lots of examples which don't follow the 'basic' rules.

Constructing questions is the one 'variant' that we can't avoid teaching, and which we need to teach in the earliest stages. Native speakers of English sometimes take for granted the way we construct questions. In fact, this involves complicated changes to the order of words in clauses, and many learners develop a command of question forms only very slowly.

Learners who have a good level of English often welcome encouragement to vary the patterns and basic orders they use in order to achieve particular emphasis. This is particularly relevant to learners who need to write English.

20.2 What are the major variants?

Question forms

In many languages the distinction between questions and statements is made only through intonation in speaking and punctuation in writing. However, in English, we use grammar to make this distinction (and often we don't use any 'special' features of intonation at all).

We divide question forms into four kinds. Three of these depend on the type of verb phrase involved:

Type 1: Verb phrases comprising *am, is, are, was* or *were* as a complement verb.

We reverse the normal order of subject and verb:

Are you ill?   Was anyone at home?

Type 2: Verb phrases which include one or more auxiliary verbs (including modal verbs).

We reverse the order of the subject and the (first) auxiliary verb:

Can Dad stay?   *Have you been drinking beer?*

Type 3: Single-word verb phrases (simple present and past tense of all main verbs apart from *be*).

We introduce a 'dummy' auxiliary (*do* or *did*) to make the question:

Did you swim?   *Do you take sugar?*

We can add question words such as *why, how, where, when* to the beginning of questions which belong to Types 1–3.

Type 1:   *Why are you ill?*
Type 2:   *When should I phone you?*
Type 3:   *Where did you swim?*

Questions with *who* and *what* may require other changes.

Type 4:

We use Type 4 questions to get information about the subject (not, as in Types 2 and 3, the object) of a sentence. The question word itself is the subject of the question. Type 4 questions involve no change to the basic order of words in a statement.

Who killed Kennedy?   *What's happening?*

Learners sometimes confuse Type 3 and Type 4 questions:

object		subject	
Who	did	Kennedy	kill?

subject		object
Who	killed	Kennedy?

'Fronting' information, pushing it back and putting it under the spotlight

Chapter 19 describes the 'basic' order of sentence constituents in which the subject establishes what the clause is about, and the predicate (i.e. what follows the subject) then introduces the new or most important information.

On many occasions we don't want this kind of clause – we don't want to begin with the subject. In these cases there are various ways we can move other information to the beginning of the clause. We call this process of bringing information forward 'fronting'.

The first clause of the first sentence in the last paragraph begins with 'fronted' information – here an adverbial is put before the subject of the main clause in order to 'orientate' you to what follows:

(Fronted) adverbial	subject	verb phrase	direct object
On many occasions	we	don't actually want	this kind of clause

Fronting is a normal and frequently occurring feature of English. We usually front information for one of two (contrasting) reasons:

- because this (and not the subject) establishes common ground and orientates the listener or reader to what is coming in the rest of the clause;
- to give information extra prominence by placing it in an unexpected position (i.e. at the beginning instead of near the end of a clause).

We look at fronting in more detail in 20.3 below.

As well as fronting information, we also do the opposite – we push information towards the end of clauses. We do this usually to make it easier to understand and process information which is long, dense or complicated, or which contains little or no familiar 'orientating information' (i.e.):

> . . . there remains a gap between people's aspirations and their awareness of what new opportunities may be available to them.

To avoid the difficulty of processing the long subject of this sentence a 'dummy' subject (*there*) is used to push this to the end of the clause.

We look at how we use the dummy subject *there* and also *it* to push information back in more detail in 20.4 below.

As well as bringing information forward and pushing it back, we can also put it under the spotlight by using specific grammatical focusing devices. In the following, the expressions immediately following *was* are 'spotlighted' in this way:

> *It was **on Tuesday** that we saw him.*   *When we saw him was **on Tuesday**.*

We look at these 'spotlighting devices' in more detail in 20.5 below.

20.3 Fronting information

Adverbials

In Chapter 19 we saw that adverbials generally come at the end of the clause.

> *That's an excellent idea **on the whole**!*

In fact the position of adverbials is very flexible, and we often 'front' them. There is nothing very strange or unusual about the following:

> ***On the whole** that's an excellent idea!*
> ***All of a sudden** she saw a movement in the shadows.*

Changes to word order after 'negative' adverbials

Some adverbials (including single-word adverbs) can have a negative or limiting meaning.

negative adverbials:	limiting adverbials:
never; nowhere; nothing; not often; not for nothing; not once; no way; never once; on no account	*hardly; seldom; rarely; hardly ever; scarcely ever; only now; only occasionally; only once; only rarely*

When we front these, we change the order of the following subject and (auxiliary) verb exactly as we do in questions (see 20.2).

fronted adverbial	verb	subject	complement
In Britain alone	*is*	*selective state education*	*reviled.*
. . . only in Britain	*is*	*there*	*segregation of pupils into two races.*

We make these changes to word order more systematically in writing than in speaking.

Adverbial and verb combinations

We front adverbial and verb combinations in speaking and writing, usually to orientate the reader to the important new information.

Adverbial	verb phrase	subject
In this street	*lived*	*the first printers and stained-glass craftsmen . . .*

Complements

This pattern with a fronted complement often occurs in short, pithy remarks, exclamations and interjections. It is primarily a feature of spoken English.

complement	subject	verb phrase	object	adverbial
A funny language	*English*	*is.*		
Really ill	*I*	*felt*		*last night.*

We also sometimes choose the order: complement + verb + subject.

Worried to death were their parents.

Examples like this only occur with forms of *be*, subjects that are not pronouns and complements that are phrases.

Direct objects

We can front direct objects. This occurs primarily in speech.

direct object	subject	verb phrase	adverbial
A right mess of it	*they*	*made.*	
An awful accident	*we*	*saw*	*on the way here.*

20.4 Pushing information back

Dummy subject there

All languages have some device to push information further back in a clause and to signal to listeners or readers that they need to pay extra attention because everything coming will be difficult to process – either because it is new (there may be no link between this information and what is familiar, no point of reference to 'orientate' them) or particularly dense (we try to avoid beginning a clause with a long and/or complicated subject).

In English, this device is the dummy subject *there* and a verb – either a form of *be* or one of the following no-object verbs: *exist, remain, live, happen, come.*

The extracts in the left-hand column use this device. In the right-hand column these are re-written to show the effect of beginning with new information or a long or complex subject:

There are over 50 distinct ethnic groups living in China.	Over 50 distinct ethnic groups live in China.
It is true that in India . . . ***there existed*** a certain respect for and understanding of Hindu traditions.	. . . a certain respect for and understanding of Hindu traditions existed.
At root for the British ***there*** always ***remained*** the preservation of power and the reputation of officials.	. . . the preservation of power and the reputation of officials always remained.
Impressive as Stonehenge is, ***there comes*** a moment somewhere about eleven minutes after your arrival when you realize . . .	. . . a moment somewhere about eleven minutes after your arrival comes . . .

Dummy subject it

We can use *it* as a dummy subject to avoid beginning a clause with a subject which includes a clause in its own right, and is therefore difficult to process. We then attach this information to the end of the complement or object – i.e. at the back of the clause where it is easier to understand.

For example, instead of:

(complex) subject	verb phrase	object
That your ceiling fell down last week	*makes*	*no difference.*

we can say or write:

dummy subject *it*	verb phrase	object
It	*makes*	*no difference that your ceiling fell down last week.*

and instead of:

(complex) subject	verb phrase	complement
Information that is expressed in long, complex subjects	*is*	*difficult to process*

we can say or write:

dummy subject *it*	verb phrase	complement
It	*is*	*difficult to process information that is expressed in long, complex subjects . . .*

20.5 Putting information under the spotlight

It + be + *spotlighted information* + that *or* who (*'clefting'*)

A simple clause is one unit.

> *Julia phoned us.*

'Clefting' is a way of dividing a clause into two parts – the first part beginning with *it* and a form of the verb *to be* (e.g. *It was*), and the second part beginning with *who* or *that*.

> *It was Julia who phoned us.*

Whereas in most clauses the information that comes at the end is what is new or important, in cleft sentences we put what is already known at the end (e.g. *someone phoned us*). What is new and important comes immediately after *It is, It was* etc. – and this is what is under the 'spotlight' (e.g. *Julia*). This spotlighted information can take the form of many types of sentence constituent (subject, adverbial etc.).

subject:	*It was*	*Julia*	*who phoned us on Saturday.*
adverbial:	*It was*	*on Saturday*	*that Julia phoned us.*
direct object:	*It was*	*us*	*that Julia phoned on Saturday.*
indirect object:	*Was it*	*Mary*	*(that) you gave the file to?*
subordinate clause:	*It was*	*in order to cheer up Julia*	*that we phoned them.*

Because it comes at the end of the sentence, the information that follows *who* or *that* is also prominent even though it is not new information.

Question word + *information* + be + *spotlighted information* (*'pseudo-clefting'*)

We use pseudo-clefting in a very similar way to clefting, again turning the spotlight on a particular part of a clause in order to draw attention to the information it conveys. We usually begin the adapted (i.e. pseudo-cleft) clause with a question word (e.g. *what, where*) and we introduce the spotlighted information at the end with a form of the verb *to be* such as *is, was, has been* or *will be*.

As in the case of clefting, this spotlighted information can take the form of many types of sentence constituent (subject, adverbial etc.), e.g.

subject:	*What drove us crazy was*	*the noise.*
adverbial:	*When you may see him is*	*on Sunday.*
direct object:	*What he needs is*	*a good shake-up.*
indirect object:	*Who you should really give the gardening prize to is*	*the person with the best window boxes.*
complement:	*What she really feels is*	*profound disappointment.*
subordinate:	*Why we came late is*	*because we had to finish the work ourselves.*

We can normally reverse the order of the two parts of a pseudo-cleft sentence:

What drove us crazy was the noise.

The noise was what drove us crazy.

20.6 Flexibility: adverbials

We generally teach that adverbials come at the end of the clause (e.g. *I'll be there on Saturday). We also teach that they can be fronted (e.g. On Saturday I'll be there*).

Although we may choose not to teach students to use adverbials in other sentence positions, we need to be aware that adverbial expressions can occur in a variety of intermediate positions (after the verb phrase or even within it).

Subject	**verb phrase**	**adverbial**	**complement**
That	*'s*	*on the whole*	*an excellent idea!*

	verb phrase			
Subject	**auxiliary verb**	**adverbial**	**past participle**	**object**
I	*have*	*on occasions*	*eaten*	*raw fish.*

We generally avoid using adverbials between verbs and objects, and we usually teach that this is a mistake. However, even this 'rule' is flexible, and we come across other examples that appear to contradict this 'rule'.

Subject	verb phrase	adverbial	direct object
We	*need to design*	*with you*	*an innovative approach.*

20.7 Typical difficulties for learners

Comprehension

As long as learners are familiar with standard patterns of ordering sentence constituents, variants on these don't usually prevent them from understanding short sentences (although they may miss intended subtleties of emphasis). Variants may create difficulties of comprehension in longer and more complex sentences, particularly if it isn't immediately clear what the subject of the clause is (we explore these difficulties in Chapter 29), and the following two kinds of variant can also confuse learners:

Word order after 'fronted' negative adverbs

In sentences like *Rarely did he speak*, learners may be deceived into thinking that a question is intended when it isn't.

Pseudo-cleft sentences

Learners may be puzzled or misled by affirmative sentences which begin with a word that they instinctively associate with questions.

> *What you need is a good, long bath!*
> *When they'll arrive is anybody's guess.*

Speaking and writing

With the exceptions we look at below, variants are unlikely to lead to mistakes when learners speak and write. What is a more common and may be a more significant (if less noticeable) problem is that learners 'play safe'. Partly from fear of making mistakes, they often miss (or reject) opportunities to highlight, emphasise or to play down particular sections of information by varying the order of constituents and words. They may also simply be unaware of the means for doing this.

It is when we read what our students have written most of all that we need to be sensitive to unnecessary simplification and missed opportunities. And it is in our feedback to individual learners on their writing that we can often encourage or show them how they can achieve clearer or more elegant expression of their ideas and intentions, by fronting information, pushing it back or spotlighting it.

Question forms

It is very common for learners to ask questions without making the necessary changes (or additions) to word order. These mistakes are obvious when the question contains a question word (*What, why, who* etc.).

  * *When she came?*   * *How you can say that?*

When there is no question word, it may not be clear that the learner intends to ask a question.

  * *She went to London?*

Learners may use rising intonation to express that statements like this are intended as a question, and listeners may either simply not notice this or they may understand that the learner is querying or checking information.

Learners sometimes also make questions by placing the subject after a whole verb phrase instead of after the first auxiliary verb.

  * *What is doing your sister?*

Having worked hard to grasp the grammatical changes they need to make in using object questions (e.g. *What did he do?*), learners may over-generalise this rule, introducing (inappropriate) auxiliary verbs into object questions.

  * *Who did see them?*   * *What did (it) happen?*

Word order after 'fronted' negative adverbs

If learners choose to 'front' adverbs with negative meaning they may forget to invert the subject and verb, or may not know that this is needed.

  * *Not only he could swim when he was three but he was also beginning to play the piano.*   * *Rarely I have been so disappointed in anyone!*

20.8 Consolidation exercises
(see pp. 482−486 for possible answers)

Language in context

1 (see p. 482)

The following extract is from a brief summary of events in the professional life of the operatic soprano Montserrat Caballé. Some of the adverbials are printed in italics. All of these are fronted.

> *For seven years* her musical ambitions (which had begun with training for the ballet) were sponsored by the wealthy Bertrand family, on the sole condition that she never neglected Barcelona's opera house, the Liceo. *In 1956* she joined the Basle Opera, where at first she had to supplement her minute income by waitressing. *Over the next few years* she sang everything from Salomé (her favourite role) to Mimì, and *in one season alone* her Aida was heard a total of twenty-six times!

a Why do you think the author has chosen to front these adverbials?

b Would it make any significant difference if these phrases occurred at the end of clauses?

2 (see p. 483)

Look at the following sentences and:

a Identify any 'variant' features in the ordering of sentence constituents or words.

b Explain why the speaker or writer may have chosen this order.

   (i)   With the coming of Dean Moriarty began the part of my life you could call my life on the road.

   (ii)   I remember everything about that day, Eden's wedding day. Sweet-pea colours we bridesmaids wore and I was the one in pale purple.

   (iii) What keeps a film critic going and enjoying his job is optimism.

   (iv) 'You know, I think you've had enough for one day. Sleep back at Passford House is what you need.'

3 (see pp. 483–484)

The two extracts below have been adapted from the originals.

a This extract is from a discussion of the state of British industry in the 1990s. The original includes two cleft clauses.

> . . . I meet increasing numbers of small and medium-sized companies which have had the aspiration, drive and tenacity to establish worldwide positions and leadership in niche markets. The country's economic future (re)lies on these hidden champions.
>
> Our failure to grow small businesses into large has been the root cause of our decline coupled with a strong hangover of a very strong anti-manufacturing culture. There is still too little provision of start-up finance and almost no long-term finance.

    (i)   Re-write the text to include two cleft clauses as you think they may have occurred in the original.

    (ii)   Explain the choices you make.

b This extract is from a discussion about whether it is useful for us to compare pairs of languages. The original includes two pseudo-cleft clauses.

> James was saying that side-by-side comparisons of pairs of languages in isolation was ineffective in predicting learner behaviour, and that a frame of reference that would encompass the universal properties of all languages was needed.

    (i)   Re-write the text to include two cleft clauses as you think they may have occurred in the original.

    (ii)   Explain the choices you make.

4 (see p. 484)

This sentence begins a chapter in a biography/social history. Read the sentence and answer the questions that follow it:

> It was in the spring of 1923 that Leonard and Virginia Woolf came out to see me.

a Has this visit been mentioned before?

b Has the date been mentioned before?

c What enables you to answer questions *a* and *b*?

Learners' English (see pp. 484–485)

The following text was written by a learner of English about her early experience as a teacher. She writes clearly and generally accurately, and makes one definite – but not altogether idiomatic – change to the normal order of sentence constituents.

I am going to write about my first year of teaching.
I especially remember about this time how unhappy I was, and
the fear of this unhappiness recurring makes me continue to
take courses of professional development.
I was teaching in a high school in a poor suburb of Helsinki.
Appalling was the emotional deprivation that many of the
children suffered – they never got to see their parents, and they
often had to beg money to buy food. But their behaviour in
school was the particular problem for me of course.

a Identify the change.

b How might she achieve the same shift in emphasis more idiomatically?

c What other opportunities are there in this text for making changes to the order of basic constituents in order to bring information into the spotlight where appropriate?

Analysing exercises (see pp. 485–486)

Learners of English sometimes carry out exercises which require putting a jumbled string of words or groups of words into the appropriate order. Look at the following exercise.

(i) Wednesday in arrive did end parcel on the the
(ii) Prose I the turgid found
(iii) Wonderful Scotland is place walking for a

a Arrange the words in an appropriate order.

b Consider whether any alternative orders are also possible.

c Explain the alternative orders you have chosen.

EXAMPLE:

mat the on sat cat the

a The cat sat on the mat

b On the mat sat the cat

c The order of constituents in **a)** is

subject	verb phrase	adverbial
The cat	sat	on the mat

In **b)** the adverbial is fronted (we would do this when it is the *mat* rather than the *cat* which forms the link with what came before):

adverbial	verb phrase	subject
On the mat	sat	the cat

21 Passive constructions

was damaged

got elected   had the car washed

got his leg broken

21.1 Key considerations

In this chapter we look at two distinct types of passive construction: 'standard' constructions (e.g. *our car was/got broken into*) and 'causative' constructions (e.g. *we had/got our car repaired*).

Teaching materials often concentrate on the form of standard passive constructions, and practice activities often involve mechanically transforming active constructions into passive ones. Learners sometimes end up with the impression that passive constructions are some kind of optional, deviant version of active constructions. While we usually do need to give learners plenty of practice in forming passive constructions correctly, we also need to encourage learners both to notice and understand when and why we choose them, and how often we use them. We also need to encourage them to use the constructions in appropriate contexts themselves.

Because the form of passive constructions is quite complex, coursebooks often teach the passive form of particular tenses one at a time. Taking into account the abilities and strengths of particular students, teachers sometimes decide to teach the underlying rules (e.g. 'we use a form of the verb *be* + past participle'), and require learners to apply these to any tense.

We generally introduce causative passive constructions when learners are already confident in using standard passive constructions in a range of tenses.

Some materials use the term 'passive voice', but the term is used to mean different things. In this book we use the term 'passive constructions', and include forms with *be, get* and *have* as auxiliary verbs.

21.2 What are standard passive constructions?

What do they do?

Clauses are either active or passive, and in active constructions, the subject of an object verb is usually the agent, the 'doer'.

> A: *You rang the bell.*
> B: *I left my keys at work.*

The subject of a clause usually establishes 'what the clause is about'; it often refers to something which is already known to the listener or reader. What follows this is the new or important information. The key information in the exchange above is that the person *rang the bell* and the *reason* for this.

In passive constructions, the subject still establishes 'what the clause is about', but it is the recipient of the action, not the agent. We choose passive constructions when the new or important information is:

- what happened to the subject: *I've been **sacked**.*

- who or what did it: *'Turandot' was composed **by Puccini**.*

- how it was done: *The conference was **badly organised**.*

We also choose them when the agent is unknown or unspecified.

> *No one was injured.*

In addition, we choose passive constructions to avoid very long subjects – a passive construction allows us to put a long and/or complex phrase at the end of a clause where it is easier to understand than at the beginning.

> *Many people have been refused help by **the new commission which was set up to look into possible abuses in the allocation of council housing**.*

'Rules of thumb'

In order to help learners to develop a feeling for when to use passive constructions, in addition to the rules above, course materials generally give them or help them to work out 'rules of thumb' which focus on particular contexts of use and particular verbs.

We use passive constructions:

- to describe processes:
> *The beans **are picked** in late summer and **are left** to dry in the sun.*

- in various formal (often academic) styles of discourse, e.g. to introduce evidence, argument, or opinion:

    *It **is** sometimes **argued** that . . .*

    *A distinction can **be made** between . . .*

  or to describe procedure in formally reporting scientific experiments:

    *Thirty eight subjects **were interviewed** in the first round of interviews.*

- to avoid the implication of personal involvement or responsibility:

  *The vase **got broken**, Mum.*

  *I'm afraid the work on your car won't **be completed** today.*

- with certain verbs – verbs we use when the person who did the action is generally unimportant. They often describe claiming, blaming, acts of destruction or emotional reactions:

  *He **is alleged** to be in a sanatorium.*

  *We **have been inundated** with gestures of support.*

Learners often also find it helpful to consider that while in speech we can use stress and intonation to highlight whether information is new, in writing we depend on ordering information:

  Spoken: SHAKESpeare *didn't write 'Edward II',* MARlow *did.*

  Written: *'Edward II' **wasn't written** by Shakespeare, it **was written** by Marlow.*

Learners are sometimes told that we choose passive constructions in order to give extra prominence to the subject. This is not true.

What do they look like?

The basic pattern

We form passive constructions with a form of *be* (e.g. *is, has been, is going to be*) or *get* (e.g. *gets, got, will get*) followed by the past participle of the main verb.

  The whole house was / got flooded.

If the agent is specified, this comes at the end of the clause and follows *by*.

  *Several protesters were taken away **by** the police.*

Verb types

We can use object, two-object and object-complement verbs in standard constructions (see the five verb types on pp. 94–97):

object:	*The wall **was toppled**.*
two-object:	*The winner **was given** a silver cup.*
object-complement:	*I think Helen is going **to be appointed** Chair of the Commission.*

Two-object verbs (e.g. *ask, bring, give, hand, offer, pass, show, take*) are followed by both an indirect and a direct object.

She gave me a book.   *They offered Charles a job.*

We can make two kinds of passive clause with these verbs depending on which information we want to highlight:

	subject		**direct object**
	I	*was given*	*a book.*
Can	*Charles*	*be offered*	*a job?*

	subject		**indirect object**	
	A book	*was given*	*to*	*me.*
Can	*a job*	*be offered*	*to*	*Charles?*

We don't use no-object and complement verbs in any kind of passive construction.

Choosing between *be* and *get* as auxiliary verbs

Some teaching materials pay little attention to the use of *get* in passive constructions. Materials also sometimes suggest that *get* is a colloquial alternative to *be*. While this may be true in some cases, we also choose *get* to suggest:

- that the action is unexpected, involuntary or possibly unwelcome:

  *When he picked up the phone we **got cut off**.*

- an achievement based on something that has been built up beforehand:

  *She **got elected**.*

- an achievement in the face of difficulty:

  *I finally **got admitted** to hospital.*

In the following sentences, we could choose between *be* and *get* fairly freely:

*I'm not going to **get/ be tricked**.*

In the following, which describes something that is desired, *get* is not an alternative:

> *The house is being redecorated.* NOT * *is getting redecorated*

Verbs which we use with a full infinitive only in passive constructions

Some verbs which are often or usually followed by a *that* clause in active constructions (*believe, consider, say, think, understand*) are followed by an infinitive when the verb is passive.

Passive	Active
*She **is thought to be** a genius.*	*People **think (that) she is** a genius.*
*He **was said to have** been fiddling the books.*	*People **say that he was** fiddling . . .*

Some verbs which are often or usually followed by the bare infinitive in active constructions (e.g. *help; make*) are followed by a full infinitive when they are passive.

Passive	Active
*He was **made to clear** up the mess.*	*They **made him clear** up . . .*
*He was **helped to get** the premises ready this time.*	*They **helped him get** . . .*

Passive constructions with *it* as the subject

Verbs like *believe, consider, say, think, understand* are also often used in passive constructions with an impersonal subject (*it*), particularly in more formal, written styles.

> *It **is understood** that no one speaks during the time for private prayers.*

Reduced relative clauses

We often 'reduce' relative clauses which include a passive verb. We leave out the relative pronoun and the verb *be*. This makes the clause more succinct.

> *They produced various plans [] drafted by different consultants.* (*[which had been] drafted . . .*)

We avoid reduced forms of future tenses.

> NOT * *Let's wait for the names of the people [] chosen in next week's ballot.* (*[who will be]) chosen . . .*

Using *by* and other prepositions after passive constructions

Because course materials generally pay a lot of attention to the use of *by* to introduce the agent in a passive construction, learners sometimes over-use it – particularly in cases where we use *with* or *in* after verbs like *contained, cover, decorate.*

> * *They covered all the furniture **by** old sheets.*

Sometimes we need to make it clear that we can use any preposition after a passive construction – our choice depends on the meaning we want to express.

> *The fruit was cut up **on** the table.*
> *   **in** the kitchen.*
> *   **into** cubes.*

Passive constructions and adjectives

Generally it is clear when past participles are used in passive constructions. The past participle in the following, for example, conveys a strong sense of action and is very much a part of the verb.

> *She was **knocked down** on the way home from school.*

Many adjectives are derived from past participles (e.g. *astonished, bothered, closed* etc.) and some of these words now function mainly (or even exclusively) as adjectives.

> *Her childhood was emotionally **deprived**.*
> *She's feeling very **jaded**.*

A lot of words can be used both as a past participle in passive constructions and as an adjective. Usually the context makes it clear which of these is the case. In the first sentence which follows, *locked* clearly describes a state – it is an adjective. But in the second, *locked* describes an action and is part of a passive construction.

> *The door was obviously **locked**.* (adjective)
> *The doors are **locked** as soon as the visitors leave each night.* (passive)

21.3 What are causative passive constructions?

What do they do?

As we saw in 21.2, in standard passive constructions the subject is the recipient of some action (e.g. *I've been sacked.*). In causative constructions the *object* is the recipient of an action – the subject is in some way responsible for what happened, but didn't do it.

Subject		Object	
He	*got*	*me*	*sacked.*

As the subject of causative constructions also usually establishes 'what the clause is about', it often refers to something that we already know.

We generally use causative constructions when we describe:

- what we arrange for someone to do for us:
  *She goes to hospital and **has** her blood pressure **taken**.*
- unfortunate experiences:
  *He **got** his leg **broken** playing football.*

What do they look like?

The basic pattern

We use a form of *have* or *get* followed by an object and then the past participle of the main verb.

We had / got the whole house renovated.

If the agent is specified, this comes at the end of the clause and follows *by*.

Can't we get the rubbish taken away by the council?

Verb types

In causative constructions we use only object verbs.

publish: *I've had two of my stories published in science fiction collections.*

Choosing between *have* and *get* as auxiliary verbs

We often use *have* interchangeably with *get* to describe things we arrange to be done for us, although we tend to choose *get* when some element of difficulty or achievement is involved (compare the commonplace *has her blood pressure taken* with the problematic *She never managed to get her symphonies played*).

In describing unfortunate experiences we tend to avoid *have* and use only *get*.

21.4 Features common to both standard and causative passive constructions

Tense

As the examples which follow illustrate, we use passive constructions with any tense of the verb and with infinitive and -ing forms.

> *When are you going to **have** that door **fixed**?*
>
> *The gardens are to **be landscaped**.*
>
> *I hate **being patronised**.*

Some people dislike putting two forms of *be* together (e.g. *be being* or *been being*) particularly when they write. They avoid standard passive constructions in the future continuous or present perfect continuous.

> *I asked the nurses to hurry because I didn't want to **be being dressed** when you arrived.*

Word order: multiword verbs and other verb + preposition combinations

Object verbs sometimes consist of two (or more) words.

> *I **looked after** my mother.* (multiword verb)
>
> *She won't **listen to** me.* (verb + preposition combination)

In passive constructions we still need to include the preposition, even though it isn't followed by an object.

> ***Has** my suggestion been **taken up**?*
>
> *She's **having** the wiring **looked at**.*

21.5 Typical difficulties for learners

Comprehension

Learners may fail to recognise a passive construction, thinking that the subject of a sentence is the agent when it isn't. For example, in the following, they may understand that the man was the attacker:

> *A man **was attacked** by three women.*

This problem is particularly acute:

- where the facts contradict normal expectations (as in the example above).

- in listening as opposed to reading, where the learner can look back and check.
- in listening when learners may fail to hear the auxiliary verb (e.g. *was*) which makes the sentence passive.
- where the past tense form and the past participle are the same e.g. *attacked* (but not *bit/bitten*).

It is often difficult for learners and teachers to identify when these problems occur. However, we can analyse texts for potential problems, and then in class consciously check whether or not our students have understood.

Speaking and writing

Non-use

For most learners knowing when to use passive constructions is the greatest problem, and they often don't use them where they would be appropriate. The following description of wine production, for example, was written by a learner with a very good command of grammar and vocabulary, and who was able to form passive sentences accurately and appropriately in controlled exercises. She had no particular personal association with wine production, and wanted to write simply about agriculture and economic activity in her country:

In my country we produce very good quality wine. We grow the vines mainly in the West of the country where the winters are milder. People pick the grapes at the end of the summer – they have to pick them at exactly the right time. When they have picked them they have to process the grapes very quickly. We keep some wines for a long time to improve before we put it into bottles. We can buy my country's wines in many other European countries.

Despite her command of passive forms, the learner did not spontaneously use any. This non-use of passives misleadingly gives the impression that she has some personal involvement or interest in wine production.

Misleadingly, learners also often 'forget' causative constructions.

(*) *I cut my hair yesterday.* (Meaning: *I had my hair cut yesterday.*)

We can help learners by frequently pointing out missed opportunities for using passive constructions. We also need to ensure that we:

- pay attention to the occasions when we use passive constructions as well as to their form.
- present passive constructions to learners as an independent and valid way of presenting information in their own right rather than as though they are active constructions which have undergone some form of 'transformation'.

If we are teaching learners whose first language (e.g. many European languages) has a form which *looks* very similar but which is used differently (and usually far less), we need to point this out, perhaps by comparing texts in the two languages.

Leaving out auxiliary verbs

Learners may leave out the auxiliary verb before the past participle.

> * *England beaten by Costa Rica in the semi-final.*
> * *Catherine loved very much by Mr Heathcliff.*

In some cases the learners may be misled by reading newspaper headlines, in which the auxiliary verbs are normally omitted (*England beaten by Costa Rica* is an acceptable headline).

Learners may use the verb in the appropriate tense and simply follow it with *by*.

> * *The film makes by Scorsese.*
> * *It believes by many people that my country is all desert.*

This may also happen where the agent is not specified.

> * *Portuguese and many African languages speak in Angola.*

Choosing the wrong auxiliary verb

Learners sometimes mix up *be, been* and *being*.

> * *Our house is be renovated.*
> * *Their documents haven't being accepted.*

This problem may be affected by the fact that we tend to pronounce these words very indistinctly when they are auxiliary verbs.

Choosing the wrong preposition

Some learners may systematically use the wrong preposition to introduce the agent in passive constructions.

> * *Kennedy was killed from a man called Oswald.*

They may also over-use *by*, particularly where *with* is necessary in order to indicate the *means* (as opposed to the agent) by which something happened.

> * *He was attacked by a knife.*

Choosing the wrong verb

Learners sometimes try to construct a passive form of no-object verbs.

> * *He was died in 1963.*

Word order

Many learners make mistakes in the order of words in 'causative' constructions, typically combining the auxiliary *have* or *get* with the past participle.

> * *I am going to have cut my hair this afternoon.*
> * *She got mended her suitcase.*

Some learners who 'know the rule' still make this mistake because the correct order of words 'feels' wrong to them.

Special cases

Speakers of languages closely related to English may translate literally from their own languages.

> * *I am born in 1952.* (French and Italian)
> * *I born in Montevideo.* (Spanish)

21.6 Consolidation exercises
(see pp. 486–490 for possible answers)

Differences in meaning (see pp. 486–487)

Look at the following groups of sentences and for each group consider the questions.

(i)   Her shoes were cleaned.

Her shoes got cleaned.
She had her shoes cleaned.

(ii)   The tree was damaged in a storm.
The tree got damaged in a storm.

(iii) The phone rang for ages but nobody answered it.
The phone rang for ages but it wasn't answered.

(iv)   He had his partner arrested.
He got his partner arrested.

a Are any of these sentences incorrect or inappropriate?

b What similarities or differences in meaning and effect are there between sentences in the group?

Learners' English (see p. 487)

Read the text written by a learner of English on page 295.

a Re-write it in order to make it more natural. Use passive constructions as appropriate.

b How important is using passive constructions as a factor in making the text more natural?

Language in context

1 (see pp. 488–489)

Read the three texts which follow. The first is part of a written introduction to a TV programme *(Walk on the Wild Side)* which concerns attacks on young people and how they are affected by these attacks. The second is part of a report which describes some research into how animal metaphors are used in different languages. The third is an extract from an official document which sets out university examination regulations. Answer the questions which follow.

(i)

Mick was attacked with a cut-throat razor. Kevin was slashed by someone who jumped through his front window. Steven had his face cut by a Stanley knife; Nick's attacker used a glass-cutter. All four victims bravely talk about their feelings and how their lives and attitudes were changed by the attacks.

(ii)

> Examples from the results of the second questionnaire are given in the Appendix. The results challenged the widely held view that animal metaphors are largely used to describe inferior or undesirable human habits and attributes . . . Although negative attributes were suggested more frequently than positive ones, many animal attributes were viewed in a very positive light, and it also appeared that many animal terms could be used, within the same culture and language group, to criticize or praise, according to context.

(iii)

> Every dissertation shall be typewritten, in English, with proper attention to style and presentation; it shall be sent through the candidate's Tutor to the Secretary of the Faculty Board, accompanied by a list of books and articles used in its preparation, and in accordance with detailed arrangements approved by the Board, so as to arrive not later than the third day of the Full Easter Term in which the examination is to be held.

a For each of these passages give a general reason why so many passive constructions are used.

b Identify all the passive constructions in (i) and give precise reasons for their use.

c Which of these constructions is causative in form?

d Could an active construction be used in place of any of these without significantly changing the meaning or effect of the sentences?

e Could any of the auxiliary verbs used in these passive constructions be replaced by another auxiliary without significantly changing the meaning or effect of the sentences?

f This passage contains three instances of *by* and one of *with*. Could any of these prepositions be replaced with the other (e.g. using *by* instead of *with*) without significantly changing the meaning or effect of the sentences?

g Re-write (iii) as if you were speaking to someone informally. How many passive constructions do you use in the re-telling?

2 (see p. 489)

The following is part of a written introduction to a TV programme (*Inside Story*) which deals with domestic violence.

> Each year in the USA, <u>abusive partners beat over six million women and kill over 4,000/over six million women are beaten by their abusive partners and around 4,000 are killed</u> *(1)*. To deal with this hidden crime, <u>a unique and groundbreaking court was established/people established a unique and groundbreaking court</u> *(2)* in Miami, Florida. *Inside Story* travels to the Domestic Violence Court where the judges are determined to break this horrific cycle of violence. The court deals with wife beaters by sending them for treatment to reform their abusive behaviour. Since the court was set up, the number of victims prepared to prosecute has more than doubled, <u>and the judges are told by many women/many women tell the judges</u> *(3)* that their lives have <u>literally been saved/they have literally saved their lives</u> *(4)*.

a The parts of the text which are underlined provide alternative constructions. In each case choose which one is more appropriate and give reasons for your choice.

b Are the following constructions from the text passive?

'. . . judges *are determined* to break this horrific cycle . . .'

'. . . the number of victims *prepared* to prosecute has more than doubled . . .'

c Give reasons for your answers.

3 (see p. 490)

There are three passive constructions in the following sentences.

   (i)   She's been a bit nervous ever since we got burgled.

   (ii)   Once you've got your modem installed, you'll need to open an account with an Internet service provider. . . . Most Internet companies will provide you with full instructions on how to get connected.

a Identify these and classify them as either 'standard' or 'causative'.

b In each case, why do you think the speaker or writer chose *get* as the auxiliary verb?

22 Discourse markers

firstly   in addition
however   on the other hand
right   anyway   you know
sadly   naturally

22.1 Key considerations

Noticing and understanding discourse markers helps learners to understand the logical structure of what they read and listen to, the order of events and the attitude of the speaker or writer to what they are describing.

Learners need to be clear that they can't always rely on discourse markers to signal logical relations, order of events and attitudes as we often rely on our readers or listeners to infer these from the context or from some shared or general knowledge.

Learning to use discourse markers helps them to show how the points they make relate to each other and to the overall argument or narrative in writing or speaking at length.

Our teaching materials and our learners' reasons for learning English (in particular whether spoken or written English is a priority; whether or not they need to use English in formal contexts) usually determines which discourse markers we teach. As with any item of vocabulary, how much we help them to appreciate subtleties of meaning (e.g. the difference between *however*, and *nonetheless*) and usage (e.g. where we can put them in a sentence) depends on their level of English and what other discourse markers they already know.

In teaching discourse markers we usually have to take into account:

- how frequently they are used (e.g. we use *however* more than *nonetheless*).
- how they are used in relation to particular kinds of text and context (e.g. we use expressions like *I'm afraid* primarily in speaking or in writing when we are personally involved with the topic and with our audience; we use a word like *hence* primarily in formal writing and speech).
- whether they can introduce or separate substantial 'blocks' of text (e.g. *however, furthermore*) or whether they tend to be used with shorter stretches (e.g. *as well*).

- whether they generally precede clauses (e.g. *so, thus*), occur within clauses (e.g. *also, therefore*) or whether they usually come at the end of clauses (e.g. *too*).

22.2 What are discourse markers?

What do they do?

We use discourse markers

- to 'signpost' logical relationships and sequence – to point out how bits of what we say and write relate to other bits ('textual discourse markers').
- to 'manage' conversation – to negotiate who speaks and when, to monitor and express involvement in the topic and the interaction ('conversation management discourse markers').
- to influence how our listeners or readers react ('preparatory discourse markers').
- to express our attitude to what we say and write ('attitude markers').

Although we can place many discourse markers within clauses, they usually refer to or comment on the whole clause – or even a whole sentence, paragraph or stretch of speech.

What do they look like?

A lot of discourse markers are single words, which can also be classified as adverbs, e.g. *anyway, finally, fortunately, furthermore, naturally, obviously, secondly.*

We also use a variety of phrases as discourse markers. These are often:

prepositional phrases:	*in fact; on the whole; on the contrary*
short finite clauses:	*what is more; I'm afraid*
adverbial phrases:	*all the same*

Terminology

There is no universally agreed way of classifying discourse markers; nor is there an exhaustive inventory of them. Inevitably, we have to over-simplify when we divide them into categories of meaning and use, and in reality the categories may overlap.

The term 'discourse marker' itself is also used in different ways. Most grammars and materials intended for teachers and learners, including this book, use it to cover a broad spectrum of kinds of words and expressions.

In some grammars, discourse markers are considered under the heading 'adjuncts'. Other grammars use 'discourse markers' to mean 'conversation management discourse markers' (e.g. *right, OK, you know*), and refer to words and expressions like *therefore, however,* and *of course* as 'linking signals'.

22.3 Types of discourse markers

Textual discourse markers

We use discourse markers to highlight a range of textual functions. Below we list the main functions and the markers we most frequently use to express these. See pages 314–316 for examples of many of these in context (bold print in the text below identifies markers that are exemplified).

Numbering and ordering points

We use a variety of words and expressions to number points we want to make.

General use:

> *First;* **firstly***; second (third; fourth etc.);* **secondly** *(thirdly; fourthly etc.); (and) finally; last; lastly*

Mainly used in speaking: > *First of all; in the first place; last of all*

We use numbering and ordering discourse markers in writing more than in speaking. This is because writing usually gives us more time to plan and monitor the number of points we are making. In both speaking and writing we often use a 'beginning' word or expression like *firstly* or *first* without then numbering the points which follow. Equally, we may use a word or expression like *lastly* or *last* when we haven't numbered any of the preceding points.

We also use discourse markers to show the order in which things happened.

> General use: *then; next*
> Mainly used in speaking: **afterwards**

Adding something

We use a variety of discourse markers to indicate that we are adding something to what we have already said or written.

General use:

> ***also***; *moreover; furthermore; further; moreover; **in addition**;*
> ***additionally; alternatively; instead***

Mainly used in speaking:

> ***besides***; ***too***; *what is more; **on top of this/that***

The most common discourse markers we use to show we are 'adding something' closely related to what has come before are *also* and *too*. We generally place *also* before the 'additional point', and *too* after it.

Other discourse markers have a similar function but are used in more formal contexts. We use *moreover, furthermore* and *in addition* to introduce the last of two or more substantial stretches of text. These markers often begin a new paragraph.

We sometimes choose the more emphatic discourse markers *what is more* and *on top of this* (*that*) when we are 'capping' what has been said before i.e. adding not just another point but adding the most telling point of all. We tend to use these expressions in speaking or when we want to lend a conversational feel to our writing.

Besides usually introduces information which adds weight to what we have already said or written, but which is a different kind of point. We often use *besides* when we are persuading, giving advice or arguing something.

We use *alternatively* or *instead* to mark that something is an alternative. We tend to place *instead* after the second of the two points, and often use it to reinforce the conjunction *or*.

Linking similar things together

Discourse markers can show that something is similar to what has gone before. They save us from having to repeat what we have said and written, e.g. **similarly**; equally; **likewise**.

Introducing something that contrasts with expectations

We use discourse markers to introduce information or points of view which contrast with

- what we have already said or written.
- what would normally be expected.

We use them to draw attention to (apparent) inconsistency. We often use them in conjunction with *but* (e.g. *but* actually; *but* nevertheless).

General use:

> ***however; in fact; on the other hand; rather; in contrast; on the contrary; still***

Mainly used in formal contexts: > ***nevertheless***; *nonetheless*; ***yet***

Mainly used in speaking:

> ***though; actually; all the same;*** *anyway; as a matter of fact; at the same time*

The discourse marker we use most frequently and generally to express a contrast is *however*. We tend to use *nevertheless, nonetheless* and *yet* in more formal contexts. They usually refer immediately back to what has been said or written before. We also use *though* to mark that something contrasts with what has gone before, usually at the end of the point we are making, and often use it in conjunction with *still*.

We use *actually, as a matter of fact* and *in fact* when we want to contrast what people may have imagined with the reality. We use *on the other hand* to introduce a contrasting opinion or point of view.

Learners sometimes use *rather, in contrast* and *on the contrary* as though they were the same as *however*, but generally they have a more specific function. We use *rather* and *in contrast* to explain or justify an alternative we have chosen.

On the contrary introduces something which is not so much unexpected as the opposite of what has gone before. *All the same* and *anyway* have several functions and can appear at the beginning or end of the information they refer to. Placed at the end of this information, they mark that this information contrasts with what precedes it and they suggest that an element of choice is involved.

Causes and results

Discourse markers can draw attention to the fact that something is caused by or naturally follows on from something else.

General use:	***so; then;***
Mainly used in formal contexts:	*consequently;* ***therefore; hence; thus***
Mainly used in speaking:	*as a result; in that case.*

The most common discourse marker we use to identify causes and results is *so*, and it is also the most general in meaning.

We tend to use *therefore* and *consequently* in more formal contexts. *Thus* is particularly formal and *hence* both more formal still, and also rarer.

We use *then* and *in that case* to introduce some kind of plan or intention based on the preceding information. This often marks a response to what someone else has said.

Generalising

We use discourse markers to make it clear that something is generally true.

General use:	***on the whole***; *in general; generally;*
Mainly used in speaking:	*by and large.*

Exemplifying and narrowing down

We use discourse markers to introduce examples and specific instances.

General use:	*notably; for example;* ***for instance***; *e.g.;*
Mainly used in speaking:	***say***.

Re-stating

We sometimes re-state or re-formulate what we, or others, say or write in order to make it clearer, and we use discourse markers to show that we are not actually expressing something new.

General use:	***in other words***; *in a sense;* ***that is***; *i.e.*
Mainly used in speaking:	*I mean*

We use *that is, i.e.* and *I mean* before the reformulation or restatement.

Rounding off

'Rounding off' a discussion is something we generally do in formal contexts (e.g. meetings). We use a variety of expressions to introduce this.

> *in summary; to summarize;* **in conclusion**; *to conclude; to sum up*

We often round off what we have said or written with a summary of the main points. We also focus on action arising from the discussion.

Conversation management discourse markers

There is almost no context in which we speak without monitoring the attention of our audience, and in some way directing this. Even in formal lectures and speeches we look at the audience and modify what we say according to their responses.

In conversation, we are constantly involved in a process of:

- negotiating which of us speaks and what we speak about.
- giving, asking for or responding to feedback on interest, understanding and reactions.

Much of this 'conversation management' takes place without words:

- We make a variety of noises (intakes of breath, sighs and sounds like *mmmm* or *ah*).
- We vary the speed and pitch at which we speak.
- We use eye contact, facial expressions and gesture.

We also use words and expressions in managing conversation.

> *actually; anyway; by the way; I mean; OK; now; right; so well; yes; you know; you see*

Problems with meaning

Learners face a range of problems in understanding and using these words and expressions:

- one word or expression can have several meanings (we sometimes rely on context to make a particular meaning clear, and sometimes say the word in a particular way e.g. we draw it out and/or use a particular intonation feature).
  OK can mean 'I accept your objection' or can introduce a change of topic or direction in a conversation.

- some 'meanings' can be expressed by more than one word or expression.
  We can use both *right* and *OK* to mean 'I accept your objection'.
- many words and expressions we use to manage conversation can have completely separate meanings and uses.
  Right can mean the opposite of *wrong* or *left*; *by the way* can describe a means, e.g. *I could tell he was ill <u>by the way</u> he was sweating.*
- there is regional, social and individual variation in the use of conversation management discourse markers.
  Now is used particularly by teachers to indicate moving onto a conclusion, and it can seem inappropriately didactic if someone uses this in this way in informal conversation.

Course materials often ignore conversation management discourse markers. Others teach them as fixed expressions with a definite function, e.g. We use *If I could just come in here* to start speaking in a conversation.

In fact, the function of conversation management discourse markers is always very dependent on context, and any generalisations we make about their meanings are inevitably inexact. Consequently, many teachers prefer to draw attention to them in context (*What does the speaker mean when she says <u>well</u> here?*) rather than teaching them actively.

Words and meaning

The following list describes some of the more common conversation management discourse markers and some of their more common uses. It is intended to help you to notice and analyse how these are used when you listen to people speaking; it is not a direct teaching tool as examples need to be studied in real contexts.

well
- to express reservation about what we or someone else has said.
- to show that we are considering what someone else has said.
- to indicate that we are thinking and don't want to be interrupted.
- to indicate that we are taking up the topic that is already under discussion.

OK
- to invite someone else to come into a conversation.
- to show that we are taking up an invitation to come into a conversation.
- to mark the end of a stage of discussion.
- to mark the beginning of a stage of discussion.

- to show that we accept an objection or reservation.
- to make a tentative gesture towards finishing a topic or conversation.

right
- to show that we understand or agree.
- to check that people understand or agree.
- to show that someone's assumptions are correct.
- invite someone else to come into a conversation.
- to show that we are taking up an invitation to come into a conversation or are claiming our turn.
- to mark the end of a stage of discussion.
- to mark the beginning of a stage of discussion.
- to show that we accept an objection or reservation.
- to make a tentative gesture towards finishing a topic or conversation.

you know
- to create an atmosphere of intimacy or solidarity.
- to suggest that the listener is already familiar with the topic or opinion.
- to invite people to confirm that they understand or are in agreement.
- to initiate conversation after a period of silence.

I mean
- to indicate a high degree of personal involvement in what we are talking about – to show that we are expressing personal opinions or feelings.
- to express indignation and invite a sympathetic response.
- to prevent someone from interrupting.

so
- to show that we are getting back to the main topic after a digression.
- to claim a pause before beginning a new topic.
- to indicate that what we are going to say is related to what we (or someone else has just said).

actually
- to show that we about to refute or disagree with something that has been said.
- to show that we are refuting or disagreeing with something that has just been said.
- to show that we are initiating a topic that is related to what we have been talking about.

anyway
- to show that we are getting back to the main topic after a digression.
- to introduce an opinion which is held despite reservations we have expressed or objections that have been made.
- to show that we want to end a conversation.

Preparatory discourse markers

Preparing for something unwelcome

We use discourse markers to alert people that we're about to tell them something they may not like, e.g. *I'm afraid; (I'm) sorry.*

We often use *I'm afraid* to soften what we are going to say, for example, when we tell people things that we think will be unwelcome, that we think will make them feel disappointed or angry.

> *I'm afraid I can't come round tonight after all.*
>
> *I'm afraid you'll have to take the examination all over again.*

We generally don't use *sorry* to express this 'softening' function.

We use *sorry* or *I'm sorry* when we are disagreeing with what someone has said or when we are criticising them.

> *Sorry, but I think your attitude is unacceptable.*

Learners sometimes misunderstand this, thinking that *sorry* always functions as a way of apologising.

We often use *but* after *sorry* (as in the example above), but never after *I'm afraid.*

Introducing strong points of view

As well as softening the effect of what we want to say, we also sometimes want to reinforce it. We can use *honestly* and *frankly* for this purpose. 'Gone with the Wind' illustrates this with one of the most famous lines in any film:

> **Frankly** *my dear, I don't give a damn.*

Attitude markers

There is an infinite number of words and expressions we can use to express our attitude towards or interpretation of what we are saying or writing.

> *naturally; of course; obviously; clearly; undoubtedly; preferably; (not) surprisingly; miraculously; predictably; (un)fortunately; thank God; as luck would have it; regrettably*

The following are all spoken examples except for the last, which is from a newspaper article:

> **Unfortunately** we didn't win.   He **obviously** hadn't had much sleep.
> **Surprisingly** no one claimed it.   Her story **regrettably** failed to
> convince us.   You can **of course** pay at another time.

> Small companies depend on overdrafts and there is little risk capital on
> offer. **Sadly** there is no sign of change and four out of five small businesses
> which start up fail within five years.

22.4 Sentence position

Textual and attitude discourse markers

We can place most textual and attitude discourse markers in a variety of positions.

> **Moreover**, I wanted to speak to him before he left.
>
> I wanted **moreover** to speak to him before he left.
>
> I wanted to speak to him **moreover** before he left.
>
> I wanted to speak to him before he left **moreover**.
>
> I **moreover** wanted to speak to him before he left.
>
> **Surprisingly**, the car started.
>
> The car **surprisingly** started.
>
> The car started **surprisingly**.

We can point out the sentence position of discourse markers in texts that learners read, so that they realise that this is flexible, and we can explore why writers choose one position rather than another. However, some markers can't be used in such a wide range of sentence positions, and the safest rule of thumb to give learners is to put most textual and attitude discourse markers before the point they introduce (e.g. *Moreover, I wanted to speak to him before he left; Surprisingly, the car started*).

We need to point out exceptional cases (e.g. *anyway, instead, too, though*) which generally come after the information they refer to.

Conversation management discourse markers

We can divide conversation management discourse markers into those that invariably come before the clause they refer to, and those which may also come at the end. This is a useful rule of thumb, but analysis of real conversation may reveal examples that contradict this:

Markers which usually come before or at the beginning of what they refer to:

> **OK** *Let's get going.*   **Right**. *Who's ready?*   **So** *where were you born?*
> **Well**, *I'm waiting for an answer*   **I mean**, *I agree with you.*

Markers which may come before or after what they refer to:

> **Actually**, *he agreed.*   *I'll go there* **anyway**.   **You know**, *something*
> *worries me.*   *I've done this before* **you know**.

Preparatory discourse markers

As the name suggests, preparatory discourse markers generally come at the beginning of what they refer to.

> **Sorry**. *You promised me you'd be here.*   **Frankly** *we're not interested.*

22.5 Punctuation

In practice, whether we use commas with most discourse markers depends both on individual preference and, in any instance, on how integrated we feel the marker is into its surrounding context. Probably it is more helpful for us regularly to draw our students' attention to whether or not commas are used with discourse markers in texts that they read, and to encourage them to read aloud what they write (*is there a pause?*) than to give them rules or even rules of thumb.

We don't use commas after *I'm afraid* and *Thank God*.

22.6 Typical difficulties for learners

Comprehension

Discourse markers sometimes underline logical relations or attitudes that are already apparent in the conversation or text, in which case misunderstanding them or failing to notice them is not a significant problem. However, we also sometimes use discourse markers in order to make these things clear. In this case it may be crucial that we notice and understand them.

Misunderstanding may also occur because learners are mistaken about the meanings of certain discourse markers. For example, they may associate *sorry* with apologising, and they may misinterpret people using *sorry* to disagree or criticise.

Speaking and writing

Meaning

Precise distinctions in meaning between discourse markers are often extremely subtle, and learners usually build up an awareness of these only as a result of exposure to the items and noticing how they are used over a considerable period of time. In the meantime, they may use them in ways which are misleading or stylistically awkward. The easiest way to identify problems of this nature is often by analysing written composition. For example, in the following, the learner has used *besides* as though it merely introduces additional information (like *moreover*), whereas, in fact, we generally use it to introduce additional arguments:

> The itinerary looks very interesting. We are going to visit six cities in seven days and, besides, we will have guided tours of the most important sights.

This learner has used *on the contrary* as though it reinforces the meaning of *but*, whereas we generally use it to introduce something which is the opposite of what has gone before:

> People told me to avoid going into the docks areas late at night but on the contrary I am big and I can run fast so I thought I would be safe there.

In spoken English, it is often more difficult to put our finger on the cause of awkwardness in using discourse markers. Very advanced learners, for example, sometimes use *by the way* to introduce new topics into discussion when *you know* would be more appropriate (we generally use *by the way* to introduce topics we have been thinking about or have previously discussed, *you know* for sudden thoughts, recollections and realisations). We often find it difficult to give useful instant feedback to learners when they make mistakes of this kind.

Style

Learners may understand the meaning of a discourse marker, without realising that it tends to be used only in particular contexts. It sounds very odd when someone consistently uses discourse markers where a simple conjunction (e.g. *and* or *but*) would do as well. Equally, some of the more colloquial expressions can seem out of place in formal (e.g. academic) prose, and some of the more formal markers will seem out of place in casual conversation.

> The outbreak of war was due to three main factors. Firstly there was a long history of tribal tension which the removal of strong, central power unleashed. Then, there was deep dissatisfaction among military personnel, many of whom had not been paid for over a year. *To top it all*, the sacking of the entire cabinet was more than anyone could bear.

To top it all is inappropriate in this formal context.

> The whole office was in a bloody mess again last night. *Thus* I had to stay behind and clear everything up.

Thus is inappropriate in this informal context.

Word order

While the position of many discourse markers is very flexible, the position of others is more restricted. Learners may use these in inappropriate positions.

* * I anyway wanted to speak to him before he left.
* * I by the way wanted to speak to him before he left.

Form

Learners may forget the precise words and form of words in phrases.

* * Thanks God I had backed up all the important files.
* * I'm afraid but I have had enough.

22.7 Consolidation exercises
(see pp. 490–491 for possible answers)

Language in context

1 (see p. 490)

The following sentences are all extracted from a transcript of teachers discussing their students and deciding which class they should go into after the holiday. Define the function of each of the discourse markers printed in italics.

It's not his best composition but I think we should display it *anyway*. *(1)*

She makes a lot of mistakes when she speaks. *Anyway*, her writing has been considerably better this term. *(2)*

She's a bit tearful today. I *mean* she's had some bad news from home. . . . *(3)*

Hmm. Yeah, I *mean*, I don't, I don't think we should necessarily put her into a lower class . . . *(4)*

A: She's working as a consultant now . . .
B: *Right*. *(5)*
A: . . . she's been doing it for a couple of months.

A: I think she should pass.
B: *Right*. Convince us. *(6)*
A: *Right*. She expresses herself as well as any of the other students. *(7)*

A: I don't think we need to say more about Maria.
B: *OK*. Carlos. Now, what I want to discuss about Carlos . . . *(8)*

A: My feeling is that she would be better in a slower group.
B: *OK*. I think she maybe feels a bit intimidated. *(9)*

---

2 (see p. 491)

The passage which follows compares how words are stressed in Spanish and English.

> Spanish is a syllable-timed language. In general, all syllables take about the same length of time to pronounce (though extra length may be used for emphasis); to an English ear, there is therefore not a great difference in prominence between stressed and unstressed syllables. In English, on the other hand, stressed syllables tend to be pronounced more slowly and distinctly, while unstressed syllables are reduced and often pronounced with a neutral vowel /ə/ or /ɪ/. Since content words (nouns, verbs, adjectives and adverbs) are stressed in English, they are therefore relatively prominent as compared with the unstressed grammatical words (articles, pronouns, prepositions, auxiliary verbs). So the stress and rhythm of an English sentence give a lot of clues to structure and meaning. When Spanish speakers pronounce English sentences with even stress and rhythm, the clues are missing, and English listeners find them difficult to understand because they cannot so easily decode the structure. (For example, in *Ann is older than Joe*, *is* and *than* may be as prominent as *old*.)

a Identify the discourse markers.

b What functions are they performing?

3 (see p. 491)

The text which follows looks at how private schools should fix course prices. Discourse markers have been removed from the text and are found in the box below.

> In advocating market-related pricing the point is correctly made that costs give you the bottom line only. They should NOT . . . *(1)* be used alone in determining prices. The market is a far more powerful instrument in deciding selling prices than the costs of production.
>
> . . . *(2)*, it is argued that schools should offer something unique which the competition cannot match.
>
> . . . *(3)*, schools ought to try to develop unique selling propositions (USPs) which the competition cannot offer, and then price them according to what the market will bear. This often implies selling at a higher price and if such USPs can be maintained and are viewed as valuable *by the customer*, then premium pricing should apply.
>
> . . . *(4)*, in practice it is difficult for schools to offer something quite unique. . . . *(5)* , their costs are likely to be heavily dependent on staffing quality and levels. . . . *(6)*, once an edge is achieved the competition will be swift to move on price.

| further | therefore | however | similarly | moreover | naturally |

a From the box, choose the discourse marker that you think is most appropriate for each of the gaps.

b What factors did you have to consider in making your choices? How sure were you about the general meaning the missing item should express?

c Look at page 491 and check your answers. What has this exercise taught you about the amount of information contained in discourse markers of this type?

23 Ellipsis and substitution

Yes.   Maybe.
[ ] Don't know.   [ ] Good one.
The train [ ] delayed by faulty
signals.

23.1 Key considerations

The biggest problem that ellipsis and substitution pose for learners is often one of comprehension. Because they may expect information to be more explicitly stated than it is, they may be confused when it is left out (ellipsis) or when a short grammatical word (e.g. *one, do*) is used in its place (substitution).

In their own speaking and writing learners may avoid ellipsis and substitution, using more repetition than is necessary. This usually doesn't lead to misunderstanding, but it can make the increased effort involved in listening or reading tedious, and can give an impression of excessive formality, particularly in speaking.

From the earliest stages of their studies we need to draw learners' attention to where ellipsis and substitution occur in materials we use, gradually encouraging them to incorporate these features into their own writing and speaking.

We usually also teach some of these features explicitly, for example when we teach 'short answers' to questions (e.g. *Yes, I have*) or phrases like *So do I* and *Neither can Bob*.

Although ellipsis and substitution occur in all languages, the kinds of words we can leave out and use as 'substitutes' varies from language to language.

Throughout this chapter square brackets ('[. . .]') are used to show the information which has been left out in examples of ellipsis.

23.2 Ellipsis

What is ellipsis?

In speaking and writing we generally try to provide only as much information as is necessary to convey what we want to express, and this involves leaving out words and phrases that we think form part of the complete grammatical unit. This 'leaving out' of words and phrases is 'ellipsis'. We can divide ellipsis into two distinct kinds: 'situational' and 'textual.'

Situational ellipsis

Situational ellipsis occurs mainly in speaking. In the example which follows, the pronoun *I* is left out. This is an example of situational ellipsis because only the context makes it clear what is missing:

A: *What time is it?* B: *Don't know.* ([I] Don't know.)

The clearest and simplest examples of situational ellipsis are found in the answers to questions, where one word (or a few words) stands for a whole phrase.

A: *Could you help me?* B: *Possibly.* ([I could] possibly [help you].)

A: *When are you coming back?* B: *Tuesday.* ([We are coming back on] Tuesday.)

In informal conversation we often leave out grammatical words such as articles, pronouns, prepositions, auxiliary verbs and forms of the verb *be* used as a complement verb. We leave these out at the beginning of sentences in particular.

A: *You OK now?*	[Are] You OK now?
B: *Can't grumble. Better than this time last year.*	[I] Can't grumble. [I'm] Better [I was] than this time last year.
A: *Your leg?*	[Was the problem] Your leg?
B: *Stuck here with my leg. Missed all the parties, Christmas parties.*	[I was] Stuck here with my leg. [I] Missed all the parties, [that is, the] Christmas parties.

The more informal the conversation and the more we refer to the immediate environment in which the conversation is taking place, the more use we make of situational ellipsis.

Dialogue in novels provides plenty of examples.

'Pity you had to dash off last night, Trev,' said Al. '. . . . Good thing Mrs Swinburne came along.'

Textual ellipsis

Textual ellipsis occurs in both speaking and writing. Words are missed out in grammatically predictable sentence positions.

After *and* and *but*

Textual ellipsis occurs most frequently after *and* and *but*, when we leave out subjects, verbs, articles and nouns if these are already specified in the previous clause.

You ought to clean your teeth and brush your hair.	(You ought to clean your teeth and [you ought to] brush your hair.)
Nick wanted a strawberry ice cream and Chris a chocolate.	(Nick wanted a strawberry ice cream and Chris [wanted] a chocolate [ice cream].)
I ordered a dozen crates but they only brought ten.	(I ordered a dozen crates but they only brought ten [crates].)

Adverbial and relative clauses

We sometimes leave out the subject and a form of the verb *be* as an auxiliary verb after conjunctions such as *when, while, after* and *before* in adverbial clauses.

> *When matching colours, you should take both items out of the shop and compare them in natural light.* (When [you are] matching colours . . .)

In defining relative clauses we sometimes leave out the relative pronoun and, again, a form of the verb *be* as an auxiliary.

> *The police are interviewing a man seen just after the robbery.* (. . . a man [who was] seen . . .)

We usually refer to these forms as 'reduced' forms of adverbial and relative clauses respectively. Although grammars don't always consider them as examples of ellipsis, for teaching it is useful to do so. Unlike situational ellipsis, which tends to make language use more informal, these are mainly a feature of formal, written English and can seem stilted in informal conversation.

This kind of reduction is briefly considered again on page 337 and page 291, and more extensively in Chapter 24 and Chapter 26.

23.3 Substitution

What is substitution?

Substitution goes hand in hand with ellipsis – substitution refers to the words we use (e.g. *so, one, do, did*) as signals indicating that something has been left out and identifying what kind of information this is.

yes *and* no

The clearest and simplest instances of substitution are the words *yes* and *no*, both of which can stand in for long sentences or sequences of sentences.

> A: *Have you ever thought of trying to get a job abroad?*
>
> B: *No.* ([I have never thought of trying to get a job abroad.])

Not all languages have equivalents to *yes* and *no*, or use them in equivalent contexts.

Replacing adverbials of place and time

We use words and expressions like *here, there* and *over there* to replace precise details of place, and words and expressions like *then* and *at that time* to replace details of time.

> *She invited me to her house but I wouldn't go **there** if you paid me.* (i.e. . . . go to her house.)
>
> *She invited me round last night but I just couldn't spare the time **then**.* (i.e. . . . spare the time last night.)

Replacing longer stretches of text

We use *this* and *that* to refer to ideas or information expressed over several clauses or which can't be precisely related to a specific part of the sentence.

> *We've had a few unexpected problems. **This**/**that** is why I've called another meeting.*

When we point to or indicate real objects (*This is where I live*), we use *this* for things near to us and *that* for things further away. When we use *this* and *that* as substitute forms, they are often interchangeable, but we may also choose:

- *this* for new, key information: ***This** is what I really want to achieve.*
- *this* to show sympathy or 'ownership' towards something: ***This** is all I can suggest.*
- *that* to disassociate ourselves from something: ***That's** rubbish.*

23.4 Ellipsis and substitution combined

Ellipsis and substitution are closely related, and in this section we look at cases where it makes sense to consider them together rather than separately.

Replacing predicates

A predicate is everything in a clause that follows the subject.

Subject	Predicate
The cat	*sat on the mat.*
A stitch in time	*saves nine.*
He	*laughed.*

We use auxiliary verbs (including modal verbs), combinations of auxiliary verbs and forms of the verb *be* to replace predicates.

When we replace a predicate with a modal verb or 'tense' auxiliary verb we don't add anything extra to indicate what is missing.

> *She'd like to take a few days off work but just **can't**.* (. . . can't [take a few days off work])
>
> *She walked all the way here in the snow but she really **shouldn't have**.* (. . . shouldn't have [walked all the way here in the snow])

Where more than one auxiliary verb is involved we can sometimes choose how many of them to use in replacing the predicate.

> A: *Have you been drinking?* B: *No, I **haven't**/I **haven't been**.*

However, if we replace a predicate including a verb in the present or past simple tense we use *do*, *does* or *did*. Since this involves adding an extra word, it is an example of substitution.

> *Sue didn't notice anything unusual but everyone else **did**.* [notice something unusual.]

Replacing infinitive clauses, that *noun clauses and noun clauses derived from questions*

We use *to* or *not to* to replace infinitive clauses, *so* or *not* to replace *that* noun clauses after *think* and *hope*, and the question word itself to replace noun clauses derived from questions.

> *I invited them all to come but they didn't want **to**.* [come].
>
> *Why did you give me a present when I told you **not to*** [give me a present]?
>
> A: *Is she coming round?*
> B: *I think **so**/I don't think **so**/I hope **not**.* (I think/hope [that she is(n't) coming round].)
>
> *They said they'd ring but I've no idea **when*** [they'll ring].

This use of *to*, *not*, *not to* and question words are instances of ellipsis. The use of *so*, however, is an example of substitution.

Using pronouns and possessive adjectives to replace nouns and noun phrases

We use pronouns and possessive adjectives to avoid specifying or repeating information that is already clear. Grammars don't always consider the use of pronouns as an example of substitution, but it is very closely related.

Subject pronouns:	*I, you, he, she, it, we, they*
Object pronouns:	*me, you, him, her, it, us, them, one, ones*
Possessive adjectives:	*my, your, his, her, its, our, their*
Possessive pronouns:	*mine, yours, his, hers, its, ours, theirs*

The old man said *he* (**1**) was going to take *his* (**2**) cat to the vet and ask *her* (**3**) if *she* (**4**) could look after *him* (**5**) while *he* (**6**) was in hospital, but then *he* (**7**) asked *me* (**8**) if *you* (**9**) could possibly look after *it* (**10**) with *yours* (**11**).

1, 6, 7	[the old man]	5, 10	[the old man's cat]
2	[the old man's]	8	[Martin]
3, 4	[the vet]	9	[Kirsty]
		11	[Kirsty's cat]

Learners are sometimes unsure about the difference between the following:

one	(indefinite, singular)
ones	(indefinite, plural)
it	(definite, uncountable and singular)
them	(definite, plural)

Examples

*Is this key the right **one**?*

*I don't like all your paintings but the last **ones** you did were brilliant.*

*He offered me some information but I didn't want **it**.*

*We considered renting mopeds but we were a bit frightened of **them**.*

We also make *this*, *that* (see p. 321) *these*, *those* and quantifiers (see Chapter 5) into pronouns. For example:

a few,   a little,   much,   many,   a lot,   any.

*He offered me some cake but I didn't want **any*** (i.e. any [cake])

*Haven't you got any money? I thought you had **plenty**.* (i.e. plenty [of money])

We may want to draw our learners' attention to examples of all these pronouns and possessive adjectives whenever they occur in texts that they are reading.

Expressing similarity, agreement, and disagreement

We use *so* to express similarity with an affirmative statement, and *neither* or *nor* to express similarity with a negative statement. In this case we use *So/Neither/Nor* followed by an auxiliary verb or a form of *be* as a complement verb and then the subject of the new sentence.

A: *My brother can stand on his head.* B: ***So** can the Prime Minister.* (The Prime Minister can also [stand on his head])

A: *I'm staying in.* B: ***So** am I.* (I am also [staying in])

A: *I'm not staying in.* B: ***Neither/nor** am I.* (I am also not [staying in])

When we express similarity with something stated in the simple present or simple past tense we need to use *do/does* or *did*.

A: *I like Abba.* B: ***So does** Sheila.* (Sheila also [likes Abba])

A: *I got caught up in the traffic.* B: ***So did** I.* (I also [got caught up in the traffic])

Comparative structures

We often leave information out in comparative structures.

Paris is big but London is bigger [than Paris].

We also use pronouns to avoid repeating actions.

*I can run faster than **them**.* (. . . than [they can run].)

See also page 323.

Referring forward

We usually leave out information that has already been mentioned or implied in a text. However, we also sometimes leave something out and refer to it later. This happens particularly when we use a subordinate clause before a main clause.

*When you want **one**, help yourself to a cake.* (. . . want [a cake])

*If you need **to**, you can always use our bathroom.* (. . . need [to use a bathroom])

324

23.5 Typical difficulties for learners

Comprehension

Learners often have considerable problems in understanding language that contains a lot of ellipsis and substitution. This is particularly the case with listening (in reading we can 'go back' and try to sort out the causes of any misunderstanding), and these features are especially problematic for learners who don't already know a European language.

We can help our students by exposing them to language in which ellipsis and substitution take place and by guiding them to recognise and understand these features so that they have realistic and informed expectations about authentic language use (e.g. by asking them *What information is missing? What does this word refer to?* and encouraging them to explore and discuss the text to find the answers).

The texts on pages 326–330 provide a further example of some of the difficulties learners of English may face with understanding ellipsis and substitution.

Speaking and writing

Avoidance

We choose what to leave out and what to substitute according to our assessment of how much our readers or the people we are talking to already know. Learners tend to be very cautious about this, and may provide more information than is necessary. We may choose not to discourage this caution with learners who have difficulty in expressing themselves, but we need to recognise this over-explicitness, and at some point we will want to encourage them to leave more out and to make greater use of substitute forms.

23.6 Consolidation exercises (see pp. 492–495 for possible answers)

Language in context

1 (see p. 492)

The greater the intimacy between participants in conversation and correspondence, and the greater the mutual familiarity with the topic, the greater the scope for ellipsis. The following interaction assumes a large amount of common knowledge.

A: Drink?
B: Lager.
A: Pint?
B: Half.
C: My round.
A: About time.
B: Pint in that case.

a Identify the context.

b Re-write the conversation so that there is less ellipsis and the whole conversation would be more easily understood by an outsider.

2 (see p. 492)

The following conversation took place between two colleagues who had had an argument the last time they met. It has been re-written to include more words than is strictly necessary. Re-write it omitting any unnecessary words so that it is more 'conversational':

A: I didn't see you yesterday.
B: You probably didn't want to see me yesterday.
A: I looked for you everywhere.
B: You didn't look for me hard enough.

3 (see pp. 492–493)

The following is from a crime novel. An unsavoury character named Gillespie is speaking to his late wife's solicitor (Mr Duggan). Gillespie claims that his late wife (Mathilda) not only robbed him but boasted of doing so in her diaries. Look at how the author has used situational ellipsis in the dialogue.

'Read her diaries,' he growled. 'They'll prove she stole them off me. Couldn't resist boasting to herself, that was Mathilda's trouble. Put every damn thing on those miserable pages, then read them over and over again to remind herself how clever she was. Wouldn't have left out a triumph like this. Read the diaries!

The younger man kept his face deliberately impassive. 'I will. As a matter of interest, do you know where she kept them? It'll save me the trouble of looking for them.'

'Top shelf of the library. Disguised as the works of Willy Shakespeare! He took a card from his wallet. 'You're a solicitor, Mr Duggan, so I'm trusting you to be honest. That's where I'm staying. Expect to hear from you on this in a couple of days or so. Grateful if you'd treat it as a matter of urgency.'

a Identify instances of situational ellipsis.

b In this context, how does this situational ellipsis contribute to the characterisation of the two participants in the conversation?

4 (see p. 493)

In the following extracts, examples of ellipsis and substitution have been singled out. In each case explain and specify what information is left out or implied.

(i) This extract is from an article written by a film critic:

Here's a useful rule of thumb: never trust those *(1)* – usually comedians, entertainers and the like – who say, "I love people." And here's another *(2)*: never trust film critics who say. "I love movies."

. . .

What keeps a film critic going and enjoying his job is optimism. Each film, you fervently hope, will be the one *(3)* that makes up for all the dross you saw last week.

Usually it isn't. *(4)*

(ii) A character in a novel pretended to like the river that her father was passionate about in order to try to win his love:

She yearned for his love and approbation. She had listened dutifully, *(5)* asked the right questions, *(6)* had instinctively known that this was an interest he assumed that she would share. But she realized now that the deception had only added guilt to her natural reserve and timidity, *(7)* that the river had become the more terrifying because she could acknowledge its terrors and her relationship with her father *(8)* more distant because it *(9)* was founded on a lie.

(iii) A sport psychologist is quoted in an article about addiction to exercise:

"We're all under a tremendous amount of pressure, from the media and from everyone around us, to fit in with our society's idea of the body beautiful. Unfortunately for many people the only way they can possibly achieve this ideal is through sustained and rigorous exercise."

This *(10)* is especially true for those who live their lives in the public eye . . .

5 (see pp. 493–494)

In the following extracts, the examples of ellipsis and substitution have *not* been identified. Answer the questions about each extract.

(i) On the tables of a café:

Every member of our Food Services Team shares one common aim – to ensure that your visit here today is an enjoyable one.

(ii) From an article about the effect of music:

> After a study that showed that fast music led to shoppers moving around a supermarket more quickly than did slow music, a follow-up showed that fast music caused diners to eat more quickly.
>
> Another study showed a similar effect with fast music in a bar – drinking was quicker than it was to slow music. In a cafeteria, diners took more bites per minute than they did to slow.
>
> Playing classical music and a selection from the Top 40 in a wine cellar revealed that people buy more expensive bottles to classical, while sad music in a stationery shop led to a bigger purchase of greetings cards.
>
> Sad music also led to people being more helpful than did other types.

(iii) From an interview with ten- and eleven-year-old children:
Usually I forget some capital letters and punctuation, but this time I knew it really mattered and I mustn't, and didn't.

(iv) This is from a book which describes the author's travels in Britain. 'Close' refers to the houses which surround a cathedral.

> I would probably forgive Salisbury anything as long as they never mess with the Cathedral Close. There is no doubt in my mind that Salisbury Cathedral is the single most beautiful structure in England and the close around it the most beautiful space.

(v) From an article about the problem of providing a meal for both children and adults:

> There are three ways of dealing with the problem. One is to find a bland menu that children eat happily and grown-ups grudgingly. The second is to cook whatever you feel like eating and let the children fend for themselves.

a Identify examples of ellipsis and substitution (ignore personal pronouns like *I* and *they*, but include the use of impersonal pronouns like *one* and *it*).

b Classify the example (e.g. situational ellipsis; substitution of a *that* clause with *so*).

    c Explain and specify what information is left out or implied.

Analysing course materials (see p. 495)

The following is part of a text from an elementary level coursebook, where it is used as a source of examples of future tenses and prepositions of time. It includes several examples of ellipsis and substitution.

(Janet and Bill are talking on Monday April 19th, at nine o'clock in the morning)

JANET:	Is everything all right?
BILL:	Yes, I think so. I'm picking up the visas on Wednesday morning and the tickets in the afternoon, and I'm getting the traveller's cheques from the bank tomorrow.
JANET:	Oh, good. Don't forget that the children are going to stay with Mother on the 22nd – you're driving them.
BILL:	Oh, yes. How long for?
JANET:	Just for two days. Back on Friday night.
BILL:	That isn't long.
JANET:	Darling – you know it's John's birthday on the 24th.
BILL:	So it is. We must have him home for his birthday. What are we giving him?
JANET:	A bike.
BILL:	Oh yes, that's right. When are you going to do the packing?
JANET:	At the weekend, at the last possible moment. You're going to help, I hope.
BILL:	Oh yes. Yes, of course.

    a Identify the following features:

        (i)   – substitution of a *that* noun clause

        (ii)   – ellipsis of subject and verb phrase in a co-ordinated clause

        (iii) – situational ellipsis of another subject and verb phrase

        (iv) – a question which includes ellipsis of an entire clause

        (v)   – an expression which confirms information and includes substitution of a whole clause

    b What pronouns are used to substitute *the children* and *John*?

    c The word *that* occurs twice in the text. What does it stand for in each case?

    d If you were using this text with an elementary class, would you draw your students' attention to any of these features? Which ones? (Give reasons for your answers).

PART D

Complex sentences

Introduction to Part D

Complex sentences generally cause particular problems for learners whose first language is not closely related to English, and these problems relate to comprehension as well as production. Teaching materials often neglect these problems.

Main and subordinate clauses

Complex sentences are those which contain one or more subordinate clauses.

A main clause is a group of words that can stand on its own. It usually contains at least a subject and a verb.

A subordinate clause is a particular kind of group of words that we attach in some way to a main clause. In the previous three sentences:

- these are main clauses:

  A main clause is a group of words

  It usually contains at least a subject and a verb.

  A subordinate clause is a particular kind of group of words

- these are subordinate clauses:

  that can stand on its own.

  that we attach in some way to a main clause.

Types of subordinate clause

Chapters 24–27 look at types of subordinate clause in isolation from each other. In reality, not only do clauses of different types frequently occur together, but it is often only because they are in combination that difficulties for learners arise.

Chapter 28 looks at the defining/non-defining distinction that can apply to a range of clause types.

Chapter 29 looks at examples where different types of clause are integrated. The Consolidation Exercises for Chapter 29 thus also consolidate the content of Chapters 24–28.

We consider clause types under the following headings:

Heading	Examples	Chapter
Finite adverbial clauses	*They left when we arrived.* *While I agree with you, many people don't.*	24
Noun clauses	*I believe (that) he's coming tomorrow.* *I don't know whether/why he's coming.*	25
Relative clauses	*They gave me a book, which I read in one sitting.* *They gave me a book (that) they found in a second-hand shop.*	26
Non-finite clauses	*They found an old man walking around in the dark.* *They found the solution without even thinking about it.*	27
Defining clauses	*Mary's the girl (who's) talking to the old woman.*	28
Non-defining clauses	*I found the solution, which made me feel much happier.*	

24 Finite adverbial clauses

as I said   as long as you need it
when the time is right
since you're here
in order that no one is disappointed
despite the fact that you came

24.1 Key considerations

Learners often find it more helpful to learn the meaning of particular (subordinating) conjunctions and to practise using them appropriately than to think explicitly in terms of adverbial clauses.

Although we may choose not to use the terms *coordinating* and *subordinating* when we teach, learners need to understand that some conjunctions have a coordinating function (see p. 262) and that others are subordinating conjunctions. Equally, they need to understand the difference between coordinated and subordinate clauses.

Learners need to know which subordinating conjunctions allow the adverbial clause (e.g. *so that – I wanted to make everything **so that** it would last*), to come before the main clause (e.g. *when* – not only *I came **when** you called* but also ***When** you called, I came*).

Learners often find it easy to carry out exercises in which they have to insert an appropriate conjunction, and they may find it easy to carry out exercises where they combine two sentences into one consisting of a main clause and a subordinate adverbial clause. They may still need a lot of encouragement, however, to use subordinating conjunctions when they speak or (more especially) write at greater length and more freely.

24.2 What are adverbial clauses?

What do they do?

Adverbial clauses are a category of subordinate clauses. They are linked to a main clause and tell us something about the information in that main clause. In this respect they are similar to adverbials

main clause	adverbial
I bought the tickets	*with some reservations.*

main clause	adverbial clause
I bought the tickets	*even though they cost more than I wanted to pay.*

What do they look like?

Adverbial clauses start with a conjunction such as *when, although* or *in order that.* These are known as subordinating conjunctions because (unlike *and, but* and *or*) they link two clauses of unequal importance. Some subordinating conjunctions consist of one word, e.g.

> *after although as before if once since though when whereas while*

and others of two or more words, e.g.

> *as if as soon as as long as in that in order that so that such that*

We usually teach *even though* as a two-word conjunction, but we can combine *even* with other conjunctions too (*even if; even when*), and we can also use *just* with a number of conjunctions (*just as; just as soon as; just when*).

24.3 Other factors

Meaning

The general meanings expressed by subordinating conjunctions (and therefore by the adverbial clauses themselves) include: time, place, manner, reason, contrast, condition, purpose and result.

See pages 336–337 for more detail about the meanings of subordinating conjunctions.

The order of clauses

Many conjunctions allow us to reverse the order of the main clause and the adverbial clause. We generally put the clause which contains any information we can take for granted first. The clause which contains the new or more important information generally comes second.

> *Even though they cost more than I wanted to pay, I bought the tickets.*
> *I bought the tickets even though they cost more than I wanted to pay.*

Other conjunctions normally only come after the main clause. These include *where, as if, as though, so that, in order that.*

> *He wanted to stay where he had always lived.* NOT * *Where he had always lived he wanted to stay.*

> *We staggered home **as if** we were drunk.* NOT * ***As if** we were drunk we staggered home.*

Punctuation

When the subordinate clause comes before the main clause, it is usually separated from the main clause by a comma.

> ***Although it's very late**, I still want to go home.*

Tense and time conjunctions

After time conjunctions we use present tenses to refer to the future.

> *I'll call you **as soon as** he arrives.*

> ***Before** you come in, please take off your shoes.*

When we refer to events in the past, the precise information contained in the conjunction itself can also affect the tenses used. For example, *after* and *before* contain precise information about the sequence of events and so we don't need to rely on the tenses to provide this information. We can use the simple past tense in both clauses.

> *Your daughter left **before** you woke up.*

When doesn't indicate the order in which things happened so we often need to use the past perfect in order to show that something happened before something else.

> *Your daughter had left **when** you woke up.*

Two-part conjunctions

In English we usually use only one conjunction to link two clauses – for example, it is necessary to remove *since* or *so* from the following sentence:

> ** Since the weather had turned extremely cold so we decided not to go out.*

However, the following conjunctions are exceptions to this: *not only . . . but (also); so/such . . . that; either . . . or.*

> *He **not only** brought the Christmas tree and all the decorations, **but** he **also** brought a pile of presents for the children.*

> *The players were **so** excited **that** they ran round the field hugging each other.*

> *They had **such** a stressful day **that** they turned on the TV as soon as they got home and watched rubbish all night.*

> *You can **either** bring the report round tonight **or** I'll pick it up tomorrow.*

We sometimes use *then* after *if* to emphasise the conditional meaning, e.g.

> **If** *I'd seen the red lights,* **then** *I would've stopped, wouldn't I?*

'Reduced' adverbial clauses

We leave the subject and the verb *be* (e.g. *are; was; have been*) out of adverbial clauses when the subject is the same as the subject of the main clause.

This results in 'reduced clauses' (see also p. 320), which are also examples of non-finite clauses (see p. 363).

Present participle clause:

> *I happened to catch your radio programme* **while** [ ] **driving home.**
> (. . . while [*I was*] driving home)

Past participle clause:

> **Even though** [ ] **badly damaged in places**, *the chest fetched £3,500 at auction.* (Even though [*it had been*] badly damaged . . .)

Verbless clause:

> **Once** [ ] **finally under way**, *the ship quickly made up for lost time.* (Once [*it was*] finally under way . . .)

24.4 Typical difficulties for learners

Comprehension

Learners sometimes fail to recognise subordinating conjunctions and/or the relationships that they express (e.g. contrast, reason, purpose), particularly when they are listening to English. Their problems may be partly due to unconscious (and mistaken) expectations about:

- the order of clauses (e.g. they may 'expect' subordinate clauses always to follow main clauses).
- the position of conjunctions (e.g. they may 'expect' the conjunction to separate the two clauses or to introduce the main clause).
- pronunciation (e.g. they may 'expect' conjunctions to be pronounced more clearly, and may fail to hear weakened forms such as /ə/ in /əsuːnəz/ – *as soon as*).

Speaking and writing

Over-using coordinating conjunctions

Learners sometimes need encouragement and guidance to help them to use subordinating conjunctions and adverbial clauses. They may 'play safe', using a small number of coordinating conjunctions, and ordering clauses in a strict chronological sequence. The following example of a student's work illustrates this:

> We went to Charing Cross Pier at the correct time but the boat didn't come so we waited but it still didn't come and we went to the station and we caught a train. We arrived in Greenwich and then we learned that the museum closed at 5.00 and we had ten minutes in the exhibition and we had some drinks by the river and we took the train back to Charing Cross Station.

Choosing inappropriate subordinating conjunctions

Learners sometimes choose the wrong conjunction, perhaps influenced by their own language. In the following, for example, the learner has used *in case* as though it meant *if*:

* *In case the new Le Carré novel is published when you're in England, can you buy me a copy, and I'll pay you back.*

Learners may also 'create' conjunctions – the following use of *even* (in place of *even though* or *even if*) is particularly common:

* *I'll do it for him even he can't afford to pay for it.*

Leaving out conjunctions

Learners sometimes leave out conjunctions. When this happens, we can sometimes work out from the context what relationship between the clauses is intended (e.g. contrast, reason, time etc.). In the following, for example, the context would help us to understand whether the missing conjunction were *if, after, as soon as* or something else:

* *He arrives. We'll eat.*

Repeating conjunctions

Although some conjunctions are used in pairs (e.g. *not only . . . but*), we usually use only one conjunction to link two clauses. Some learners (perhaps influenced by their own language) may be inclined to use two conjunctions instead of one.

> * *Although he joined the class late but he caught up quickly.*

> * *Because he arrived at the airport early so he took an earlier flight.*

Using prepositions as conjunctions

Learners may use linking prepositions as though they were conjunctions.

> * *They brought us a present despite they've got no money.*
> (Meaning: . . . although they've got no money. / . . . despite having no money.)

> * *Very few people turned up at the exhibition due to our publicity was so late.*
> (Meaning: . . . because our publicity was so late. / . . . due to the late publicity.)

24.5 Consolidation exercises (see pp. 495–499 for possible answers)

Differences in meaning

1 (see pp. 495–496)

Look at the list of conjunctions which follows.

as long as; as soon as; even though; although; while; since; as; until

a Divide them into groups according to the general meanings they express (e.g. time, reason, purpose etc.). Some of them can belong to more than one group.

b Within each group, what differences in meaning are there between the different conjunctions?

c What particular problems would you expect learners to have in using any of these conjunctions appropriately?

2 (see pp. 497–498)

Look at the following pairs of sentences:

(i)   I was terribly hungry. I started eating before you got here.

(ii) My mother left school when she was thirteen. She has had a very successful career as a writer.

a Join each pair together using as many conjunctions as you can (you can change the order of the clauses if you want).

b What differences do the different conjunctions make to the meaning of the sentences?

Language in context

1 (see p. 498)

The first extract that follows is from a novel and describes a character called Stephen spotting someone he knows through a restaurant window. The three sentences below are all from an article about getting connected to the Internet. Subordinating conjunctions have been omitted from the extracts.

> Stephen was halfway through lunch at a seat in the window . . . (1) he saw a familiar figure bustle past, her head lowered, with a basket on her arm. Her face was concealed by a scarf but he recognized her by her walk and the tartan sash at her waist.
>
> He left some coins spinning on the table . . . (2) he pushed back his chair and went out into the street. He saw her disappear from the corner of the square and go down a narrow side street. He ran to catch her up. He drew level . . . (3) she was pulling the bell handle outside a double door with flaking green paint.

> (4) you've got your modem installed, you'll need to open an account with an Internet service provider.

> (5) the sleazy and the outlandish both have a presence on the Net, what is often ignored is that much of its content is simply good fun.

> (6) you can buy modems very cheaply these days, the key factor is speed.

a Choose the most appropriate conjunction from the box below to fill each of the gaps.

although	as	just as	once	when	while

b Briefly justify your choice by referring to the context and the meaning expressed by the conjunction you have chosen.

2 (see pp. 498–499)

The following is part of the Introduction to the published diaries of the British actor and comedian Kenneth Williams, who died in 1988. This passage describes Williams' voice and discusses his tendency to ad lib or say things that were not in his script. Read the passage and answer the questions that follow it:

His vocal agility was Williams' outstanding gift, and so dominant that it almost unbalanced him as a performer. In his early days as a concert-party artist for Combined Services Entertainments, he specialised in imitations of voices, both male and female. When he progressed to the 'legitimate' stage, the question 'Which voice shall I use?' continued to determine his approach to each new role. But once he hit on a vocal register, he did not necessarily stick to it. He might shift from tone to tone, and from a languorous delivery to an agitated jabber, much as he did in conversation. While still a beginner in repertory, he felt he should be given the licence to let his own qualities as an entertainer show through the allotted part: he called it 'personality playing'. It clearly unnerved some directors, who were apt to take him aside and question him as to the seriousness of his commitment to the theatre. Later on, in his West End roles, Williams would become a notorious ad-libber. As his autobiography shows, he remained proud of his exercise of this privilege, even when it ruined a scene or a sketch or a working relationship. Naturally he raged at anyone else who departed from the script, arguing, probably rightly in many cases, that they were simply no good at it. Williams had many of the instincts of the music-hall comedian. He knew about laughs. When there were no laughs, or when a director aimed for a straight-faced reading of a scene where laughs would otherwise have been available, he became troubled and troublesome.

a Identify a two-part conjunction.

b Identify a 'reduced' adverbial clause. What words have been 'left out'?

c Identify a sentence which includes two adverbial clauses with subordinating conjunctions.

d Identify two sentences in which an adverbial clause with a subordinating conjunction follows the main clause.

e Identify three sentences in which a main clause follows a single finite adverbial clause with a subordinating conjunction.

f Which of the conjunctions in the passage are modified in some way (e.g. in 'just as' *as* is modified by *just*)?

g In all these sentences you have identified, consider whether any alternative conjunctions could have been used, and whether these would have changed the meaning of the sentence at all.

25 Noun clauses

> . . . that you didn't know.
> . . . whether or not you want to.
> . . . why it didn't work.
> . . . what we all need.

25.1 Key considerations

Many learners find it easy to construct noun clauses in controlled exercises but when they speak and write may both over-use them and make mistakes in their construction.

We often leave out the conjunction *that* at the beginning of noun clauses or pronounce it so weakly that learners don't hear it. Some learners may fail to understand the structure and meaning of sentences when this has been left out or 'swallowed'. They may welcome a lot of help and guidance in spotting where it is implied in real conversation and text.

25.2 What are noun clauses?

What do they do?

These clauses are known as noun clauses because they can often take the place of nouns (or noun phrases) in a sentence.

I don't know	*the time.*
I don't know	**when he's coming.**

In some grammars noun clauses are considered as types of direct object. Like direct objects, they often contain the most important information in the sentence.

In some grammars, infinitive and *-ing* forms which follow transitive verbs are considered as noun clauses. In this book they are dealt with separately (in Chapter 11).

One common use of noun clauses is in reporting what someone has said or written. (See also pp. 219–220).

What do they look like?

Noun clauses are subordinate clauses which generally follow the main clause and are linked to it by one of the following (kinds of) conjunctions:

Question words:	*I don't know **when** he's coming.*
if or *whether*:	*I don't know **whether** I want to go out.*
that:	*I don't know **that** he's here yet.*

25.3 Types of noun clause

Noun clauses derived from questions

These clauses contain an implicit question and the conjunction we use is either a question word (*where, what, when* etc.) or *if* or *whether*.

Question words:	*I have no idea **where** I put it.*
if:	*Do you remember **if** you left it anywhere?*
whether:	*They wonder **whether** you need help.*

Although they usually follow the main clause, a noun clause can form part of the clause, acting as the subject or complement of a verb (see pp. 255 and 258).

> ***Whether I want to go out or not** needn't concern you.*
>
> *The issue is **what time you're coming back**.*

We use noun clauses as complements in pseudo-cleft sentences. This is explained and illustrated on p. 280.

That *clauses*

The term '*that* clause' is potentially misleading because we can leave out the conjunction *that* and we often do:

> *I'm sure **(that) I had it earlier**.*

As in most course materials, we use the term '*that* clause' here to refer to the type of clause that can be introduced by *that*, whether or not the conjunction is actually used.

We often use *that* clauses after adjectives and nouns which express:

- feelings e.g. *angry, disappointed* (adjectives); *feeling, sensation* (nouns).
- mental states e.g. *convinced, determined* (adjectives); *conviction, hunch, idea* (nouns).
- necessity e.g. *crucial, essential* (adjectives); *importance, necessity* (nouns).
- some aspect of possibility, fact or truth e.g. *likely, probable, certain, sure, true* (adjectives); *possibility, certainty, fact* (nouns).

We also use them after verbs which:

- express feelings e.g. *feel, sense*.
- express mental states e.g. *believe, learn, think*.
- we use to report what someone says or writes e.g. *mention, say, tell*.

Examples

adjective:	*I'm **pleased** (that) you were able to come.*
noun:	*I had a **hunch** (that) you'd call.*
verb:	*They **believe** (that) they are right.*

We can also use *that* clauses as complements.

*The point I want to make is **that we're in trouble**.*

Verbs in *that* clauses – present simple, base form and *should* + bare infinitive

After certain adjectives (e.g. *crucial, essential* and *important*) and certain verbs (e.g. *insist, recommend, suggest*) we can choose from three forms of the verb (without significantly altering the meaning).

present simple	*It is crucial (that) she **comes.*** *I insisted (that) she **submits** her assignments on time.*
base form	*It is crucial (that) she **come.*** *I insisted (that) she **submit** her assignments on time.*
should	*It is crucial (that) she **should come.*** *I insisted (that) she **should submit** her assignments on time.*

Pronunciation of *that*

When we use *that* as a conjunction we almost always pronounce it as a weak form (/ðət/) i.e. very softly and very rapidly, barely articulating the consonants.

When we leave *that* out

We use *that* more in writing than in speaking, but we only really have to use *that* in long, complicated sentences where we need to signal the structure of the syntax explicitly in order to make our message clear. For example, the following would be a lot more difficult to understand if we removed *that*:

> The reason that you are receiving your second warning is because you have again openly communicated to the staff that you disagree with corporate policy that you agreed to in a meeting that you attended.

25.4 Typical difficulties for learners

Comprehension

Leaving out that

When we leave *that* out of *that* noun clauses, learners sometimes fail to understand the structure and meaning of the sentence. The more often *that* is left out, the more problematic it is to understand the sentence. The sentence that follows, for instance, would be easier to understand if *that* had been included:

> *Did you hear [] the boss said [] somebody's going to be appointed who doesn't know [] people are being made redundant.*

Question-word noun clauses

Learners may also associate question words so firmly with questions that they are 'thrown' by what initially appears to them to be a question.

> *I don't know where he is.*

They may also associate *if* so firmly with conditional sentences that they are 'thrown' by what initially appears to them to be conditional.

> *I have often wondered if he was gay.*

Speaking and writing

Over-using noun clauses

In English many different kinds of clause can follow verbs, adjectives and nouns, and some learners consistently over-use noun clauses in contexts where some other kind of clause is correct or is more natural:

> * *They want that we swap our offices around.* (instead of *want us to swap . . .*)

> (*) *Is there any possibility that you get the work finished by this afternoon?* (instead of *Can you get . . .*)

Word order

Learners often use the word order of questions (i.e. they put an auxiliary verb before the subject) in noun clauses which are introduced by a question word.

> (*) *Do you know when is he coming?* (instead of . . . *when he is coming?*)

They may also leave out *if* or *whether*, and may use the word order of questions.

> (*) *I can't remember did he speak to me.* (instead of . . . *remember if (whether) he spoke to me.*)

We usually teach that we need to use the standard word order of statements in noun clauses. However, native speakers also sometimes use this word order, and (at least in speech) most people consider this acceptable. So, many teachers correct mistakes only if learners make them systematically when they write. Otherwise, they may choose to ignore them.

Stressing that

We normally never stress *that* when we use the word as a conjunction. Learners, however, may stress the word and their listeners may be confused, thinking that the learner is using *that* as a demonstrative adjective (e.g. *I remember <u>that</u> Michael*) or as a pronoun (e.g. *I remember that.*).

> * *I remember* THAT *Michael came round to see us very early one day.*

25.5 Consolidation exercises
(see pp. 499–500 for possible answers)

Language in context

1 (see p. 499)

Many of the following sentences contain noun clauses.

(i)   Do you know where he is?

(ii)   I can't believe he said that!

(iii) She didn't know if he was coming.

(iv) She would meet him if he was coming.

(v)   What they did was completely unfair.

(vi) I'd like you to prepare me something that is typical of your country.

347

a Identify the noun clauses.

b Identify any other clauses which resemble noun clauses (e.g. conditional clauses or relative clauses).

2 (see pp. 499–500)

The first of the following extracts is from a book describing a journey around Britain using public transport. The second is from an interview in which someone talks about the great classical singer Peter Pears. The third is from an account by the journalist John McCarthy of his imprisonment. He and his cellmate have just caught a glimpse of McCarthy's girlfriend on TV.

(i)

> I was mildly astounded to discover that many substantial communities had no rail services at all – Marlborough, Devizes and Amesbury to name but three.

(ii)

> That he was a great man, and in a way a great human being, is beyond doubt, but he had foibles like all of us.

(iii)

> We talked over the remaining shots trying to tie the words to the pictures. The fact that the story should be on the news the one night we'd risked a look, was amazing. It had to mean something, had to be a good omen. Yet the hard fact was that nobody knew what had happened to us. We were excited that Jill was getting something going and taking the Thatcher government to task.

a Identify noun clauses in these extracts.

b In each case, explain why the noun clauses are used (rather than some other construction).

3 (see p. 500)

The following is adapted from the diary entry of an actor. The expression 'appear on boards' refers to acting in the theatre.

Siobhan McKenna told me John Fernald had written to her saying her performance was a travesty, and he had been greatly hurt by hearing she had adversely criticised his production. Fernald must be psychopathic I think, to write such things to anyone that has to appear on boards. She kept saying I must not tell a soul about the letter, and I said I wouldn't. Of course I shall.

a Identify the noun clauses in the text.

b Re-write these, inserting *that* wherever it is possible to do so.

c Consider what difference (if any) this makes to the readability of the text.

d Speculate as to how many of these conjunctions were used in the text as originally written.

26 Relative clauses

> . . . *who arrived.*
> . . . *that mattered.*
> *who(m) we liked.*
> . . . *which I thought would break.*

26.1 Key considerations

Long before we expect or require learners to use relative clauses, we can help them to recognise and understand them by systematically drawing their attention to where and why they are used in real conversation and texts. Native English-speaking teachers often underestimate the difficulty that relative clauses can pose for comprehension.

Course materials often introduce relative clauses only at late intermediate or advanced levels, and may expect the students to learn all the important features together. In fact we can teach relative clauses bit by bit, starting at quite low levels where, for example, learners can use them to identify people in response to the question *Who . . . ?*

> Who's Mary? – She's the person *who's dancing.* She's the person *who's getting into a car.*

It is easy to confuse learners unnecessarily by teaching general features of clause construction such as ellipsis and 'defining' versus 'non-defining' at the same time as teaching relative clauses. Students can learn these general features beforehand and in simpler grammatical contexts.

26.2 What are relative clauses?

What do they do?

Relative clauses describe or provide information about something or someone that we have usually already specified.

> *I like working with students **who appreciate what I do**.* (*who . . .* refers to *students*)
>
> *Her husband died, **which was the beginning of her depression**.* (*which . . .* refers to *Her husband died*)

Relative clauses are similar in function to adjectives.

> *I like working with students who appreciate what I do./ with appreciative students.*

Relative clauses also enable us to combine clauses without repeating things, e.g. instead of saying:

I tried to help a child. The child was crying her eyes out.

we say: *I tried to help a child **who was crying her eyes out**.*

and instead of saying:

I had to translate the whole text. Translating the whole text was difficult for me.

we say: *I had to translate the whole text, **which was difficult for me**.*

We sometimes use relative clauses in order to identify things (or people) – to distinguish them from other, similar things (or people).

*Mancunians aren't people **who live in Manchester**; they're people **who were born there**.*

What do they look like?

Sometimes we can recognise relative clauses because they begin with a relative pronoun such as *which* or *that* (see p. 352), but often it is only their sentence position and what the context tells us about their function that enables us to identify them.

Where do they come in sentences?

Relative clauses usually follow whatever they qualify, so they come immediately after the main clause if they qualify the whole of the clause or the last part of it.

*The bus came at last, **which was an enormous relief**.*

*I like working with **students who appreciate what I do**.*

They are embedded in the main clause if they qualify the subject.

*People **who know several foreign languages** make better language teachers.*

Relative clauses are also known as 'adjectival' or 'attributive' clauses.

26.3 Relative pronouns

What are relative pronouns?

The following words can act as relative pronouns:

that which who what whom whose where when why

Learners may be confused by the fact that all the words we can use as relative pronouns can be used for other purposes too, e.g.

- *who, whose* and *which* can introduce questions.
- *that* can refer to specific things (*that* man) or stand in place of them (give me *that*).

When do we have to use a relative pronoun?

Possessive meaning: *whose*

Whose usually combines with the word or words which follow it to become the subject of the relative clause, and can't be left out. It stands in place of a possessive form (e.g. *our*, Shirley's). Instead of saying:

*Relative clauses may create problems for learners. **Their** first language is not closely related to English.*

we say: *Relative clauses may create problems for learners **whose** first language is not closely related to English.*

If we can use 's to denote possession, we can also use *whose* in a relative clause. However, we use *whose* as a relative pronoun more widely than we use 's.

| *a shirt label* | → | *a shirt **whose** label . . .* |
| *the roof of the house* | → | *the house **whose** roof . . .* |

The relative pronoun as subject of the relative clause (*who, which, that*)

The verb in a relative clause needs to have a subject:

main clause		relative clause	
	object	subject	verb
* *I tried to help*	*a child*	-	*was crying.*

A child is the object of *help,* and can't function also as the subject of the next clause. We need to use a relative pronoun in order to provide a subject:

main clause		relative clause	
	object	subject	verb
I tried to help	*a child*	*who (that)*	*was crying.*

This rule is generally expressed as 'if a relative pronoun is the subject of a relative clause we can't leave it out'. When the relative pronoun is the subject of a clause, we choose between *who, which,* or *that.* See below for further information about choosing between them.

When can we leave out a relative pronoun?

We can choose whether or not to use a relative pronoun when the verb in the relative clause already has a subject. *I* and *we* are are subjects of the relative clauses in the following sentences:

main clause		relative clause		
I tried to help	*a child*	*(that)*	*I*	*found in the street.*
Paris is	*a city*	*(that)*	*we*	*always go back to.*

This rule is usually expressed as 'we can leave out a relative pronoun if it is the object of a relative clause'.

We leave out optional relative pronouns in speaking more than in writing, and only when the sentence is simple enough not to need them in order to signpost the grammar. For example, we would be unlikely to leave out *that* in the following report of a telephone message:

> He said he had put your keys in a box *that* you'll find somewhere on a shelf *that* you apparently put up for him in the garage.

How do we choose which relative pronoun to use?

General considerations

In choosing which relative pronoun to use we need to ask:

- Does the relative pronoun refer back to a person or to a thing?
- Does it refer to a possessive relationship?
- Does it refer to or stand in for a place, a time or the reason for something?

who, which and that

If the subject of the relative clause is a person, we can use *who* but not *which*.

> *I'd like to give these blankets to people **who (that)** really need them.*

If the subject of the relative clause is a thing we use *which* but not *who*.

> *Are you going to throw out the food **which (that)** has gone off?*

We can use *that* in place of *who* and *which* in these examples.

that

We can use *that* in defining clauses (see Chapter 28) to replace any relative pronoun except *whose*.

> *Was it the day **that (when)** I saw you for the first time?*

whom

We can use *whom* instead of *who* to link a relative clause to a main clause when the relative pronoun is not the subject of the relative clause.

> *Is that the person **who/whom** you invited?*

We use *whom* mainly in formal contexts, and in spoken English it may seem pedantic. We often leave it out or use *that* instead. For another use of *whom* see 26.4.

where, when and why

We sometimes use question words as relative pronouns.

Is this the room	**where**	*the murder happened?*
I remember a day	**when**	*we all went for a picnic.*
I want to know the reason	**why**	*you came here.*

We may need to add a preposition if we leave these out or use *that* instead.

> *Is that the room [] the murder happened in?*
> *Is that the room **that** the murder happened in?*

what

We use *what* as a relative pronoun to mean 'the thing(s) that'.

> *Give him **what** he wants.*

26.4 Other factors

Position of prepositions

We use particular prepositions with particular verbs and expressions (e.g. *listen to*; *speak to*).

When we use these verb/preposition combinations in relative clauses, the preposition usually comes at the end of the clause.

> *That's the person I spoke **to**.*
>
> *Have you got the weapon she was attacked **with**?*

Some people dislike placing the preposition at the end of a clause and may avoid this through introducing the relative pronoun and by placing the preposition before it.

> *That's the person **to** whom I spoke.*
>
> *Have you got the weapon **with** which she was attacked?*

This is particularly common in formal, written English. We use *whom* after prepositions rather than *who* (NOT ** . . . the person to who I spoke.*)

the

We often use *the* to introduce the information that relative clauses qualify, and learners generally learn that this is necessary. As in the following example, *the* alerts us to expect a relative clause, identifying which person the speaker is talking about:

> *Do you know **the** person **who just left the room**?*

We use *the* to signal that the clause that follows is going to specify which thing or person we are referring to.

While the 'rule' that we use *the* before relative clauses is a useful rule of thumb, it is not water-tight. At some point, we need to ensure that our students recognise and understand the function of clauses without *the*. We don't use *the*, for example, when the relative clause identifies a category or class of people or things, or refers to 'one among two or more'.

People who live in glass houses shouldn't throw stones.	This defines a category of people i.e. those who live in glass houses
I saw a man who I was once on a course with yesterday.	This identifies one among the several men on my course

'Reduced' relative clauses

When a relative pronoun is followed by a form of the verb *be* (e.g. *is, was, has been*), we often leave out both the pronoun and this (part of the) verb. The result is a non-finite verbless or participle clause, and can cause difficulty for learners in understanding the sentence.

verbless clause	*Lets discuss only issues [] relevant to the topic on the agenda.*	[*which are*]
participle	*The house [] broken into last week has been boarded up.*	[*which was*]
clauses	*We don't speak to the people [] living in the cottages.*	[*who are*]

In these cases we make an exception to the rule that we can't leave out a relative pronoun when it is the subject of a clause (see p. 353).

See pages 291 and 320 for further consideration of reduced relative clauses. See page 414 for punctuation rules relating to relative clauses.

26.5 Typical difficulties for learners

Comprehension

Learners whose first languages are very different from English may have particular difficulty in recognising and understanding relative clauses.

Comprehension is a problem particularly when relative pronouns are left out. Learners may not only fail to understand the message, but may be baffled by the structure of the sentence if they try to analyse it.

The parcel [] somebody left still hasn't been claimed.

Languages [] we don't know always seem to be spoken fast.

Problems of comprehension are compounded when the relative clause is reduced through ellipsis.

The drivers of the cars [ ] crashed into never got compensation. ([which got])

The person [ ] arrested escaped. ([who had been])

Speaking and writing

Using unnecessary pronouns

When we use relative clauses we have to leave out subject and object pronouns that refer back to what we are describing or qualifying. This is because the relative pronoun itself refers back to this.

Learners sometimes use the pronouns as they would if the two clauses were separate sentences.

* * *I work for a company which it controls the local sugar trade.* (. . . which controls the local sugar trade.)

* * *Amaral is the name of the man who she married him.* (. . . man (who/whom) she married.)

Using the wrong relative pronoun

The most common mistakes in this category are using:

* *what* instead of *that*.
* *who* to refer to things.
* *which* to refer to people.

Many native speakers use *what* as a relative pronoun instead of *that*, but this is not standard English. Learners may use *what* inappropriately for things by analogy with the (correct) use of *who* for people.

* * *That is the problem what I have to understand.*

Some European languages (e.g. French) use a different pronoun according to whether it is the subject or object of the relative clause, but make no distinction according to whether the clause qualifies a person or a thing. Speakers of these languages are particularly prone to make mistakes like the following:

* * *I want a car who is more reliable than my old one.*

* * *I want to speak to the person which I wrote to.*

Not all mistakes in choosing relative pronouns can be explained by the influence of the learners' first languages. They may simply result from the fact that in English we have to choose from a *number* of relative pronouns.

26.6 Consolidation exercises
(see pp. 501–503 for possible answers)

Language in context

1 (see p. 501)

 a Identify the relative pronouns in the following sentences.

 b Which ones can be left out?

 c In which of these instances could another relative pronoun be used in its place? Which pronoun?

   (i) If you can wait a minute I'll look for the person that you want.

   (ii) People who park on double yellow lines are a menace.

   (iii) Nobody who leaves before the end of the concert is eligible for the offer of free tickets.

   (iv) They don't keep the addresses of the people whose letters they've answered.

   (v) I don't remember much about her. She had a name which I'd never heard before.

   (vi) I swear that that isn't true. Nothing that she says is true.

2 (see pp. 501–502)

 An advanced learner saw the following on a noticeboard in the staff room of a university and she found it particularly difficult to understand. Identify any features related to relative clauses which might have contributed to this difficulty.

```
Following suggestions made to the working party elected
at the previous meeting, it has been decided that the
proposal drawn up in November will be re-drafted and
submitted to members for consideration and further
modification.
```

3 (see p. 502)

 The first of the following extracts is from an interview in which the speaker, Jack Richards, argues that we can teach language in either an explicit or an implicit way. The second is from some publicity for 'personal development' seminars, and the third is from a satirical

article about smokers and gossip in the work place. Read the extracts and then answer the following questions.

(i)

> There may be a situation where one teacher presents things explicitly and very effectively, and students learn from explicit modelling and so on, and that happens to be the style that that teacher does well and children appreciate from that particular teacher. The next teacher may set about doing it in a more implicit way, and again perhaps does that better than he could do the other style of teaching and so on. So I think the results may be the same – the children may have learned whatever it was that the teacher set out to teach but in both cases the teachers took them by a different route.

(ii)

> To follow what moves, excites and inspires us, is to create a life which is joyful and satisfying.

(iii)

> I HAVE a serious complaint about smoking, and may have to sue a tobacco company. It is this. In offices where smoking has been banned, smokers have a huge advantage. For one thing they do not work as much, because they are no longer allowed to puff as they work. For another they are the only people who know what is going on.

a Identify the relative clauses in these extracts.

b Mentally re-write these texts using no relative clauses.

c In general terms what difference does this make?

d Which of these relative clauses follows an expression that is not introduced by *the*? In each of these cases, how would you explain the non-use of *the* to a learner?

Learners' English (see pp. 502–503)

The following was written by an Asian learner of English who was asked to describe his favourite moment from a film. The learner knew very

little grammar and made extensive use of a bilingual dictionary. Some mistakes have been corrected:

My favourite – or best memorable film scene is from the film
Gandhi. It is set in there was civil war in India one a time. There is
one walked along a wearing very tattered clothes many people
thronging thronging avenue. This is my favourite moment

a Re-write the sentence *There is . . . avenue* so that it reads more naturally, and explain in general terms what kinds of change you are making to the original.

b What problems is this learner likely to face in learning to use relative clauses?

27 Non-finite clauses

> *At that time in Australia, . . .*
> *Barely hatched from their eggs, . . .*
> *Although willing to give a hand, . . .*
> (solution is) *to get up earlier.*

27.1 Key considerations

Non-finite clauses can bewilder learners and can even distract their attention from what they do understand. We can help learners to overcome these problems by systematically drawing their attention to non-finite clauses in texts that they read, and by encouraging them to develop and use a mental checklist of functions these clauses frequently have. This, and careful attention to the contexts they are used in, can help them to work out the precise meaning of a particular clause.

In order to speak idiomatically and to write in appropriate styles, learners need not only to recognise and understand non-finite clauses, but also to use them. We can provide them with controlled exercises which, for example, involve using non-finite clauses to combine two sentences into one. We can also help them by monitoring and guiding them during the actual process of writing, and at a later stage we can show them where they could have used non-finite clauses in order to express themselves more succinctly and fluently. There are several different kinds of non-finite clause. Learners may find it helpful if we teach them separately, and if they concentrate on using different types at different times.

Learners often seek 'rules' to help them decide where to put the non-finite clause within the sentence. In fact, decisions about sentence position necessarily depend on context and emphasis, and often need to be made sentence by sentence.

27.2 What are non-finite clauses?

What do they look like?

Non-finite clauses are those in which the only verb is in a participle or infinitive form, or those which have no verb at all. We call them non-finite clauses because they don't contain a finite verb (i.e. a verb which has a subject and a tense form, or is imperative). The main categories of non-finite clause are:

- present participle: ***Leaping out of bed***, *he grabbed the bat.*

- past participle: **Barely hatched from their eggs**, *they started chirruping.*

- full infinitive: *The solution is **to get up earlier**.*

- bare infinitive: *I didn't see anyone **come into the room**.*

- verbless: **At that time in Australia**, *they missed the news.*

We look at different types of non-finite clause in more detail below.

Participle clauses

	participle clause	main clause
present	***Breaking*** *into a broad grin,*	*she invited the visitors into her home.*
past	*Barely **hatched** from their eggs,*	*the chicks opened their beaks and started chirruping.*

We can use a perfect form of a present participle (*having* + past participle). This indicates that the action took place before what is described in the main clause.

> **Having drunk** *all their store of water*, *they started collecting snow.*

We can use a passive form of present and past participles (*being* + past participle; *having been* + past participle).

> **Being rejected** *in this way*, *I consider I have rights too.*
>
> **Having been invited** *for so many years*, *I felt I couldn't turn them down again.*

Participle clauses are usually reduced adverbial or relative clauses.

> *I met him **while living in Egypt**.* (adverbial: *while I was living . . .*)
>
> *I saw the children **huddled against the wall**.* (relative: *. . . children who were huddled . . .*)

We can use present participle clauses as:

- the subject of another clause.
  Getting started on the Internet *doesn't cost a fortune.*

- the complement of another clause.
  *The biggest problem in learning a language is **remembering all the words**.*

Present participle clauses are also called '*-ing* clauses'.

Infinitive clauses

We use both the full infinitive (e.g. *to drink*) and the bare infinitive (e.g. *drink*) to make infinitive clauses.

We use full infinitive clauses:

- as the subject of another clause:
  To give up now *seems stupid.*
- as the complement of another clause:
  *Our only option is **to get up even earlier in the mornings.***
- attached to another clause:
  *I came all the way **to find out what had happened.***

See also Chapter 11 – we can use infinitive clauses in all the contexts where we can also use a simple infinitive.

We use bare infinitive clauses:

- after *rather than*:
  ***Rather than open a new packet**, why don't you finish up the remains of this one?*
- as the complement of a pseudo-cleft sentence:
  *What you should do is **try to open it with a knife.***
- attached to another clause – after 'sense' verbs (e.g. *hear; see*):
  *I didn't see anyone **come into the room.***

We can use a perfect or passive form of an infinitive in non-finite clauses (*to have* + past participle; *to be* + past participle).

> *It would have been rude **to have left the party any earlier**.*
>
> *I want **to be taken out** and given a good time.*

The first example above shows how we often use perfect forms of the infinitive, in combination with conditional forms, for hypothetical speculation about the past.

Non-finite clauses with subjects

Participle and infinitive clauses can have subjects. We normally place these immediately before the participle or infinitive:

non-finite clause		main clause
subject		
The old man	*having finally nodded off,*	*everyone began discussing what he'd said.*
The house	*sold at last,*	*we were able to start planning to move out.*
For us	*to try to find someone at short notice*	*is asking a lot.*

(We usually use *for* to introduce the subject in full infinitive clauses.)

Rather than the team	*play in the rain*	*they postponed the match.*

Non-finite clauses and their subordinate clauses

Non-finite clauses may, themselves, contain subordinate clauses.
Moreover, these subordinate clauses may be finite clauses, e.g.

non-finite clause			main clause
	finite (relative) clause		
Having put the child	*who was crying*	*to bed,*	*he began preparing a meal for the other children.*

main clause		non-finite clause
		finite (adverbial) clause
Can I ask you	*to come in and see us*	*when you have a few moments?*

Verbless clauses

When we 'reduce' clauses, we sometimes leave the verb out altogether.
These are known as verbless clauses.

> ***Although <u>willing to</u> lend a hand***, *he's never around when you actually need help.* (Although [*he is*] willing . . .)

> ***Without <u>hope</u>***, *he staggered on.* (Without [*having*] hope . . .)

We often introduce verbless clauses with:

- a conjunction, e.g. *although*.

- a preposition, e.g. *without.*
- a prepositional phrase, e.g. *at that time.*

What do they do?

Defining non-finite clauses

Defining clauses identify something or someone – they say which thing or person we are talking about. They usually immediately follow the information they qualify, and are not separated from this by a pause or comma.

		defining clause	
present participle:	My sister's the one	wearing a sari.	
past participle:	You look like something	dragged out of a pond.	
infinitive:	The guest house	to stay in	is the last one in the row.
verbless:	Don't buy anything	pale or soggy.	

Non-defining non-finite clauses

We use non-defining non-finite clauses for a number of purposes, and the following show examples of some of the more common uses. We use non-defining non-finite clauses mainly in written English.

Things happening simultaneously:

1 *She froze, the jar in her hand, as if she had been caught in an act of private violation.*
2 *She pictured the big house happy and lively, with Lord and Lady Rockingdown giving parties, going off to hunt, choosing ponies for their two small children . . .*
3 *There are a lot of people still queuing up for concert tickets.*
4 *Firmly ensconced in her favourite armchair, she simply refused to get up and open the door.*

One thing happening immediately after another:

5 *Once away from the city and into the fresh, country lanes, we opened all the windows and breathed deeply.*
6 *Leaping out of bed, he grabbed the baseball bat and began hammering on the wall.*

Cause and effect:

7 *With <u>feathers on every surface in the room</u>, it was obvious to everyone what had happened.*
(<u>With</u> introduces the meaning of <u>cause and effect</u> into the verbless clause.)

8 *<u>Working in a bank</u>, he knew a great deal about how people behave when they are embarrassed.*
(Cause and effect are simultaneous.)

9 *<u>Having worked in a bank</u>, he knew a great deal about how people behave when they are embarrassed.*
(The cause precedes the effect.)

10 *<u>Driven to a frenzy by the loud music and flashing lights</u>, the two began dancing uncontrollably, down the aisle towards the stage.*

Descriptive detail:

11 *The eyes in the mirror stared back at her, <u>guilty and a little ashamed</u>.*

12 *The 1930s dressing table with its triple mirror held a plastic tray patterned with violets <u>containing a jumble of half empty bottles of hand and body lotions</u> . . .*

13 *All credit to the English cricket team, <u>coolly captained by Atherton</u>.*

Making something possible:

14 *She believes she got over the fever <u>by eating nothing but spinach and comfrey</u>.*

15 *She caught up on her work <u>through staying up till 2.00 in the mornings and cutting down on her sleep</u>.*
(<u>By</u> or <u>through</u> express the sense of making something possible.)

Expanding information:

16 *Satisfaction is a concept <u>impossible to define precisely</u>.*

17 *He saw her <u>disappear from the corner of the square</u> and <u>go down a narrow side street</u>.*

18 *I don't want to find you <u>helping yourself to food ever again</u>.*

19 *<u>To apply for your Golden Promise Credit Card</u>, simply fill in the attached form and return it to the address at the bottom of the page.*

20 *I would give anything <u>not to have failed the exam</u>.*

Where do they come in sentences?

Verbless and participle clauses

When these refer to the whole of the main clause, they can come before it, after it or in the middle, depending on the emphasis we want to give to different parts of the sentence. On the whole the further towards the end something occurs, the more weight it carries as 'new information' (see Chapters 19 and 20 for more detailed description and illustration of this).

> ***Their eyes burning with passion***, *they danced from one side of the room to the other.*
>
> *They danced,* ***their eyes burning with passion***, *from one side of the room to the other.*
>
> *They danced from one side of the room to the other,* ***their eyes burning with passion***.

When the non-finite clause refers to part of the main clause we normally have to place it immediately after the information it qualifies. Changing the position of the non-finite clause changes the meaning of the sentence.

> *The old woman* ***leaning calmly against the wall*** *looked at Ralph and asked him what he thought he was doing.*
>
> *The old woman looked at Ralph* ***leaning calmly against the wall***, *and asked him what he thought he was doing.*
>
> *The old woman looked at Ralph and asked him what he thought he was doing* ***leaning calmly against the wall***.

If the subject of the main clause is a pronoun (e.g. *she* in the example below), we need to put the non-finite clause before rather than after this.

> *Leaning calmly against the wall, she looked at Ralph and asked him what he thought he was doing.*

Full infinitive clauses

We generally place full infinitive clauses before or after the main clause.

> ***To claim your free gift***, *just hand this voucher to the cashier at your local shop or supermarket.*
>
> *Just hand this voucher to the cashier at your local shop or supermarket* ***to claim your free gift***.

Bare infinitive clauses

Bare infinitive clauses usually come after the verb *be* when they form the complement in pseudo-cleft sentences.

*The thing to do in New York is **take one of those boat tours right round Manhattan Island***.

Bare infinitive clauses with *rather than* can go before or after the main clause.

***Rather than pick you up on the way to the school**, why don't I collect you now? Why don't I collect you now **rather than pick you up on the way to the school**?*

27.3 Other factors

Agreement between subject and participle

Many people think we shouldn't rely on context alone to make clear what is the implied subject of a non-finite clause. They think that this implied subject must be the same as the subject of the main clause. So they would regard the following as acceptable because it is the three conspirators who raise their glasses, and the child that was seated on the wall:

non-finite clause	subject of the main clause	
Raising their glasses in a gesture of solidarity and friendship,	*the three conspirators*	*swore eternal brotherhood.*
Seated perilously on the edge of the wall,	*the child*	*screamed as she heard the resounding crack of the branch break above her.*

They regard the following as unacceptable, arguing that it is not clear respectively who raised their glasses and who was sitting on the wall:

non-finite clause	subject of the main clause	
Raising their glasses in a gesture of solidarity and friendship,	*the door*	*burst open and the crowd fell into the room.*
Seated perilously on the edge of the wall,	*there*	*was a resounding crack as the branch broke above her.*

In fact, as long as the context makes clear what the implied subject of the non-finite clause is, in spoken English at least, people rarely notice this let alone object to it.

Non-finite clauses which stand alone

Course materials generally teach that non-finite clauses need to be attached to a finite clause, and so far this has been true of all the examples in this chapter.

In fact we do use non-finite clauses as complete sentences. We do this when common knowledge and assumptions or the context makes it clear what we are referring to.

For example, in cinema, theatre and TV guides the first sentence following the title of a film, play or TV programme is often a non-finite clause on its own.

Last in the series of the entertaining topical magazine show.

Continuing the second series of the award-winning comedy.

The grand final of the quiz that tests teams on their knowledge of the black music scene . . .

We can also use non-finite clauses as complete sentences for dramatic effect. In the following, the absence of subjects and verbs allows the descriptive phrases to make more striking visual impact:

'Hold your noise!' cried a terrible voice, as a man started up from among the graves at the side of the church porch. 'Keep still, you little devil, or I'll cut your throat!'

A fearful man, all in coarse grey, with a great iron on his leg. A man with no hat, and with broken shoes, and with an old rag tied around his head.

27.4 Typical difficulties for learners

Comprehension

Comprehension is a problem most of all when non-finite clauses occur in long, complex sentences, and when other clauses – finite or non-finite – are embedded within them. Often learners don't recognise and understand the structure of the sentence. Or they may recognise the structure but have difficulty in locating, for example, what the non-finite clause refers to or describes (see also p. 364).

Past participle clauses often pose a particular problem of recognition, as we see in the following text. This is about proposals to build a new underground railway line in London. These proposals are part of what is known as the CrossRail project, and the text is from a newspaper article describing some problems in relation to the project. The text contains three past participle clauses, and these have been printed in italics:

> The CrossRail project, *designed to speed millions of travellers on a new East-West line under London*, has suffered a devastating double blow.
>
> A detailed and authoritative report *commissioned by the Government* has concluded that it is "a visionary project which may be ahead of its time".
>
> It says that the scheme, *originally planned to open in six years*, is now unlikely to be justified until at least the year 2010. And it warns that the project is not likely to attract the private investment which the Treasury has demanded to help cover the £2 billion cost.

The problem for many learners is that they tend to read the verbs in each of these clauses as regular past tense forms. In this text, for example, learners might understand (at least initially) that it is 'the CrossRail project' which has designed (something); that it is 'A detailed and authoritative report' which has commissioned (something) and that it is 'the scheme' which planned to open (something).

Present participle clauses are usually more easily recognised, although learners often still need to stop and consciously puzzle out how the information in these relates to the information in the respective main clauses. In the following text (the beginning of an article, humorously describing a church service for clowns) this is true of the three straightforward present participle clauses which add descriptive detail (*2*, *3* and *6*):

> It is Sunday, *backstage at Dalston Holy Trinity Church's 49th Clown Service* (**1**). I am surrounded by 100 clowns, *honking their horns* (**2**), *falling over banana skins* (**3**), and so on. 100 clowns and 50 photographers, *crowded into a tiny back room* (**4**). It is a media circus (honk! honk!) *a frenzy of organised pathos* (**5**). The vicar, John Willard, is attempting to smile amiably through the chaos, but the tension on his face is palpable.
>
> "Excuse me," he announces. "Um. Excuse me. I have an announcement to make . . ."
>
> "Announcement! Announcement!" yells Fizzy-Lizzy The Clown, *honking her horn* (**6**).
>
> Announcey-nouncey! Mousey Mousey Mousey!" screams Billy the Clown, *his bow tie flashing* (**7**).

In this text it is the verbless clauses (**1**, and **5**), the past participle clause (**4**) and the present participle clause containing a subject (**7**) which pose the biggest problem to learners. These also add descriptive detail, but learners may not appreciate this. In **5** this may partly be because there is no comma before the clause (a comma would help to make clear its non-defining function).

Example **1** may confuse learners because the implied . . . [*and I am*] *backstage* . . . may not be evident to them, and in **4** it is the fact that there is no finite verb in the sentence at all which may confuse learners. In **7**, learners may simply be unused to finding the subject (here *his bow tie*) with a participle clause and they may fail to recognise that this is what this clause is. In cases like this, learners may think that something has been missed out in the printing process.

Speaking and writing

Avoidance

If we compare a few pages of writing by learners and by native speakers, or a few minutes' worth of their speech, we usually find that learners use non-finite clauses far less than native speakers. However, when we read and correct our students' compositions, we often notice mistakes in vocabulary, spelling, word order or tense construction, and may miss the fact that they are not trying to use appropriate structures such as non-finite clauses.

The following, in which only spelling mistakes have been corrected, was written by a learner of English. It describes a pageant that takes place annually in her village:

> This folkloric spectacle, what it has been watching by over than one million tourists, is taking its place in a building of the nineteenth century. It has all kinds of attractions, food service and full bar with alcoholic permit inclusive.
>
> The spectacle is acting by people of the mountains. They are come into the city two weeks in every year for make spectacle.
>
> In case you are definitely wanting attend this 'spectacle' you have to buying your tickets as soon possibly.

It would be easy to re-write this in correct and natural English without the use of non-finite clauses. However, compositions like this are also an opportunity for us to point out to learners when they could use non-finite clauses. The following is a re-written version of this learner's composition. Non-finite clauses are printed in italics.

> This folklore performance, *seen by over a million tourists*, takes place in a nineteenth century building. It has all kinds of attractions, *including a restaurant service and licensed bar*.
>
> The performance is given by people from the mountains who come to the city for two weeks each year *in order to put on the performance*.
>
> Buy your tickets as soon as possible *to make sure of your place at this event*.

Choosing the wrong forms

The following are some of the most common mistakes:

Using *for + -ing* instead of a full infinitive.

> * *We went to Woolworth's **for buying** our spring bulbs.*

Using *for +* bare infinitive instead of a full infinitive.

> *Go to England **for study** English better.*

Using a present participle instead of a past participle.

 * *The train robbery, **thinking** to be the greatest of the century, took place in 1963.*

Using a full infinitive instead of a present participle.

 * *I watched them **to dance**.*

27.5 Consolidation exercises
(see pp. 503–506 for possible answers)

Language in context

1 (see p. 503)

The text which follows is a short extract from a novel. A character catches sight of someone he knows through the window of the restaurant where he is eating. Read the extract and answer the questions.

> Stephen was halfway through lunch at a seat in the window when he saw a familiar figure *bustle past,* **(1)** *her head lowered,* **(2)** *with a basket on her arm.* **(3)** Her face was concealed by a scarf but he recognized her by her walk and the tartan sash at her waist.
>
>   He left some coins *spinning on the table* **(4)** as he pushed back his chair and went out into the street.

 a What kind of clause is each of the sections written in italics? (e.g. verbless)

 b In each instance, explain why the author has chosen this kind of clause.

2 (see p. 504)

The text which follows is the beginning of an article about the effect of modern production methods and marketing strategies on the tradition of lager production in the Czech Republic. Read the text and answer the questions.

> Pilsner, the most abused beer style in the world, is in danger of being equally defiled in its country of origin. The dash to embrace every aspect of free-market capitalism in the Czech Republic now threatens the noble traditions of Bohemian brewing, turning some of the finest beers into just a few more international-style lagers.
>
> To most people, the terms Pilsner, Pilsener or plain Pils stand for exceptionally pale and often rather bland lagers. As a result of the prominence of Holsten of Hamburg, you could be forgiven for thinking that Pils was a German beer style. But the origins of Pilsner lie in Bohemia, not Germany, and in the Czech Republic the term is used as a protected generic style confined to beers brewed in the industrial city of Pilsen. There are two breweries in the city, Pilsner Urquell and Gambrinus, now part of the same privatised company, and both have rushed to modernise in a way that threatens the unique character of the beers.

("Pils" and "Pilsner" are the names of types of lager.)

a Identify the non-finite clauses which occur in the text.

b Classify each of these clauses e.g. 'infinitive clause used to explain *how to*'; 'verbless clause used to express cause and effect' (you may want to refer to the list of clause types and functions on pp. 361–364).

3 (see pp. 505–506)

The following is an adaptation of part of a newspaper article about plans to construct a new bridge or some other form of transport link across the River Thames. The original text contains a number of non-finite clauses. Here, however, some of these have been re-written and are printed in italics. Answer the questions about each of these adaptations.

A new bridge is emerging as Westminster Council's main contribution to London's Millennium scene. *The bridge will link the cultural centres on either bank of the Thames (1)*.

The council's Millennium Committee agreed last night to earmark £30,000 for a study of possible link concepts – which the council may be prepared to fund to the tune of up to £5 million pounds.

A brief will be prepared by the council over the next few weeks. *This brief will invite ideas from consultants about how a bridge could be devised and funded (2)*.

The brief will not restrict applicants in terms of design or location and Westminster is hoping a lively and imaginative line-up will emerge.

The link could be a foot-bridge along the lines of another. *It is being proposed by the City Corporation (3). It would link Bankside and the St Paul's area (4)*. But the option of a monorail or cable car has not been ruled out. *This opens up the possibility of running the link from locations as far away from the river as Seven Dials in Covent Garden or even Piccadilly Circus (5)*.

Locations on the South Bank would have to be coordinated with the winner of the architectural competition. *This winner has recently been announced (6)*.

a Re-write the text to make it more natural. Incorporate a non-finite clause in re-writing each phrase printed in italics.

b Define the type of clause you have used.

c What other types of non-finite clause might it be possible to use here?

Learners' English (see p. 506)

Learners' English (see p. 506)

The following was written by a student who had been asked to comment on his difficulties in reading comprehension. The student has tried to use non-finite clauses, but they are not completely natural and appropriate.

> General cultural knowledge helps you to understand texts,
> not mattering what they are about or whether you have
> specialised knowledge of the subject you have obtained
> through years of study. Problems with reading can often be
> solved you think about what you already know so that you
> have an idea about what you are going to read.
> Understanding difficult vocabulary you can use a dictionary
> or you can try to understand it looking at the context.

a Identify examples of unnatural or inappropriate use of non-finite clauses and also any case where he has avoided using them.

b Re-write these portions of text so that they read more naturally.

c How would you explain to the learner the nature of his 'mistakes' so that he can use more appropriate structures subsequently in similar contexts?

28 Defining and non-defining phrases and clauses

(a pen) which works
(the house) with a green door
(my bike), which had a puncture, . . .
(they left), with Eric hurrying them out

28.1 Key considerations

The basic distinction between defining and non-defining is a simple one, and we shouldn't exaggerate either its importance or its difficulty. Learners sometimes feel that there are far more problems associated with this distinction than is necessarily the case.

One reason for this is that teachers sometimes introduce the distinction between defining and non-defining clauses when learners are already grappling with the form and uses of relative clauses. It may be more helpful in the first instance to introduce the defining/non-defining distinction with examples that are simpler than relative clauses.

28.2 What are defining and non-defining phrases and clauses?

What do they do?

Defining phrases and clauses

Clauses and phrases sometimes single out a particular thing or person from two or more similar things or people, showing which one or ones we are talking about.

> *It's the last house **on the right**.*   *This is the hotel **we stayed in**.*

The phrase and clause printed in bold are defining (they are sometimes also known as identifying or restrictive).

Non-defining phrases and clauses

Non-defining clauses and phrases are not just clauses and phrases that 'don't define'. More specifically, they are clauses and phrases which 'don't define' even though the same words in the same place, if spoken or punctuated differently, might do so.

Defining: *Our house is the one **with the new paint**.*
              (The new paint distinguishes our house from all the other houses.)

Non-defining: *Our house is the last one in the street, **with the new
                 paint**.*
                 (Incidentally, it also has new paint.)

What do they look like?

The following can have either a defining or non-defining function:
phrases in apposition, preposition phrases, participle clauses, infinitive
clauses and relative clauses. We look at each of these in turn below.

Phrases in apposition

'Phrases in apposition' are phrases we use to re-state something we have
said immediately before.

Often the two things are equivalent, or one of them is included in the
other.

> *They gave me a bottle of elderflower cordial, **my favourite drink**.*

> *Someone told me to try PANADOL, **a pain reliever**.*

Often the second phrase simply provides additional information about the
first – as in both these examples. These phrases are non-defining.

We usually separate non-defining phrases like this from the phrase before.
We use a comma in writing, and when we speak our intonation makes it
clear that we are thinking of these phrases as separate units.

Phrases in apposition can also have a defining function. In the following,
the phrases *the electrician* and *the politician* are each in apposition to
John Major, and they each define or identify which *John Major* we are
concerned with.

> *I'm John Major **the electrician**, not John Major **the politician**.*

In the following, the first phrase in apposition is non-defining (there is
only one 'Daniel Day Lewis') whereas the second is defining (people in
Britain often know several John Smiths):

> *I once saw Daniel Day Lewis, **the actor**, walking through Leicester Square
> with John Smith, **the then leader of the Labour Party**.*

Preposition phrases

Preposition phrases can also have either a defining or a non-defining
function.

In the first of the following examples *with the yellow stripe* has a defining function, identifying which of several bags belongs to me. In the second example *with all the kids* is non-defining.

> *The bag with the yellow stripe is mine.*
>
> *This is a photo of my sister with all the kids.*

Participle clauses

In the following sentences, the participle clauses identify, respectively, which woman *we gave everything to*, and which tree *has borne fruit*. These defining clauses are not usually separated from the rest of the sentence by intonation in speech, or by commas in writing.

> *We gave everything to the woman **begging on the stairs**.*
>
> *The tree **planted in memory of the earthquake victims** has finally borne fruit.*

In the following, the participle clauses are non-defining. We use intonation (or in writing, a comma) to separate them from the rest of the sentence.

> *They burst into the open, **shouting and singing as if they had escaped from jail**.*
>
> *He found the missing watch, **buried under a pile of rubbish**.*

Infinitive clauses

The following includes a defining infinitive clause: *We abandoned a specific plan.*

> *We abandoned the plan **to renovate the barn** because we couldn't get planning permission.*

In the following, the non-defining clause merely provides additional information about her intention.

> *Her original intention, **to stay in Paraguay till Christmas**, still seems like the best one to me.*

Relative clauses

Defining and non-defining relative clauses are similar to other kinds of defining and non-defining clauses and phrases in terms of meaning, intonation and punctuation.

The following contains two defining relative clauses. The first identifies *which scarf* (the one you liked), and the second identifies *the person who received it* (the organiser of my stay).

> *I gave the scarf **you liked** to the person **who organised my stay***.

The following contains a non-defining clause, providing additional, descriptive detail.

> *The house, **whose doors and windows had been wide open the last time we had passed it**, stood empty and dead-looking in the moonlight.*

All relative pronouns can be used in defining clauses. We don't use *that* in non-defining clauses.

28.3 Other factors

Style

Learners are often taught that we only use non-defining clauses in written English. Although it may be true that we use them less frequently in speaking, we certainly do use them in the spoken language. And although there are ways of saying the following which may be more common in speech (*It was an enormous relief that* . . .), these sentences are still good examples of spoken English.

> *The bus came at last, **which was an enormous relief**.*
> *I gave this vase to my brother, **who gave it to Mum, who gave it back to me**.*

Non-defining relative clauses are rarer in spoken English when they qualify the subject of the main clause (and are embedded within the main clause), particularly if they are quite long. This is because these clauses can make the sentence quite difficult to understand by postponing the important information that usually follows the subject. The two examples which follow are both from written texts.

> *The Borough Council, **whose resources have dwindled further in the recent cutbacks**, are now considering closing another of their advice centres.*
> *The house, **whose doors and windows had been wide open the last time we had passed it**, stood empty and dead-looking in the moonlight.*

However, the following are from informal conversation:

> *Peter, **who's our accountant**, is dealing with it.*
> *Our fridge, **which hasn't worked properly for years**, has finally packed up.*

Ambiguous cases

Teachers as well as learners sometimes feel frustrated because they can't work out whether a particular phrase or clause is defining or non-defining. In fact, although (as in all the examples so far in this chapter) the distinction is sometimes very clear, there are also cases in which phrases and clauses are not clearly one or the other. This is true of the parts of the following:

> *We watched some herons taking off from the lake **behind the cemetery**.*
>
> *I saw a very good dance **which I'd like to get the music for**.*

We look at how we use punctuation to distinguish between defining and non-defining phrases and clauses on pages 414–415, and at how we use intonation to do this on page 407.

28.4 Typical difficulties for learners

Comprehension

The context (as well as punctuation or intonation) generally makes it clear whether phrases and clauses are defining or non-defining. Learners may 'miss' this distinction in their reading or listening, but this rarely causes significant problems of comprehension. If we do identify misunderstanding, we can often prompt learners to work out whether the words are defining or not by looking at the context (and punctuation or intonation).

Speaking and writing

Avoidance

Learners often avoid using the kinds of phrase and clause that can be defining or non-defining, preferring longer but grammatically simpler ways of expressing themselves. We may need to encourage them to make use of these constructions and provide them with appropriate practice. In commenting on their written work, we can usefully point out any missed opportunities.

Relative clauses

Sometimes we can ignore the defining/non-defining distinction in our teaching, relying on context to make this clear when necessary. However, in the case of relative clauses we need at some point to introduce this distinction as it affects which relative pronouns we choose (we can't use *that* in non-defining relative clauses).

Many teachers pay attention to non-defining relative clauses only after students feel confident about using relative clauses to define. They may also choose to 'slip in' this distinction in the context, say, of phrases in apposition, well before the students grapple with relative clauses.

28.5 Consolidation exercises
(see pp. 507–508 for possible answers)

Differences in meaning (see p. 507)

Look at the following pairs of sentences and consider what difference, if any, there is in their meanings.

(i) She kept on telling jokes, which made everyone really angry.
    She kept on telling jokes which made everyone really angry.

(ii) They said they loved their children, who were obedient and well-behaved.
    They said they loved their children who were obedient and well-behaved.

(iii) They all came out of the lecture, chatting and laughing.
    They all came out of the lecture chatting and laughing.

(iv) She was a very hard-working student, who made excellent contributions to group discussion.
    She was a very hard-working student who made excellent contributions to group discussion.

Language in context (see pp. 507–508)

In the following passage a doctor writes about asthma in the East End of London. Read the passage and answer the questions.

> It tends to get better at the age of seven, but a lot of East End children with prolonged childhood asthma go on to suffer from severe teenage bouts and adult lung disease. Even the ones that don't can lose a lot of schooltime which surprisingly quickly stunts their education . . . And the condition is dangerous. Children can quite rapidly become distressed and start to get potentially fatal complications. And the aerosol treatments which are so very effective in adults can't really be used under about ten years, so inhaled powders to dilate the lungs or oral bronchodilators and anti-inflammatory drugs, which are fiddly and need careful dosing, must be used.

a Identify any defining and non-defining clauses or phrases.

b Identify any cases where the comma which often marks non-defining clauses has been left out.

29 Integrating the elements

Chapters 24–28, (see also 20 and 23) look at the individual 'elements' that we 'integrate' in <u>this</u> chapter.

29.1 Key considerations

Understanding and constructing complex sentences often pose a major challenge to learners whose first language is not closely related to English. We can help these learners by systematically paying attention to complex sentence construction, feature by feature, over a considerable period of time. We can also exploit any texts that they read, identifying complex sentences and explaining how these are constructed and what they mean, or guiding learners to work this out for themselves.

Learners whose first languages are closely related to English (i.e. most European languages) generally have far less difficulty with complex sentences. They may still, however, have problems of comprehension when sentences are particularly long or tightly constructed. They may also avoid using features of complex sentences, or may avoid using them in natural combinations.

29.2 What are complex sentences?

Complex sentences contain two or more clauses. One of these is a main clause, which is finite and can stand on its own. The other clause or clauses are subordinate to this or in some way dependent on it. Chapter 19 looks at the structure of main clauses in detail, and Chapters 24 to 27 look at types of subordinate clause.

29.3 What makes them difficult for learners?

Multiple clauses

In practice, many sentences contain a combination of different kinds of clause. Learners who can understand and use complex sentences containing one subordinate clause may have more difficulty when two or more subordinate clauses or types of subordinate clause are used together.

If you see him, can you let him know I'm on my way.

She used to make a terrible mess of everything she did until she learned that a little patience doesn't come amiss.

adverbial clause		main clause	
conjunction			noun clause
If	*you see him,*	*can you let him know*	*(that) I'm on my way.*

main clause			adverbial clause	
	relative clause	conjunc- tion		noun clause
She used to make a terrible mess of everything	*she did*	*until*	*she learned*	*that a little patience doesn't come amiss.*

Embedding

At its most straightforward, embedding refers to phrases slipped into the middle of clauses either in apposition (re-stating) or in parenthesis (less important supporting information).

	Embedded phrase	
We stopped off at a small town,	*Canetas,*	*on our way to the border.*
And finally, on Sunday	*– the last day of our holiday –*	*we had some decent weather.*

Embedding can also involve using clauses within clauses. In the following, the relative clause is embedded within the main clause. Although this embedding is relatively simple, we may already need to slow down a little to work out who or what went bankrupt:

	Embedded clause	
The company	*on whose behalf he had been doing the research*	*went bankrupt.*

Finite clauses can be embedded within non-finite clauses, and these can contain further clauses. In theory this process of multiple embedding could go on for ever, but in reality we put a brake on it when we think that the sentence may be becoming difficult to understand.

Other factors

Ellipsis, substitution and changes to the normal order of words and
basic constituents of clauses are not technically part of complex
sentence construction. However, where these features co-occur with
features of complex sentences they may contribute to making the
sentence difficult to understand.

29.4 When do we use complex sentences?

Generally, the more complex the ideas we want to convey, the more
complex we make the sentences we use to convey these ideas. We
use complex sentences in speaking as well as in writing, but it is in
writing that we can normally afford to increase the degree of
complexity. This is because the reader may need to look carefully at
different parts of the sentence in order to see how they fit together
and to work out what the sentence as a whole expresses. This is
possible when reading but isn't normally possible in listening.

How much we use complex sentences is also a matter of individual style.
For some people complex syntax is a necessary part of elegant expression
and a sign of linguistic mastery. For other people, the same features of
style can seem over-elaborate and unclear. In recent decades people have
tended to use shorter and simpler sentences in written English, and this is
generally considered 'good style'.

29.5 Typical difficulties for learners

Comprehension

For many learners, complex sentences can pose severe problems of
understanding. The problems increase according to how many
subordinate clauses the sentences contain and whether these are
embedded or not. Ellipsis and substitution, and changes to the basic
order of words and clause constituents can compound this problem.
So can non-standard language use.

The text below illustrates these difficulties. It is from a journal for English
teachers. Like sentences in most very condensed summaries, the first two
sentences in this paragraph contain a lot of features of complex
sentences. The texts on pages 388–393 illustrate and analyse these factors
further.

> This paper describes an experiment in which users investigated and evaluated the resources available in a university self-access centre, producing leaflets and reports for other potential users and the centre's staff as a piece of language-learning 'project work'. The involvement of students in improving the infrastructure, in providing support to other users, and in publicising the facilities available, creates potential for more efficient use and more democratic control of the learning resources which it is the task of such a centre to provide. It also provides additional opportunities for language learning and for learning-how-to-learn.

Features of complex sentences contained in this text:

Main clause	This paper describes an experiment
Relative clause	in which users investigated and evaluated the resources
Non-finite verbless clause	available in a university self-access centre,
Non-finite (participle) clause	producing leaflets and reports
Adverbial (prepositional phrase)	for other potential users and the centre's staff
Adverbial (adverbial phrase)	as a piece of language-learning 'project work'.
Main clause, which itself includes: • ellipsis of *the involvement of the students* for the second and third times • a relative clause 'reduced' to a verbless clause: (*available*)	The involvement of students in improving the infrastructure, in providing support to other users, and in publicising the facilities available, creates potential
Adverbial (prepositional phrase)	for more efficient use and more democratic control of the learning resources
Relative clause	which it is the task of such a centre to provide.

Speaking and writing

Avoiding and simplifying

Some learners avoid using complex sentences and over-depend on simple sentences composed of one clause or of clauses strung together with coordinating conjunctions. This may not only be stylistically inappropriate, but it may also prevent the learners from expressing themselves as effectively as they would wish.

The text which follows was written by a student who was asked to describe her difficulties in understanding written English. (She uses *familiar* to mean something like *'apparently and misleadingly familiar'*

> I don't have any problems with vocabulary in my reading. I just try to find the meaning through the context. If I can understand the whole idea, I just forget it. I never look a word up in the dictionary because it just distracts me. Familiar words always cause me difficulties. I think that's because I always think in my language.

The text is generally clear. However, the exaggerated simplicity of the style (apart, perhaps, from the final sentence) also reads oddly. Either she doesn't know how to construct more complex sentences, or she is being cautious. Her teacher might want to encourage her to write more naturally using complex sentences, and would have to teach the relevant features as necessary.

Over-ambitious construction of sentences

Other learners may attempt to construct complex sentences before they have sufficient command of the linguistic means to do so. The result of this may be that they fail to express what they want to express.

The text which follows was written by another student in the same class. The two students have similar linguistic and educational backgrounds, and had been set the same task.

> I think that the problems with vocabulary are relative, because many words
> are possible to understand and find their meaning (**1**) looking at the context.
> (**2**) But obviously you can't understand the context if you haven't
> assimilated some essential vocabulary.
> This vocabulary that I think a reader must know to understand at least the
> context it's given (**3**) by practice only.

The writer of this text is altogether more ambitious than his classmate, and the length and degree of complexity of his sentences are correspondingly more natural. He makes extensive use of noun clauses, participle and infinitive clauses and ellipsis. He also uses adverbial and relative clauses where they are appropriate.

On the other hand, this text isn't easy to read. The difficulties are partly because the writer lacks a command of vocabulary and idiomatic expression and has some general problems with grammar (e.g. his use of *the*), but they also relate to the way sentences are constructed. Specific problems include:

(**1**) The learner ambitiously links infinitives (*to understand*; *find*) after *possible*, but wrongly uses *find their meaning*. After *possible* the infinitives already have an implied object (*many words*) and we can't add a new one (*their meaning*). What the learner perhaps needs here is a preparatory 'it' construction – *It is possible to understand and find out the meaning of many words . . . .*

(**2**) The learner really needs a preposition here – *from the context* or, if he wants to use the participle clause, *by* or *through* (*looking at the context*).

(**3**) This repetition of the subject (*it* – *This vocabulary*) after the relative clause is ungrammatical and can give the impression that *is given* refers to *the context* rather than to knowledge of the vocabulary.

In some other languages, the longer and more complex the sentences, the 'better the style'. Learners may be influenced by what is considered 'good style' in their own language, and may feel that they have to use complex sentences in English when this isn't appropriate. So, while we have to teach the essential features of sentence construction, we may also have to discourage our students from making sentences over-complex.

29.6 Consolidation exercises
(see pp. 509–514 for possible answers)

Language in context

1 (see p. 509)

Read these passages and answer the questions that follow. The first is an extract from a novel, and describes part of a wedding from the point of view of a bridesmaid. The second is from a book about group dynamics in the classroom.

(i)

> When I walked up the aisle behind Eden, one of a bevy of whom Evelyn who married Jonathan Durham, Patricia Chatteriss and a Naughton cousin called Audrey were the others, I saw Chad in a front pew on the bride's side but a long way from Vera who with Jamie was correctly sandwiched between Helen and my mother.

(ii)

> I have the feeling that a lot of the tensions in groups, particularly at intermediate level where students are making the difficult transition from a situation where language can somehow be dealt out in chunks to a situation where language becomes altogether more insubstantial and progress cannot be measured so easily, may be due in part to this unsatisfied feeling, that is the need to possess something that cannot be possessed.

a Both extracts consist of a basic main clause and a basic subordinate clause (each of these contains several further embedded clauses). Divide each extract into these two basic clauses.

b Is the basic subordinate clause in (i) an adverbial clause, a relative clause or a noun clause?

c Is the basic subordinate clause in (ii) an adverbial clause, a relative clause or a noun clause?

d The first clause in (i) contains a verbless clause. Identify this.

e This verbless clause contains an embedded relative clause. Identify this.

f This relative clause contains a further embedded relative clause. Identify this.

g Is this further embedded relative clause defining or non-defining?

h Identify a past participle clause in this first basic clause of extract (i).

i Extract (ii) has been printed below in a different format. Work out and explain the system and rationale that underlies the fact that phrases have been indented from the margin (to different degrees). Refer to each line of the text:

```
           1  2   3   4  5
1    I have the feeling
2        that a lot of the tensions in groups,
3            particularly at intermediate level
4                where students are making the difficult transition from a
                                                                situation
5                    where language can somehow be dealt out in chunks
4                to a situation
5                    where language becomes altogether more insubstantial
                                     and progress cannot be measured so easily,
2        may be due in part to this unsatisfied feeling,
3            that is the need
4                to possess something
5                    that cannot be possessed.
```

2 (See pp. 510–512)

The three sentences which follow are from different contexts. Each of them was picked out by an advanced learner of English as being difficult to understand. Study each sentence in turn and answer the questions.

(i) This sentence summarises a talk given at an international conference for language teachers.

Ranging over two millennia, and casting a glance or two at Kelly, while concentrating chiefly on current times, I discussed and on the whole defended several distinct lines of thought on foreign-language learning and teaching (English serving as the example) which are still regarded by many as unorthodox and impracticable.

(ii) This sentence considers the reaction of an immigrant community to a possible policy of enforced repatriation.

> How disturbing it is for the gainfully employed, and those whose attempts to find work have been arduous and time-consuming, to discover that enforced repatriation is not only a possibility but is in danger of becoming an integral part of the policy of the new government, is slowly becoming apparent throughout the community.

(iii) The third sentence is from a review of a particular restaurant on Barbados.

> Only when I'd finished, and offered the remains of my smoked flying fish and fresh tropical fruits to the local birds – who were threatening to re-enact their roles in the Hitchcock movie if I didn't leave plenty for them – did I become aware of the blindingly blue stretch of the Caribbean over-looked by customers from the terrace.

a What is the structure of this sentence? (What clauses are there and how are they related?)

b How well-expressed is this sentence?

c What is there in the construction of this sentence that might pose particular problems for learners?

Learners' English (see pp. 512–514)

The following texts were written by different learners of English. They had been asked to comment on their difficulties in learning the language.

(i)

> When I read books, newspapers, I don't understand many words. So I sometimes use a dictionary. But usually I imagine the meanings for words. I find a word many times in a book or newspaper, I use a dictionary. I don't have familiar words between English and my language. So it's difficult to memory and use it.

(ii)

> Sometimes teachers ask me about the things I don't know at all.
> Then I can't join the conversation. I just listen to other students'
> opinions. It is quite difficult for me to have time to express my point
> of view because we're educated that we have to be quiet during
> class. If we want to speak during the class we have to put our hands
> up and beg some period of time to the teacher or the teacher points
> out one, particular student.

(iii)

> (iii) My biggest problem is with vocabulary; although a lot of words
> are the same as in my language however sometimes the meanings
> change a little – or I should say a lot – and this confuses me
> especially when I am talking and I don't pay too much attention to the
> exact words I use for this purpose so I need to learn a lot of new
> words and learn to use the old ones what I know them better. I hope
> in this class I will have the opportunity for improve a lot.

a Re-write each of the texts so that they read naturally, and then examine the changes you have made.

b In general terms what strengths and weaknesses does each of these learners have in constructing English sentences?

c What specific problems do any of these learners have? (Is there anything in particular that you would want to teach this learner?)

PART E

Extension exercises

Extension exercises

The following exercises help you to become more aware of issues that affect our choice of one grammatical feature rather than another, more aware of difficulties your own learners have with specific grammatical features, and more constructively critical of how grammar is treated in the range of materials available to your learners.

These exercises are roughly tuned so that they extend the content of any of the chapters. More detailed extension exercises for each of the chapters in this book can be found on the Cambridge University Press Website http://www.cup.cam.ac.uk/elt/.

Exploring English

Obtain two or more short texts from different sources. These can be written (e.g. a letter from a friend; a serious newspaper article; a recipe) or transcribed spoken English (e.g. a magazine interview or your own transcription of a recording of friends talking or of an unscripted radio discussion).

You can:

- count the number of times your chosen grammar feature occurs, and for each text work out a ratio between this and some related feature (for example you might compare the use of *a* and *the* or of two tenses);
- justify why this feature is chosen each time it occurs;
- sub-classify the feature (for example you might divide adverbs into adverbs of frequency, attitude markers etc.);
- look at how the speaker/writer's tone or message would be affected if other choices had been made;
- identify and account for any non-standard features (e.g. conditionals – *If I'd have had*; past tense forms – *didn't used to*; relative pronouns – *The girl what I saw*);
- compare the occurrence of this grammar feature between the two texts, and account for any differences (e.g. some features are assumed to occur more frequently in written text than in spoken, or in formal

contexts than informal). This exercise enables you to begin testing this out.

Researching how people use English

If you have access to a corpus of English and a concordancing programme, you can learn a great deal about how English is really used by calling up real examples of words and seeing what words they occur with (e.g. how often are comparative forms followed by *than*?; how often is *than* followed by a subject pronoun such as *I* as opposed to an object pronoun such as *me*?).

If you don't have this access, you can choose proficient users of English from different regional and social backgrounds and, for example, read them or show them a list of sentences and ask them to rate each as 'correct', 'incorrect' or 'dubious'. Insist on a rapid, spontaneous response.

Record their answers, and then ask them to explain any which are not correct. Try to account for any disagreement between them, or between their answers and your own.

Whether or not you use a corpus, choose a grammar feature where use varies – for example, comparatives, prepositions, modal verbs or singular/plural agreement, e.g. (comparatives)

	correct	dubious	incorrect
(i) He runs *quicker* than me.			
(ii) He runs faster than *I*.			
(iii) He's *more old* than me.			
(iv) He's *pleasanter* than me.			
(v) He runs *faster* than me.			
(vi) He's *more pleasant* than me.			
(vii) He's *older* than me.			
(viii) He runs faster than *me*.			

Exploring learners' English

You can carry out any of the following exercises both before and after teaching a particular grammar feature, in order to evaluate the effect your teaching has on your learners' awareness, understanding and speaking or writing. Choose two or three learners to focus on.

Comprehension

Ask your students to listen to or read something in which your chosen grammar feature is used prominently. Focus initially only on general understanding.

You can:

- isolate the instances of your chosen grammar feature and ask specific questions to test their understanding of this.
- isolate the instances of your chosen grammar feature and ask students to explain why this has been used (where feasible, they might do this in their own language).
- ask your students to underline or pick out anything they don't understand.

Speaking and/or writing

You can use learners' written compositions of different kinds or can record them speaking and transcribe this. In some cases, the choice of topic may be important – for example, if you are exploring their use of passive constructions, asking them to describe some kind of process (e.g. *What happens to letters when you post them?*) is likely to create opportunities for their use.

You can:

- count how often they use your target grammar feature in contexts where its use would be natural.
- count how often they use it in inappropriate contexts.
- count how frequently they construct its form correctly or make mistakes in this.
- underline problems in their writing, and ask them to correct this and to explain their basis for doing this.

After teaching the feature, you can ask them how easy or difficult they have found it to:

- understand the use and meaning of these forms.
- understand the construction of these forms.
- remember these forms.
- use these forms in speaking and in writing.

You can also ask them to compare the use of these in English with any equivalent forms in their own language(s).

Course materials

You may decide to look at one coursebook, or may choose to compare two or more. In comparing course material it is useful to look at:

- materials intended for two different types of learners (e.g. adults versus adolescents; elementary versus upper-intermediate).
- materials produced by different publishers for similar markets.

Consider:

- how easy is it to find the grammar feature by looking in the contents section or index of the book?
- how accurate, comprehensive, clear and useful are the rules provided?
- how clearly does the material clarify the difference between closely related forms (e.g. *each* and *every*; *past perfect simple* and *past perfect continuous*)?
- are learners guided to work out the meaning of the language for themselves?
- what opportunities are provided for learners to practise the grammar feature in controlled exercises and to use it more freely? Do they provide opportunities for students to work together?
- what kinds of texts are provided? Are these real or are they especially constructed to provide examples of a particular rule? If they are especially constructed, how natural are they?
- how much attention does the book pay to this grammar feature compared to others? Do you think this degree of attention is appropriate?
- how much attention is paid to the meaning(s) of this feature?
- how much attention is paid to relevant aspects of spelling?
- how much attention is paid to relevant aspects of pronunciation?
- does the book cover the feature in one section, or is attention to it divided between different sections of the book (or different books in a series)? At what levels is it considered and at what levels are more complex or exceptional forms introduced?

Comparing reference materials

Select two dictionaries or two grammars intended for learners. Choose one or two grammar features and compare how they are treated in the two books. You may choose a general heading such as *type 2 conditional* or *relative clause* to research in the grammars, using the contents section or the index to find what you are looking for. In a dictionary you can simply look up a number of words in a particular class such as *quantifiers, modal verbs, prepositions; discourse markers* or *relative pronouns.*

Consider:

- how much information is given?
- how comprehensive and accurate is this?
- how clearly is this expressed?
- how much use is made of examples?
- how much attention is paid, respectively, to form, meaning, collocation, style factors, ordering of sentence constituents and words, pronunciation and spelling?
- which of the dictionaries or grammars would you recommend to students who wanted to buy one for their own study? Why?

PART F

Pronunciation, spelling and punctuation

I   Pronunciation

Plural nouns (See Chapter 1 p. 8)

Regular forms

The regular plural ending has three possible pronunciations:

+ /ɪz/

We add /ɪz/ to singular nouns which end in the following sounds:

/tʃ/ *churches*	/dʒ/ *judges*	/s/ passes	/z/ *mazes*
/ʃ/ *wishes*	/ʒ/ (*rouges*)		

+ /s/

We add /s/ to singular nouns which end in the following sounds:

/p/ *lips*	/t/ *parts*	/k/ *locks*

We also add /s/ to many words which end in /θ/ and /f/:

/θ/ *cloths*	/ʃ/ *ruffs*

The sounds /p/, /t/, /k/, /θ/ and /f/ are all *voiceless* i.e. we say them without making a 'humming' noise in the throat.

+ /z/

We add /z/ to words which end in all other sounds:

/n/ *tons*	/g/ *frogs*	/v/ *waves*	/əʊ/ *toes*

At some point everyone needs to learn when we pronounce regular endings as /ɪz/ (e.g. *oranges*).

Although course materials often also pay attention to the distinction between /s/ and /z/, many learners automatically make this distinction. Even if they don't, this rarely leads to any problems of being understood – teachers sometimes regard this distinction as an unnecessary complication for their students and gloss over it in practice.

Words that end in /f/ and /θ/

Singular nouns which end in /f/ or /θ/ have a tendency to change their pronunciation in plural forms. Sometimes this is optional.

| /f/ | ⇒ | /v/ | *roofs* | (/ruːfs/) | or | /ruːvz/ |
| /θ/ | ⇒ | /ð/ | *baths* | (/bɑːθs/) | or | /bɑːðz/ |

Sometimes corresponding changes in the spelling oblige us to make the change.

- f(e) + ves

| Some singular nouns which end in *f* | *loaf* ⇒ *loaves*
 leaf ⇒ *leaves* |
| Singular nouns which end in a combination of vowel + *fe* | *wife* ⇒ *wives*
 life ⇒ *lives* |

Some words that end in /f/ and /θ/ never change their pronunciation in the plural form.

| all singular nouns that end in *ff* | *puff* ⇒ *puffs* (/pʌfs/)
 cloth ⇒ *cloths* (/kloθs/) |

Using dictionaries

Learners also need to use a dictionary to check the pronunciation of plural forms of words that end in *th* and *f*.

Adverbs which end in *ly* (see Chapter 3 p. 30)

Most people pronounce:

- *ly* (e.g. weak*ly*) as /li/ i.e. a weak form of /liː/
- *cally* (e.g. physi*cally*; ironi*cally*; fantasti*cally*) as /kli/.

a, *an*, and *the* (see Chapter 4 pp. 45–46)

a and *an*

Whether we use *a* /ə/ or *an* /ən/ depends on the pronunciation of the sound which immediately follows. The key factor is whether or not this sound is a consonant (we consider /j/ and /w/ as consonants for this purpose).

The spelling itself is unimportant. Even though *umbrella* and *union* begin with the same letter (*u*), and so do *hour* and *horse* (*h*), we say:

an umbrella	The first sound of *umbrella* is /ʌ/
a union	The first sound of *union* is /j/

an hour	The first sound of *hour* is /aʊ/
a horse	The first sound of *horse* is /h/

Most people pronounce /h/ in *hotel* but some people say *an hotel* (/ənəʊtel/).

the

Although we use *the* as the definite article no matter what sound follows, we pronounce this differently according to whether or not a consonant follows.
Before a consonant we pronounce *the* /ðə/. Before a vowel we pronounce it /ðɪ/, and sometimes add a linking /j/:

Before a consonant	*the problem*	/ðəprobləm/
Before a vowel	*the egg*	/ðɪeg/ or /ðɪjeg/

Stressed and isolated forms

We don't usually stress articles but if they are stressed or if we are isolating the word for some purpose, we also pronounce them differently.

	a	an	the
Stressed or isolated form	/eɪ/	/æn/	/ðɪː/
Neutral form	/ə/	/ən/	/ðə/ (/ðɪ/)

*I didn't say **two** tickets, I said **a** (/eɪ/) ticket.*

*You're not **the** (/ðɪː/) Tom Stoppard are you?*

Comparative and superlative adjectives and adverbs (see Chapter 6 p. 68)

The following are normally 'weak' i.e. we pronounce them so rapidly and quietly that they are only just distinguishable in the flow of speech. The vowel sound in both cases is /ə/:

'er' (/ə/) *bigger* – /bɪgə/

than (/ðən/ or even /ðə/) *bigger than me* /bɪgə ðəmiː/

The following is also normally 'weak'. The vowel may be pronounced /ə/ or /ɪ/:

'est' (/əst/ or /ɪst/) *biggest* – /bɪgəst/ or /bɪgɪst/.

We often leave out the final sound (/t/) of . . .*est*, *most* and *least*, particularly if it is followed by a consonant:

> The **biggest** prize – /bɪgəs praɪz/
>
> The **most carefully** painted – /məʊs keəflɪ/
>
> The **least practical** suggestion – /liːs præktikl/

In words which end in the sound /ŋ/, we add /g/ before the comparative or superlative ending:

> long ⇒ longer /lɒŋ/ ⇒ /lɒŋgə/ (not /lɒŋə/)
>
> strong ⇒ strongest /strɒŋ/ ⇒ /strɒŋgə/ (not /strɒŋə/)

Past forms (see Chapter 8 p. 101)

We spell regular verbs with *ed* at the end of their past tense form but we pronounce the end of the past tense form in one of three distinct ways. In each case our choice of final sound depends on the sound that ends the infinitive:

+ /ɪd/

We add /ɪd/ to the infinitive when the infinitive ends in /t/ or /d/:

> waited (/weɪtɪd/); hoarded (/hɔːdɪd/)

+ /t/

We add /t/ to the infinitive when the infinitive ends in one of the following sounds: /p/; /k/; /θ/; /f/; /s/; /ʃ/; /tʃ/ (like /t/, these sounds are all produced without vibration/humming in the throat i.e. they are 'voiceless'):

> pricked (/prɪkt/); laughed (/lɑːft/)

+ /d/

We add /d/ to the infinitive when the infinitive ends in any other sounds (like /d/, these sounds are all produced with vibration/humming in the throat i.e. they are 'voiced'):

> moved (/muːvd/)

It is important to teach our students when to use /ɪd/ and when not to. With regard to distinguishing between /t/ and /d/, however, many learners automatically make the distinction. It may be unnecessary to teach this, and may even mystify students if we decide to draw attention to the distinction.

Modal verbs (see Chapter 10 pp. 119–135)

We generally pronounce modal verbs in two ways.

'Strong' form

Modal verbs have one pronunciation when:

- they occur without a main verb: *Yes, I **can**.* /kæn/
- we stress them for particular effect: A: *You can't swim.*
  B: *I **can** swim.* /kæn/

'Weak' form

Generally, we don't pronounce modal verbs as strongly as in the examples above. In most contexts, we stress some other part of the sentence, and then we *weaken* the modal verb (i.e. we say it very fast and very softly). The vowel is often reduced to /ə/ or is practically omitted. The final consonant is also often left out, especially if the verb which follows begins with another consonant.

	Strong form	Weak form
can	/kæn/ (*Yes, I can*)	/kə/ (*I c' see*)
could	/kʊd/ (*Yes, I could*)	/kə/ (*I c' see*) /kəd/ (*I c'd eat*)
shall	/ʃæl/ (*Yes, I shall*)	/ʃə/ (*I sh' know*) /ʃəl/ (*I sh'l know*)
should	/ʃʊd/ (*Yes, I should*)	/ʃə/ (*I sh' go*) /ʃəd/ (*I sh'd eat*)
would	/wʊd/ (*Yes, I would*)	/wə/ (*I w' go*) /d/ (*I'd go*)

The weak form rather than the strong form is the most neutral.

The present simple 'third person *s*' (see Chapter 12 pp. 153–166)

In the third person (i.e. after singular subjects like *he, she, it, the dog, Fred*) we add *s* to the infinitive.

Infinitive	3rd person form
live	*lives*

The pronunciation of the final *s* varies according to the final sound of the infinitive. It may be pronounced /ɪz/, /s/ or /z/ in accordance with the rules described for regular plural forms of nouns on page 402.

Learners very frequently fail to pronounce this final *s*, even when they have reached a very high level of proficiency in the language. This may sometimes be a problem of pronunciation, but it may also be a problem of grammar (i.e. a problem of remembering that it should be there). It may also be affected by the fact that the final *s* conveys no meaning – it is purely a formal requirement. Teachers sometimes pay a lot of attention to this 'problem', but it is one which seems to resolve itself only if and when an individual learner chooses to make formal accuracy a major priority.

Defining and non-defining clauses (see Chapter 28 pp. 377–383)

In speaking we usually make a distinction in whether something is defining or non-defining by the way we use intonation. A defining phrase is part of a larger group of words. We use intonation to show that this is all one group.

A: *Which fridge packed up?*

one intonation group

B: *The one that hasn't worked properly for years.*

Non-defining information usually forms a group on its own. We use intonation to show this, and we may also pause briefly between each information group.

separate intonation group

The fridge, which hasn't worked properly for years, has finally packed up.

II Spelling

Plural nouns (See Chapter 1 pp. 10–11)

Regular plural forms end in the letter *s*. Sometimes we just add **s** to the singular form (*pen* ⇒ *pen***s**), but we also sometimes add *es* and we change the spelling of some singular words which end in *y* to *ies*.

+ es

We add *es* to singular nouns which end in the following letters or combinations of letters.

ch chur***ches***   *s* pas***ses***   *x* bo***xes***   *sh* wi***shes***
z buz***zes***

We also add *es* to some singular nouns which end in *o*.

*potato**es***   *tomato**es***

-y + ies

We change *y* to *i* and add *es* to singular nouns which end in a combination of consonant + *y*.

party ⇒ *part**ies***   *lady* ⇒ *lad**ies***

Using dictionaries

Learners need to use a dictionary to check whether we add *s* or *es* to any particular words ending in *o*.

Adverbs which end in – *ly* (see Chapter 3 p. 31)

+ *ly*

Many adverbs are written in the same way as adjectives with the addition of the letters *ly*, e.g.

absolute ⇒ *absolute**ly***   *equal* ⇒ *equal**ly***
obvious ⇒ *obvious**ly***   *successful* ⇒ *successful**ly***

Also : *professionally; properly; usually.*

y ⇒ i + *ly*

Sometimes we need to make other changes to the adjective in order to add *ly*. We take off the final *y* on many adjectives and replace this with *ily*.

happy ⇒ *happ**ily***   *dry* ⇒ *dr**ily***   *gay* ⇒ *ga**ily***

There are some exceptions to this rule, e.g. *coyly; wryly. Drily* can also be written as *dryly.*

-e + ly

We take off the final *e* on some adjectives and add the letters *ly.*

true ⇒ *truly*   *due* ⇒ *duly*   *whole* ⇒ *wholly*

We simply add *ly* to most adjectives which end in a consonant + *e*, e.g. *absolutely.*

-e + y

We take off the final *e* on adjectives that end in *le* and add the letter *y.*

capable ⇒ *capab**ly***   *possible* ⇒ *possib**ly***

+ ally

We add *ally* to most adjectives which end in *ic*:

intrinsic ⇒ *intrinsic**ally***   *fantastic* ⇒ *fantastic**ally***

There are a few exceptions e.g. public*ly*.

Comparative and superlative adjectives and adverbs (see Chapter 6 p. 68)

We often refer to *er* and *est* forms (e.g. *older; oldest*). However, in many cases we need to add slightly different combinations of letters.

+ r
+ st   Words which already end in *e*   *brave* ⇒ *braver, bravest*

-y + i + er
-y + i + est   Words which end in **consonant** + **y**   *dry* ⇒ *drier*
                                                  pretty ⇒ *prettier*

+ consonant + er
+ consonant + est
	The final consonant of a one-syllable word is doubled where the word end is a **single vowel + single consonant**	*fit* ⇒ *fitter*
		thin ⇒ *thinner*
		but not
		calm ⇒ * *calmmer*
		    (two consonants)
		green ⇒ * *greenner*
		    (two vowels)

-ing forms (see Chapter 8 pp. 98–104; Chapter 11 pp.136–152)

In many cases we simply add '-*ing*' to the infinitive.

go ⇒ *go**ing***   *open* ⇒ *open**ing***

-e + ing

In other cases, we also need to modify the spelling of the infinitive before we add -*ing*.

Some infinitives end in a combination of vowel + consonant + **e**. In these cases we leave out the **e** before **ing**.	*live* ⇒ *liv**ing*** *improve* ⇒ *improv**ing***

+ consonant + ing

We double the final consonant of the infinitive in the following cases:

One-syllable infinitives which end in a single vowel + single consonant combination	*pat* ⇒ *patting* *stop* ⇒ *stopping*
Multi-syllable infinitives when:	
• the final syllable is stressed and ends in a single vowel + single consonant combination	*begin* ⇒ *beginning* *refer* ⇒ *referring*
• the final syllable ends in a single vowel + **l** (British English only – American: traveling)	*travel* ⇒ *travelling*
Doubling the final consonant of the infinitive is optional in multi-syllable words which end in **s** (stress not on the last syllable)	*focusing; focussing*

+ k + ing

We add **k** to infinitives which end in **ic**	*panic* ⇒ *panicking*

Past forms (see Chapter 8 pp. 98–104)

Regular verbs are sometimes referred to as **ed** verbs. The past simple form ends in **ed** and is the same as the past participle form.

talked   *liked*   *sinned*

Learners sometimes understand that we make the past tense form of regular verbs by simply adding **ed** to the end of the infinitive. In the case of some verbs (e.g. *talk – talked*) this is fine. However, we often need to make other changes as well – the precise changes we make depend on the spelling of the infinitive:

+ d

We add only **d** to the infinitive when the infinitive ends in **e**.

liked   *phoned*

- y + ied

We replace **y** with **i** and add **ed** when the infinitive ends in consonant **+ y**.

cry ⇒ *cried*   *dry* ⇒ *dried*

+ consonant + ed

We double the final consonant and add **ed**:

in single syllable verbs	When the infinitive ends in a single vowel + single consonant combination. *sinned*; *rammed*
in multi-syllable verbs	When the final syllable of the infinitive is stressed and ends in a single vowel + single consonant combination. *referred* (c.f. *offered* – final syllable not stressed)
When the infinitive ends in *l* *rebelled*; *travelled*; *labelled*	In American English the final *l* is only doubled if the final syllable is stressed e.g. *re<u>belled</u>* but *<u>traveled</u>* and *<u>labeled</u>*.

+ k + ed

We add a **k** to the infinitive and then *ed* when the infinitive ends in a vowel **+ c**.

panicked; *picnicked*

+ ed

We add *ed* to the infinitive of all other regular verbs. These include:

Single syllable verbs	When the infinitive ends in a vowel + vowel + consonant combination, e.g. *moaned*; *greeted* When the infinitive ends in a vowel + consonant + consonant combination, e.g. *calmed*; *warned*
Multi-syllable verbs	When the final syllable of the infinitive ends in a consonant and is not stressed, e.g. *offered*; *opened*

The present simple 'third person s' (see Chapter 12 pp. 153–166)

The spelling of the final *s* varies according to the final sound of the infinitive. We sometimes add *es* to the infinitive, and we sometimes add *s*:

+ es

We add *es* to infinitives which end in the following letters or combinations of letters:

ch	watches
s	kisses
sh	wishes
z	fizzes
x	faxes

We also added *es* to most infinitives which end in a combination of consonant + single *o*, e.g. *goes*; *does*.

-y + es

We remove final *y* and add *es* to infinitives that end in consonant + *y*.

cry	⇒	*cries*
worry	⇒	*worries*

+ s

We add *s* to other infinitives, e.g. *loves*; *reads*; *pays*; *rages*

Have changes to *has*.

III Punctuation

Plural nouns (See Chapter 1 p. 13)

In writing, we place an apostrophe ('):

- before the possessive *s* on singular nouns, e.g. *a girl*'s *book; a man*'s *best friend*, and on irregular plural nouns, e.g. *The People*'s *Republic; women*'s *clothes.*

- after the possessive *s* on regular plural words, e.g. *the books*' *covers; the dogs*' *tails* and on singular nouns ending in *s*, e.g. *the series' end; James' friend.*

The pronunciation rules for *'s* are the same as those for regular plural endings (see Pronunciation p. 402).

Linking two or more adjectives together (See Chapter 2 p. 22)

In writing we generally separate the adjectives in a list by commas when they all qualify the same noun.

A dark, gloomy, terrifying, clearing.

We leave out commas when one adjective qualifies another.

A pale blue vase.

Direct speech (See Chapter 17 pp. 216–230)

We generally indicate direct speech by enclosing it in either single or double inverted commas: '. . .' or ". . .".

If this direct speech is enclosed in double inverted commas, then we use single inverted commas to enclose any further direct speech that is embedded in this (*"What do you mean, 'Mary's had enough'?"*) or vice versa.

Increasingly, people use a colon (:) to introduce direct speech (see the newspaper report on p. 224). More traditionally, we use a comma to introduce this, or we place a comma before the second inverted comma when followed by a phrase like *he said*.

> *He said, 'I like you.'*
> *'I like you,' he said.*

See the extracts from novels and a newspaper in Chapter 17 for examples of how direct speech is normally punctuated.

Relative clauses (See Chapter 26)

Some relative clauses simply provide information which is additional to the information in the main clause (non-defining relative clauses). We generally use a comma to separate these clauses from the main clause.

> *She gave the uneaten food to the children, who cooed with delight.*

Some relative clauses identify something from other, similar things (defining relative clauses). In this case we don't use a comma to separate the clauses.

> *The child **who was crying** eventually found her mother.*

We always use a comma before a relative clause that qualifies the whole of the main clause.

> *The bus came at last, which was an enormous relief.*

Defining and non-defining clauses (See Chapter 28)

Grammars and coursebooks for learners of English usually suggest that non-defining clauses and phrases are separated from the main clause by commas (all the examples in Chapter 28 follow this rule).

This is sensible advice to give to learners, and enables them to choose between defining and non-defining clauses and phrases in writing.

In fact, however, we often leave out the commas where the context makes it clear that a clause or phrase doesn't have a defining function. As the following demonstrates, this practice is very widespread, through a range of genres ([ ] shows where a comma could be used but wasn't in the original):

a)   Newspaper report

> The Bank of England's huge operation for the pound [   ] which
> ended in Britain's humiliating departure from the Exchange Rate
> Mechanism on Black Wednesday [   ] has left the Government facing
> losses of up to £5 billion.

b)   Information on packaging

> Hovis Wheatgerm Bread has 4 times as much Germ as 100%
> Wholemeal Bread [   ] which gives it the distinctive taste that
> all the family enjoys.

c)   History

> The London Docks, however, faced increasing pressure from
> Tilbury [   ] which could handle larger boats.

d)   'Literary' fiction

> Oldmeadow shoved the man away [   ] who moved a foot or two
> then came back again.

e)   Popular fiction

> She found a crumpled tissue and blew her nose violently. She
> never cried. Strong Alice hadn't cried since after Charlie [   ] which
> was obviously post-natal.

f)   Formal correspondence

> I enclose a note of my charges [   ] which I would mention I
> have limited to the absolute minimum and I look forward to
> receiving a cheque in settlement in due course.

PART G

More on
sentence constituents

1   Discourse markers – examples in context

(See Chapter 22)

Numbering and ordering points

> Two other trends give me cheer: *firstly* the impact of Far Eastern inward investment on the supply chain has forced more suppliers to adopt standards and consistency of quality . . .
>
> *Secondly* in our largest companies we are developing a number of significant world class champions.

I lost my temper and *afterwards* I felt really stupid.

Adding something

> Mix [stuff such as cheese and meat] either with stale bread and freeze it to feed the birds in winter. *Also* help them with birdbaths, berrying shrubs and birdboxes.

> During the first two blocks . . . there are lectures and seminars . . . These satisfy the need to establish perceptions of what language is, what teaching is, and alternative approaches to the teaching of English.
>
> *In addition*, the second block, leading up to the practicum, devotes substantial time to developing a familiarity with techniques for observation and evaluation, training and supervision.

. . . most of us find it hard to plan our financial futures with total confidence. ***Additionally***, with the continuing uncertainty surrounding house prices up and down the country, it is ever more important to be aware of every investment opportunity.

You can grill the fish for five minutes in a very hot grill or on a barbecue. ***Alternatively*** *you can poach it.*

I can cook if you want or we can go out ***instead***.

If your tooth really hurts you should make an appointment with the dentist. ***Besides****, it's high time you had a check up.*

. . . working with kids on my children's TV show *Small talk* sharpens my wits. My elder daughter Emma's six-year-old son Tom keeps me on my toes, ***too***.

The fundamental problems still remain. Inadequate investment in training, woefully inadequate investment in state of the art machinery and in the development of new products and processes – and ***on top of this*** we still lack a supportive capital structure.

Linking similar things together

Classroom management cannot be reduced to a few discrete components to be imparted to teachers in a short, one-shot training session.

Likewise, even a simple skill such as the use of referential questions versus display questions is dependent upon knowing when one kind of question might be appropriate.

. . . the course is not subject-specific. ***Similarly***, the course is not language-specific.

Introducing something that contrasts with expectations

Just like those rich American ice creams, Sainsbury's Indulgence is made with real dairy cream and the highest quality, freshest ingredients.

However, at only £1.99 for a 500ml tub (that's up to £1.50 cheaper than the US brands) you don't have to be a rich American to afford it.

there is the naive belief that the irrelevant words and images that the keyword method requires somehow waste space in the memory. *In fact*, experiments show that the learning of such 'vehicle' words does facilitate the learning of others, and does not overburden the memory.

applied research is more rigorous and does not claim to contribute directly to the solution of problems. Action research, *on the other hand*, is less interested in obtaining generalisable, scientific knowledge than knowledge for a particular situation or purpose.

I am not presenting my findings at this point as prescriptions for teachers to follow. *Rather*, I encourage teacher educators to use the interactional arrangements presented in this chapter as suggestions.

adults kept written records of child second language learners' linguistic output. *In contrast*, here the term emphasises first-person authorship.

*I thought she was going to complain but **on the contrary** she seemed quite pleased.*

*We've had to cut out most luxuries. We **still** get a daily newspaper, **though**.*

Small companies depend on overdrafts and there is little risk
capital on offer. Sadly there is no sign of change and four out
of five small businesses which start up fail within five years.
　　Nevertheless, I can now produce examples of manufacturing
companies in every region which have proven their ability to
take on the toughest world competition and win.

*You promised to end corruption in government. **Yet**, already we learn that
three senior posts have gone to members of your family.*

Well, the lions and giants for me have always been the ones that live in
my mind, not the ones that live outside me. They have been my own
depressions, my own lack of courage, my own anger. These have been
the lions and giants I've had to fight with, and I think they were for
Bunyan, too, *actually*.

*I could have taken Monday off work but I decided to go in **all the same**.*

Causes and results

*. . . plants growing in compost-rich soil need less pest and disease control.
So, rather than taking exercise, use your muscles to turn your compost
heap instead.*

A: *It's raining again.*
B: *Shouldn't you wait till it stops **then**?*

Memory improvement is generally regarded as a low-level activity, as
mechanical, non-intellectual, and *therefore*, especially in academic
circles, as non-educational (perhaps rather as drilling is seen). It is
therefore ignored in spite of the fact that it is known to be of value
for many activities that occur in educational studies.

The emphasis in this phase of reflection however is on description. **Hence**, the journal is more like a ship's log, where what happened and who is involved form the main part of the record.

in the last twenty years a substantial degree of professionalization has taken place. **Thus**, the theoretical basis of the field has moved from the study of phonetics and grammatical theory

Generalising

*The inspectors made a few criticisms but **on the whole** they were very satisfied.*

Exemplifying and narrowing down

Humans, as we all know, have much in common with animals: the needs for food and shelter, security and self-preservation, **for instance**.

*Why don't we meet again on, **say**, Saturday?*

Re-stating

A: I've got too much to do.
*B: **In other words** you don't want to go out.*

*She didn't have a heart attack – **that is**, it wasn't a 'coronary thrombosis'*

Rounding off

*. . . we're running out of time so, **in conclusion**, I'd just like to ask you to think over my proposition . . .*

2   Subordinating conjunctions – meaning

(See Chapter 24 pp. 334–342)

The following shows the main meanings expressed by subordinating conjunctions:

		Example
time	after; as; as long as; as soon as; before; since; until; when; while	The children ran away **as soon as** they heard the window smash.
place	in the same place as; where; wherever	He wanted to stay **where** he had always lived.
reason	as; because; since	I teach a lot of pronunciation **because** I think it's important.
manner	as if; as though	We staggered home **as if** we were drunk.
contrast	although; despite the fact that; even though; though; while	He did what I asked him **although** he looked very sullen about it.
condition	as long as; given that; if; provided that; unless	I don't go out of the house **if** it's raining.
purpose	in order that; so that	The teachers arrived early **in order that** they could decorate the hall before the party.
result	so; so that	I damaged the car **so that** now it's very difficult to open the door.

Some conjunctions can express more than one meaning (and so occur in more than one of the boxes above).

Since	
time	*I haven't wanted to eat anything **since** I've had flu.*
reason	*I refuse to buy the children presents **since** they get so many from other people.*

Some conjunctions are very similar in meaning (e.g. *as, because* and *since*). Others, although generally similar, are not interchangeable. For example, we can use both *while* and *although* to express contrast in the context of expressing opinions or making reservations but when we express general contrasts, we can use *although* but we can't use *while*.

> ***While/Although*** *I agree with you up to a point, I do think that there are other factors we ought to take into account.*
>
> *She won the prize **although**, no one thought she could do it.*

The conjunctions of time, in particular, express different kinds of meaning. The following table shows some of the most important of these:

	when	as	while	as soon as	until	since
1 Simultaneous events	✓	✓	✓			
2 Non-simultaneous				✓	✓	✓
3 Immediate sequence	✓		✓			
4 Duration	✓	✓	✓		✓	✓
5 No duration	✓	✓				
6 'Time before'					✓	
7 'Time after'						✓
8 Extending to the present						✓

1 *Marion watched TV **when/as/while** I did the ironing.*
   *I did the ironing **as/when/while** Marion watched TV.*

2 *I left **as soon as** I saw Carla.*
   *She waited **until** the phone rang.*
   *She has been ecstatic **since** the phone rang.*

3 *I left **as soon as/when** I saw Carla.*

4 *Marion watched TV **when/as/while** I did the ironing.*
   *I did the ironing **as/when/while** Marion watched TV.*

*She waited **until** the phone rang.*

*She has been ecstatic **since** the phone rang.*

5 *He left **as** I arrived.*

   *He left **when** I arrived.*

6 *She waited **until** the phone rang.*

7 *She has been ecstatic **since** the phone rang.*

As long as suggests that the duration of the event described lasted only for a particular period of time.

*I'll stay with you **as long as** you need me – but no longer than that!*

Once generally suggests completion – the achievement of some kind of goal.

*You can start doing gentle exercise **once** the stitches have been removed.*

PART H

Key to consolidation exercises

1 Nouns

Pronunciation

a

Those whose plural form is pronounced /s/ or /z/	Those whose plural form is pronounced /ɪz/
knives; moves	*wedges; oranges; wishes; lunches*

b The singular form of the words in the right-hand column all end in one of the sounds which is followed by /ɪz/ in the plural form: wedge, orange – /dʒ/; *wish* – /ʃ/; *lunch* /tʃ/.

c

Those whose plural form is pronounced /z/	Those whose plural form is pronounced /s/	Those whose plural from can be pronounced either /s/ or /z/
pins; pillows	*locks; pits; coughs; cloths; scruffs; growths*	*hearths; mouths; baths*

d The singular form of the words in the first column end in a voiced sound (i.e. one which is accompanied by 'humming' in the throat), and those in the middle column end in a voiceless sound. The singular form of the words in the third column end in /θ/. Some words which end in /θ/ have two possible plural pronunciations /θs/ or /ðz/.

Language in context

a

1 The following is a possible answer to this question:

generally countable	generally uncountable	both
breast	unhappiness; dissatisfaction; understanding; soil; meat	society; life; fish; exposure; lamb; steak; misunderstanding

2 The meaning of, *life, fish, lamb, steak,* and *misunderstanding* as countable nouns is closely related to the meaning of the words as uncountable nouns. On the other hand *a society* is quite different from *society,* and *an exposure* is different from *exposure.*

b

Understanding (second and third uses), *misunderstanding* and *soil* are all used as countable nouns in the second text. *Understanding* and *soil* are countable to suggest a *kind* of understanding and a *kind* of soil. *Misunderstandings* is plural (countable) to suggest particular instances of misunderstanding.

countable nouns	uncountable nouns
technique; cuts; barrage; steaks; chops; cutlets; choice; cut; exterior; problems; sardines; fish (second instance); *way*	*grilling; food; exposure; heat; meat; heat; breast; lamb; fish* (first instance); *mackerel*
unhappiness; therapists; patients; therapist; position; patient; past; life; patient; therapist; offer; belief; patient; situation; soil	*therapy; dissatisfaction; society; misunderstandings; understanding; understanding; unhappiness; misery*

Some of the nouns in the 'countable' column are clearly countable (for example, they are used in a plural form like *problems* or are preceded by *a* or *an* like *a cut* and *an understanding*). Some of the nouns in the 'uncountable' column are clearly uncountable (for example they are followed by a singular verb but are not preceded by *a* or *an*).

However, in other cases the text offers no conclusive evidence (and it makes no difference to the meaning) e.g. *the food;* this *barrage;* this *offer.* The second instance of *fish* and *belief* have been classified here as countable but it could be argued that they are *un*countable.

Changing attitudes

c

(i) Few people use *media* as the plural form of *medium*. We generally use it as an uncountable noun meaning *the press* (particularly TV and radio).

(ii) This use is quite normal among native speakers, even in formal contexts. However, learners preparing for conservative (written) examinations should consider the names of companies to be singular.

(iii) Although this is often heard, many people still consider this to be incorrect (we generally still use *criterion* as the singular form, and *criteria* as the plural).

(iv) Most people consider this the standard and correct form. Some people use *syllabi* as the plural of *syllabus*.

2 Adjectives

Language in context

a The following are adjectives: *foggy; drab; misty; huge; dim; red; rumbling; dingy; dark; ugly; broken-down; hissing; heavy; thick; pale-blue; hopeless; loathsome; damp; entire; wet*. Some grammars consider the following as adjectives: *first; enough*.

The passage also contains a number of *adjective-like* forms. These include the participle forms *filled, glowing, reduced* and *suspended*, and the modifying nouns (see p. 12) *coin* and *gas*.

b Without the adjectives this would be a characterless description. It is the adjectives which, above all, create the pervasive feeling of drabness, dampness and cold. And this feeling is arguably more important than the details.

c *Rumbling* and *hissing* are also present participles. *Broken-down* is a past participle.

d *Foggy; misty. Hopeless* is derived from *hope*, which can be either a noun or a verb.

e *Loathsome*.

f *Broken-down* (Although *pale-blue* is written in a hyphenated form here, it would be more usual to consider *pale* as a separate word).

g *Loathsome* refers to the *odour*. The final part of this sentence is a relative clause (see Chapter 26) and the verb in this clause (*found*) is an object-complement verb. We understand the following: *Queenie found the odour loathsome*.

h The only words in this passage with 'adjective' suffixes are *misty, foggy* and *loathsome*. None of the adjectives has a prefix.

Learners' English

The learner uses a number of adverb forms in place of adjectives: *seriously*; *brightly* (x2); *smilingly*; *passionately*.

She attempts to make the following plural: * *longs*; * *blonds*; * *blues*; * *reds*.

She uses the following *after* rather than *before* the nouns they refer to: (these forms are written in a corrected version) – *very hard-working and serious person; a little crooked nose; bright red lips.*

We need to use *long, blond* rather than *blond, long* (general before specific).

We would say a *little crooked* nose rather than *little and crooked*. We might also choose *small* rather than *little* to make it clear that this describes the *nose* rather than *crooked* (her nose is *little* and it is *crooked*; it is not *a little crooked* as opposed to *very crooked*).

She mistakes the form of *hard-working*.

She incorrectly constructs a number of expressions with *with*: * *clothes with brightly colours* ⇒ *very colourful clothes* or *brightly coloured clothes*; * *with lips brightly reds* ⇒ *bright red lips*; * *I am usually a character with passionately* ⇒ *I have a very passionate nature*.

She needs either to write *it is easy to recognise* . . . or to use an adverb and adjective instead of an adjective and verb: *easily recognisable face*.

We use measurements before adjectives – we say *one metre 39 tall* (also *three feet long; six centimetres wide* etc.).

3   Adverbs

Language in context

1

a

(1) attitude marker   (2) manner   (3) focusing   (4) manner

(5) manner   (6) frequency (This can also be analysed as focusing adverb (*hardly*) + adverb of relative time (*ever*).)   (7) time

(8 & 9) focusing   (10) focusing

Answers to questions *b* and *c* involve subjective considerations of style. Your own answers may be different:

	Answers to **b**	Answers to **c**
(1)	The following don't have so specific a meaning as *traditionally* but could be used in its place: *usually; conventionally; normally.*	*traditionally* could precede *I* with little change to meaning (although this would give more emphasis to the adverb)
(2)	*on a personal basis* and *on a one-to-one basis* are possible alternatives	*individually* could precede *to renew* or separate *to* and *renew* (although many people would consider this 'splitting' of the infinitive to be unacceptable)
(3)	*particularly* can't be replaced (*especially* is similar in meaning but most people would want to avoid putting this adverb together with *special*)	the word order can't be changed
(4)	*all together* is a possible alternative	the word order can't be changed
(5)	*one-by-one* is a possible alternative	the word order can't be changed

(6)	*rarely* or *seldom* are possible alternatives	the word order can't be changed
(7)	*at the moment* and *these days* are possible alternatives	*nowadays* could precede *I hardly ever*
(8 & 9)	*to some extent* is a possible alternative	the adverb could follow *I*
(10)	*too* could be used but would need to be placed after *processing*	*also* could follow *want*

2 a, b

effectively (manner); **simply** (manner); **simply** (focusing); **completely** (degree (absolute)); **still** (relative time); **boldly** (manner); **elegantly** (manner); **beautifully** (manner); **softly** (manner); **confidently** (manner); **outside** (place)

c The texts still make sense, but the adverbs provide a substantial amount of 'colouring-in' detail. Without adverbs the texts would be more straightforwardly descriptive. We would lose much of the author's opinion and attitude.

Changing attitudes

a, b

(i)	*Hopefully* is used as an attitude marker. (*Hopefully* as an adverb of manner is universally acceptable, e.g. *She waited hopefully.*)
(ii)	This includes a split infinitive i.e. the adverb *further* is placed between *to* and the base form of the verb
(iii) & (iv)	Adverbs of manner with the same form as adjectives are used in these sentences. *-ly* forms also exist (e.g. *steeply; quickly*).

There is no real consensus as to what is correct in these cases, although learners who are preparing for conservative, accuracy-based examinations should probably avoid these uses.

4   Articles

Language in context

1   This is introducing new information. The noun (*person*) is singular.

2   This is introducing new information. The noun (*voice*) is singular.

3   Although this is introducing new information, the noun (*eyebrows*) is plural and so no article is needed.

4   This is introducing new information and the noun (*mason*) is singular. In some languages *a/an* would be left out before the name of an occupation (*mason*).

5   *the* signals that this is not <u>*any defect*</u>, but a particular one. Since no prior mention has been made of *defects*, this alerts us to search for 'qualifying' information which we find in the following relative clause (*that he could not be depended on*).

6   We leave out articles in many expressions which include *work* (*begin/ start/finish work*).

7   *on a certain day* contains a fixed expression (*a certain . . .*). We always use *a certain* before singular nouns (e.g. *at <u>a</u> certain time*; *in <u>a</u> certain place*) and we always use no article when we use *certain* with this meaning before plural or uncountable nouns (*at* [ ] *certain times*; *in* [ ] *certain weather*).

8   *the* signals that this is not *any furniture*, but a particular instance. Since no prior mention has been made of *furniture*, this alerts us to search for 'qualifying' information, and from the context we conclude that this is *the furniture* <u>*in the house that he has been engaged to work on*</u>.

9   *the far end of* is a fixed expression. This use of *the* can also be explained by the fact that the *far end* is qualified by *of . . .*

10   *the* signals that this is not any *house*, but a particular instance. Since no prior mention has been made of *house*, this alerts us to search for 'qualifying' information, and from the context we conclude that this is *the house* <u>*that he has been engaged to work on*</u>.

Learners' English

1   The learner is referring to the previous week and should have written *Last week*. *The last week* would be appropriate in a context where she wished to refer to the final week of an established period of time (*We didn't have very good weather on our holiday but the last week was dry*).

   The learner may be translating literally from her own language.

2   This is not incorrect but it is unidiomatic. We normally talk of *going to the cinema* or *theatre*, thinking of the act of seeing a film or a play.

   This learner may, however, be acting on the principle that we use *a* before singular nouns when the information is 'new'. After all, *I decided to go to a museum* is completely idiomatic.

3   A teacher might be tempted to correct this to something like *without any problems* or *with no problems*, both of which are more accurate in that she is unlikely to have only one problem. However, the expression itself is an odd one and might be a literal translation from the learner's first language.

   A more idiomatic way of expressing her meaning might be something like *without too many difficulties*.

4   This is not incorrect but it is unidiomatic. We normally refer to the act of *reading/looking in/consulting the newspaper* (fixed expressions). The 'common ground' principle would lead a learner who didn't know this to use *a/an*.

5   The learner probably wants to say that the actors *spoke Italian* or that the film was *in Italian*. She may not know these set phrases and may not realise that *Italian* can be a noun, acting as the name of the language.

6   This is incorrect, at least if the learner intends to refer to *life* generally, in which case no article should be used.

7   She wants to say that she saw a programme on TV about tuberculosis, but lacks the knowledge and command of appropriate set phrases (*watch [ ] television* and *on [ ] television*). In fact the meaning is quite clear, and her use of *a* follows the 'not common ground' principle.

8   This is general and needs no article. The effect of *the* is to alert our sensors for 'common ground', and it is disconcerting to discover (from the context) that there is none.

9   Given that the learner applies the rule for using indefinite articles before *TV* (albeit inappropriately in this instance), it is perhaps surprising to find a singular noun without any article (or other determiner) here. Perhaps she leaves out *a* because there are already two words before the noun (*very interesting film*).

10   The learner probably doesn't know that we don't use an article when we describe *belonging* to an institution. As in the case of *tuberculosis* she chooses *the*. Perhaps she is influenced by expressions such as *go to the cinema, the pub* etc.

11 &   In these two instances the articles are used correctly. (12) is an
12   idiomatic use (one might expect *among their families*) and perhaps the learner absorbed this or picked it up from the programme itself.

5   Quantifiers

Language in context

1

a The quantifiers are: *all* (ii); *most* (iii); *every* (iv); *few* (v); *some* (vi).

b *all* (i) is a pre-determiner (see p. 60); *a large number of* (vii) is similar in meaning to *a lot of*, and could be considered as a quantifier.

c *every teacher has her own implicit theory* . . . would be similar in meaning (ii), but emphasises the teachers as individuals rather than as a collective body. Conversely, *all teachers have a fund* . . . could be used in (iv); *not many teachers* . . . could be used in (v) with little change in meaning, although it would perhaps sound more colloquial; *a lot of* might be considered as an alternative to *a large number of* in (vii).

2

	Answers to **a** The following quantifiers were used in the original sentences:	Answers to **b**
1	Both	This has to be a quantifier that can be followed by a plural noun. *All* would also be possible since there is not enough context to show *how many* sides are involved, and *many, a few, few, several* and *a lot of* could also be used.
2	All	This has to be a quantifier that can be followed by a plural noun. The context makes it clear that *both* is not possible. *Many, a few, few, several* and *a lot of* could be used here, but the sentence would then be ambiguous (it could then be interpreted that Britain also has a gymnasia system i.e. *apart from* could mean 'in addition to').
3	Some	Given the amount of context provided, *many* or *a lot of* could also be used here. If this sentence were read aloud, *some* would be stressed (implying *some* – but *not all* teachers).
4	much	This use of *much* has a formal ring to it, and *a lot of* might be predicted in its place. *Some* (stressed) would also be possible, and would suggest a *limited* degree of pride.
5	any	*Every* could also be used. *Any* adds the sense of '*if* any spiders appear'.

Differences in meaning

	Answers to **a**	Answers to **b**
(i)	Both sentences are correct.	A simple explanation of the difference would be that the first sentence is an enquiry and the second a request. However, many people feel that they use these two forms interchangeably. Other people feel that they might use *some* here because they are concerned with a restricted kind of paint (for concrete floors).
(ii)	All three sentences are correct.	The first two sentences are very similar in meaning, although some people feel that the second puts more emphasis on the methodical, one-by-one attention to the drawers. Many people feel that the third sentence emphasises the completeness of the act, but it is still extremely close in meaning and effect to the other two sentences.
(iii)	Both sentences are correct.	They are identical in meaning. Many people feel that the second is less likely to be used in spoken English.
(iv)	Both sentences are correct.	They are identical in meaning. Some people feel that the second is less likely to be used in spoken English.
(v)	Both sentences are correct (although learners are often encouraged to use sentences like the second rather than the first).	Many people feel that the first sentence expresses an interest in his having scored a lot of goals, whereas the second expresses interest more generally in quantity.
(vi)	Both sentences are correct.	The second sentence suggests that there are other photographs which she doesn't have at the moment (restricted use).
(vii)	Both sentences are correct.	The second sentence is less common than the first in informal, spoken English. The second sentence suggests that he is lacking in sense (i.e. he doesn't have enough). The first sentence does not have this suggestion of insufficiency.

Learners' English

	Answers to **a**	Answers to **b**
(i)	It is difficult to imagine any context in which this would sound natural or correct.	Most teachers would encourage learners to use *a lot of* before uncountable nouns in noun phrases functioning as objects.
(ii)	This sounds very odd, but conceivably might appear in some kind of written report.	Unless the learner was a very sophisticated user of English who had chosen this form for appropriate reasons, we would probably correct this and encourage the learner to use *a lot of*.
(iii)	This use of *many* (in a noun phrase functioning as the subject of the sentence) is more natural than its use in (ii), even though it is still more a feature of the written than the spoken language.	We would probably mark this as correct (unless we particularly wanted the learner to practise the 'rule of thumb' that "we use *a lot of* in affirmative sentences and before subjects").
(iv)	This is absolutely natural and correct.	
(v)	The use of *much* in a noun phrase functioning as the subject of a sentence is quite natural, but this is still a feature of the written rather than the spoken language.	We would probably mark this as correct (unless we particularly wanted the learner to practise the 'rule of thumb' that "we use *a lot of* in affirmative sentences and before subjects".
(vi)	Most teachers would correct this, encouraging the learner to use a singular form of the noun (and verb).	Not everyone, however, recognises this as incorrect, and plural forms of the verb are sometimes used after *neither* ('Neither side seem to be putting the passenger first' – said in a report on a proposed rail strike BBC TV 9.00 News 18 June 1994).
(vii)	This sounds odd, but conceivably might occur in speech.	Unless the learner was a very sophisticated user of English who had chosen this form for appropriate reasons, we would probably correct this and encourage the learner to use *everybody*, pointing out that *all* is not normally used as a pronoun.

6   Comparatives and superlatives

Learners' English

	We might tell the learner:
1	double the final consonant before *est* (or *er*) when the adjective has one syllable and ends in a single vowel + consonant.
2	we don't use *more* and *most* in addition to *er* and *est*.
3	we change *y* to *i* before *er* and *est* when *y* follows a consonant.
4	*good* has completely irregular comparative and superlative forms (*better* and *best*).
5	with adjectives of three or more syllables we have to use *more* or *most* to make the comparative or superlative form.

Language in context

Answers to **a**	Answers to **b**	Answers to **c**
1–5 superlative	adjectives	It would be unusual to use *correctest, loyalest* and *ardentest* in any circumstances (because of these adjectives' endings: . . . *ect*; . . . *al*; . . . *ent*). *Most brave* and *most firm* would be possible, although a little unusual.
6 & 7 comparative	**6** adverb **7** adjective?	In this context *faster* is an adverb describing the manner of *shop*. Two meanings are possible for *more expensive wine* (the first of these may be more likely but there is no way of really knowing which is intended) • more wine (expensive wine) *more* = quantifier • wine that is more expensive – *more expensive* is a comparative form.

8 & 9 comparative	adverbs	Some people would use *quicker* in these contexts, but the adverbial form *more quickly* is more generally accepted (describing the manner, respectively, of moving around and of eating).
10 comparative	adjective	Only the adjective form is possible after *was*. * *More quick* is not used.
11 comparative	quantifier	This is the only possible form.
12 comparative	adjective?	See **7** above.
13 comparative	adjective	This is the only possible form.
14 comparative	adjective	This is the only possible form (we use *more* and *most* with adjectives that end . . . *ful*).

2

a 1 . . . . 30 per cent lower *than today in the 1990s*

   2 . . . . seven years earlier (i.e. *younger) than on average today*

   3 . . . . the cheapest car *that was available at that time*

   4 . . . . far fewer cars *than there are on the roads today*

b *they did* could be left out

3

Answers to **a**		Answers to **b**
(i) better educated	comparative/ adjective?	*Well educated* is effectively a two-word adjective, and *better educated* the comparative form of this. It could also be argued that *better* is the comparative form of the adverb *well.*
(slightly) richer	comparative/ adjective	*than the Robertses* is only implied
more	comparative/ quantifier	than the Robertses is only implied

(holidays) the strongest	quantifier superlative/ adjective	
(ii) (three times) more likely	comparative/ adjective	
better able	comparative/ adjective	*than men* is only implied. *better able* is an idiomatic expression, similar to *more able*, but suggesting that the ability is more intrinsic.
fastest	superlative/ adverb	This is an adverb of manner, and *the* isn't needed. We understand that men of this age lose cells fast in all parts of their brains – the *frontal lobe area* is singled out for the prize!
(iii) be nastiest	superlative/ adjective	This is part of a relative clause (*that can be . . .*), and *the* is not necessary. Since this refers to relationships with two participants, some people would prefer to use *nastier*. (*. . . than the other person* is implied).

7 Prepositions

Learners' English

The following is divided into sections, each focusing on a particular kind of problem. Within each section, answers to questions *a* and *b* are considered together.

Dependent prepositions and fixed expressions – wrong choice of preposition

Several of these mistakes involve dependent prepositions or idiomatic expressions. In each case the learner has chosen a preposition which makes sense in this position, but which happens to be incorrect:

Mistake	Correction
interested **about** sport	interested + in
I have taken part **at**	take part + in
I went **in** America	go + to
in the end of this year	at + the end of
knowledge **in** grammar	knowledge + of

Possessive forms

Several mistakes involve the use or non-use of *of*. This preposition has a particularly wide range of uses, and learners often find it difficult to know exactly when or when not to use it:

Mistake	Correction	Comment
the manager **from**	**of**	This mistake is typical of learners whose first language uses one preposition to cover the meanings roughly expressed in English by *of* and *from*.
training weekends **of** these sports	**for**	The learner doesn't seem sure of how to use *for*.
a bank**'s** branch	the branch *of* a bank	In both these cases the learner appears to have overgeneralised the use of the possessive *'s* (see p. 15).
political relevant**'s** issues	issues **of** political relevance	

Leaving out dependent prepositions and putting in extras

In some instances the learner leaves out a dependent preposition where one is required and inserts one where it is not – she appears to have learnt verbs without having learned what follows them.

Mistake	Correction	Comment
listening music	listen + **to**	
I want to return in	return there (no preposition)	The usual dependent preposition after return is *to* (He returned to America). However, no preposition is needed before *there*.

After/by the end of

In the following case, the learner probably does not know the expression *by the end of.* She may have chosen *after* as a conscious 'second best substitute'. However, it is also possible that she is unaware of the need to make this distinction in meaning:

Mistake	Correction
After the next two weeks	*by the end of*

Around

The following is correct, but could be ambiguous (*around* could mean the same as *all over* or could refer, specifically, to circumnavigating the world). The learner intended the former.

Mistake	Correction
travelling **around** *the world*	*all over*

Language in context

1

a

    1 with   **2** from   **3** on   **4** on   **5** to   **6** of

b The words either side of the gap generally help us to decide what is missing – this decision is particularly easy in the case of the dependent prepositions associated with the verbs *suffer* and *depend*. In the case of **5**, however, we need to look at the whole text in order to decide whether the missing word is *to* or *from*.

c Although prepositions *generally* don't convey much meaning, correct choice can also be crucial on occasions. This is particularly true of prepositions of *movement* and *place* (e.g. **5** *from* or *to*?).

2

a *Given, of, in, for, like, into, of, on, of, from, on, of, with, of, on, of, with, of, on, before, into, for, of, at, of, to, into, of, to, of*

b *To* is part of the infinitive in the following:

    has tended *to* focus; how *to* do; but *to* run; allows it *to* access.

In is part of the multiword verb to *throw something* in (to *include* something).

c The following are part of 'fixed' idiomatic expressions:

on the net (*on* the Internet); *for* instance; *at* least.

d The following prepositions are 'dependent':

forgive *for*; fade *into*; focus *on* (preposition repeated – *on* the sleazeball end . . .); connect *to*; transform *into*; capable *of*.

e These prepositions convey very little meaning, and can almost be considered as part of the verb.

f Most of these prepositions couldn't be replaced.

Given could possibly be replaced by *considering*.

<u>*in*</u> the past could possibly be replaced by <u>*during*</u>.

Differences in word class

In **ii, iii, vi, vii, viii, x, xi** the words in italics are prepositions.

In **i** the word in italics is an adverb.

In **iv** the word in italics is part of the infinitive form.

In **v** and **ix** the words in italics form part of multiword verbs (see Chapter 9). We sometimes think of these as prepositions, but we also refer to them as *particles*.

In **vii** the word in italics is a straightforward preposition if the meaning of the sentence is literal (i.e. he stood in the road and looked along it). It is the particle of a multiword verb if the sentence refers to consulting a directory or the index of a map.

8 Verbs

Language in context

a The following are verbs:

do(n't); watch; being; behaving; laugh; (to) be; eating; do(n't); cook; hate; do(n't); shop; have; been; known; (to) fill; sit (down)

b The following are main verbs:

watch; being; behaving; laugh; eating; cook; hate; shop; known; (to) fill; sit (down)

c The following describe a state:

    being; hate; known.

d The tense/passive form components are: *(to) be; have; been.*

e *don't* is used three times to make a statement negative.

f *to be* and *to fill* are the only full infinitives.

    watch, cook and *shop* are also infinitives – they are bare infinitives occurring after the auxiliary *don't. Sit (down)* is also an infinitive. We understand the implied repetition of *I have been known to (sit).*

g The following shows how the verbs are used in this context.

Object verbs	No-object verbs
watch (*much telly*)	*cook*
hate (*supermarkets*)	*shop*

In another context, *watch* could be a no-object verb (*I'm watching.*) and *cook* could be an object verb (*I'm cooking lunch*). The meaning of *shop* changes when it is used as an object verb (a colloquial version of *betray*) *He'd shop his mother for £20.*

Pronunciation

a

One-syllable words	Two-syllable words
looked; smoothed; washed puffed; tapped; purred	*fitted; faded; printed; hated*

b All the two-syllable past forms are verbs which have one-syllable infinitive forms ending in /t/ or /d/.

c

Words which end in /t/	Words which end in /d/
looked; washed; puffed; tapped	*smoothed; purred*

d The infinitive forms of the past tense verbs which end in /t/ all end in a voiceless consonant (other than /t/) and those which end in /d/ all end in a voiced sound.

Spelling

Most of these mistakes are the result of learners over-generalising rules.

cryed	The learner has added **ed** to the infinitive without changing the **y** to **i**.
offerred	The learner has doubled a final consonant on an unstressed syllable
peelled	The learner has doubled a final consonant which follows two vowels
staied	The learner has changed **y** to **i** before **ed**, when this letter follows a vowel
refered	The learner hasn't doubled the final consonant on a stressed syllable

Similarity in form

The following matches together verbs which change in similar ways in the formation of past and past participle forms.

become	–	*run*
drive	–	*freeze*
begin	–	*drink*
teach	–	*catch*
bend	–	*burn*
sleep	–	*mean*
broadcast	–	*cut*

9 Multiword verbs and multiword verbal expressions

Learners' English

Answers to **a**	Answers to **b**
I went out my wife	We can say *My wife and I <u>went out</u>*, but need to add *with* before an object (*I went out <u>with</u> my wife*).
we had to save our money	This is correct, but the Type 1 multiword verb *save up* would be more idiomatic (*save up to pay . . .*).
set our new home	The Type 3 multiword verb *set up* would be appropriate here, and this is probably what the learner was trying to say.
we get on happily together	The learner has chosen the appropriate multiword verb (*get on*), but this multiword verb is normally used with adverbs such as *well, badly, wonderfully, appallingly*. We don't normally use it with more specific adverbs like *happily*, perhaps because the meaning of this adverb is already implied in the multiword verb itself.
we seldom have argument	*Argument* exists as an uncountable noun but in the multiword verbal expression with *have* it is always countable. *We seldom have arguments* would be correct. The student could also have written *we seldom argue*.
we make them up rapidly	The learner has chosen the appropriate multiword verb but we always use *it* as the object. He wants to say *we soon make <u>it</u> up*.
have set them up all	*set them up* is the appropriate multiword verb, but we don't normally follow this with an adverbial (*on life's highway*). If we want to use this adverbial we need to use some other verb such as *launch* . If we use the Type 3 multiword verb *set up*, the adverb *all* needs to come immediately after the object (*them*), separating the verb and particle (*we have set them all up*).

we compensate the lost time	*compensate* is possible here but needs to be followed by the preposition *for*. The Type 4 multiword verb *make up for* would be more idiomatic.
we expect many more happy years	This is perfectly correct but the learner may want to say that they *look forward to many more happy years*.
I didn't fabricate	*fabricate* is an object verb and so needs a direct object (*fabricate this*). It would be more idiomatic to use a multiword verb here i.e. *I haven't made this up*.

Looking at examples

Answers to **a** & **c**	Answers to **b**
(i), (vii) & (viii) are Type 1 multiword verbs.	None of their meanings are literally the sum of the constituent verbs and particles.
(iii) & (iv) are both multiword verbal expressions.	(iii) is clearly more literal in its meaning than (iv).
(ii) & (vi) are not multiword verbs.	(ii) & (vi) are superficially similar to (i), (vii) & (viii). However, in these sentences the verbs and accompanying adverbs are used completely literally (*Where did she walk? – away*).
Put up with (x) is a Type 4 multiword verb.	It makes no sense to separate *with* from *put up*.
(v) & (ix) are Type 1 multiword verbs.	Although they are superficially similar to *put up with* (x) *reach out* and *drop in* belong to Type 1 not Type 4. They can exist on their own (*Although she knew she wouldn't be able to catch anything, she still reached out; If you're in this area, why don't you drop in?*). Here, the multiword verbs are followed by adverbial expressions which provide more information, and these expressions begin with a preposition (*to; on*). These prepositions create a link with what follows, they are not part of the multiword verb.

Language in context

This text is a good example of the fact that we don't use multiword verbs and verbal expressions only in informal contexts. The exercise confirms how classifying different forms is not always cut and dried.

Answers to **a** & **b**	Answers to **c**
(1) We can classify this as a Type 2 multiword verb (*come into*). However, since with this meaning, *come into* is used with only a limited range of objects (*come into being, existence, force, sight*), we can also think of these as fixed, multiword verbal expressions.	Alternative ways of expressing this (*how languages are born, the origin of languages* etc.) fail to convey the same sense of involuntary creation and gradual evolution.
(2) This is often classified as a multiword verb (*lead to*). However it doesn't fit into any of the four basic Types. We generally (as here) use it in a passive form but in an active form the verb and particle have to be separated by the object (*lead* + object + *to*) whether or not this is a pronoun. It may make more sense to consider it as a non literal use of the verb *lead*. The word *to* introduces the place or goal, and is part of an adverbial.	It is difficult to think of any alternative word or expression which would convey the same meaning.
(3) This Type 3 multiword verb (*put* + object + *forward*) is used here in a 'reduced' passive form (. . . *hypotheses* [*which have been*] *put forward*).	We could also use *advanced* or *proposed* as an alternative to *put forward* with little change to meaning or tone, but these might also seem inappropriately formal.
(4) multiword verb. This expression is very frequently used in the passive form to describe this particular kind of causality/ dependence. This doesn't fit into any of the four basic Types as we have to use an object between the verb and the particle (*base* + object + *on*), whether or not the object is a pronoun. Unlike *lead . . . to* (2 above), *base . . . on* has no separate literal use, and so we are obliged to classify it as a multiword verb.	It is difficult to think of any alternative word or expression which would convey the same meaning.

(5) It could be argued that this is not a multiword form here, but simply the verb *look* and the preposition which normally follows it (*at*). However, since its meaning in this context is not entirely literal (referring to the process of *considering* rather than to *vision*) we can also classify this as a Type 2 multiword verb.	*Consider* could be used here, but conveys less sense of conscious attention.
(6) See (1) above.	

10 Modal verbs

Forms and meanings

   (i)a   (ii)f   (iii)h   (iv)d   (v)h   (vi)e   (vii)g   (viii)e   (ix)i

Comparing exercises

The standard explanation of the difference between *must* and *have to* is that *must* is used when the authority is imposed by the speaker and that *have to* refers to some external authority.

According to this explanation, passage i) is the more natural and therefore the more useful and appropriate as teaching material. All the same, some people use *must* to express 'external' authority, and they mightn't find the second passage unnatural.

Differences in meaning

a

   Most people would use (i) if they are personally responsible for imposing (or withdrawing) the obligation, whereas (ii) and (iii) are appeals to external authority.

   The standard explanation is that (v) implies that she brought it, but that this was unnecessary and that (iv) implies that she knew this in advance and so she didn't bring it. People sometimes also use (iv) when the action was unnecessary.

Most people use intonation to distinguish between degrees of probability and will only choose between these modal verbs on stylistic grounds. Some people choose between them to express different degrees of probability.

b

(i)   is likely to be pronounced: You might have visited him.

(ii)   is likely to be pronounced: You MIGHT have visited him.

Language in context

1

Answers to **a**	Answers to **b**	Answers to **c**
(i) *However interesting it* **may** *be*	This use of *may* after words like *however, wherever* etc. doesn't express any 'modal meaning'.	*might*
it **would** *be even more interesting*	hypothetical statement	None
(ii) *You* **could** *have asked me*	past possibility (implied: *but you didn't*)	*might*
it **wouldn't have** *hurt you*	hypothetical speculation about the past	None
I **would** *disgrace you*	This can be explained both as 'future in the past' and as a hypothetical statement	*might* is possible, but suggests less probability
Your rejection . . . **would** *still* **have** *been unfair*	hypothetical speculation about the past	None
I **could** *have said . . .*	hypothetical speculation about possibility in the past	*would have been able to*
I **can't** *even reach you*	ability/possibility	*not* (even) *able to*
(iii) *. . . the snake* **must have** *been an inspiration*	logical deduction about the past	None
He **need** *waste no time*	necessity	*didn't need to* would be a more likely form

*All he **had to** do*	necessity	*needed to do*, also possible here, isn't usually considered a modal verb
(iv) *Do I **have** to come in?*	*Must* and *have to* are more or less interchangeable in this context, although some people might feel that *must* is chosen here because the speaker is imposing her own (i.e. internal) authority.	
*I've already told you you **must**.*		
*But does it **have** to be now?*		
(v) ***Can** you two stay . . .?*	Invitation/question about possibility	*Would you like to* would also be an invitation.
*Well, I **might could**.*	This very unusual form expresses possibility with considerable reservation i.e. 'it all depends . . .'	
(vi) *The fact that the story **should** be on the news*	This use of *should* in certain kinds of subordinate clause following *that* doesn't express any 'modal meaning'	
*It **had to** mean something,*	*logical deduction of necessity*	*must*

11 Infinitive and *-ing* forms of verbs

Differences in meaning

(i) The *-ing* form in the first sentence suggests that she was smoking at the same time as she went out. The infinitive in the second sentence suggests that the reason she went out was that she wanted to smoke.

(ii) There is very little difference in meaning between these two sentences. However, the first is probably more common than the second, and some people may actually choose between the forms, using the *-ing* form if they are referring to a factual event (people who have come to work when they are drunk), and the infinitive in a more speculative context.

(iii) The first and second sentences both describe a routine. The first is more common in American English and the second in British. In British English we might choose the first sentence in order to describe an event which is more unusual. We might also use the first sentence to suggest that it is the fact or the effect of *having a run* that we like, whereas the second sentence suggests that we are more interested in the physical sensation.

The third sentence is a very common way of expressing a wish.

The fourth sentence would be odd in most contexts, but is possible as a way of expressing feelings about an imagined healthier lifestyle.

Acceptability

(i) In this sentence *to* is a preposition, and would normally be followed by an *-ing* form (*committed to reducing*). However, particularly in speech, it is common for people to use a full infinitive in this context.

(ii) We usually use a full infinitive after *want*. However, if we are thinking of an action (*working*) which will be in process at a particular point in the future, we might use the progressive form of the infinitive (*I want him to be working . . .*). In speech it would be fairly normal to leave out the *to be* in this sentence.

Only very proficient users of English would be likely to choose this form consciously and correctly. Many learners of English may use this form incorrectly i.e. when they simply mean *I want him to work . . .*

(iii) Normally we would say *I'd appreciate it if you knocked . . .* , although it would also be correct (if rather stilted) to say *I'd appreciate your knocking . . .*

This object + infinitive combination after *appreciate* is not correct. However, in speech people sometimes make slips like this.

(iv) After *too* + adjective we usually use the full infinitive e.g. *I'm too tired to go out . . . . . .* However, we use the preposition *for* to introduce a noun (*I'm too tired for dinner*), and in speech it may happen that people combine the preposition *for* with the *-ing* form in this way.

We probably want to encourage our learners to use the standard forms in each of these four cases. With students at very advanced levels, we might want to explore contexts in which sentences such as this are used, but we would still probably discourage learners from copying them.

Language in context

1

Answers to **a**		Answers to **b**
be	line 2	bare infinitive: follows a modal verb (*would*)
to get (down)	line 3	infinitive: we have to use an infinitive after the adjective *unusual*. This is part of an 'It + be + adjective + infinitive construction'. An alternative would be to use the -*ing* form as a subject (*Getting down to business right away would be considered . . .*)
be	line 3	bare infinitive: follows a modal verb (*may*)
drinking	line 5	-*ing* form: part of the subject of a clause
engaging	line 6	-*ing* form: part of the subject of a clause
developing	line 6	-*ing* form: follows a preposition (*to*)
getting (down)	line 7	-*ing* form: follows a preposition (*before*)
exist	line 9	bare infinitive: part of simple present tense
To suggest	line 12	full infinitive: subject of a sentence, conveying an element of speculation
to acknowledge	line 14	infinitive: after the adjective *important*. This is part of an 'It + be + adjective + infinitive construction'. An alternative would be to use the -*ing* form as a subject (*Acknowledging that such cultural differences exist is more important . . .*).
exist	line 15	bare infinitive: part of simple present tense

The following occur in the text as adjectives: *working* (line 7) and *misleading* (line 13).

2

	Form in the original text	Answers to **b**
1	*think*	We have to use the bare infinitive in this *make +* object + verb construction.
2	*handling*	We have to use an *-ing* form after a preposition (*of*).
3	*buying*	*as above*
4	*to cook*	We use infinitives after question words (*what*).
5	*Accommodating*	Part of the subject of the clause (we could also use an infinitive here with little difference in emphasis).
6	*to find*	This is part of a clause complement referring to an activity. *Finding* would also be possible, but would sound more factual and emphatic.
7	*to cook*	*as above*
8	*eating*	We need to use an *-ing* form after the expression *feel like*.
9	*let*	The subject of this clause is *the second* (*way*). The complement divides into two: *to cook . . . . .* and *to let . . . .* . We can leave out *to* in the second of this pair of verbs, which explains the use of *let*.
10	*fend*	We have to use the bare infinitive in this *let +* object + verb construction.
11	*to make*	This is an example of the clause complement referring to an activity. *Making* would also be possible, but would sound more factual and emphatic.

12 The present, including uses of the present perfect

Differences in meaning

The following answers involve an element of speculation since no context for the sentences is provided. The explanations given are the most likely, but others may also be possible.

(i)   The first sentence describes a fact about the person. It tells us about one of her habits. The second expresses something temporary. Depending on the context, this may be what she is doing now, or it may describe, for example, an ex-smoker's temporary relapse.

(ii)   & (iii) We generally teach the second of these uses as being correct, and may provide the rule of thumb that *want* and *like* are 'state verbs'. If we use them to refer to general wants and likes (*I want peace*; *I like music*) we do have to use the present simple. However, if they refer to something temporary (e.g. wanting to leave a party; feelings about a particular concert that is still unfinished), we can use continuous tenses. In these cases the first sentence in each pair is appropriate and correct.

(iv)   The first sentence refers to a period of time which began in the past and continues into the future. The second refers only to the time 'until now'.

(v)   Both sentences are correct and in most contexts probably interchangeable. We sometimes choose the continuous form in order to stress temporariness, but this is clearly not the case here (60 years).

(vi)   The second of these sentences stresses the regularity or frequency of the action. We often use this combination of tense and adverb to express irritation. We may see the action as in some way temporary (i.e. one day she'll stop doing this). The first sentence expresses a fact about the person. It tells us about her routine behaviour.

(vii) The first sentence tells us something about the person's possessions (in American English we would probably make this clearer by saying a *bathtub*). Depending on the context, the second sentence could mean the same as the first or it could refer to the regular action of taking a bath (e.g. *In the mornings he has a bath not a shower*). The third sentence can only refer to the action of taking a bath (e.g. *Sorry, he can't come to he phone just now. He's having a bath*) since we wouldn't use *have* in a continuous form to express possession.

Language in context

a

1 present continuous	This use implies 'at any particular point in time' within a temporary period.	
2 present simple	This describes routine behaviour, a fact about the person.	
3 *will* (*'ll*) + infinitive	Superficially this sentence resembles a conditional type 1 sentence (see Chapter 18). In fact, however, this refers to the present, not to the	

future. *Will* is used here to describe regular or habitual actions.

4	present simple	This is a permanent state, a fact about the person.
5	present simple	This describes routine behaviour, a fact about the person.
6	present simple	This a general fact about their lives.
7	present continuous	This refers to events which are temporary and which are occurring at specific points of time i.e. those times when they don't know what is happening.

b We tend to introduce adverbs of frequency with the present simple, and learners sometimes get into the habit of using them only with this tense (e.g. *never, from time to time* and the second instance of *always* in the text). The first instance of *always* occurs with the present perfect, which is another common usage.

Learners often associate *now* with the present continuous, where it often simply repeats the meaning expressed by the continuous form of the verb itself. We also use *now* with the present simple, usually to express that something has changed – to express some kind of contrast between past and present. Here, *now* suggests that she used to do flower arranging.

c

(i)	*Are recording.*	The continuous form suggests that recording is a temporary process i.e. there are periods where they are making recordings, and then periods where they are not.
(ii)	*Has* and *swim.*	Both these verbs describe general facts – a feature of the house and a habit respectively.
(iii)	*I've been.*	The present perfect expresses the idea of 'until now'.

13 The future

Form and meaning

1–e   2–e   3–f   4–b   5–d   6–c   7–c   8–c   9–a

Language in context

1

Answers to question:	**a**	**b**	**c**
1	present continuous	This is an enquiry about *arrangements* or *plans*.	Other tenses could be used – for example, if the questioner thought of the holiday as determined by someone else he might ask *you're to go away, aren't you?*, or if he thought of it as being 'as a matter of course': *you'll be going away, won't you?*.
2	present continuous	This is an *arranged* future.	
3	*will*	This might be a prediction not based on present or past evidence. Alternatively, the speaker may simply be avoiding repetition of *going*.	He could also use *going to*. This absence of restrictions is probably something he has already thought about, if not planned.
4	present simple	The expression *on the time that* functions like a time conjunction, after which we use present tenses to refer to the future.	

5	continuous form of *will* (*will be . . . ing*)	The rule of thumb we'd use to explain this would be *future 'as a matter of course'.*	He might have used the present continuous or *going to*. In this case he he might be thinking of the departure time more as an arrangement or a plan.
6 & 7	*will*	These predictions appear to be based on present or past evidence (knowledge of personalities and interests in the group) – the speaker may be avoiding repetition of *going to.*	He could also use *going to* – although we generally avoid repeating this so frequently.
8	present continuous	This is an *arranged* future.	The future continuous could also be used (future as a matter of course) without making perceptible difference overall.
9	continuous form of *will* (*will be . . . ing*)	The rule of thumb we'd use to explain this would be *future 'as a matter of course'.*	*Will* and *going to* would also be possible although these lack the neutrality of *will be answering* and the latter suggests more a sense of Gorbachev's intention, of his having planned this. *Is going to be answering* would be completely acceptable in terms of meaning, but might seem stylistically out of place in this context (English written for a public audience).
10	present simple	This is part of a fixed itinerary.	The present continuous could also be used but would convey less of a sense that his arrival is an inevitable fact.

11	present simple	This is also part of a fixed itinerary.	*Will* or *going to be* could be used with little perceptible difference in meaning or emphasis in the context as a whole. *Going to* might be stylistically out of place.
12 & **13**	*will*	Both these events are planned, and we generally teach that *going to* would be appropriate in a context like this. However, the formality of the report probably also influences this choice.	*Going to* might be used in place of *will* in a more colloquial context.

2

Answers to question:	**a**	**b**	**c**
1 & **2**	*'re going*	*'re going to go*	This makes it less certain that *arrangements* have been made. Also, many people avoid this expression.
3	*will be*	*is going to be*	Although this may already be planned, the speaker probably chooses *will* rather than *going to* because *going to* would make the form of this passive construction more complex and more awkward.
4	*are going*	*will go; will be going;* present simple	This clearly seems to be something that has been arranged or at least planned. However, the other tenses could be used without making much difference since the context already makes this clear. The simple present has some suggestion that this is an inevitable, programmed fact.

5	*will be*	*going to*	It is already clear that this is a planned event, and so the speaker doesn't depend on choosing *going to* to make this clear. Also, the verb occurs in a subordinate clause, where we tend to use *will* rather than *going to*.
6	*will have*	*going to*	as above (**5.**)
7	*'ll do*	*going to*	as above (**5.**)
8	*are going to talk*	*will*	Perhaps she chooses *going to* here for variety (the three previous verbs all use *will* or *'ll*).
9 **10** **11** **12**	*going to get* *going to live* *going to be* *going to be*	We would normally expect more variety of tense (in particular the use of *will* as well as *going to*), and this would make no difference to meaning. The speaker is a nine-year-old boy, and this repetition of *going to* is a characteristic of children's speech.	

14 The past: past simple, present perfect simple and present perfect continuous

Language in context

1 a, b

1 **Past simple** is used because this event took place within a clearly identified, finished period of time (1969 or soon after). No other tense could plausibly be used here.

2 **Present perfect simple** is used because no past time is specified i.e. these are general facts about his life – an unfinished period of time. The past simple might be used if the writer wanted to 'distance' these facts, to suggest that they belonged to a finished period in his life.

3 **Present perfect continuous** is used because this is a repeated activity which has only recently stopped. Present perfect simple or past simple

would not make it clear that writing the column was a regular activity. The past simple would also suggest that this activity belonged to a period in Davies' career which is now over.

4 **Present perfect simple** See 2 above.

5 **Past simple** is used because this event occurred within a clearly identified, finished period of time – Williams' life. The present perfect could only be used if Williams were still alive.

2

	Answers to **a**	Answers to **b**
1	**Past simple** (*met*)	
2	**Past simple** (*came*)	
3	**Present perfect continuous** (*has been happening*)	The person who asks this question is interested in a *string* of recent events. The present perfect simple (*what has happened . . .?*) would also be possible, but in this case, the speaker would be interested in one or two key, single events, and may be referring to a specific topic that both people recognise.
4	**Past simple** (*met*)	
5	**Present perfect continuous** (*have been eating*)	In choosing this tense, the speaker focuses on the *recentness* and *duration* of the event. He might also have chosen the present perfect simple (*have eaten*) Here, the focus would be on the fact of eating garlic rather than on features of time.
6, 7	**Present perfect simple** (*have heard / have talked*)	The finished time *yesterday* leads us to expect the past simple (*heard*). However, this is an example of where we choose a form which doesn't follow this rule of thumb because, despite the specified time, we *feel* that the event is within a present time frame.

Learners' English

a (i) is the most obviously incorrect sentence since the use of the present perfect implies an unfinished period of time. Shakespeare's life is a finished period of time.

(ii), (iii) and (iv) all contain forms that contradict the rule of thumb we give to learners – that we use the past simple when the event occurred within a *finished* period of time. Following explanations given by coursebooks, we would expect

- *I haven't called you earlier but I've just got . . .* (ii)

- *Have you ever been to . . . ?* (iii)

- *I mended it . . .* (iv)

b Sentences (i) and (iv) would probably pass unnoticed if spoken outside the language classroom. (ii) and (iii) are standard American English, and would be said by a speaker of any English variety if they were thinking of:

- a particular finished period of time e.g. a particular holiday or business trip (iii).

- being back home as a new (and unfinished) phase of the day (ii).

(iv) would be used if the speaker were thinking of the 'mending' as belonging to a present time.

c (ii), (iii) and (iv) are not really mistakes, but a teacher might 'correct' them if the learner was struggling to grasp and apply the basic rule of thumb, and this correction was sure to help. Teachers would normally correct (i).

15 The past: past perfect simple, past continuous and past perfect continuous

Differences in meaning

In (i) the two events are practically simultaneous whereas in (ii) the departure took place before the arrival (I was no longer there). In (iii) the arrival occurred during the act of leaving (e.g. I might have been locking doors or saying 'goodbye').

In (iv) his speaking English was a fact at the time she pointed it out whereas (v) refers to a previous occasion on which he spoke English or possibly to the fact that he used to speak English. In (vi) the pointing out took place during the time of speaking.

In (vii) we understand that she had recently stopped painting the room, but not that she had necessarily finished the work. In (viii) we understand that the job of painting the room was completed. In (ix) we understand that the task of painting the room was begun but not finished. In some contexts we could choose between (vii) and (ix) without significantly affecting the meaning.

Learners' English

	Answers to **a**	Answers to **b**	Answers to **c**
(i)	Since the second event (the car losing control) happened at some point *during* the journey, the past continuous (*was travelling*) is appropriate here.	Learners sometimes over-use the simple past as part of a natural tendency to simplify the tense system. Alternatively, the learner may simply not have learned this use of the past continuous.	A useful rule of thumb for this learner would be: 'Use the past continuous for an action which is in progress when something else happens to interrupt it.'
(ii)	The simple past and not the past perfect is appropriate in this chronological sequence of events.	It is likely that this learner has learned or has internalised the rule that the past perfect is used for actions previous to other actions in the past, but that she has not understood that it is used to *clarify* the sequence of events.	'Use the past perfect when this *helps to make the sequence of events clear*.'
(iii)	The sentence doesn't make sense. *We had been staying in Kabul* is what, in fact, the learner meant.	The learner appears not to know the use of the past perfect continuous.	'Use the past perfect continuous when you describe something that took place over a period of time and then stopped before or at a specified point in the past, especially if you also use the conjunction *when*.'

Language in context

1

Answers to **a**	Answers to **b**	Answers to **c**
1 past perfect simple	The verb refers to an event two years before the key event – the end of Prohibition.	To some extent the meanings of words (*end/begin*) make the sequence of events clear, and so the simple past could be used. The past perfect makes the sequence still clearer, however.
2 simple past	The previous verb (*had begun*) has established the time sequence.	The past perfect could also be used, but this would only repeat a distinction which has already been made.
3 past perfect simple	This shows that the failure took place before the time that is specified (*less than two years later*).	The simple past could not be used here since it is only the tense which makes the sequence of events clear.
4 past continuous	The gangsters were making their millions before the key time reference (the failure of Prohibition) and were continuing to do this at and perhaps after that time.	The simple past could be used here, but this would be a balder, factual statement – we would lose the sense of 'this was happening at around that particular time'. The past perfect would change the meaning, suggesting that they were no longer making money at the time of the failure of Prohibition.
5 simple past	This describes a fact that was true at that time.	The past continuous could also be used, but this would emphasise that the defiance was happening before and after the key time reference (the failure of Prohibition), making it seem more temporary.
6 past perfect continuous	This describes an extended event that continued until (more or less) the war began.	No other tense would make the sequence of events clear in the same way.

7 past perfect simple	The meaning of this in terms of *time* is the same as **6** above. However, the verb here is *be*, which we don't use in continuous tenses.	The simple past (*was*) would also be possible here as the previous verb has established the relevant time period (before the war) and there would be no risk of ambiguity.
8 past perfect simple	This makes it clear that the event is prior to *waking up* i.e. part of her dream.	No other tense would make the sequence of events clear in the same way.
9 past perfect continuous	Unlike **8** above, which describes something momentary, this is extended over a longer period of time.	The past perfect simple might be possible here if the author didn't wish to make a contrast with **10** below, where the change in tense instantly makes it clear that this is a different event in the past.
10 past perfect simple	This is still previous to the key time reference of the paragraph (her *waking up*).	No other tense would make the sequence of events clear in the same way.
11 past continuous	This is a past event that is interrupted by something else happening.	We might expect the past perfect continuous (*had been working*) to be used here since this appears to be over (he was on his way to the airport to *leave*). Perhaps the past continuous is chosen because (closer to the present) it has more immediacy and lends greater impact to the shock of the seizure.

2

a Tense used in the original text	Answers to **b**
1 past continuous *was playing.*	This shows that the activity began before Christmas and continued after it. Any other tense would alter the meaning.
2 simple past *woke.*	This describes an event within a finished period of time (Christmas Day).

3 past perfect simple *had snowed.*	This shows that the snowing had finished before the key time reference (waking up). The past perfect continuous could also be used here, and would draw attention more to the duration of the event rather than to the fact of it.
4 past perfect simple *had put.*	This shows that this happened before the moment of discovering it. The present simple could also be used, but we would then have to pay a lot of attention to context to work out the sequence of events.
5 past perfect continuous *had already been living*	This describes something that occupied a period of time continuing up to specified point in the past (their meeting). The past perfect simple (*had already lived*) is also possible as we often use *live* in simple tenses (see p. 202).
6 past continuous *was apologising*	The appearance of apologising was in progress at the moment of death.
7 past perfect simple *had lived*	This verb takes us back to an earlier part of her life.
8 past perfect simple *had loved*	This is part of an earlier period in the narrative (before her death). The simple past would also be possible here since the time sequence of events is clear.
9 past perfect simple *had disowned*	As above (**8**).

16 The past: *used to* and *would*

Learners' English

The following is one person's way of re-writing the texts.

> We used to live in a small house on a modern housing estate, but
> we had a garden. I grew anemones and a yellow flower – I don't
> remember the name. My mother often used to want to pick the
> yellow flowers and she would want to put them in vases in the
> house but I didn't permit her to do this. Sometimes I would buy
> her flowers from the florist's so that she didn't ask me to let her
> pick my flowers.

> I used to have long hair and I wore glasses and I would ride my
> bicycle to school. I liked watching television and I used to play
> basketball in the park.

Language in context

1

Answers to **a**	Answers to **b**
1 simple past	*Used to have* (permanent state) would also be possible here without affecting meaning.
2 simple past	As above.
3 simple past	Both *used to* and *would* are also possible here. However, the context makes the repeated and distant nature of the action clear, and so these forms would not supply any extra information.
4 *would*	The simple past is also possible here, and would make little difference to meaning or effect. *Used to* might be confusing in this context, possibly suggesting that this was a *previously used* method of steering.

5 *used to*	*Would* is also be possible here. The simple past would not be appropriate here as the context does not make it clear that this was on repeated occasions.
6 *used to*	Both the simple past and *would* are also possible here without significantly altering meaning or effect.

2

a Original form used	**b**
1 *used to see* **3** *used to go* **5** simple past *stood* **6** *used to look* **7** *'d* (*would*) *see*	Any of the three forms is possible in each of these cases, although we would avoid simply repeating the same one. Expressions like *almost every day, a lot,* and *sometimes* convey that this was habitual, and so the simple past can be used as well as *used to* and *would*.
2 simple past *was*	*Used to be* is also possible but would probably be avoided after its use in the previous line. We don't use *would* to express permanent states.
4 simple past *had*	After *when* we tend to choose the simple past. *Used to* and *would* are possible but less likely.
8 *would be* **9** *would come* **10** *would see*	Despite the expression *night after night* in the previous sentence, context is insufficient to make the habitual meaning clear, and so the simple past could not be used. *Used to* is a possible alternative for any of these verbs.

17 Reported and direct speech

Language in context

1

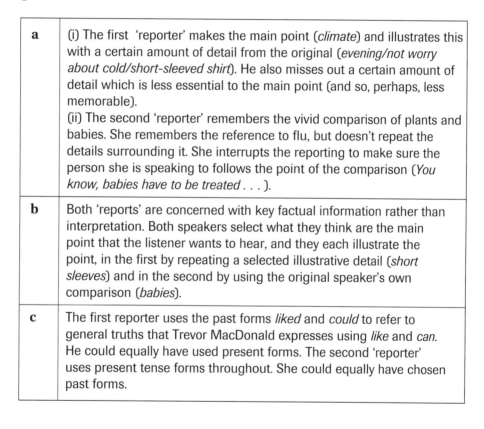

a	(i) The first 'reporter' makes the main point (*climate*) and illustrates this with a certain amount of detail from the original (*evening/not worry about cold/short-sleeved shirt*). He also misses out a certain amount of detail which is less essential to the main point (and so, perhaps, less memorable). (ii) The second 'reporter' remembers the vivid comparison of plants and babies. She remembers the reference to flu, but doesn't repeat the details surrounding it. She interrupts the reporting to make sure the person she is speaking to follows the point of the comparison (*You know, babies have to be treated . . .*).
b	Both 'reports' are concerned with key factual information rather than interpretation. Both speakers select what they think are the main point that the listener wants to hear, and they each illustrate the point, in the first by repeating a selected illustrative detail (*short sleeves*) and in the second by using the original speaker's own comparison (*babies*).
c	The first reporter uses the past forms *liked* and *could* to refer to general truths that Trevor MacDonald expresses using *like* and *can*. He could equally have used present forms. The second 'reporter' uses present tense forms throughout. She could equally have chosen past forms.

2

a	Mr Kimber . . . . . . said *I should write a book.*
	He said that *if I wrote a 2,000 word synopsis of my life story he would let me know whether he would give me a contract.*
	he said *he could never publish such a book, it was too scandalous.*
	He said *that if I gave him the 2,000 words that had frightened Mr Kimber and a transcript of what I had said on the radio, and photographs of myself, he would undertake to sell the book.*
b	Bob Kaine . . . said, *"I have my spies and I will put them out."*
	he said, *"You'd better come and see me."*
c	The speaker is a gifted story-teller, who varies his style and brings his characters to life by putting words into *their* mouths (i.e. using direct speech).

3

Answers to **a**	Answers to **b**
(i) *asked; said; said;* *seemed surprised* * *;* *didn't think* **	This summary appears to follow the turns in the conversation, and gives the impression that the writer wants to retain as much of the original conversation as space allows (did he have access to a written transcript of the conversation in writing this summary?) There is little evidence of *interpreting*. *'seemed surprised'* may reflect what was said (e.g. 'Oh really?') A reporting verb is implied in *He didn't think..*
(ii) *introduced;* *announced; invited;* *thanked; said*	This summarises in the broadest of brush strokes – we learn what *happened* in the conversation rather than what was said. The reporting verbs give the impression of an exchange of official statements and actions rather than any real communication. *Said* introduces the most informative piece of text.

4

Comparing exercises

Answers to **a**	Answers to **b**
(i) practises some of the mechanical aspects of reported speech, independently of context.	Exercises like this are necessary for learners who need to carry out similar transformations in tests and examinations. However, many learners find such exercises mystifying and they can create problems where there need be none.
(ii) provides a natural context for using reported speech, and enables the teacher to see how well learners report speech and to identify and respond to any problems they may have.	Learners usually find exercises like this useful.
(iii) focuses students' attention on natural (i) and unnatural (ii) ways of reporting speech.	Learners often find exercises like this useful, particularly if at some point they have been encouraged to transform direct speech mechanically and literally.

18 Conditional sentences

Review of form

The tables on pages 232–236 provide an example of each type, and label the form of the verbs.

Differences in meaning

(i)   The first sentence implies *take your umbrella, it may rain* (and so you'll be prepared). The second suggests that choosing whether to take your umbrella depends on whether or not it is raining.

(ii) One sentence is the opposite of the other. In the first sentence they'll phone if their train is cancelled, and in the second (as it says) they won't.

(iii) The meaning of the two sentences is very similar but the first stresses the conditionality, implying more than the second sentence that helping at any other time is out of the question. The speaker is imposing the condition.

(iv) The second sentence suggests that we *won't* need her to come in tomorrow, and so this is purely hypothetical. The first sentence is concerned with real possibility – we may need her to come in.

(v) The conventional explanation for the first sentence is that I am *still* ill – it suggests that the illness is part of the present. The second sentence suggests that *being ill* belongs to the past and I am now probably better (in fact we sometimes use sentences like the first to refer to the past when the context makes it clear that we are doing this, but we probably wouldn't want to *teach* this).

Form and function

The following are likely answers. You may also think of types not mentioned here.

	Answers to **a**	Answers to **b**
(i)	Type 2 (Type 1)	*I'd get a microwave if I were you.* (*You'll feel better if you have a rest.*)
(ii)	Type 1	*We'll buy the more expensive one as long as you don't charge for delivery.*
(iii)	Type 3	*If you'd been paying attention, we wouldn't have got on the wrong bus.*
(iv)	Type 0	*Seeds don't germinate unless the temperature is right.*
(v)	Type 1	*I'm going to phone the police if you don't turn the music down.*
(vi)	Type 1	*It'll break if you step on it.*
(vii)	Type 3	*I'd've got here sooner if they hadn't been digging up the road.*

Language in context

	Answers to **a**	Answers to **b**	Answers to **c**
(i)	*Had it done so, we wouldn't have stood a chance.*	This is a standard variant on the Type 3 conditional.	*Had* + subject + past participle is used here to speculate about an 'unreal' past – imagining that the demonstration had become an all-out confrontation. There is little difference in this context between this and *If it had done so . . .*
(ii)	*Were he living . . ., [he] would certainly . . . have cautioned . . .*	According to the conventional division, this is a 'mixed' conditional. The first clause is a variant on the subordinate clause of a Type 2 sentence, and the second is a standard Type 3 main clause.	The first clause refers to the present, and the verb is continuous because the writer is concerned with the moment rather than any general truth. The use of *were* + subject makes the conditional more remote than *if* + subject. The second clause refers to the past – Potter isn't alive so he *wasn't* able to caution the writer . . . .
(iii)	The whole sentence is conditional.	*hadn't <u>have</u> been* is a common variant on the standard Type 3 *hadn't been*.	For many people this is the standard Type 3 form, particularly when they speak. However, many people also disapprove of it, and most teachers discourage learners from using it.

(iv)	The whole sentence is conditional.	The use of the imperative, here, means that there is nothing in the *form* to show us which type this is associated with (we can use *could* in the conditional clauses of Types 1,2 and 0).The meaning of the sentence allocates it to Type 0 – it refers to a general fact.	This is the first sentence in the article, and the writer probably chooses this form for dramatic effect. *Walk into . . .* is a more arresting and more vivid beginning than *If you walk into . . .*
(v)	*. . . she would, if you wouldn't be so hard on . . .*	At first sight this looks like a non-standard Type 2 conditional, in which *would* is wrongly used in the subordinate clause.	*would* here is the past of *will*, describing stubbornly persistent behaviour. (*You will be hard on her!*) *. . . if you weren't so hard* doesn't convey this sense.
(vi)	*would have banned faced . . . reached . . . been required . . . replaced . . . would study . . .*	There are seven conditional clauses. Six of them belong to Type 3 and one to Type 2	Although there is no explicit conditional clause, *If the law had been passed . . .* is clearly implied. There is no obvious rule which determines that some of these imagined consequences are seen as belonging to the past (*would have faced*) while *would study* belongs to the present.
(vii)	*I'd have stayed . . .*	This is a Type 3 conditional clause.	*. . . except that it began . . .* can be paraphrased as *. . . if it hadn't begun . . . ,* and is thus equivalent to a conditional clause with *if*.

(viii)	*If . . . are forgotten, fearful consequences can result . . .*	This is a Type 0 conditional sentence.	This form could be either Type 1 or Type 0. The context and the meaning make it clear that it is Type 0 i.e. it refers to a timeless fact.
(ix)	The whole sentence is conditional.	This refers to the future, and is a variant of the basic Type 1 form.	Although probably no coursebook would teach the form that occurs in this *if* clause, it is completely idiomatic and correct. The combination of *going to* and *be coming* communicates a strong sense that this may already be planned and inevitable.
(x)	*. . . if any form . . . came to be . . . , the concept will become . . .*	The verb in the *if* clause appears to belong to Type 2, and the verb in the conditional clause to Type 1.	It is difficult to explain this linking of something which appears to be seen both as impossible (*came*) and possible (*will become*). Perhaps the writer shifts from thinking of this as impossible to possible in the process of writing about it.
(xi)	The whole sentence is conditional.	Type 1 (continuous form of the verb in the conditional clause).	The verb in the conditional clause is in a continuous form because the act of subordinating is seen as a temporary rather than a permanent condition. Nonetheless, it is a general or *permanent* truth that individuals choose to act in this way.

19 **Basic principles and patterns**

Language in context

1

Answers to **a**	Answers to **b**	Answers to **c**	Additional comment
(i) *'re sitting*	*sit*	no-object	*on* is part of the adverbial *on my chair*, not part of the verb.
(ii) *Don't call*	*call*	object-complement	*me* is the direct object and *stupid* the complement. The verb is in the (negative) imperative form.
(iii) *will put up*	*put up*	object	*put up* is a separable multiword verb, and so the direct object pronoun *me* separates the verb and preposition.
(iv) *'ve given*	*give*	two-object	*me* is the indirect object and *the money* the direct object.

Answers to **d**:

(i) *You; my chair*
(ii) *me*
(iii) *Beth and Albert, me, the night*
(iv) *They; me; the money*

Answers to **e**:

(i) *on my chair*
(ii) *none*
(iii) *for the night*
(iv) *at last*

2

a *I; Your lies; I; I; Anyone else*

b *you (doubt you); you (seen through you); your lies;*

c *me*

d *really convincing; an idiot*

e *at the time; about your promise *; after a while; at once; ever again*

f *(Don't) . . . try*

* In this analysis *about your promise* is classified as an adverbial. Some grammars would also consider the whole phrase *thinking about your promise* as a direct object of *started*, and some would consider *your promise* to be the direct object of the verb + preposition combination *think about*. Some grammars would consider the phrase *to tell me your lies* the direct object of *try*.

However is a discourse marker. In some grammars it might also be considered as an adverbial.

3

a

1 *There were two remarkable outbreaks of thunderstorms in July 1968.*
2 *June had ended on a fine, hot note*
3 *a cold front drifted eastwards into western Britain early on July 1*
4 *(it) triggered an unusually severe and prolonged series of thunderstorms in the west and north.*
5 *Darkness descended in daytime*
6 *there were reports of very large hailstones.*

b

1

Subject	Verb phrase	Complement	Adverbial
There	*were*	*two remarkable outbreaks of thunderstorms*	*in July 1968*

2

Subject	Verb phrase	Adverbial
June	*had ended*	*on a fine, hot note*

3

Subject	Verb phrase	Adverbial	Adverbial	Adverbial
a cold front	*drifted*	*eastwards*	*into western Britain*	*early on July 1*

4

(Subject)	Verb phrase	Direct object	Adverbial
(it)	*triggered*	*an unusually severe and prolonged series of thunderstorms*	*in the west and north.*

5

Subject	Verb phrase	Adverbial
Darkness	*descended*	*in daytime*

6

Subject	Verb phrase	Adverbial
there	*were*	*reports of very large hailstones*

Learners' English

1

	Answers to **a**	Answers to **b**
(i)	*very well*	*knew Peter's character very well*
(ii)	*a chicken stolen*	*a stolen chicken*
(iii)	*[he] talked about; [it] was night; [they] received*	*he talked about; it was night; they received*
(iv)	*the letter*	*the letter explained everything*
(v)	*the character of Peter; parents' Peter*	*Peter's character; Peter's parents*
(vi)	*asked [* to his wife]*	*asked his wife*

2

a

* My speciality engineering hydraulic.	The learner has left out the complement verb (*is*) She has reversed the order of the modifier (*hydraulic*) and noun (*engineering*)
* Engineering hydraulic very important new science.	The learner has again left out the complement verb (*is*) She has again reversed the order of the modifiers (*hydraulic*) and the noun (*engineering*).
* Using engineering hydraulic in the future will communications system develop my country.	It isn't completely clear whether the learner means that the communications system will develop the country or vice versa, although the latter seems more likely (in which case the subject is in a strange position at the every end of the clause). All the adverbials come at the beginning (*using hydraulic engineering; in the future*)

	The verb phrase is split (*will . . . develop*) She has again reversed the order of the modifier (*hydraulic*) and noun (*engineering*).
* *Will profit everyone.*	*everyone* seems to be the only subject, and needs to come before the verb, not after it
* *Will construct a glorious future engineering hydraulic.*	The subject (*hydraulic engineering*) again comes at the end of the clause. She has again reversed the order of the modifier (*hydraulic*) and noun (*engineering*).
* *Recently expanding this field of science.*	The subject (*this field of science*) again comes at the end of the clause. The learner had left the auxiliary verbs out of the verb phrase (<u>*has been*</u> *expanding*).
* *In the future I will with great pleasure give to my country.*	We generally teach that adverbials like *with great pleasure* come at the end of a clause, but the learner again splits the verb phrase (*will . . . give*). We need to use a direct object (as well as an indirect one – *to my country*) with *give*, but there isn't one here.

b The following is one way in which the text might be re-written.

> My speciality is hydraulic engineering. This is a very important new science. My country will develop a modern communications system using hydraulic engineering in the future. This will benefit everyone/Everyone will benefit. Hydraulic engineering will lead to the construction of a glorious future. This field of science has recently been expanding. In the future I will contribute to my country with great pleasure.

20 Major variants

Language in context

1

a Each of these fronted adverbials is an expression which refers to time and plays a key role in structuring the information in the whole section of text. In this fronted position they act as markers of the various stages in her career, each of them orientating us to expect *another* stage.

b The effect of changing the position of the adverbial is slightly different in each case:

*Her musical ambitions (which had begun with training for the ballet) were sponsored by the wealthy Bertrand family **for seven years**, . . .*	In this position the information about time is more prominent and emphasises that the *sponsorship* lasted seven years rather than that the sponsorship of *her musical ambitions* lasted this length of time.
*She joined the Basle Opera **in 1956***	Again in this position the information about time is more prominent, and the fact (joining the Basle Opera) less so.
*She sang everything from Salomé (her favourite role) to Mimì **over the next few years***	This sentence seems odd with this very general information about time occupying this prominent position.
*her Aida was heard a total of twenty-six times **in one season alone***	The exclamation mark at the end of this clause compounds the effect of changing the position of the adverbial – here what is surprising is the fact that this happened in one season more than that she sang this role 26 times.

2

	Answers to **a**	Answers to **b**
(i)	Both the adverbial (*With the coming of Dean Moriarty*) and the verb (*began*) are fronted.	This is the opening sentence of a novel. Beginning this way, as though we already knew something about *Dean Moriarty* and his *coming*, instantly draws us in and arouses suspense (What happened with the coming of Dean Moriarty? What is it we are supposed to know already?). It also pushes back the less arresting (but more difficult to process) subject (*the part of my life you could call my life on the road*).
(ii)	*Sweet-pea colours*, the direct object of *wore* is fronted in this sentence.	The effect of bringing this new, unfamiliar information to the front of the sentence is to 'jolt', to 'surprise' – creating a strong visual image.
(iii)	This is a pseudo-cleft clause.	This draws attention to *optimism*. This is new and important information, and would get squeezed out of the limelight as the subject of a simple clause (*Optimism keeps a film critic going . . .*).
(iv)	The second sentence is a pseudo-cleft clause (*Sleep . . . is what you need*). Here the more common order (*what you need is sleep*) is reversed.	The pseudo-clefting suggests that *sleep back at Passford House* is a complete cure. By choosing this order (*what you need* at the end), the author draws additional attention to the proposed cure (compare this sentence with *You need sleep back at Passford House* – but you may need other things too!). Sleep . . . is semi-familiar information, building on and implied by the previous sentence (*you've had enough . . .*).

3 a

Answers to **(i)**	Answers to **(ii)**
The original text read: *It is on these hidden champions that the country's economic future (re)lies*	This cleft sentence enables the writer to spotlight *these hidden champions* and also to give prominence to *the country's economic future* by putting this at the end (crucially, separating *on* from *(re)lies* like this also draws attention to the relationship of dependence).

| The original text read: *It has been our failure to grow small businesses into large that is the root cause of our decline* | This cleft sentence enables the writer to spotlight *our failure . . . large* and also to give prominence to *the root cause of our decline.* |

b

Answers to **(i)**	Answers to **(ii)**
The original text read: *What James was saying was that side-by-side comparisons of pairs of languages in isolation was ineffective . . .*	This pseudo-cleft device allows the writer to make it clear that he is getting at James's *essential* (but possibly only *implicit*) message. *What James was saying* implies *What James was <u>really</u> saying . . .*
The original text read: *what was needed was a frame of reference that would encompass the universal properties of all languages*	This pseudo-cleft device puts greater emphasis on the *needing* than a simple clause would. It puts the long and complex noun phrase (*a frame . . . languages*) further back in the sentence. It is easier to process here than as a subject.

4

a Yes. **b** No. **c** This cleft sentence spotlights *in the spring of 1923.* The visit has been mentioned before, but not the date.

Learners' English

a

complement	verb phrase	subject
Appalling	*was*	*the emotional deprivation that many of the children suffered.*

This fronting of the complement and verb phrase is rare in written English, and seems inappropriately literary here.

b In informal spoken English we might use a dummy subject (*it*) to push back the long noun phrase.

It was appalling, **the emotional deprivation that many of the children suffered.**

We can also use a pseudo-cleft sentence (the 'normal' way of pushing information back and focusing on the information that would be conveyed by both the subject and the complement of a simple clause).

> *What was appalling was the emotional deprivation that many of the children suffered.*

c

Original version	Idiomatic reformulation	Comment
I especially remember about this time how unhappy I was,	*What I especially remember about this time is how unhappy I was*	Pseudo-cleft sentence
the fear of this unhappiness recurring makes me continue to take courses of professional development.	*it is the fear of this unhappiness recurring that makes me continue to take courses of professional development.*	Cleft sentence
But their behaviour in school was the particular problem for me of course.	*But of course it was their behaviour in school that was a particular problem for me.*	Cleft sentence; fronting of adverbial (*of course*).

It might not be appropriate for the writer to have made *all* these changes – the text might then be more emphatic than she wished. It might be necessary for her to select which information she wanted to give particular prominence to, and to *select* the changes accordingly.

Analysing exercises

Answers to **a**	Answers to **b**	Answers to **c**
(i) *Did the parcel arrive on Wednesday in the end?*	*In the end did the parcel arrive on Wednesday?.*	If we begin with *In the end* we are using this expression to link the question to what has immediately gone before, and the actual day (*Wednesday*) seems to be more prominent. However, in speaking we can also use stress and intonation to draw attention to what is important, and so the order of words is less significant.

(ii) *I found the prose turgid.*	*The prose I found turgid.*	The fronted direct object (*The prose*) in the first sentence implies some kind of contrast (*I quite liked the poetry, but the prose I found turgid*). The fronted complement (*Turgid*) in the second sentence is unusual and as well as establishing that *Turgid* is what the sentence is about, the unnaturalness of this order draws additional attention to the word.
	Turgid, I found the prose.	
(iii) *Scotland is a wonderful place for walking.*	*A wonderful place for walking is Scotland.*	The fronted complement (*A wonderful place for walking*) in the second sentence is unusual, and as in (ii) this both establishes what the sentence is about and (because we are struck by its unusualness) also increases its prominence.

21 Passive constructions

Differences in meaning

a These sentences all make sense.

b

(i) The first sentence provides no information about whether she wanted her shoes to be cleaned or not. The second suggests that this simply 'happened' – perhaps even despite her wishes. The third sentence, however, very definitely means that this was done on her initiative and in accordance with her wishes.

(ii) There is no perceptible difference between the sentences in meaning. This is because the context (storm) makes the involuntary and unexpected nature of the event clear.

(iii) There is little difference between the sentences. Some people might choose the first if they are visualising a group of particular people who might have answered it.

(iv) The sentences could have exactly the same (causative) meaning. Depending on the context, however, the second sentence could also be taken to mean that his partner was arrested as an accidental consequence of something he did.

Learners' English

a) There is no definitive way of re-writing this text. The following is one of various possible examples:

> Very good quality wine is produced in my country. We grow the vines mainly in the West of the country where the winters are milder. The grapes are picked at the end of the summer – they have to be picked at exactly the right time. When they have been picked, the grapes have to be processed very quickly. Some wines are kept for a long time to improve before they are put into bottles. You can buy my country's wines in many other European countries.

b Using passive constructions is a major factor in making this description of a process more natural. However, a completely natural description may include some evidence of personal involvement – in this re-writing:

- the following sentence is retained from the original: *We grow the vines mainly in the West of the country . . .*;

- the impersonal subject *you* is also used: *You can buy my country's wines . . .*

Language in context

1

> **a** In (i) we are interested in the acts of violence and not in the identity of the attackers. The names (Mick, Kevin and Steven) establish who the victims were. It wouldn't make sense to begin each clause with *someone* (e.g. *someone attacked Mick . . .*) as we are not interested in who did it, and this information doesn't in any sense establish 'what the clause is about'. In (ii) passive constructions are used for similar reasons – we are interested in the results and not in the people who completed the questionnaires. This use of passive constructions is very typical of reporting research in academic journals. (iii) is written in a very particular style. The long complex sentences and the use of *shall* are part of a conventional way of expressing official regulations. Using passive constructions also belongs to this 'official regulations style'. The function of the text is to *instruct* the reader (the tutors or the students), and although this isn't explicitly stated, we understand the implied *students should* . . . The use of passive constructions makes the document relevant to both students and tutors – if they were addressed directly (*you . . .*), there would need to be two separate documents, one for tutors and one for students.

> **b** *was attacked; was slashed; had his face cut; were changed* In the first three cases we are interested in what follows the subject – the acts of violence. In the fourth instance the passive construction attaches importance to the fact that the attacks changed something. The writer chooses to stress this rather more than the fact that what *was changed* was their *lives and attitudes*.

> **c** The third construction (*had his face cut*) is causative in form, but the meaning is definitely not that he caused this to happen. The writer probably chooses this form partly for stylistic reasons, to avoid repeating the same 'standard' passive form over and over again.

> **d** Only the fourth of these constructions could be replaced by an active construction. See **b** above for a description of the difference this would make in emphasis.

> **e** *Got* could be used in place of *was* and *had* in the first three instances. However, the sense of these incidents being unwelcome is already implicit in the context, and so we don't need *got* to make this clear.

> **f** The use of *by* in *Steven had his face cut by a Stanley knife* is odd since it introduces the *instrument* used in the attack rather than the *agent*. *With* would be a more likely choice here. The other prepositions couldn't be changed.

g There is no definitive way of 'translating' this passage into spoken English. The following is one of many possibilities. It is addressed to a student, but the text could equally well be changed to address tutors:

You have to type your dissertation, in English, and you need to pay attention to style and presentation. You have to send it through your Tutor to the Secretary of the Faculty Board, together with a list of books and articles you have used in preparing it. It has to arrive on or before the third day of the Full Easter term which the examination is in. In this example, no passive constructions are retained. Any translation of official regulations into casual advice, instruction or explanation would probably involve a decrease in the number of passive forms.

2

a The following are the sentences as they occur in the original:

1 over six million women are beaten by their abusive partners and around 4,000 are killed.	This passive construction establishes the women as 'what the sentence is about' and draws attention to the acts of violence that they suffer from.
2 a unique and groundbreaking court was established	*To deal with this hidden crime* establishes 'what the sentence is about'. What follows is the key information, and this doesn't include *people* (which is both vague and unnecessary).
3 many women tell the judges	Since the preceding text is about these women, it would be odd to draw attention specifically to them at this point by using a passive construction.
4 *they have literally saved their lives*	Both alternatives would make good sense here, but the writer chooses an active construction which draws attention to *saved their lives*.

b Both *determined* and *prepared* are adjectives in this text and not part of passive constructions.

c There is no sense of anyone or anything *determining the judges* or *preparing the victims*. The meaning of these words is quite different from that of the related verbs.

3

Answers to **a**	Answers to **b**
(i) . . . we *got burgled.* (standard)	This describes something unfortunate, unwelcome and unexpected.
(ii) . . . you've *got* your modem *installed;* (causative) . . . how to *get connected* (standard)	Both cases imply an element of *difficulty* and therefore of *achievement.*

22 Discourse markers

Language in context

1 Answering this question is inevitably a matter of informed speculation. It is rare that we can be definitive in an exercise like this, but more context and information about tone of voice and facial expression would make the task easier.

    1 The speaker is indicating that she acknowledges the reservation (not his *best*) but is discounting it.

    2 This indicates the change to a new topic.

    3 This 'particularises' the information that comes before it, explaining and giving background to it.

    4 This is a 'filler' – the speaker gives herself time to think and perhaps fends off the chance of interruption.

    5 This acknowledges or confirms the information.

    6 This seems to be preparing the ground for a challenge (*Convince us*).

    7 This seems to indicate that the challenge is accepted.

    8 This seems to close one topic (*Maria*) and to make way for a new one (*Carlos*).

    9 This seems to express agreement.

2

Answers to **a**	Answers to **b**
In general	This is a *generalisation* (*though* introduces cases that don't fit in with the general rule).
therefore	This introduces a *result* – a logical consequence.
on the other hand	This introduces *contrasting* information.
therefore	This introduces a *result* – a logical consequence.
So	This introduces a *result* – a logical consequence.
For example	This introduces an example of the general rule that has been given.

The passage contains the following conjunctions (See also Chapter 24). These are related to discourse markers in function:

> *though; Since; When; and; because*

3

a

1	therefore	**4**	However
2	Similarly	**5**	Moreover
3	Naturally	**6**	Further

b You probably tried to work out what the logical relationship was between the information on either side of the missing discourse marker. You probably found it quite difficult to decide which discourse marker went where.

c We sometimes think of discourse markers as 'extras', marking more clearly relationships in the text that are already apparent. However, this is not really true; often it is only the discourse marker that establishes what the logical thread is in a text. In this instance, it is difficult to identify the correct discourse markers precisely because they *do* carry so much meaning.

23 Ellipsis and substitution

Language in context

1

a This conversation took place between three male friends in an English pub. Among the key areas of common knowledge are the measures in which beer is served in pubs, the ritual of buying rounds, and C's habitual avoidance of buying his round.

b The following is one of many ways in which this conversation might be re-written:

> A: Would you like another drink?
> B: Yes please. I'd like a lager.
> A: Would you like a pint?
> B: No thank you. I'd like half a pint.
> C: I think it's my turn to buy a round.
>
> A: It's about time you bought a round.
> B: Since you frequently avoid buying a round I'll change my order from half a pint of lager to a pint of lager.

2

> A: Didn't see you yesterday.
> B: (You) probably didn't want to.
> A: Looked everywhere.
> B: Not hard enough.

3

a [*She*] Couldn't resist boasting to herself, that was Mathilda's trouble.

[*She*] Put every damn thing on those miserable pages, then * read them over and over again to remind herself how clever she was.

[*She*] Wouldn't have left out a triumph like this.

[*They're on the*] Top shelf of the library.

[*They're*] Disguised as the works of Willy Shakespeare!

[*I('ll)*]Expect to hear from you on this in a couple of days or so.

[*I'd be*] Grateful if you'd treat it as a matter of urgency.

* this omission of *she* is an example of how we often avoid repeating a subject pronoun and is a case of *textual* rather than *situational* ellipsis.

b Only Gillespie uses ellipsis. In this context (i.e. in contrast to the speech of the lawyer, in which there is no situational ellipsis) this gives an impression of haste and gruffness.

4

1	substitution/ellipsis	. . . those *people* . . .
2	substitution/ellipsis	. . . another *rule of thumb* . . .
3	substitution . . .	the *one* ⇒ the *film* . . .
4	ellipsis	. . . isn't *the one (i.e. the film) that makes up for all the dross you saw last week.*
5	ellipsis	. . . *she had* . . .
6	ellipsis	. . . *she* . . .
7	ellipsis	. . . *she realized now* . . .
8	ellipsis	. . . *had become* . . .
9	substitution	*it* ⇒ . . . *her relationship with her father*
10	substitution	*This* ⇒ *the only way they can possibly achieve this ideal is through sustained and rigorous exercise (it could not be used here, as the first word in a paragraph referring back to a general point in the previous paragraph)*

5

Answers to **a**	Answers to **b**	Answers to **c**
(i) *an enjoyable* **one**	substitution of noun phrase	*an enjoyable visit* (i.e. this is indefinite and singular)
(ii) *than* **did** slow	substitution of a predicate	slow music *led to shoppers moving around a supermarket* (note the inversion: slow music *did* ⇒ *did* slow music)
a follow-up [ ] *showed*	ellipsis	a follow-up *to this study*
a similar effect [ ]	ellipsis	a similar effect *to the effect discovered in the previous study*

*than **it** was*	substitution of noun phrase	*drinking*
*they **did** to*	substitution of a predicate	⇒ *took*
buy more expensive bottles [ ]	ellipsis	more expensive bottles *of wine*
to classical [ ]	ellipsis	to classical *music*
bigger purchase of greetings cards [ ]	ellipsis	than happy music
other types [ ]	ellipsis	other types *of music*
*than **did** other types*	substitution of a predicate	⇒ other types (of music) *led to people being helpful* (note the inversion: other types *did* ⇒ *did* other types)
(iii) *I knew **it** really mattered*	substitution of noun phrase	One way of analysing this is: *it* ⇒ (*remembering*) *capital letters and punctuation*. Another way of interpreting this is one that doesn't really involve substitution; *this time it mattered* can be understood as an expression we use to indicate that an occasion is important.
I mustn't [ ]	ellipsis	*forget capital letters and punctuation*
and didn't [ ]	ellipsis	*forget capital letters and punctuation*
(iv) *and* [ ] *the close around it* [ ] *the*	ellipsis X 2	and *there is no doubt in my mind that* the close around it *is* the . . .
the most beautiful space [ ]	*ellipsis*	*in England*
(v) *One* [ ]	ellipsis	one *way of dealing with this problem*
and [ ] *grown-ups* [ ] *grudgingly*	ellipsis	*that* grown-ups *eat* grudgingly
The second [] *is*	ellipsis	The second *way of dealing with this problem*
and [] *let*	ellipsis	*The second way of dealing with this problem is . . . to* let . . .

Analysing course materials

a

    (i)   *I think **so***

    (ii)   *I'm picking up the visas on Wednesday morning and [**I'm picking up**] the tickets . . .*

    (iii) *[**they're coming**] Back on Friday night.*

    (iv) *How long [**are the children going to stay with Mother**] for?*

    (v)   ***So it is***

b the children ⇒ them
John ⇒ him

c That isn't long ⇒ a stay of two days.
that's right ⇒ the fact that we're giving him a bike.

d Answers to this question will depend on the students you are teaching, and what does or doesn't cause them difficulty. In each case you could ask them what is 'missing' (ellipsis) or what a substituted word stands for, teaching through further examples any features that are not obvious to them. In terms of asking students to use any of these features, at this level you might choose to focus firstly on short questions and short answers to questions (e.g. *How long for?* and *Just two days* rather than *How long are the children going to stay with Mother for?* and *They are going to stay with Mother just for two days*).

24 Finite adverbial clauses

Differences in meaning

1

a

Time:	*as long as; as soon as; while; since; as; until*
Contrast:	*even though; although; while*
Reason:	*since; as*
Condition:	*as long as*

b

Time:	*As long as* describes something that continued (only) for the same length of time as something else. *As soon as* describes something that happens immediately before something else. *While* describes something (with duration) that happened at the same time as something else. *Since* describes the starting point for something that continues until now. *As* is similar in meaning to *while* but doesn't necessarily involve duration. *Until* describes something that happened that marked the end of something else.
Contrast:	*Even though* and *although* are similar in meaning, although *even though* always expresses a high degree of contrast, introducing something that we wouldn't normally expect. *Although* (as in the sentence before this one – *although* **even though** *always expresses a high degree of contrast*) sometimes expresses a reservation about something. We couldn't use *even though* in this context. *While* usually introduces an opinion or point of view expressing partial agreement.
Reason:	*Since* and *as* are largely interchangeable as conjunctions of reason.
Condition:	We use *as long as* to express a strong degree of reservation, suggesting *only if* . . .

c Given the fine distinctions in meaning between conjunctions which express the same general meaning (e.g. between *as*, *while* and *as long as*), it is not surprising that learners sometimes confuse them. It is unlikely that their own languages make precisely the same distinctions, and it is only through repeated 'noticing' of how the conjunctions are used that learners can really build up a sense of what they can and can't express. Learners may also miss off one or more of the words in multiword conjunctions (for example using *even* instead of *even though*, or *as soon* instead of *as soon as*).

2 The following are possible combinations:

(i)

Answers to **a**	Answers to **b**
I was terribly hungry **and** started eating before you got here.	And expresses the order in which the events happened. The fact that one thing was the reason for the other is only implied.
I was terribly hungry **so** I started eating before you got here.	No distinction is made between the importance of the two events.
I started eating before you got here **because/since/as** I was terribly hungry.	Here, the clause expressing reason is a justification of the action (started eating). The key information is in the main clause (I started eating).

(ii)

Answers to **a**	Answers to **b**
My mother left school when she was thirteen but has had a very successful career as a writer. My mother has had a very successful career as a writer but left school when she was thirteen.	The two clauses in each of these sentences contain information of equal importance. We order the clauses so that what we think of as the 'surprising factor' comes second, after the conjunction.
Although/even though/despite the fact that she has had a very successful career as a writer, my mother left school when she was thirteen. Although/even though/despite the fact that she left school when she was thirteen, my mother has had a very successful career as a writer.	In the these sentences, the conjunctions introduce the 'supporting information'. The key point is expressed in the main clause. In these cases, where there is a naturally surprising relationship between the information in the two clauses, choosing one of these subordinating conjunctions rather than another makes little difference to the overall meaning of the sentence.
My mother has had a very successful career as a writer although/even though/despite the fact that she left school when she was thirteen.	Choosing one conjunction rather than another makes little difference to meaning.

My mother left school when she was thirteen although/even though/ despite the fact that she has had a very successful career as a writer.	In this sentence, there is a sense of asserting the truth about 'when my mother left school' – the speaker is talking to someone who is familiar with this information but is sceptical about it. In this case, *even though* and *despite the fact that* are more appropriate than the less forceful *although*.

Language in context

1

a Conjunction used in original text:	**b** Possible justification:
1 *when*	simultaneous events. No duration is involved in *saw. As* can't be used to introduce something that interrupts a longer event.
2 *as*	simultaneous events. No duration is involved in *saw. When* could also be used but might suggest that one action followed the other rather than that they were simultaneous.
3 *just as*	*just* highlights the precise coincidence of timings
4 *Once*	*Once* suggests that some kind of *achievement* is involved. *When* could also be used but wouldn't carry this implication.
5 *While*	The first clause expresses a reservation which is effectively discounted in the second clause. *Although* could also be used.
6 *Although*	The two clauses suggests a general contrast.

2

a . . . *and* **so** *dominant* **that** . . .

b **While** *[he was] still a beginner* . . .

c **When** *there were no laughs, or* **when** *a director aimed for* . . .

d . . . *much* **as** *he did in conversation* . . . *even* **when** *it ruined a scene* . . .

e **When** *he progressed to the 'legitimate' stage* . . . *But* **once** *he hit on a vocal register* . . . **As** *his autobiography shows* . . .

f **much as** *he did in conversation* . . .; **even when** *it ruined a scene* . . .

g *When he progressed to the 'legitimate' stage . . . After or once could be used here, but both conjunctions are more specific in their meaning, after suggesting that there might be a time lapse between the two events, and once suggesting some kind of achievement of a goal.*

Similarly, *when* or *after* could replace *once* in *once he hit on a vocal register* . . . . The connotations would be slightly different (as in the previous example).

When could replace *while* in *While still a beginner* . . ., but this would take away the suggestion of duration implied in *while*.

If could replace *when* in the last three examples where this conjunction occurs. However, this would take away the sense of these occasions as factual events.

25 Noun clauses

Language in context

1

a The following are noun clauses: (i) *where he is* (ii) *he said that!* (iii) *if he was coming* (v) *What they did*

b The sentences also contain one conditional clause (iii) *if he was coming* and one relative clause (vi) *that is typical* . . .

2

Answers to **a**	Answers to **b**
(i) *that many substantial communities had no rail services at all*	This follows the verb *discover*
(ii) *That he was a great man* (The following is also an implied noun clause: [*that he was*] *a great human being*)	*Beyond doubt* functions like an adjective. We would generally say *It is beyond doubt that* . . . Here the noun clause is fronted.
(iii) **1** *that the story should be on the news;* **2** *that nobody knew;* **3** *what had happened to us;* **4** *that Jill was getting something going* (The following is also an implied noun clause: [*that Jill was*] *taking the Thatcher government to task*).	**1** This noun clause follows the noun *fact* and is embedded within a complex noun phrase; **2** & **3** the noun clause *what had happened* follows the verb *know* and is embedded within another noun clause; *that nobody knew* . . . follows the noun *fact;* **4** this follows the adjective *excited;*

Fernald must be psychopathic is also a noun clause (I *think (that) Fernald must be psychopathic*), but can't be introduced by *that* in this 'fronted' position.

. . . that has to appear on boards is a relative clause, not a noun clause.

3

a The following are noun clauses
  – *John Fernald had written to her . . .*
  – *her performance was a travesty . . .*
  – *he had been greatly hurt . . .*
  – *she had adversely criticised . . .*
  – *I must not tell a soul . . .*
  – *I wouldn't.*

b *That* can be inserted at the beginning of each of these clauses

c The only case in which *that* seems to make much difference to the readability of the text is before *he had been greatly hurt*. This is the only clause that doesn't immediately follow a reporting verb, and without *that* it is not immediately apparent whether this is a fact as reported by the author or whether it is something John Fernald asserted in his letter.

d *That* occurs at the beginning of each clause in the original text.

26 Relative clauses

Language in context

1

Answers to **a**	Answers to **b**	Answers to **c**
(i) . . . *person **that** you want.*	*You* (not *that*) is the subject of the relative clause, and so *that* can be left out and in most circumstances it probably would be.	*Who* or *whom* could replace *that.*
(ii) *People **who***	*Who* is the subject of the relative clause, so it can't be left out.	*That* could be used in its place.
(iii) *Nobody **who** leaves . . .*	As above (ii)	*That* could be used in its place.
(iv) . . . *people **whose** letters . . .*	Only the word *whose* has this possessive meaning and linking function, and so it can't be left out or replaced.	–
(v) . . . *a name **which** I'd never . . .*	*I* (not *which*) is the subject of the relative clause, and so *which* can be left out and in most circumstances it probably would be.	*That* could replace *which.*
(vi) *Nothing **that** she says . . .*	***She*** (not *that*) is the subject of the relative clause, and so *that* can be left out and in most circumstances it probably would be.	–

2

This text contains three reduced relative clauses, none of which the learner 'spotted':

> Following suggestions [*which were*] made to the working party [*that was*] elected at the previous meeting, . . . the proposal [*which was*] drawn up in November . . .

Making sense of these reduced clauses helps to untangle the meaning of the rest of the sentence (which includes a great deal of further ellipsis).

3

a)

(i)	*where one teacher presents things explicitly and very effectively* *that that teacher does well* *[that] children appreciate from that particular teacher.* *that the teacher set out to teach*
(ii)	*which is joyful and satisfying*
(iii)	*where smoking has been banned* *who know what is going on*

c Using relative clauses enables us:

* to avoid repetition (e.g. *In offices where smoking has been banned* ⇒ *Smoking has been banned in some offices. In <u>these offices</u> . . .*)

* to be very specific (e.g. *a life <u>which is joyful</u> – not just <u>any</u> life*).

d

(i)	***a situation** where one teacher presents things explicitly and very effectively*	a situation = one of a class of situations
	***whatever it was** that the teacher set out to teach*	whatever it was = *the* things
(ii)	***a life** which is joyful and satisfying*	a life = one of a class of lives
(iii)	***offices** where smoking has been banned*	offices = a class or category of offices

Learners' English

a There is no definitive way of re-writing any of this text. The following is a re-written version of the whole text. The sentence *There is . . . avenue* is re-written in two ways. The first of these alternatives uses full relative clauses (*which . . .; who . . .;* and *who . . .;*), and the second uses *reduced* relative clauses (*. . . an avenue* [] *thronging with people* [] *walking along, and* [] *wearing very tattered clothes.*

My favourite – or most memorable scene from a film is from *Gandhi*. It is set in India at a time of civil war. [*There is an avenue which is thronging with people who are walking along, and who are wearing very tattered clothes.*] [*There is an avenue* [ ] *thronging with people* [ ] *walking along, and* [ ] *wearing very tattered clothes.*] This is my favourite moment.

b The learner systematically places information *before* what it qualifies (also in *there was civil war in India one a time*) and needs to learn that in English any information expressed in a clause comes after what it qualifies. This is likely to feel very strange, and the learner is probably going to face problems in dividing clauses up and in ordering them

Speakers of many languages find the arrangement of information in main and relative clauses unsettling and difficult to grasp. Expectations about where information lies in sentences are strong and instinctive. When listening, it is particularly difficult to make the necessary adjustments to inherent expectations.

27 Non-finite clauses

Language in context

1

	Answers to **a**	Answers to **b**
1	bare infinitive	This clause is attached to the clause *saw a familiar figure*. This clause includes the 'sense' verb *see* (*saw*).
2	past participle (including subject – *her head*)	This adds additional, descriptive detail. She has lowered her head herself.
3	verbless (introduced by a preposition -*with*)	This adds additional, descriptive detail.
4	present participle	This describes a simultaneous action, which also expands previous information (*He left some coins*).

2

Answers to **a**	Answers to **b**
the most abused beer style in the world	verbless clause used to expand information (i.e. about Pilsner)
to embrace every aspect of free-market capitalism in the Czech Republic	infinitive clause used to expand information (i.e. about the 'dash')
turning some of the finest beers into just a few more international-style lagers	Present participle clause. This clause fulfils a range of functions – it describes something simultaneous, but something which also is both a result and which expands information (i.e. about the threat to the traditions of Bohemian brewing)

confined to beers (brewed in the industrial city of Pilsen)	past participle clause used to explain/expand information (i.e. use of the term 'Pilsner' in the Czech Republic)
brewed in the industrial city of Pilsen	defining past participle clause (i.e. the term 'Pilsen' is confined not to any beers but to those which are brewed in Pilsen)
Pilsner Urquell and Gambrinus	verbless clause used to expand information (i.e. naming the two breweries)
now part of the same privatised company	verbless clause used to expand information (i.e. about the two breweries)

The following prepositional phrase would normally be considered as an adverbial:

As a result of the prominence of Holsten of Hamburg.

It might also be interpreted as a verbless clause used to describe a cause (i.e. *why you might think Pils was a German beer in style*).

3

Answers to question **a**.

The following is extracted from the original text:

> **1** *A new bridge* **linking the cultural centres on either bank of the Thames** *is emerging as Westminster Council's main contribution to London's Millennium scene.*
> **2** *A brief will be prepared by the council over the next few weeks,* **inviting ideas from consultants about how a bridge could be devised and funded**.
> **3, 4** *The link could be a foot-bridge along the lines of the one* **being proposed by the City Corporation to link Bankside and the St Paul's area**.
> **5** *But the option of a monorail or cable car has not been ruled out,* **opening up the possibility of running the link from locations as far away from the river as Seven Dials in Covent Garden or even Piccadilly Circus**.
> **6** *Locations on the South Bank would have to be coordinated with the winner of the architectural competition* **recently announced**.

	Answers to **b**	Answers to **c**
1	Present participle clause providing additional information.	An infinitive clause would also be possible here (. . . *to link* . . .), but would suggest that this was more the bridge's purpose than some incidental fact.
2	Present participle clause providing additional information.	–
3	Present participle clause expanding information (this is a reduced relative clause i.e. one [*which is*] being proposed . . .).	This clause could also be placed immediately after *A brief*, but the author chooses to put it after the whole main clause, probably because it is long and would make the sentence more difficult to understand if it separated the subject and the verb.
4	Infinitive clause expanding information (and in this case describing the purpose of the bridge).	A present participle clause would also be possible here (. . . *linking* . . .), but would not convey the sense of this being the bridge's purpose.

5	Present participle clause providing additional information.	–
6	Past participle clause providing additional information (this is a reduced relative clause i.e. *competition* [*which has been*] *recently announced . . .*).	–

Learners' English

Answers to **a**	Answers to **b**	Answers to **c**
not mattering what they are about . . .	This present participle (introducing the following *what* clause) is inappropriate here. The learner has used *not mattering* as though it means something like *regardless of* (or, possibly, *no matter*).	The problem here is really one of vocabulary – we might respond to this problem by teaching the appropriate expressions.
you have obtained . . .	This is completely acceptable. The learner could also omit the subject and auxiliary verb (*you have*), making this into a past participle clause (*knowledge of the subject obtained through years . . .*).	Since learners are sometimes reluctant to use ellipsis of this kind, we can help them by showing them where they could leave out words in what they write.
you think about . . .	A present participle clause introduced by *by* (. . . *solved by thinking about what . . .*) establishes the function of making something possible.	We could help this learner by teaching that we use *by* + present participle for this purpose. For the same reasons, the learner needs to add *by* to *looking at the context* (*by looking at . . .*).
Understanding difficult vocabulary you can . . .	The learner needs to use an infinitive rather than the present participle (*To understand difficult vocabulary . . .*) in order to *explain how to*.	We could help this learner by teaching that we use infinitives for this purpose.

28 Defining and non-defining phrases and clauses

Differences in meaning

a, b

(i)   The non-defining clause in the first sentence suggests that it was the fact of her telling jokes which made everyone angry. The defining clause in the second sentence identifies that what made everyone angry was the particular jokes she was telling (i.e. she didn't tell harmless jokes).

(ii) The non-defining clause in the first sentence suggests that they loved all their children and that their children were all obedient and well-behaved. The defining clause in the second sentence suggests that among their children they loved some and not others. Those that they loved were the ones who were obedient and well-behaved.

(iii) There is no essential difference between these two sentences. Some people might argue that the comma is necessary since *chatting and laughing* has no defining function. However, it is very common to see sentences like this written with no comma.

(iv) The relative clause in these sentences isn't clearly defining or non-defining. It makes little difference whether we write it with a comma or not.

Language in context

Answers to **a**	Answers to **b**
(a lot of East End children) *with prolonged childhood asthma* – *with prolonged asthma* is a prepositional phrase which defines which children we are concerned with.	This is a defining clause, and so a comma is not used.

(the ones) *that don't* – *that don't* is a defining relative clause (*don't* stands in place of *don't go on to suffer from severe teenage bouts and adult lung disease*).	This is a defining clause, and so a comma is not used.
(schooltime) *which surprisingly quickly stunts their education* – *which surprisingly quickly stunts their education* is a non-defining relative clause.	Although non-defining, this clause is not separated from the main clause by a comma.
(the aerosol treatments) *which are so very effective in adults* - it isn't clear whether *which are so very effective in adults* is defining or not.	If the clause was separated from the rest of the sentence by commas, this would make it clear that this is simply additional information. However, the absence of commas doesn't make the clause defining either – it isn't clear that this clause singles out certain aerosol treatments as distinct from others.
(inhaled powders . . . and anti-inflammatory drugs,) *which are fiddly and need careful dosing* – this non-defining relative clause is separated from the main clause by commas.	The relative clause qualifies the subject of the main clause, and is embedded in it. Because of its position (qualifying the *subject*), the clause has to be separated from the rest of the sentence by commas.
(inhaled powders) *to dilate the lungs* – *to dilate the lungs* has a defining function, specifying what kind of inhaled powders we are concerned with (i.e. not just any).	This is a defining clause, and so a comma is not used.

29 Integrating the elements

Language in context

1

a (i) Subordinate clause: *When I walked . . . cousin called Audrey were the others,*

Main clause: *I saw Chad . . . and my mother.*

(ii) Main clause: *I have the feeling*

Subordinate clause: *that a lot . . . cannot be possessed.*

b an adverbial clause   **c** a noun clause   **d** *one of a bevy . . . others*

e *of whom . . . others*   **f** *who married Jonathan Durham*

g *non-defining*   **h** *called Audrey*

i Each degree of indentation represents a degree of embedding.

The basic subordinate clause is marked *2* (*that a lot of the tensions in groups, may be due in part to this unsatisfied feeling*).

— *particularly at intermediate level* is a phrase which qualifies the kinds of *groups* we are concerned with.

— *where students are making* . . . is a relative clause, which qualifies *intermediate level.*

— *where language can somehow be dealt out in chunks* qualifies *a situation.*

— *that is the need* introduces a relative clause re-stating and expanding this unsatisfied feeling.

— *to possess something* is an infinitive clause which qualifies *the need.*

— *that cannot be possessed* is a relative clause that qualifies *something.*

2

Answers to **a**	Answers to **b**	Answers to **c**
(i) This sentence begins with three 'fronted' present participle clauses (*Ranging over two millennia and casting a glance or two at Kelly/ while concentrating chiefly on current times*). The verb phrase contains a discourse marker (*on the whole*) which separates the two verbs (*discussed/defended*). The subject is not repeated before the second verb. There is a parenthesis, which is itself a non-finite present participle clause (*English serving as the example*). The sentence ends with a relative clause. It is not easy to identify what *regarded as unorthodox and impracticable* refers to (in fact it refers to *lines of thought on foreign-language learning and teaching*). This is partly because the parenthesis separates the relative clause from the group of words it refers to. The placing of *by many* between *regarded* and *as* also makes processing and understanding more difficult.	The sentence is not badly written, but it is long and complex, with multiple embedding – the result of having to compress a lot of information into a small space.	The difficulty is due to: • the number of clauses in the sentence; • the amount of embedding; • the placing of the subject far into the clause; • the use of *many* as a pronoun, referring to *many people*.

(ii) The basic structure of the sentence is that *something is slowly becoming apparent*. Once we have worked that out, we still face the problem of understanding what that *something* is. The most plausible meaning of the sentence is probably something like: *It is slowly becoming apparent throughout the community how disturbing something is.* *This is disturbing to two groups of people – firstly to people who are 'gainfully employed', and secondly to people who have spent a lot of time and effort trying to find work. What is disturbing these people is a discovery.* *This discovery is that enforced repatriation is more than just a possibility. Enforced repatriation is in danger of becoming an integral part of the policy of the new government.*	Most people would probably agree that this sentence is badly written.	It is extremely difficult to unravel the meaning, and the writer appears to have little sense of how much (or how little) embedding readers can process with ease. Among the specific difficulties posed by this sentence are: • the extraordinary length of the subject (everything before *is slowly becoming*) • the extraordinary complexity of the subject (with multiple embedding of finite clauses, non-finite clauses and adverbials) e.g. ellipsis *and [how disturbing it is for] those [people] whose attempts . . .; but [that enforced repatriation] is in danger . . .* relative clause *whose attempts . . .* noun clause *to discover that . . .* non-finite clauses *to find work . . . ; to discover that . . .* • the fact that all these clauses are embedded in a fronted noun clause (*how disturbing it is . . .*). It would also be more usual (and clear) to use a 'preparatory *it*' construction e.g. *It is slowly becoming apparent throughout the community how . . .*

| (iii) The basic structure of the first four lines is an adverbial clause introduced by the conjunction (*only*) *when*.
The main clause begins with an inversion (*did I become*), and the final noun phrase (*the blindingly blue . . .*) contains an embedded past participle clause (*over-looked from the terrace*). This noun phrase can be analysed in two ways – as the direct object of *aware of* or as an adverbial beginning *of . . .* | In contrast to the previous sentence, most people would consider this to be clearly and elegantly written. Nonetheless it poses problems to learners with a certain level of English. | The adverbial clause contains:
• an extremely long direct object (*the remains of my smoked flying fish and fresh tropical fruits*)
• a relative clause (*who were threatening . . .*) which depends on
• an indirect object (*to the birds*), which is widely separated from the verb (*offered*) and into which is embedded
• a further adverbial clause (*if I didn't leave*).
The main clause contains:
<u>parenthesis</u> – marked here by dashes (this parenthesis is effectively a non-defining relative clause qualifying *the local birds*)
<u>inversion</u> – (*did I become*). This depends on the 'negative adverb' *only* with which the sentence begins. Some learners, however, may not identify this and the underlying rule, and may be confused by the fact that this appears to them to be a question. The problem is made worse by the distance in the sentence which separates the adverb *only* and the inversion that depends on this (*did I become*).
<u>ellipsis</u> e.g. *and* [*only when I had*] *offered . . .* ; *the blindingly blue stretch of the Caribbean* [*Sea which was*] *over-looked by customers from the terrace* [*of the restaurant*]. |

Learners' English

(i)

a The following is one of many ways the first text might be re-written:

> When I read books and newspapers, if I don't understand some
> of the words, I try to imagine what they mean. However, if the
> word comes up again and again, then I use a dictionary. It is
> difficult to remember and use new words in English as they are
> quite different from words in my own language.

b & **c** The learner who wrote the first text writes in short, very simple
sentences. She uses some discourse markers to signpost logical
relationships (e.g. *so*), but the structure of what she writes would be
clearer if she made greater use of conjunctions (e.g. *If I find a word many
times in a book or newspaper (then) I use a dictionary*).

(ii)

a The following is one of many ways the second text might be re-written:

> When teachers ask me about things I know nothing about, I can't
> join in the conversation – I just listen to other students'
> opinions. It is quite difficult for me to have time to express my
> point of view because we're educated to be quiet during class.
> We have to put our hands up to show that we want to speak,
> and then the teacher points out one, particular student.

b The learner who wrote this text writes less simply than the writer of *(i)*.
The first sentence includes a well-formed contact relative clause (*about
the things* [ ] *I don't know . . .*) and, although the first three sentences
seem rather unnatural because they are not combined, the logical
connections are clear (helped by the use of *then*, appropriately to
indicate a logical consequence). The last two sentences in the text are
very well-formed.

c The learner's problems are generally less with clause and sentence
construction than with the grammar of particular words (*educated that*;
beg something to) and the use of articles (*the things*). Her writing would
also be more natural if she used a two-part conjunction such as *either . . .
or* in the final sentence.

(iii)

a The following is one of many ways the third text might be re-written:

My biggest problem is with vocabulary. Although a lot of words
are the same as in my language, sometimes the meanings
change a little – or I should say a lot – and this confuses me,
especially when I am talking, and I don't pay too much attention
to the exact words I use. So, I need to learn a lot of new words
and I also need to learn to use the words I already know better. I
hope in this class I will have the opportunity to improve a lot.

b The learner who wrote the third text writes fluently and with no hint of trying to avoid complexity. In fact, many of what at first sight may be considered 'mistakes' (e.g. the use of *however* in a sentence with *although*) seem far more natural if this is read aloud. Added punctuation also helps to make the structure of this text clearer.

c Many of the changes one might make in re-writing this text have more to do with converting it from an acceptable spoken style to a more formal written style rather than 'correcting' it. The key exception in terms of sentence construction is * *use the old ones what I know them better.* Here she has used *what* wrongly as a relative pronoun. A contact relative clause would be most natural here (e.g. *use the ones* [ ] *I know better),* but *that* could also be used in place of *what.*